Why Delphi? Why The Beginn

Delphi is comparatively new to the world of computer
commands a huge following all around the world. Wh
Pascal, the language that everyone knows, with a blist
the intuitive IDE? The 'openness' of Delphi's APIs and
32-bit version of the package? We don't know for sure, but one thing we are certain of
is that Delphi is giving C++ a run for its money, the Delphi fraternity is growing and
third party support is surpassing all previously recorded levels. Can you afford to not
back this horse?

The book continues on the tradition of the Wrox Press Beginner's Series, providing easy
to follow explanations, backed up by hands-on tutorials and fully-fledged solutions for
this exciting new development system from Borland. Using a relaxed and visual style,
the book takes you quickly and painlessly to outstanding results. Before you know it,
you will have enough knowledge of Delphi to create advanced applications without
batting an eyelid, compiling, debugging and preparing your works of art for
distribution around the globe!!

What is Wrox Press?

Wrox Press is a computer book publisher which promotes clear, jargon-free
programming and database titles that fulfill your real demands. We publish for
everyone, from the novice through to the experienced programmer. To ensure our
books meet your needs, we carry out continuous research on all our titles. Through
our dialog with you, we can craft the book you really need.

We welcome suggestions and take all of them to heart - your input is paramount in
creating the next great Wrox title. Use the reply card inside this book or contact us at:

feedback@wrox.com

Compuserve 100063, 2152

http://www.wrox.com/

Wrox Press Ltd.
2710 W. Touhy
Chicago
IL 60645
USA

Tel: +1 (312) 465 3559

Fax: +1 (312) 465 4063

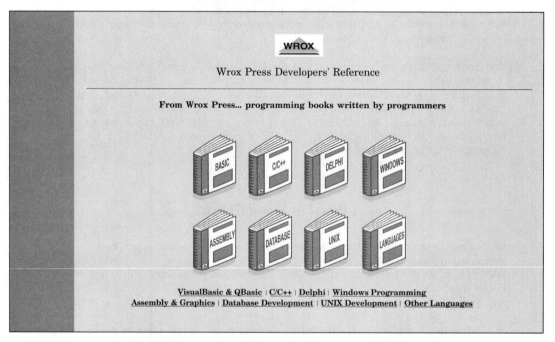

Beginning Delphi 2.0

Peter Wright

Wrox Press Ltd.®

Beginning Delphi 2.0

Published by Wrox Press Ltd. Site 16, 20 James Road, Birmingham, B11 2BA, UK
Printed in Canada
1 2 3 4 5 TRI 99 98 97 96

Library of Congress Catalog no. 95-61107
ISBN 1-874416-74-5

Trademark Acknowledgements

Wrox has endeavored to provide trademark information about all the companies and products mentioned in this book by the appropriate use of capitals. However, Wrox cannot guarantee the accuracy of this information.

Windows 95 and Windows NT are trademarks of Microsoft Corporation. Delphi is a trademark of Borland International, Inc.

Credits

Author
Peter Wright

Editors
Gordon Rogers
Tim Briggs

Managing Editor
John Franklin

Technical Reviewers
John Harris
Darren Millin
Dave Jewell

Contributing Material
John Harris
Bob Swart

Operations Manager
Gina Mance

Production Manager
Greg Powell

Design/Layout
Neil Gallagher
Graham Butler
Damon Creed
Andrew Guillaume

Proof Readers
Melanie Orgee
Pam Brand
Simon Gilks

Index
Simon Gilks

Beta Tester
Melanie Orgee

Cover Design
Third Wave

For more information on Third Wave, contact Ross Alderson on 44-121 236 6616
Cover photograph: Greg Powell

Dedication

A long time ago in a galaxy far, far away...

When this book was originally spec'd, Delphi 1 had just hit the shelves, Visual Basic still reigned supreme, various royals remained married and Delphi 2.0 was but a twinkle in Borland's eye. However, as time went by, it soon became evident that a 32-bit version of what was rapidly becoming the leading rapid application development tool would soon hit the market.

The result was a book spec turned on its head, a flurry of new research, numerous late nights, far too many cans of Doctor Pepper to be healthy for a single person and a near series of mass nervous breakdowns as deadline after deadline were slipped in a frantic effort to bring you the best of the best, the creme de la creme of Delphi books.

I think we succeeded.

Along the way, though, numerous people helped, advised, supported and generally supplied a steady stream of encouragement. This book, like any other, was definitely NOT written by one person locked in a closet for a few months, so time for the others to stand up and grab their 15 minutes.

First, the Wrox team. If you can picture in your mind a group of the most talented, dedicated, driven and patient people in the industry then you can picture the Wrox editorial team. Gordy and Tim, despite having to cope with a somewhat temperamental author, displayed dedication above and beyond the call of duty. It is their insight and talent which turned my incessant ramblings into something readable. Greg and his team also deserve heaps of credit for their hard work in laying it all out. Above all the others though, my thanks to Dave, the guy who had the vision to commission the book and the pen which authorized the checks.

At Psynet too, a cast of heroes sits in the background. Richard Bass contributed oodles of advice and also the first drafts of the final application, as well as numerous opportunities to be my moving target in the odd game of Doom. My thanks also to Kees for pushing this work ahead and for encouraging me all the way.

On the Internet, the guys who spend their lives floating around in `comp.lang.pascal.delphi.misc`, and `comp.lang.pascal.delphi.database` helped me get over many technical hurdles. The breadth of knowledge that they hold between them is really quite staggering and always incredibly valuable.

Away from the lights and the action, though, my thanks to Sharon for copious amounts of coffee, Simon for showing me that there really is life away from a keyboard, to Dagwin for just being Dagwin (see, I really, really was working - I wasn't just being bad tempered <G>).

Finally, my deepest gratitude and love for Gail. More than anyone else your drive, energy and faith in what I could accomplish put this book on the shelves.

Special Dedication

This book is especially dedicated, though, to two little people, with giant personalities. Through the tempers, the laughter, the fun and the games, my children, Chris and Eloise, remain my constant source of inspiration and energy. I love you both guys!

About the Author

Peter Wright is the managing director of Psynet Ltd. and Psynet Interactive, two software houses specializing in the development of Windows multimedia, relational database and Internet applications. He has just finished work on STALKER, the world's first group-enabled, Windows 95 off-line web browser, a product designed to complement his previous online Internet client, HAMSTER.

Peter has been developing Windows applications for five years, prior to which he wasted a great deal of time on various home computer formats, as well as one or two deathly dull operating systems derived from Unix.

When he isn't developing earth shattering Windows 95 applications, he can be found frequenting Efnet IRC on #TheCafe where he is known as the AlphaFrog, generally running up huge phone bills surfing the Internet, or out re-enacting Easy Rider on his motorcyle.

Psynet can be e-mailed via the Internet at **admin@gendev.demon.co.uk**, while Peter himself can be found at **peter@gendev.demon.co.uk**.

Beginning Delphi 2.0

Summary Of Contents

Beginning
Delphi
2.0

Beginning
**Delphi
2.0**

Introduction

Welcome

First of all, thanks for buying this book. We hope that you'll find it useful, helping you to understand the subject of Delphi programming with the least amount of heartache and a little bit of fun along the way.

This introduction covers a few of the most important features of the whole package - how you can use the book, what other material is supplied extra to the pages you are now looking at and how you can get the most out of Borland's new 32-bit compiler-driven rapid application development tool, Delphi 2.0.

Who is the Book for?

If you are new to programming in general, new to Windows programming in particular, an old Pascal programmer or just someone who wants to get more out of the glorified calculator that sits on the desk, this book is for you. It assumes no prior knowledge of computer programming, but neither does it drag you through endless amounts of theory. This is most definitely a hands-on book.

By the end of the first chapter you will have created your first Delphi/Windows application and by the end of the third, that number will be into double figures. At every stage of the learning process, we try to guide you through the mire of computer programming, while introducing new techniques, fun diversions and interesting but not completely useless anecdotes.

If you are looking for an easy to follow, hands-on tutorial backed up by a source code disk packed with examples and a web site overflowing with even more information, you're looking at the right book. Otherwise, you'd better try the next one on the shelf!

However, before you make any rash decisions, you'd better check out what we think you need to get the most out of this book.

What Do You Need to Use this Book?

To make best use of this book, we recommend that you have several items around your person while you are reading it. You shouldn't consider these necessary to your understanding - you might be able to learn the language just by reading the text through once - but we would strongly advise you to get some, if not all, of the following.

A Computer

First of all, a computer. This book has been designed as a hands-on tutorial. You'll find yourself asking questions that can only be answered by typing in a few lines of code, compiling the small Delphi application and seeing what the computer comes up with.

According to the box, you'll need a computer with at least the following spec:

- Intel 486/25-based PC or higher
- Microsoft Windows 95 or Windows NT 3.51
- 8MB of RAM (12MB recommended)
- 50MB of hard disk space
- CD-ROM drive
- Mouse or other Windows pointing device

Of course, this is only the minimum requirement for the computer. You'll find that you can get your applications to compile a lot faster on a more high-powered machine, a task that can become very tedious on this most basic spec.

Of course, that doesn't mean that you can't read the book away from your computer - we find that you sometimes need a break away from the beast, just to get your thoughts in order - but we're sure that as you get drawn more and more into the world of Delphi programming, a computer will become to you like Shakespeare's quills were to him.

A Copy of the Software

The second most important thing to have close at hand is a copy of Delphi, hopefully already installed on your machine. If you haven't got a copy of Delphi when you buy this book, you might be a little confused when you go to get one, as Borland have released three flavors.

Delphi Desktop

The first, **Delphi Desktop**, is aimed at the basic developer who isn't particularly interested in database work, isn't too worried about OCX controls and is really focusing on quick and dirty application development - the prototyper. This flavor is essentially a stripped down version of the product aimed at the student market, so the trade-off between price and features has been made in favor of price. Don't get us wrong, this product is exactly the same as the other flavors, it's just a little restrictive for our liking, but it can still see you though 90% of the chapters in this book.

Delphi Developer

The second flavor, called **Delphi Developer**, is, as the name suggests, the option of choice for the serious Delphi developer. This version of the software comes with a lot more features aimed at easing the development of professional-looking application. Some of these features include the full source code for Delphi class library (the VCL), some powerful OCX controls and improved database access through a wider range of database drivers. This flavor is a little more expensive than Desktop, but it will grow with you throughout your Delphi programming career. It will get you through all of this book and, unless you are a real client/server database fanatic, it includes everything you'll ever need.

Delphi Client/Server

The third and final flavor is called **Delphi Client/Server**. This is the most expensive version of the software by quite some way, but it does come with a variety of extra features that you might find useful it you are in the major league database world. Some of these features include tools for monitoring database transactions, upsizing and downsizing your data and even your own high-powered server-based industry-leading database server. If you aren't in this league, save your money and head for Developer, or if you're on a budget, go for Desktop.

A Familiarity with the Operating System

One thing that we will rely on throughout this book is your familiarity with the Windows operating system. One of the prerequisites for using Delphi 2.0 is to have either Windows 95 or Windows NT installed on your computer, so we'll assume that you can use this tool. We will use a number of phrases such as *double-click*, *shift-click* and *run the executable* and we'll presume you know what they mean.

If you are a little unsure on any of these terms, we suggest that you put this book down and take a look at something to help you use your particular operating system. We have done our best to introduce Delphi terminology into examples with copious amounts of description and guidance, so if you come across terms that aren't explained, they are probably operating system commands. When this happens, get help from another book, the operating system online help or, if you are like people here, your friendly operating system guru who sits at the next desk.

An Internet Connection

The final item that we would suggest you get, although you could regard it as an optional extra, is a connection to the Internet. If you do get access, you'll find that Delphi has one of the most active and helpful support networks in computing as a whole, with everyone striving to help each other out, throw new useful tools into the freeware arena, or offer free advise and even a potential working solution to your problem, just by sending one e-mail message or strafing one forum or newsgroup.

The World Wide Web has also exploded in terms of popularity over the last few years and has become an invaluable resource to those serious Delphi developers who need to stay abreast of all the latest twists and turns in the industry. Thanks to sites such as **www.yahoo.com**, which offer powerful search engines, you can quickly zero in on interesting Delphi sites that might have a lot to offer a confused Delphi developer, or a programmer with a problem.

One of the WWW sites that we would advise you to check out is **www.wrox.com** - our site. It comes replete with extra source code, sample chapters, information on industry movements and much, much more. Well worth a visit!

Installing the Disk

This book comes complete with a disk containing all the source code discussed in the chapters, as well as a few extras that we found lying around. To install the disk onto your computer, simply run the file called **install.exe**, either by double-clicking on the file in Explorer or by typing **a:\install** at a DOS prompt.

The file will then organize the extraction of the source code onto your hard drive, installing the source code chapter-by-chapter under the **begdelf** directory.

If you have any problems with the disk or the installation program, please don't hesitate to contact us. We'll provide you with a speedy solution to your problem, whatever that may be.

Using the Disk

The source code provided on the disk is broken down into chapter directories, which are in turn broken down into example directories. To locate the source code for a particular example, say **stage4.dpr** in Chapter 6, you should first navigate to the **chap6** subdirectory, then look for a directory called **stage4**. There you'll find all the source code for the example, including the target file, **stage4.dpr**.

If at any point you get lost, take a look at the **readme.txt** file that should be in the root of the chapter directory. This file documents what each directory contains, what the files held within them are used for and, hopefully, should show you the directory you are looking for.

The database chapters are a little more complicated. The source code that they use is actually split over two directories: one for the Delphi source code and one for the database itself. We'll explain why in the chapters themselves, and tell you how you should handle this setup.

Conventions Used in this Book

We have tried to use the styles and font sizes in this book to make the text as easy as possible to understand. For example, you'll notice that all classes in the text are referred to by their full title, i.e. TForm and they always appear as shown here. Hopefully, this should allow you to easily pick out these references and quickly identify exactly what is happening to what.

As well as the appropriate use of headings and (perfect, we hope!) grammar, punctuation and spelling, we have also used a number of other conventions in the book to try and make the text easy to follow.

'For Your Information' note boxes pass on useful, interesting or just fun information that you might find useful to know:

 The styles in this book have been added to make the text easier to read.

We have put all the filenames, directory references and other code snippets into a style so that you can quickly identify them:

In the previous section, `c:\begdelf` and `stage4.dpr` are referenced a number of times and, if you look in that file, you will find a reference to the `close` method.

If the code snippet covers more than a line, we want to highlight a few lines of code or to identify where some lines of code are in respect to their neighbors, we have used the following convention:

```
procedure TfrmViewer.mnuFExitClick(Sender: TObject);
begin
    close;
end;
```

If we introduce a new term, an important concept or an interesting technique, we will highlight it with a little bit of bold text:

The following concept, that of **polymorphism**, is really quite important.

The only other style that we have used is one to denote the keystrokes that you should make to achieve a given result. If you see the following in a paragraph, *F9*, we actually want you to press the *F9* function key. If you see *Ctrl+F9*, you should hold the *Ctrl* key down while you are pressing the *F9* function key.

The only other convention we have used in this book is the Try It Out/How It Works chapter subsections. A Try It Out heading indicates that the following section is one specifically designed for you to try out yourself. They have been designed to be easy to follow step-by-step examples that lead you to a working application or a functioning technique. The next section, How It Works, actually dissects the Try It Out, explaining what happened behind the scenes, filling in any gaps that were missing and occasionally adding extra techniques to your arsenal.

Tell Us What You Think

We've worked hard on this book to make it useful. We've tried to understand what you are willing to exchange your hard-earned money for and tried to live up to your expectations. However, you are part of the team on that one. If you're reading this, you've already seen something you like about the book to pick it up off the shelf. However, we know that's only the beginning of the story. What we care about is that you get the results you want.

Please, please let us know what you think of this book. Tell us what we did wrong and, hopefully, what we did right. This isn't just marketing flannel: we really do all huddle around the e-mail to find out what you think. If you don't believe it, send us a note. We'll answer and we'll take whatever you say on board to try and do better in the future.

Feedback@wrox.com

http://www.wrox.com/

Compuserve : 100063,2152

Welcome to Delphi

If you have seen the marketing campaign surrounding Delphi, you will have already been told what a great package it is. You will have been informed that it produces lightning fast Windows applications and lets you develop in a highly intuitive manner. You will have been told that exhaustive coding is now a thing of the past; Delphi provides developers with the ability to produce simple, yet powerful, applications with little or no code. You will have also been told that Delphi is the tool for rapidly developing prototype applications, multimedia applications, client/server database applications and much, much more.

But hold the hype; haven't we heard this all before? Wasn't this what Microsoft said about Visual Basic? Visual FoxPro? And what about Access? Well, yes - the difference this time is that all the hype is true.

Delphi is the fastest Windows application development system in the world. Fast, not only from a programmer's point of view (meaning that you spend less time in front of the computer actually producing an application) but also from the point of view of the user. You see, at present, Delphi is the only visual development environment to include a true **compiler** (more on this later). Sure, there are C compilers out there that claim to let you develop an application using the point and click method, but none of them really has Delphi's level of integration. In fact, none of them is what I would call a visual development system.

Maybe you still need convincing. Maybe you are already sold on the Delphi idea. Whichever point of view you have, by the end of this chapter you are just going to love Delphi to bits, want to throw those old C compilers in the bin and relegate that faded Visual Basic box to its rightful place as a glorified doorstop.

In this chapter, you will:

- Learn how to use the Delphi user interface
- Create a fully functional application with hardly any code
- Learn a little about the internals of Delphi and its more advanced facilities
- Find out how to use Delphi's extensive help system

More than this, though, you are going to find out why the future of programming is here today, and why its name is Delphi.

Getting to Grips with Delphi - A Whirlwind Tour

As I said in the introduction to the book, I do have to make certain assumptions about my readers. From here on in, I assume that you have Delphi running and that you are quite comfortable with phrases like 'Double click the mouse on the menu heading' and other Windows shortcuts. I don't expect you to be an expert in all things Windows, but you do at least need some passing familiarity with the system.

Straight after starting Delphi (well, that's not quite true - you could be in for a bit of a wait on a low powered system, but you get my point) the first thing you see is a bewildering collection of menus, icons, toolbars and other assorted windows.

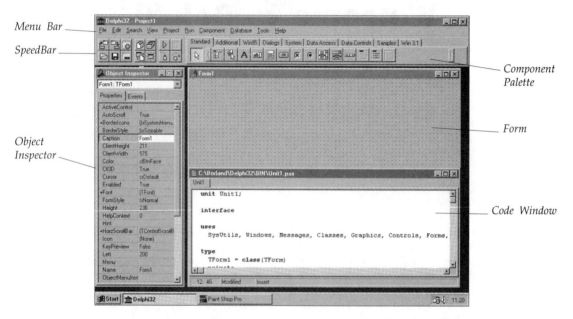

What do they all mean? What do they do? How are you ever going to learn how to use all of them? Don't panic - it's all quite logical. Also, you needn't worry if your screen doesn't look too much like mine - Delphi lets you move everything around to suit your own working preferences.

What you are looking at is the **Delphi Integrated Development Environment**, which just trips off the tongue, so we usually refer to it as the **Delphi IDE**. It's here that we design our applications - this is the coal face so to speak. The IDE holds such diverse elements as:

- The menu bar
- The SpeedBar
- The Component Palette
- The Object Inspector
- The form
- The code window

So much information, but how can you use them? Well, let's look closer at each in turn.

Form and Code Windows

Center stage, we have the **form** itself. This is to the Delphi programmer like a canvas is to a painter. It's here you create your application's user interface so that at run time, when the form becomes a window, the user can interact with the program.

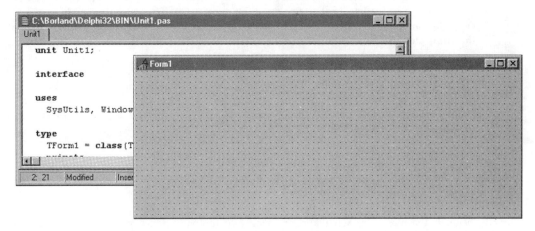

There is a hidden side to the form - the **code window**. Press *F12* to toggle between these partners in crime. Armed with Delphi, you can actually create programs simply by dropping components onto forms, but when it comes to providing a little more functionality, you need to type in some Pascal program code; easy-to-read statements that tell the computer, step-by-step, exactly what you want it to do.

Throughout the rest of this chapter, we'll introduce you to the code window and some basic Pascal statements with a variety of examples... stay tuned.

Menu Bars and SpeedBars

As is typical in a Windows program, the top section of any application's IDE is taken up with a menu bar:

The menu provides you with access to Delphi's own functionality. There are the usual file editing, saving and printing menu items, as well as specialized items to control the compiler, the debugger and the Delphi help system, to name but a few.

Before we go any further, let's look at a few of these new terms in greater detail.

Delphi is a compiler-driven rapid application development environment. This means that it uses a *compiler* to create stand-alone executables (`.exe` files) that you can run on any machine - you don't need Delphi, run-time DLLs or p-code interpreters.

When you have completed the design of your Delphi project, to create an executable application you need to invoke the compiler (press *F9*). The compiler loads in each separate part of the project, checks it for errors and then turns it into something that the computer itself can understand.

When you attempt to run the application inside Delphi's environment (pressing *F9* not only compiles the project, but also runs the resulting application), Delphi invokes the integrated debugger if anything goes wrong with the execution of the code. This tool allows you to quickly track down the error and may even offer some insight into a possible solution.

Going through each of the items in detail here would bore you to tears, so let's crack on with the rest of Delphi's rather unique interface. We'll cover other items in more detail as we use them throughout the rest of the book.

Directly beneath the menu are what appear to be two toolbars, areas of the screen filled with small strange looking, bitmap-filled buttons. The left one is a real toolbar called Delphi's **SpeedBar**. The buttons give you access to commonly used menu items, letting you load and save projects, invoke the compiler or control the debugger, all with just a single click.

Component Palette

The right-hand toolbar is not really a toolbar at all, it's known as the **Component Palette**. Just as a painter uses a palette to hold and mix colors, so the Component Palette contains the **components** that you will use to create your work of art.

What's a *component* you ask? Simple - a component is an object that you can drop on to the forms of your Delphi application. These ready-to-use pieces of code help build up your application's user interface and give your users something to play with. They are also called *controls*, a term borrowed from Visual Basic.

This begs the question - what's an *object*? Well, a computing object is best explained with an analogy to a real-world object - say a caterpillar. It's self-contained, having both attributes that excite and behavior that fascinates a lepidopterist. It can interact with the outside world, but controls its own internal workings.

After all, what good would a Windows program be if all that appeared when you run the program was a blank window? Most Windows users expect to see something a bit more dramatic - data entry areas, command buttons, menus, check boxes and radio buttons. Delphi labels all these elements as components, holding them on the Component Palette ready for action.

Notice how, above the components, there are a number of tabs. As Delphi provides you with more components to build your application than any other Windows development system, it's best to group them into neat categories. When you first start Delphi, you see the Standard tab and beneath it the standard components that all applications will probably need, no matter what they're intended for. You've got menus, labels, text boxes, and so on. Click on the Win95 tab, though, and the components specific to Windows 95 come into view.

Once again, we'll look at each component in more detail as it appears throughout the book. You can take a guess at how it is used from the icon, or by resting the mouse pointer over it to see a fly-by hint.

Object Inspector

Lastly, take a look at the window titled Object Inspector:

The Object Inspector gives you access to the **properties** and **events** of the components that will eventually make up your finished masterpiece.

Properties define the look of the component - the color of the caterpillar's coat or how many legs it has. Most of these properties are available through the Object Inspector, the tool that Delphi provides to simplify how they are organized and assigned. Events deal with the things that can happen to a component - a button can be clicked, a form can be closed. You can use the Object Inspector to set up small sections of code called *event handlers* that are run when the appropriate event occurs. We'll look at this in more detail when we look at our first sample application.

That's really all there is to it, and concludes our whirlwind tour of the Delphi user interface. The only thing left to cover is how you can customize the interface to your heart's desire.

Customizing the User Interface

What if you don't like the layout of the user interface, or the content of the SpeedBar, or you want to add more third party components to your Component Palette?

As they designed Delphi, the engineers at Borland took these questions on board and produced a very flexible user interface. To begin with, you can resize and relocate any of the elements that make up the interface just as if they were stand-alone applications - you might have noticed that my setup is different to the default layout that you'll have been given. You'll have to experiment to get it just the way you like it.

In the rest of this section, I'm going to cover customizing the SpeedBar and adding programs to the Tools menu. Customizing the Component Palette is quite a complex task, so I'm going to leave that until after we've learnt a little more about Delphi.

Customizing the SpeedBar

As you use Delphi more and more, you will quickly come to appreciate the many shortcuts and workarounds that Borland have provided for you to get the job done. You'll find that the one you use most often is the SpeedBar. With this in mind, Borland have provided you with the option of fully customizing the layout and content to make working with it as comfortable as possible.

Try It Out - Customizing the SpeedBar

There are three different ways to customize the SpeedBar: resize the bar, change the content and alter the layout of that content.

1 Move the cursor over the dividing line between the SpeedBar and the Component Palette. The cursor should change shape to the usual splitter cursor, allowing you to resize the SpeedBar. Make a little more room for another icon.

2 Right-click on the SpeedBar and select the Properties menu item, so invoking the Speedbar Editor:

3 This editor allows you to select an icon for any of the menu items of Delphi's regular menu bar. Check out the File listing. You should be able to find an icon to close down Delphi at the bottom of the list. Drag it over to the SpeedBar and drop it into the gap that we have just created.

4 Now we've got the icon on the SpeedBar, we can organize the icons into a better order. Just click on the icon you want to move and drag and drop it in its new position. You might find it useful to expand the SpeedBar to give you room to move the icons around - if you try and drop them anywhere except for the SpeedBar, Delphi deletes the icon and you'll have to get another from the editor if you want to replace it. I've organized my SpeedBar like this:

You should notice that Delphi automatically tries to align the icons together - a useful feature allied to the Snap to Grid feature of the form that we'll cover in the next chapter.

So there you go, a customized SpeedBar. Okay, an Exit icon isn't really that useful - you could just close Delphi down in the normal Windows way - but it does illustrate how to add icons. As we explore more of Delphi, you might come across other features that you want to place on the SpeedBar - and now you know how!

Calling the Outside World

Okay, let's admit it - Delphi can't do everything. Occasionally, you might need to run another application - say the Image Editor to create a bitmap for a button - and so Borland provided you with the option of calling these programs from the Tools menu.

Try It Out - Adding Another Program to the Tools Menu

1 Select Tools | Tools... from the listing of current tools available on the Tools menu:

By default, you should already have two entries for the Image Editor and the Database Desktop. We'll look at each of these tools as we use them, but for now let's concentrate on adding our own.

2   Click on the Add... button and Delphi will give you the following template to fill in all the details about your new tool:

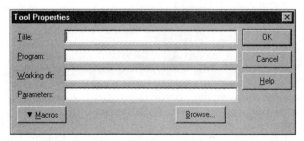

3   Click on the Browse... button and use the Select Transfer Item dialog to select the location of the executable file you want to call. For our example, navigate to your Windows directory and select that essential tool - Solitaire (**sol.exe**). Try looking for it in your Windows directory. If you can't find it, try looking for another executable file that you often run, like Word or Excel.

4   When you return to the template dialog, all you need to do is fill in the Title: with the text you want to appear on the Tools menu. In our case, this should be something like...Solitaire.

5   Close down all the dialogs and take a look at the Tools menu. If you select Solitaire (or whatever you put in the Title:), Delphi will open it up and let you get on with that really important work you have to do with this tool!

Well, there you go. A fully customizable user interface. However, it's no good being able to customize Delphi if you don't know how to create an application, so let's get some hands-on experience and write a program for real.

Writing Your First Delphi Application.

Okay, in case you have never written a Windows application in your life, I'll keep this simple. We are going to write a graphical file viewer that will:

1   Display a complete file selection dialog

2   Get the user to select a **.bmp** file

3   Display this on the form

The user can then click a button to go through the process again, or click another to quit the program. In addition, the File Open dialog should only show graphic files to the user, hiding all the other types.

Simple enough? Don't panic, calm down - Delphi makes seemingly impossible tasks like this a snap. In fact, writing a program like this in a typical C compiler could take you hours of work and hundreds of lines of code. Instead, it's going to take us only three lines of code and roughly ten minutes.

The first step in creating a new Delphi application is to do that just - create a new Delphi application. You have probably already done that, since simply starting Delphi creates a new project, complete with one blank form and an associated unit.

 If you have been playing with Delphi, you'll need to get hold of a fresh new project for our examples. Rather than restarting Delphi to get the default new project, simply choose <u>F</u>ile | New Application.

Saving Your Applications

As you go through our examples in this and following chapters, you will see that Delphi creates a number of files associated with any given project that you are working on - in fact, you might be dealing with upwards of twenty files at any one point. Fortunately, most of these files are handled by Delphi itself, but until you actually tell the IDE where to save these files, it will choose for itself, which could cause problems.

 I think that it's always a good idea to create a directory on your local drive for each of the projects that you're working on. Although this is not strictly necessary, it does help when it comes to maintaining your code sometime in the future. Another advantage is that all files that result from compiling the project are also stored in this directory - as opposed to being scattered into Delphi's own internal files.

So, as soon as the new project has been created, use <u>F</u>ile | Sav<u>e</u> Project As... to tell Delphi to permanently store all the files. In response, Delphi will ask you two questions, the first concerning the name and location of the form's files, the second asking for the same information about your project file.

 Note that the project file simply orchestrates the other files in your application, marshaling your code ready for compilation. We look at the structure of a Delphi project and its associated files in Chapter 3.

You can accept the defaults, **unit1.pas** (for the unit file) and **project1.dpr** (for the project file), in your **Delphi 2.0** directory, but, as we have mentioned, it's a good idea to place them in a purpose-built directory with intuitive names. Once the project is safely saved to disk, try compiling it - you can do this by clicking on the Run icon on the SpeedBar or simply by pressing *F9*. "But we haven't added any code" I hear you cry! When you create a new application, you are actually asking Delphi to provide you with a basic framework, including a simple project file and form which actually compiles 'straight out of the box'.

This basic project compiles to give a blank window which you can move around the screen, resize and finally (out of sheer boredom) close - you should note that that blank window takes up 153KB! - open up Explorer and take a look at the directory to which you have just saved your project and unit files, and root out the newly compiled executable file.

 When the compiled produces an executable, it gives the **.exe** the same name as your project. It you call your project **account.dpr**, then Delphi will create **account.exe**.

The size of this executable is directly attributable to the way that Delphi's compiler works. Borland have provided you with a number of precompiled units of code that are included into the executable, allowing it to stand alone. Rather than Delphi requiring us to provide the code to handle the basic functions of a window, we just need to include **forms** in our **uses** statement and, hey presto, our application works.

As we have said, this convenience does come at a price. Even if we only use the simplest functions included in **forms**, Delphi must include the whole compiled unit in the executable, which makes up a large percentage of the size of our executable file. On the upside, we can use any of the other parts of **forms** at no extra cost!!

Okay, we've digressed a little, but now's a good time to get back to our example and take a look at how this environment works, what the compiler does and what happens when we actually press the button - the first step is to add some components to the form.

Adding Components to a Form

If we take a look back at the original design brief for this program, we can see that we need three visible components on the form: two command buttons (one to invoke the File Open dialog, the other to quit the program) and a third component in which we can display our pictures.

Try It Out - Adding Components to a Form

Let's do the command buttons first; you can find them on the Standard page of the Component Palette:

1 Click on the button component in the palette just once, then click once more inside the form. Miraculously, a button appears on the form:

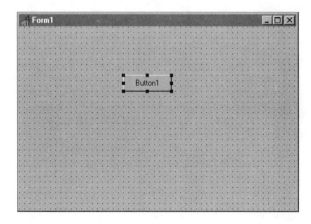

Notice the black squares around the new button - these are resize handles. Clicking and dragging any of the resize handles with the left mouse button enables you to change the size of the component.

2 Try it - adjust your button so that it looks like mine.

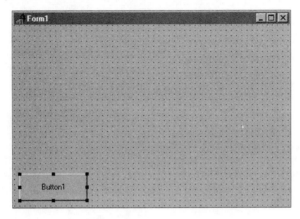

Now we need to create the second button. Rather than repeat the process, let's copy the existing one so that the new button is exactly the same size. The application then starts to take on a consistent look and feel.

3 If the resize handles are not visible on your button, click it once with the left mouse button to select it. The resize handles not only allow you to resize a component, they also show you which component on your form is currently selected.

4 Now copy the button to the Windows clipboard by selecting Edit | Copy, or by simply pressing *Ctrl+C*.

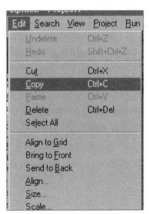

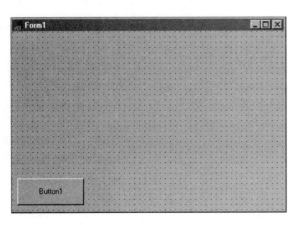

5 Click anywhere on the form so that the resize handles disappear from the button, indicating that it is no longer selected.

17

6 Now either select <u>E</u>dit | <u>P</u>aste or press *Ctrl+V*. A new button appears on the form, identical in size and on top of the old one. Delphi automatically offsets the position of the new button so that you can see it easily.

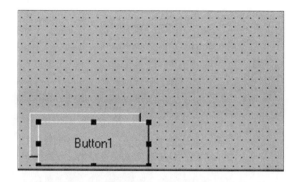

7 Obviously, it's not that good for our users if we leave the buttons one on top of the other. Drag the new button so that your form once again appears like mine:

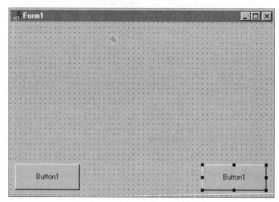

8 Okay, so far so good. Now that we have our command buttons which the user will use later to load pictures or quit the program, all that remains is to draw some components on the form which can display graphics. Click on the Additional tab on the Component Palette to bring some more components into view:

9 The Image component you can see highlighted in this screenshot is just the one we need. Draw one on your form the same way as we did the command button (i.e. click the Image component once, then click in the form):

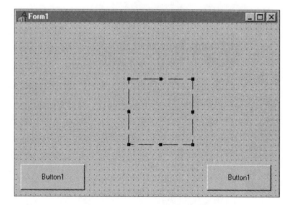

10 Once you've done that, it's probably a good idea to move and resize the control so that the image sits nicely in the form. Once again, copy mine if you want.

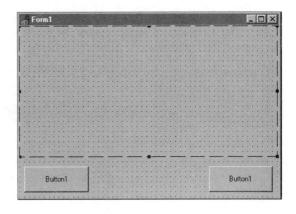

You have now completed all the steps you need to create a very simple user interface for our program. The next stage of development is to tidy it up, changing the words in the two buttons to read <u>L</u>oad and <u>Q</u>uit and changing the title bar of the form itself. You can do this when you design the form by setting the properties in the Object Inspector.

Setting Design-time Properties

Before we actually start making dramatic changes to the look and feel of our new program, let's take a little time out to play with the Object Inspector and find out exactly how it works.

Although the main part of the display is taken up with the properties themselves, the **combo box** at the top of the inspector totally changes the way it works by allowing you to select the component whose properties you want to manipulate.

A combo box, familiar to all Windows users, shows the currently selected item with a drop-down box that lists the alternatives.

On our form so far we have three components. If you drop down the combo box at the top of the Object Inspector you can see them:

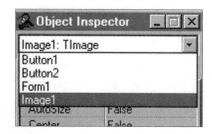

Ah! - a problem. We have only drawn three objects on the form, but the Object Inspector has other ideas and lists four. The reason for this is simply that the form itself is an object, with its own properties that you can change to customize the way the form looks and behaves at run time.

Using the Object Inspector is another way of selecting an object. Try it now - drop down the combo box and select **Button1**. The button on the form is selected, as shown when the resize buttons appear:

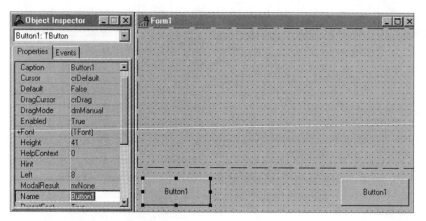

This is all well and good, but what exactly are the properties that the Object Inspector claims to display, and how do you we play with them? As we saw earlier, each property in the list changes the look and/or functionality of the selected component. How you actually change a property varies considerably:

> Some drop down a list of options, they have a button with a downward arrow. Some of these have only two values (usually True or False), and these may be toggled by double-clicking the property's current value.

> Others involve nothing more than typing the new property value into the data area, to the right of the property name.

> Lastly, those with an ellipsis on their button pop up a dialog box (called a **property editor**) which you can edit. Usually, such editors allow you to browse for files or enter lots of data at once. We'll see a simple one in action soon.

Navigating around the Object Inspector is also easy enough. After clicking in the Inspector, you can use *Page Up*, *Page Down* and the cursor keys to move around, as well as the scroll bar on the right-hand side of the Inspector. You can also jump directly to groups of properties by clicking on the Object Inspector and then press the *Tab* key followed by the first letter of the property you want to jump to, i.e. *C* for **Caption**, *F* for **Font**.

Try It Out - Using the Object Inspector

Okay, let's change some properties now to make our application start to look like a real program (we still need to write code to bring it to life, but we'll do that a bit later).

1 The first thing to do is to change the captions of the two command buttons. Select the first button (the one on the left), then find the Caption entry in the Object Inspector:

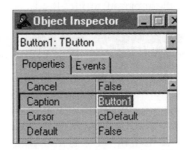

To the right of this label is the data entry area, currently holding Button1. Click on this and type in &Quit. The caption in the button itself should change, but rather than saying &Quit, it actually says Quit. The & sign that you typed in tells Delphi that the letter following it will be this object's **hot key.**

When the program is actually running, the user can press *Alt+Q* to activate that object, rather than moving the mouse over to it and clicking, or pressing *Tab* repeatedly until the object gets **focus** (i.e. is active and has that dotted box on the button). By the way, you can also change the order in which the components receive focus (using the TabOrder property) and even whether it can accept focus (TabStop).

2 Now you know the basics, change the caption of the second button to Load (so you type &Load). Remember to select the button itself before changing the properties, either by selecting the button from the combo box at the top of the Object Inspector, or by single-clicking on the button itself.

3 Finally, try changing the caption of the form to My First Delphi Application. You can select the form by clicking in the area inside the form that is not already covered by a component. For example, you could click in the space between the two buttons to select the form, but clicking in the form's title bar will have no effect. This allows you to move the form around by dragging its title bar without your component focus lapsing:

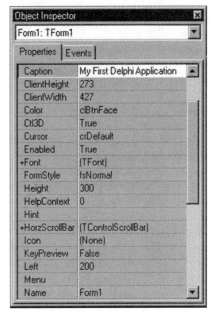

Note that, on occasion, it won't be easy to get to the form - some components can be instructed to completely cover the form, resizing as the form's dimensions change. In this case, the Object Inspector is where you should turn, selecting the form via the combo box.

Cracking the Code

Okay, now that we have our components on the form and have changed the properties of some of the components, the whole thing looks a lot more professional. It's now time to write some code and really bring the program to life. Ready, Igor....

Try It Out - Working with Code

Strangely enough, the easiest part of the application to write is the bit that stops the application, so let's tackle that first.

1 Double-click on the Quit button.

2 Change the code that Delphi presents you with to look like this:

```
procedure TForm1.Button1Click(Sender: TObject);
begin
    Close;
end;
```

3 Press *F12* to switch back to the form, because we've finished with the code part!

How It Works

When you double-click on a component, Delphi interprets this as a request to create an event handler for the component's default event. In this case, the default event is the **OnClick** event, so Delphi creates the following code:

```
procedure TForm1.Button1Click(Sender: TObject);
begin

end;
```

We're going to discuss the individual parts of an event handler in the following chapters but, for now, you should note that this code states that the button is a member of **TForm1**'s collection, the button is called **Button1** and we are dealing with the **OnClick** event.

To get the application to respond correctly to the user's request to close down the application, we need to add the appropriate Pascal statement - **Close**, in this case - to this event handler. When we compile the project, Delphi interprets this as a request to close down **TForm1** and so end the application, just as we want.

Why not try it out? Fire up the compiler and run the executable (press *F9*) - the Quit button works!!

Well, we've talked about events and event handlers, but what do they mean? If you come from a C or Pascal background, you won't have encountered this concept before, so let's look at it in a little more detail.

Event-driven Programming

In traditional programming languages such as C and earlier versions of Pascal and Basic, a programmer would write code in a linear fashion. In the best traditions of novel writing, you'd start at the beginning and progress through the middle to get to the end. Unless it was exceptionally well written, anyone using such a program would be forced to proceed through the program's functionality in a predetermined order.

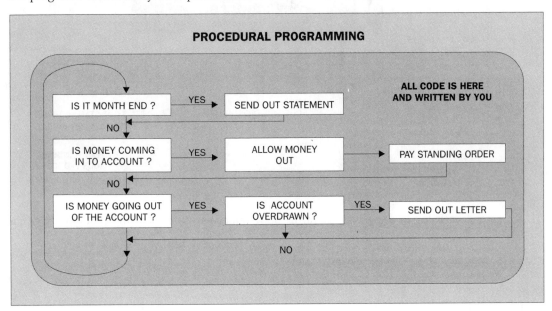

Windows applications bring with them a lot more freedom. Users expect to be able to use most parts of a program's functionality most of the time. They expect to be able to click buttons, use their mouse to move around data entry forms in any order they choose, and so on. For this reason, it is very hard to write a Windows program in the traditional manner - you soon end up with a jumbled mess of code frantically trying to figure out what the user did and run the appropriate routine to cope with it.

Event-driven programming languages such as Delphi are much nicer to work with. As you have already seen, the first step in developing an application with Delphi is to create the user interface, essentially drawing the look and feel of the application with flamboyant waves of the mouse. The programming side comes in by adding code to handle relevant events. Combining this idea with that of an stand-alone object is natural - a button should expect to be clicked as that is part of its design, so building an OnClick event into the object is a logical way of handling the event.

In this way, your application is actually developed in much the same way as a user might use it. You put a text box on a form and think "What is the user going to do with this, and what do I want the user to do?". You then code the events of the text box to tell the program how to cope with the data that the user is likely to enter, as well as, perhaps, what to do when the user enters data that is not supported.

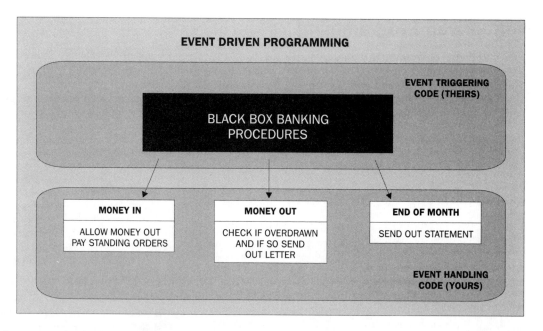

So, getting back to our sample program, it's now quite easy to explain the code you have just written:

```
procedure TForm1.Button1Click(Sender: TObject);
begin
    Close;
end;
```

The first word tells Delphi that this block of code is a **procedure**. Event handlers like this are always **procedures**.

 FYI   Procedures are small self-contained blocks of code written to do some particular task - follow the 'divide and conquer' method of solving a problem - several small procedures are more flexible and easier to write than one hulking monolith.

It's really quite similar to the type of procedures that we, as humans, may follow:

In case of fire:

1 Scream

2 Grab backups

3 If no backups exist, blow fire while making backups

4 Scream some more

5 Panic

6 Run

7 Cry

This simple procedure explains the things staff here do in the event of a fire. The alternative to a procedure is a block of code known as a **function**.

If you need to return some result of a piece of code to the program (and not just to the user interface), use a function.

For example, we could rewrite our fire procedure to include a function called CanFindBackups. So, the procedure above becomes something like this:

1 Scream

2 If CanFindBackups = 'No' then BlowFire and create Backups

3 Grab Backups

4 ...

Back to the Delphi code. Directly following the word **procedure**, we have the name of the procedure. Since we are programming for events, we need very specific names so that Delphi can use the right code for the right event. For this reason, when dealing with events we leave the naming of the event procedure in Delphi's capable hands.

In this case, the procedure name is **TForm1.Button1Click**. With a bit of reverse reading, we can deduce that this applies to the click event code for a component called **Button1**, which belongs to **TForm1**. All in all, we end up having a pretty clear-cut ownership of the event within the application. The bit in brackets after the procedure name we ignore for now - more of that in Chapter 5.

The words **begin** and **end;** mark the beginning and end of the actual code statements that we want the computer to execute when this event occurs. Delphi needs to be told where you think your procedure code actually starts and ends in order for it to make a rough guess at what you're trying to accomplish. It can then return the right error code when it doesn't understand, if you're being cynical, or perform the correct operation when it does.

Each code statement needs to end with a semicolon, to indicate that it has finished. This has the benefit that you can write a statement over several lines of code to make it fit on the screen, the compiler will ignore the carriage returns, waiting for that semicolon. Woe betide you if you don't deliver one.

Finally, we come to the bit of the code that you actually wrote. The **Close;** statement, strangely enough, closes down the **current object** (in this case, the owner of the procedure **TForm1**).

Even though you have added just one line of code, there is still a surprising amount of functionality to your program. You can drag the window around, resize it and, if you had any controls on the form, you'd be able to move around them using *Tab*. All this is handled for you by both Windows and Delphi. To activate your part of the program, click on the Quit button and the application will end because its one and only form closes down.

Extending the Application

At the moment, we have done very little to the project other than paint a few components onto the form and add code to the **OnClick** event on the Quit button. For the program to become useful, it needs to open files and display graphics.

Thankfully, the power of Delphi 2.0 means that this need not be a labor of Hercules. Later in the book we'll learn more about the common dialogs that appear in so many Windows programs. They are really very easy to use and can add an exceptional level of power and functionality to your programs with very little effort.

The dialog we are most interested in using is called File Open:

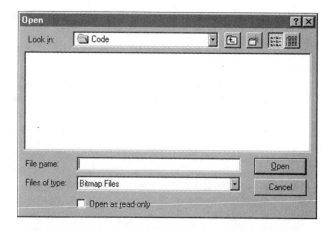

You can add the File Open dialog's functionality to your application just by dropping an OpenDialog component onto your form, just like any other component. You can find this component on the Dialogs tab of the Component Palette along with a list of all the common dialogs that Delphi supports.

When you do add the component to the form, a small icon, the same as the one on the Component Palette, appears on your form. This is a sure sign of an invisible component. It's visible at design time, but at run time the user sees nothing until you bring the dialog to life. We'll look at how to do this in a few moments, but for now, let's carry on with the design of our application.

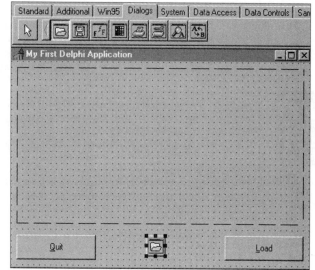

FYI If you ever mistakenly add the wrong component, either visible or not, to your form, simply highlight the component and press the *Delete* key.

As we said way back when we started work on this program, we only want the user to be able to select graphic files on the hard disk, so, in effect, we want to filter out all the other files. This is all handled for you by the dialog's Filter property.

Try It Out - Using a Property Editor

1 Add an OpenDialog component to your form (anywhere, it doesn't matter) and then click on the Filter property in the Object Inspector:

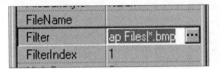

2 Unlike the other properties you have dealt with so far, the right-hand side of the data entry area contains a small button with three dots (ellipsis). Click this button to activate the Filter Editor.

It looks a lot more complex than it actually is. The left-hand column of the grid holds descriptions of the filters that you enter, while the right-hand side contains a file specification that is the filter. In our case, all we want to see are files ending in **.bmp**.

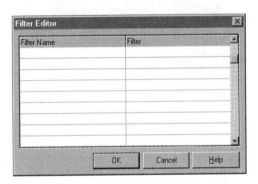

3 Click the top row of the grid in the left-hand column and enter a suitable description for the filter, say Bitmap Files, then in the right-hand column type *.bmp.

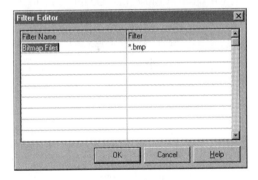

4 Now all that remains to set up the filter is to press the OK button.

FYI In case you're bored with looking at an empty Image outline while designing the form, you can use the Picture Editor (check out the Image component's Picture property) to load in a bitmap at design time. It will be loaded into the image when the form is created as well.

Method in Our Madness

Our application is now nearly ready. To complete it, we need to write code in the Load button's **OnClick** event that displays the OpenDialog and then loads the specified filename into the Image box.

Now we enter the realm of *methods*. Basically, a method is a predefined function or procedure of an object that allows you to work with the data held in an object. The way they handle the data is specific to the object and is hidden from the user, who only knows how to call the method. It's like the caterpillar we met earlier - you know it digests those leaves, but not how.

In contrast, event handlers are created by the application programmer to handle certain predefined happenings. It is here that you can call an object's methods (and set and retrieve an object's properties) as part of your Pascal code.

The **Close** command you used earlier was a method of the form. By saying **Close** we are actually running a part of the form's functionality, in this case telling the form to close itself down. All the code needed to do that is built into the object. Unfortunately, several commonly used components share similarly named methods and, therefore, we need to explore a way to explicitly call the method we wish to execute.

One of these components is the subject of our example, the OpenDialog, sharing several methods with other members of the Component Palette's Dialog tab. To invoke a specific object's methods, we need to use the following syntax:

```
<object>.<method>
```

The intervening full stop indicates that the method belongs to the object. This being the case, as we wish to cause the OpenDialog to appear on screen, we must call the component's execute method like this:

```
OpenDialog1.Execute
```

Now, that's all well and good, but those of you who are still awake may now be asking some searching questions, such as:

- What if the user hits the Cancel button on the dialog?
- How do we get at the name of the file that the user actually selected?

These questions are nothing to worry about - just remember at the beginning of this chapter I said we were only going to write three lines of code.

It's not at all obvious, but the **Execute** method of the OpenDialog is actually a function. It returns a value of True if the user selected a file and pressed OK, False if they did not. In our case, if the user does choose a file to load, we need to load the file into the Image box. If the user cancels, we should do nothing. We go into the detailed ins and outs of Delphi code over the rest of the book, but just to whet your appetite, let me introduce the **If** statement.

Using the Help Menu

In order for you to get quickly into the swing of depending on help for the syntax of all these code commands (and the 'friendly' way in which Pascal presents them), select Help | Help Topics. Go to the index page and type if, then select that help page.

FYI When you start to use the help system extensively, you will quickly notice that the index is incremental, which means that you don't have to type in the whole word before the help system has zeroed in on a small number of alternatives for you to manually choose between. You probably won't have noticed this feature if you have looked up if, but if you try something a little longer, you'll see how invaluable this tool really is.

You will find that many of the help pages offer you a number of features that will make your search a little easier. Two of the most useful are the Example and See Also links, which give you an example of the current subject in practical Pascal code terms or offer you advice as to other help pages that you might find interesting, respectively. Another feature that you might find useful, particularly if you like the See Also feature, is that of the Back button. This allows you to quickly move backwards to help pages that you have recently been looking at.

Back to the **If...then...else** statement:

```
If <condition> then
   { Block of code to run if the condition is met }
   else
   { Block of code to run if the condition is not met }
```

The **If** statement lets us test a condition and, depending upon the result of that test, it will run one of two distinct sections of code. You should note that the test must return a True or False result so that the decision can be taken between the two sections of code.

Let me illustrate. For our example, we could write

```
If OpenDialog1.Execute = True Then
   {Load the picture}
Else
   {Do Nothing};
```

The curly brackets here are comments. They allow you to put little notes in your code which the Delphi compiler will happily ignore. Comments are a great idea, not only from the point of view of the poor guy writing books for you lot to read, but also for you making notes while you write code. You will find such notes invaluable when you come back to the code after a few months - you won't get a headache trying to understand what the code does; just read the 'English' comments. No laughing at the back there - it's not as far-fetched as it sounds.

FYI In Delphi 2.0, to tie in with C++ commenting conventions, you can also comment out single lines of code using //.

So, armed with our **If** line, all that remains is to load the selected filename into the Image component. This part is shockingly simple, so stay with me:

```
If OpenDialog1.Execute Then
    Image1.Picture.LoadFromFile(OpenDialog1.Filename);
```

What are we saying here? Well, we are calling the **LoadFromFile** method of the **Picture** object, which is the part of the Image component responsible for displaying graphics. Let's try that again! The Image component called **Image1** has an object within it called **Picture** which deals with various types of picture. The **Picture** object has a method that we can use to get a graphic into the Image component, called **LoadFromFile**. However, we can't just say **LoadFromFile** in code. We must tell Delphi which object the method belongs to and, in this case, the parent object that this object is attached to.

The bit in brackets (called a **parameter**) just passes a value to the **LoadFromFile** method - you must tell the method the name and path of the file that you wish to load - and in this case, we are using the file selected by the user with the OpenDialog. We can access this information using the OpenDialog's **Filename** property - I know it can get tricky to tell the difference between methods and properties, but we'll come back to this distinction in a later chapter. For now, why don't you select the component and take a look at the Object Inspector.

FileEditStyle	fsEdit
FileName	
Filter	Bitmap Files|*.bmp
FilterIndex	1
HelpContext	0
HistoryList	(TStrings)

FYI Or you can select the component on the form, and then press *F1* to access Delphi's context-sensitive help. Just think about this for a moment - you can get context-sensitive help from either the Object Inspector, the form or from mouse-selected text in the code window; *F1* saves you time and bother, especially as I can never remember the exact Pascal syntax for every statement.

Hang on a minute, we use the Object Inspector to set the properties of our objects. We haven't set **Filename**, so how can we use it? To complicate matters, most properties can be set at either design time or run time - just like in real life, the caterpillar starts at a given size and grows bigger until it pupates. If we don't set the property at design time, we have to set the property at run time before we can use it, just like our example. We need to get some user interaction with the OpenDialog to set the **Filename** property before we can use to in the **LoadFromFile** method to view the graphic.

Just to reinforce the point, call up the help on the Image component and take a look at the Properties and Methods hot keys near the top - note how some of the properties are described as key (specific to the Image component) and how others are run time only (these properties are marked with little triangles). Whereas most properties may be assigned when designing the form, some can't. For instance, the **Owner** of the Image component cannot be determined until the program runs.

Let's use two of those key Image properties: **Stretch** and **Autosize**, set their properties within the program code and thus at run time. **Stretch** alters the bitmap to fit it to the Image component's boundaries, while **Autosize** alters the boundaries to suit the actual bitmap size. They are set to either **True** or **False** and, since they are opposites, it's one or the other. I've put them both in the program, but left one commented out:

```
Image1.Stretch   := True;
//Image1.Autosize := True;
```

As you can see from the code, both object methods and properties are written in Delphi code in the same way.

So, the next question is, where can we put this code? Think about it! We want this code to run when the user clicks on the Load button on the main form. It should make sense then that you have to code the Load button's click event. That's all there is to it; there's no catch. Double-click the Load button to bring up the code window:

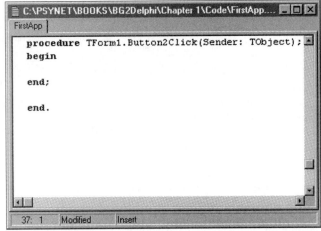

Change the event so that it looks like this:

```
procedure TForm1.Button2Click(Sender: TObject)
begin
   If OpenDialog1.Execute then
   begin
     Image1.Stretch   := True;
     //Image1.Autosize := True;
     Image1.Picture.LoadFromFile(OpenDialog1.Filename);
   end;
end;
```

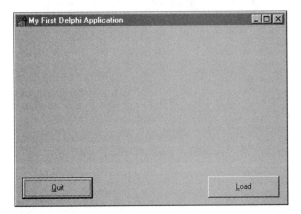

Once you have typed that little lot in, you can run your program. You already saved it earlier on, so Delphi already knows where to put the files before you compile, and it will do so. Once again, provided you typed everything in correctly, the program will run and the familiar form will appear.

This time, click on the <u>L</u>oad button:

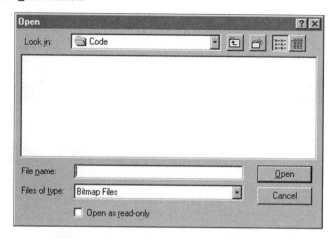

Select **logo.bmp** from the samples disk and click OK. A very short pause later and the file is displayed in your form. Try it again - click <u>L</u>oad, but this time when the File Open dialog appears click on Cancel. The picture doesn't change at all because there is no code that could run to make it change if you clicked Cancel.

So there you have it. A fully working graphic file viewer with just three lines of code, a few components and just four property changes. It probably took you a little longer than the ten minutes I originally promised, but that's only because you were reading the book and following its text rather than working intuitively on your own. By the end of the next few chapters, though, you should have enough experience to do what we just did without any help and probably a lot quicker.

The best bit is that if you put this little program up against the equivalent from a C programmer, your code will be as fast, if not faster than theirs. So much for the bum rap visual development environments being slow and clunky.

Getting Help When You Need It Most

In a Utopian programmer's world, coding would be simple. You'd sit down at your PC, specification in hand, hammer away for a couple of hours whilst pondering how delicate the grass on the lawn outside looks blowing in the breeze. At the end of the couple of hours, you would hit the magic compile button, everything would go right first time and within weeks, you'd be sailing the Med in your new 64 foot cruiser.

In real life, thought, things are different. If the bugs don't get you, the technical aspects will. Constantly reaching for the manuals each time you hit a stumbling block and then spending minutes, maybe even hours, thumbing through its well worn pages is annoying. Sitting, staring blankly at the screen without the foggiest clue why the GOC (Generally Offensive Compiler) has thrown up the latest Invalid Object Reference insult is worse still.

Don't be afraid to play around and experiment with the help system. It contains more information than the manuals along with a veritable treasure chest full of helpful code examples and hints that would otherwise take you hours of painful experimentation to learn. Never be afraid to ask Delphi for help.

Summary

We have covered a lot of ground in this chapter, and hopefully made you a lot more comfortable with Delphi and its environment than you were when we started. Just to jog your memory, we have covered:

- How to create a new Delphi project
- How to draw a user interface using Delphi's components
- How to save your work to disk
- How to move around the Object Inspector quickly and efficiently
- How to use the Object Inspector to change properties
- How to use the code window to write code
- How to use properties through code
- What events are
- How to use a common dialog
- How to run an application
- How to use the help system

Many of these topics still have gaps in them and the general idea is that, by this point, you are so fired up that you just have to turn the page and learn more. If that's the case read on, if not, read on anyway.

Delphi and Components

The simple reason why development systems like Delphi are so popular is their visual approach to programming. Instead of having to write hundreds of lines of complex code just to allow the user to interact with your program in a Windows environment, visual development systems allow you to concentrate on your program and its interaction with the user, focusing your creativity on code specific to the application and on the look of the form. For each race you run, rather than having to run two miles just to reach the starting line, your front door is now the start blocks, so to speak.

This level of functionality, particularly in Delphi, is made possible by the **components** the package includes as standard. The forms in your application are like a blank canvas upon which you drop those pre-written components, and, hey presto, the canvas comes to life. As we saw in Chapter 1, even the form will work perfectly as a window which you can drag, minimize, maximize and close. And none of it took you any time.

In this chapter, we take a look at some of the basic components included within Delphi 2.0, and how to use them. You will learn:

- What components really are
- How to navigate around Delphi's Component Palette
- How to drop components onto a form and then bring them to life through code
- How to use more of Delphi's components

By the end of this chapter you should fully understand how to use a component. Thus armed, you can start exploring not just the Palette, but the wealth of add-in components (freeware or shareware) out there. Viewing applications as a collection of diverse components, most, if not all, of which you don't have to code yourself, becomes a very seductive and practical way to look at the Delphi world.

A Quick Introduction

The easiest way to think of **components** is as the building blocks for your application. Continuing our artistic analogy, we could compare programming Windows applications without components to an artist who, in the course of painting his or her masterwork, also has to make the canvas, brushes and paints.

Many programmers have settled for this method of code creation, but those new to the industry now have a choice. Delphi still allows you to create this type of code, but it also offers you several short cuts to speed your development and reduce programming bugs. In effect, Delphi offers the artist the tools of his trade if he wants to take advantage of them.

Delphi components provide you with pre-tested, fully functional **objects** (that magic word again) which you can add to your applications to provide users with a powerful and familiar user interface. You could, of course, spend time designing and implementing your own kind of text, combo or list box, but why should you when they're already available and can save you time writing, testing and debugging your application?

Let's take a closer look at Delphi's component repository, the **Component Palette**.

The Component Palette

When you first load up Delphi, the Component Palette appears across the top of the IDE, underneath the Delphi menu bar and to the right of the SpeedBar. Since Delphi is shipped with a large number of components 'ready to go', Borland thought it would be a good idea to group all the components into categories, with each category accessible by clicking on a tab above the Component Palette itself. This is a much better way of working than in something like Visual Basic, where you can end up with a massive component toolbar that dwarfs the editing area as it grows.

Each component on the Palette will also quite happily tell you what it is. If you move the mouse pointer over a component and leave it there for a few seconds, a fly-by hint pops up giving you a clue as to what the component actually does.

In addition to all this, the Component Palette is fully configurable. If you feel, for example, that a component would be better off living on a different tab, or that you want to add to the Palette some components that you have just bought, you can do so simply by clicking on the Configure Palette... entry on the Component menu.

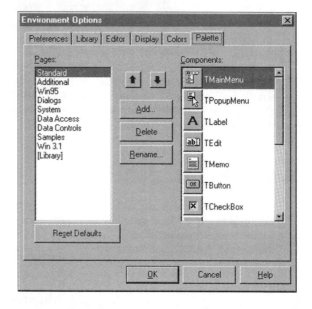

A dialog pops up, allowing you to move the components around, create new tabs and much more besides.

We'll discuss adding new components at the end of this chapter.

Before we go any further, it's worth explaining a little more about the Component Palette. Notice how the far left-hand component is not really a component at all. If you select a component by mistake, you can click on this icon to deselect the component and give you a normal 'non-destructive' mouse cursor again.

You should also notice that the far left and right-hand edges of the Palette look like left and right arrows. In the screenshot above, my screen resolution is such that I can see all the standard components on screen at once. However, if you work in a smaller resolution, these buttons become enabled, letting you scroll the components to the left and right if they don't all fit onto your screen.

 You may also get active buttons that allow you to scroll between the tabs on the Component Palette. This could be because of a small screen resolution or because you've added to many new tabs to the Component Palette - we look at one way of doing this at the end of the chapter.

Ideally, though, considering the amount of information Delphi likes to give you when you write your applications, it's a good idea to run your screen in 800x600 resolution at a bare minimum.

Using the Components

Actually applying the components to the form is really quite easy; you simply click on the component you want and then on the form where you want that component to go. The new component appears with resize handles to show that it is selected. You can also use these handles to change the shape and size of any visual component.

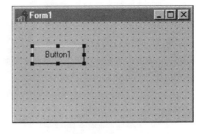

Delphi can provide a lot of automatic help when it comes to sizing and positioning components on your form. If you right-click on a component that you have just put on the form (i.e. it is selected), a menu appears with various options, including those to control the alignment:

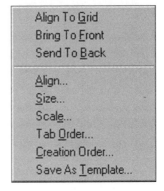

Let's put all of this theory into practice and look at how we could create the layout of Chapter 1's application user interface with a little more control.

Try It Out - Sizing and Positioning Components

1 If you haven't got Delphi running, start it up now and take advantage of Delphi's habit of creating a new application when it first starts up. If it's up and running, just select File | New Application to clear the decks - your screen will show the familiar blank form and you'll be ready to go:

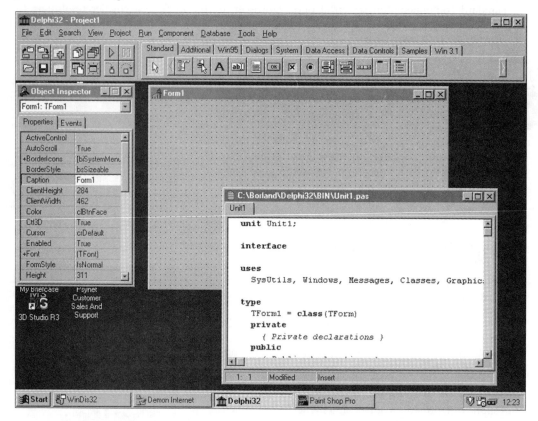

2 Let's put all the components onto the form to start off with and introduce another method of putting them there. Double-click on the Image component - it's on the Additional page of the Palette - and the component should appear in the middle of your form. Do the same for the OpenDialog component - it's on the Dialogs page, remember?

3 Next, we need to add the buttons. Let's try a new technique for this, too - hold down the *Shift* key while you select the Button component from the Standard page. Now click on the form, once on the left of the Image component and once on the right:

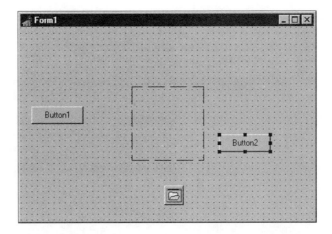

Now deselect the Button component by clicking on the cursor icon at the very left of the Component Palette.

4 Now we're ready to organize the layout of the components. Select the left button and right-click on it. As we want to alter the dimensions of our button, select the Size... menu item:

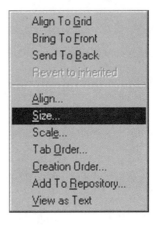

5 Enter a custom width of 113 and a custom height of 33 by clicking on the appropriate entry and then entering the value in its Edit box partner - then click OK to accept your new dimensions. This should give you a button of the same dimensions as those in Chapter 1's application.

6 In that application, both of our buttons are the same size. We could use the same technique to resize the right button, but let's try something else instead. With the left button still selected, hold down the *Shift* key and select the right button. Now release the *Shift* key, right-click on one of the selected components and choose the Size... menu option:

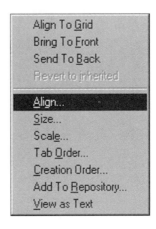

39

7 This time select Grow to largest from both the Width: and Height: options. This should give us what we want! While we've got both buttons selected, you should note that you can drag them all around at the same time as a group. Their final resting place is at the bottom of the form, so why don't you drag them there now?

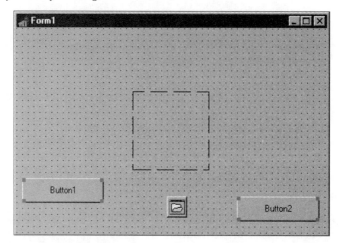

8 The next stage is to tidy up how the buttons align with each other. While we're at it, why not move the OpenDialog component out of the way as well? Again, while the two buttons are selected, hold the *Shift* key down and click on the OpenDialog component - you should now have all three components selected.

9 Right-click on one of the selected components and choose the Align menu item. Select Bottoms from the Vertical offerings and your components should line up, resting on a common base line which is taken from the position of the component that you selected first.

10 If you selected one of the higher components first, you'll need to move all of the components to the bottom of the screen. If you have all three selected, you can do this in one movement. Simply place your mouse over one of the components and, while holding the left mouse button down, drag the components to their final resting place, something like that shown below:

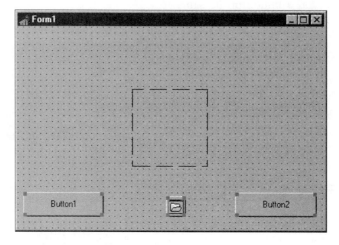

11 The last thing to sort out is the Image component. If you select it and take a look at the Object Inspector, you'll be able to find a property called Align. Change this property to alTop by selecting this option from the list provided (click on the tab that appears at the end of the property) and the Image component should jump to the top, spreading itself across the entire width of the form.

12 The final step is to resize the Image component to fit the rest of our window. Grab the bottom middle resize handle and drag the bottom of the component down closer to the buttons, which leaves the finished user interface looking like this:

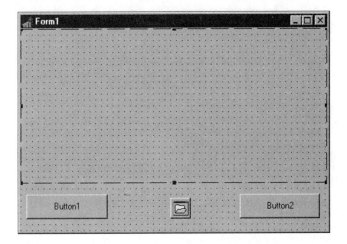

How It Works

I've covered quite a lot of techniques in this Try It Out, so let's take a bit of time to examine each in turn. First of all the *Shift* key - we used it in two different ways, which are in fact related. We first used it to add a number of components to the form without needing to return to the Component Palette. We used it again to help us to select several components on the form at the same time.

As a general rule, if you want to work with more than one component, use the *Shift* key to select them all before you start.

You must remember that this is a state feature - this means that until you turn it off, it's on, and vice versa. To turn it off, you need to either click on the cursor icon on the Component Palette if you are adding multiple components to the form, or click on the form if you have been selecting multiple components already on the form.

One of the most powerful uses for multiple component selection is when you wish to use the Size... and Align... menu items. Unless you are using the custom sizing options, you will need to have a number of components selected before the logic will make sense. How can you align a set of components if you've only got one selected?

The more astute observers among you will be asking "How do we know which component will be used as the anchor?", i.e. which component stays put and which components move? The answer to your question is in the order in which the component selection occurred. The first component to be selected is the anchor, and all the rest will conform to its position.

The final item of interest is the use of the Align property. Delphi uses this property to anchor a component to a specific part of your form. Try resizing the window - the Image component resizes with it! Again, you should have a play with this property to get used to it.

alTop, alBottom, alRight and **alLeft** all anchor the component to the relevant side of the form, and dynamically resize the component on the adjacent sides. The final side is static (i.e. Delphi won't automatically move it when the form is resized), as you can see by the way we need to pull down the bottom side of the **Image** component closer to our buttons. **alNone** cuts all links between the component and the form, while **alClient** causes all four sides of the component to resize to the dimensions of the form and dynamically resize with the form.

The easiest way to get used to these tools is to play around with them. I suggest that you get yourself a blank form, drop three components onto it and try aligning and resizing them to your heart's content.

The Grid

You may have noticed the collection of dots on the forms you're using at design time, which mysteriously vanish at run time. This is the grid and provides a convenient way to uniformly resize and position components on your form.

Using the Environment Options dialog (by selecting Tools | Options... and the Preferences tab) you can turn the grid on and off, and make Delphi 'snap' new components to the grid. This rather dramatic term just means that - when you draw and resize components on a form, Delphi will only let you move and resize in steps the size of the spacing between the dots on the grid.

Fortunately, Delphi does let you change the size of the grid - check out the **Preferences** tab on **Tools** | **Options...** again. You can choose any size between 2 and 128, but a useful range is between 4 and 16.

The dimensions and spacing of the grid really depend on your own personal preferences. Personally, I like a very fine grid: it gives me enough finesse over moving and resizing my components to prevent the form from looking too mechanical, but it still lets me easily align the components on the form.

While we are looking at this dialog, you might be interested in the three checkboxes that are deal with the grid. You can choose whether to display the grid, whether to force the new components to snap to the grid (it doesn't matter whether they're visible or not) and whether the names of non-visual components should appear below the component.

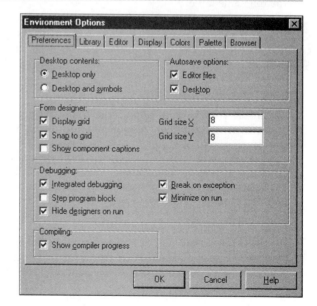

This final option can be quite useful when you have a number of non-visual components on your form. Each component's icon simply identifies what type of component it is, but with this feature, you can tell immediately which of the three OpenDialog components you should currently be working with, as each now has a label beneath it stating its name.

While you're here, you might be interested in some of the other features that Delphi offers you. For example, you can ask Delphi to show you the compiler's progress - a useful feature that indicates that something is actually happening when you press the Run button, as well giving you some other interesting information. Try compiling a project with this option on and see what you can see.

You might also be interested in the Minimize on run feature - this hides the Delphi IDE when the project is actually run from inside the package; it gives you a cleaner desktop that makes the application look more like a stand-alone executable when it is running.

 Remember that if you spot an item on any dialog that sounds interesting, you can check out Delphi's help system for more information. Just hit *F1* and see what Delphi has to say...

Dealing with Component Properties

In addition to the size and alignment dialogs, you can also change the way your components both look and behave by changing their properties in the Object Inspector.

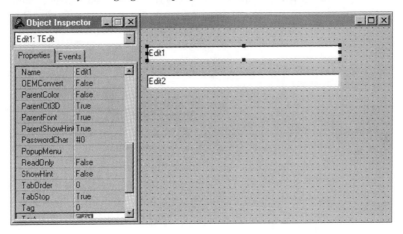

In fact, the Object Inspector will probably become your main design-time property editor. Why? Well, let's take a look at how you would resize and relocate the two buttons on your interface without using the dialogs.

Try It Out - The Object Inspector

1 Start a new application and drop two buttons onto the form. If you still have the last project open (the one where we tried to rebuild our user interface with our newly acquired skills), Delphi will ask you if you wish to save your work - you won't need the project again, so answer with the No button.

2 Using the *Shift* key, select both buttons.

3 Go to the Object Inspector and enter the following values for the given properties: Width - 133, Height - 33, Left - 8 and Top - 232. As you change each property, watch what happens to the components - if you set the properties in this order, the buttons will resize to the same shape and then move around until they appear to be one button - in fact, they are on top of each other.

4 Click on the form to deselect both components and then select Button2 using the drop-down list box at the top of the Object Inspector.

5 Go to the Left property in the Object Inspector - this now only relates to the second button - and enter the value 288. The button should now jump to the right, leaving us with two perfectly sized and impeccably aligned buttons.

How It Works

The Object Inspector is, in one way, a glorified property viewer. In this capacity, it reviews the contents of a component and documents all the properties and their current values. When you think of the Inspector in this way, it's not hard to work out what it will do when you have got several components selected - the Inspector displays the properties common to the selected components.

Here's a selection of properties that you will usually see in the Object Inspector, no matter which components you currently have selected:

Property Name	Description
Left, Top	Defines where on the form the left and top edges of the control appears.
Height, Width	Defines the height and width of the component on the form. Remember that screen coordinates have their origin at the top-left of the screen.
Visible	Defines whether the component actually appears on the form when your application is running, or whether it is hidden from view (it's still on the form, though).
Enabled	Defines whether the component responds to user input at run time, or whether it appears grayed out and disabled.
Ctl3d	Defines whether the component adopts a 3D look in design mode and when the application is running. If it is not set to display the component with a 3D look, it appears like an old-fashioned Windows 3 control (plain and nasty).

So, by changing Left, Top, Width and Height properties to the same values, you are effectively saying "Put both components in the same place and make them the same size." Then we make sure that we've only got one of the buttons selected and 'right-shift' it by making the value of the Left property a little larger.

As you can see, using the Object Inspector is quick and easy, and automatically means that your components with be exactly the same size and perfectly aligned.

The values that you give to Top and Left properties will even overrule the Snap to grid option - if you ask the Object Inspector for something, you'll get it.

For the rest of this chapter, I'm going to concentrate on some more examples of using the Object Inspector, while also digging into some of the most commonly used components and some of the more exciting features of the Delphi IDE, but before I go....

Microsoft Design Standards

While we're on the subject, using Delphi components enables you to provide the common elements of the Windows 95 user interface in your applications. And, of course, with the look goes the feel, the Microsoft design which we all know and love.

This means that just by producing a Delphi application that makes use of these components, you can reduce the time users spend learning how to use your application. You're left with the difficult task of positioning the components for maximum impact. Give a user an interface that looks totally original and after the initial "Wow, that looks nice!", you'll most likely find them getting frustrated at not being able to find their way around. Once they get used to something, they find it difficult to break the habit and let you be original.

Although, at the moment, this might not seem to be a prime consideration, you'll find that it becomes more and more important as you progress in the programming world. You'll find that many books have been completely devoted to interface design.

Check out *The Windows Interface Guidelines For Software Design* by Microsoft Press, ISBN 1-55615-679-0. It's also available from the MSDN or as part of the documentation associated with numerous Microsoft products.

You can spend time (and resources) looking out this information, but there is an easier way to adhere to the design standards.

Simply compare your layout and organization to any other commercial package - in general, everybody follows the rules, so copying somebody else can usually get you 90% of the way to a decent screen layout. To complete your layout, test it out with a couple of friends and see what they've got to say - usability studies can be really quite useful at times.

Starting at the Beginning

To get the ball rolling, let's throw together a quick application that does some fun stuff with properties at run time. What we're going to do is allow the user to control how and when they can enter information into an Edit component. You should be able to see that this could easily be extended to changing the appropriate properties based on code events rather than user interaction, but more on that later.

Try It Out - Our Basic Application

1 Get yourself settled in with a new application on screen, saved in a new directory, ready for work to begin. I suggest the following names for your files - **edit1u.pas** for the unit and **stage1.dpr** for the project - remember that when you want to save a project just after you've created it, the easiest way is to select File | Save Project As....

2 Add an Edit component to the form in the usual way and use the resize handles to size it as shown here:

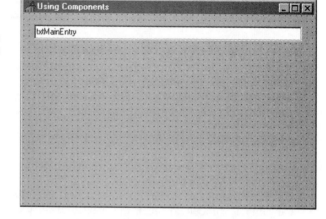

3 Use the Object Inspector to set the Name property to txtMainEntry. You can also change the Name property of the Form to EditingForm.

4 Next add a GroupBox to the form (it's on the Standard page) so it appears as shown below and change its Name to grpSelector:

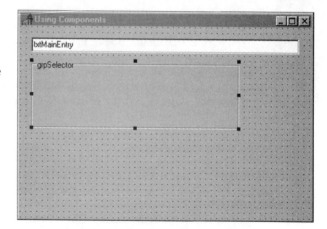

5 By default, the GroupBox comes with a built-in label. In this example, the label doesn't convey any useful information, so delete the default value in the GroupBox's Caption property:

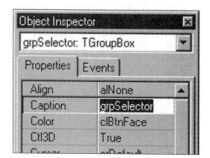

6 Now that we've got our container, we can add the RadioButtons that allow the user to control the user interface. Again, you can find these components on the Standard page of the Component Palette, but before you place the three that we need, you must make sure that the GroupBox is selected. You must also be careful to place the components inside the GroupBox when you place them - in fact, double-clicking on the Palette icon is the easiest and safest way to ensure that everything goes okay. More on this later.

7 Change the Names of the three RadioButtons to, starting from the top and working down, optDisable, optInVisible and optReEnable. You can now use your newly acquired alignment skills to organize the radio buttons neatly within the GroupBox and change the Captions of each to reflect the following interface layout:

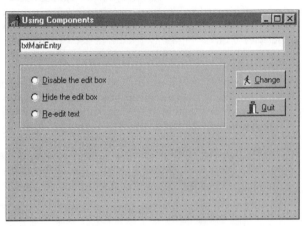

8 As you can see, I've also added two other components to my form, both of which are BitBtns. This type of component is just like a normal Button, but it also allows you to display a small bitmap (glyph) upon it. You can find this component on the Additional page of the Palette.

9 Select the first BitBtn and change its Name to cmdChange, and its Caption to Change. Now select the Glyph property, hit the ellipse and prepare to use the Picture Editor:

Click on the Load... button, select the **\Delphi2.0\Images\Buttons\Picture.bmp** and click OK, once to return to the Picture Editor and once again to return to Delphi. All we need now is the code behind this button...watch this space.

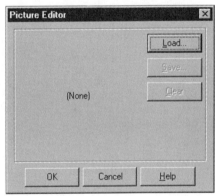

10 For the other BitBtn, change its Name to cmdQuit and change its Kind to bkClose. This provides us with a default BitBtn - all we need to do to get our finished BitBtn is to change the Caption to Quit.

11 Run the compiler and take a look at the application so far. Note that the Quit button still works, i.e. the application closes down, even though we haven't yet added any code to the application.

How It Works

In this Try It Out, I've introduced three new types of component, and we've looked at a variety of ways of using the Object Inspector. Let's take a look at the new types of component first.

I'm going to leave the GroupBox until the next section - it's a complex tool, so it deserves its own discussion - so let's move on to RadioButtons. These components are used to indicate whether or not an option is selected. You might well ask why you need them when a CheckBox does the exact same job. Well, RadioButtons are normally used to indicate which option is selected from a mutually exclusive set of choices, providing a feature that you can't really do without.

If you create a new application, drop several RadioButtons onto the form and run it - you'll soon see what I mean. When you select a RadioButton, all the others immediately become unchecked - no matter how you try, you will never get more than one RadioButton selected (see the explanation of the GroupBox for more details).

This differs from CheckBoxes, which are simply used to indicate whether an option is selected or not, irrespective of the state of any other option. For an example of how the two components are used, check out the Preferences page of the Tools | Options... menu:

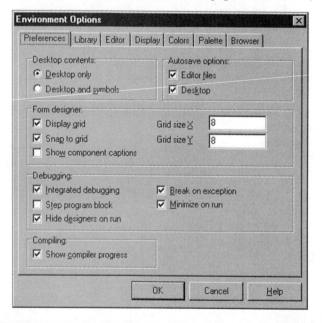

At the moment, we're not really interested in what each of these options does, but more about how the CheckBoxes and RadioButtons are put to use. Delphi offers you a set of RadioButtons under the title of Desktop Contents:. You have the choice of either just the Desktop or the Desktop and symbols. Clearly you can't have both, so a set of RadioButtons is used to provide you with a mutually exclusive set.

FYI Did you notice the **GroupBox** used to group together the **RadioButton**s into a set?

On the other hand, Delphi offers you a variety of options under the heading of Debugging, each of which bears no relationship to any of the others. Delphi doesn't care whether you want to Minimize on run at the same time as Hide designers at run, so a collection of CheckBoxes is used.

The other new type of component that I introduced was a BitBtn. As I mentioned, this is just like a normal Button, except that, along with the normal caption, you can display a glyph on it.

We used different methods of setting up the BitBtns on interface, one implicit and one explicit. The implicit method, using the Kind property, allows you to take advantage of the internal code that has been written into the description of BitBtns themselves. While defining this type of component, the developers at Borland decided that there were some kinds of buttons that you will probably want to regularly place on your forms. The buttons might include an OK button, a Close button or a Cancel button. They took it upon themselves to write the code for you, so that all you need to do is to drop a BitBtn onto a form, change a few properties and hey presto! a working button.

The explicit method is really what the Borland developers had to do to produce the 'no code' BitBtns. You have to specify a name and caption for the button, supply it with a Glyph and then write some code to be executed when the user clicks the button. Did you notice that nothing happened when you clicked the Load button as the application was running? As it had no code to work with, Delphi didn't know what you wanted to happen, so decided that nothing should!

Before we move onto the GroupBox, just a quick word about the Picture Editor. This is just a simple tool that allows you to load a property with the actual data that makes up a bitmap. As you have seen, it's not difficult to use, and the only extra functionality that it provides is the ability to clear the decks ready for a new bitmap (the Clear button) and the opportunity to rename an existing bitmap and place it in a new location (the Save... button).

Container Components and the GroupBox

As you are developing your Delphi applications, if you simply drop components onto a form, pretty soon you'll end up with a real mess of a user interface. Look at any decent Windows application and, amongst other things, you'll see frames around groups of common components. These frames are called GroupBoxes, and although we've already seen them in action, they do deserve a little more discussion.

GroupBoxes not only provide a neat way to organize the layout of the components on your forms, they also provide a great deal of control over the components they contain. Components within the GroupBox belong to the GroupBox. For example, hide a GroupBox and you hide all the components contained within it. Disable a GroupBox and all its contained components are also disabled (though they won't be grayed out).

Remember, I said that **RadioButtons** are used for mutual exclusive sets and you can never have more than one **RadioButton** selected on any given form? I lied. What I should have said is that you can never have more than one **RadioButton** selected within a given container - a form is a container in just the same way as a **GroupBox** is, but by adding a **GroupBox** to a form, you can have two **RadioButtons** selected, one that is associated with the **GroupBox**, and one that is associated with a form:

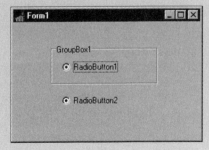

Better still, move a GroupBox and all of its associated components go with it, maintaining their relative positions. It's almost like having a mini window within a window. Dealing with them at design time can be a bit of a pain, though, if you don't know how they work.

Try It Out - Working with GroupBoxes

1 Create a new application and add a Button to the form by double-clicking on the icon in the Component Palette - it's important to use this method of adding the component this time. Notice how it appears in the dead center of the form:

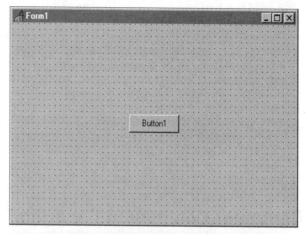

2 Now do the same thing, except this time add a GroupBox. Once again, the component appears dead center of the form, but now it obscures the button you've already created:

As you can see, the GroupBox is opaque, just like other components, the form and any normal window. It's important to note that, when selected, the GroupBox is not simply drawn around the components.

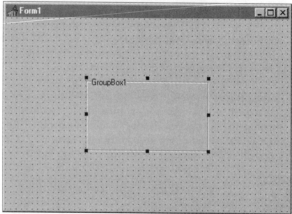

3 To get around this problem, we want to reorder the layering of the components. In Delphi you can do this by right-clicking the mouse over the control that you wish to send to the back of the list. A pop-up menu appears, like this:

If you click on the Send To Back item on the menu, then, in this case, the GroupBox will be moved underneath the button, bringing it into view:

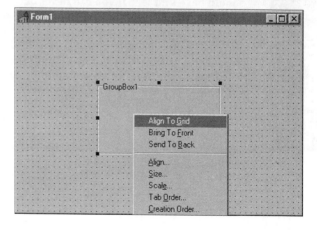

And there you have it - a button contained inside a GroupBox.

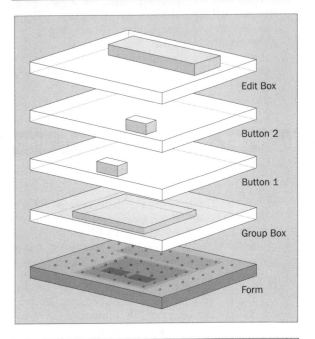

How It Works

Well, not quite. Let's think about the layering of the components on the form in another way. Picture each component you put on a form as a glass panel. This panel is the size of the form, and the component is an opaque part of an otherwise transparent panel. Putting components on top of one another stacks up these glass panels, but when you look straight down at them, you only see the controls that they contain.

Now if you have two components on different glass panels, but at the same coordinates on the form, a larger upper one can obscure the lower - this is the case with the GroupBox and the button. The simplest way around this in real life would be to move the offending glass panel underneath the others. This is what happened when we moved the GroupBox using the right-click menu.

Unfortunately, this means that the button is actually on a different panel to the GroupBox and so is free to be moved independently of the GroupBox. However, you should remember that we're talking about containers in this section. The components that are associated with a GroupBox should be tied to it, move with it, be disabled with it and so on. Take a look at this:

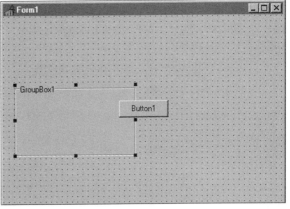

It's easy to see just how independent the two controls really are. We need to revise our model a little. Suppose that each container, whether a form, a **GroupBox** or any other type of container, is still repressed by a glass panel, but now each glass panel has an engraved area upon which you can place components. This recess into which you can place components allows the form to look exactly the same, except that now, when you move the containers around, the inlaid components must move with them.

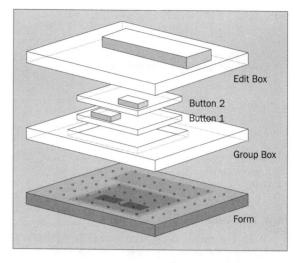

This would seem to answer our problem, but how do we make sure that the components are placed in the recess, as opposed to being encapsulated in another glass panel? Fortunately, the answer is simple. When you're adding a component to a container, Delphi asks that that container is selected - if you want to add components to a **GroupBox**, select it and drop the components on to it. If you want to then add them to the base form, deselect the **GroupBox** by clicking on the form and add the components as usual.

Try It Out - Solving the Double Glazing Problem

1 Create a new application and add a **GroupBox** to the form.

2 As the **GroupBox** is currently selected, any components that you add to the project will automatically be directly related to it. Remember that when you double-clicked on an icon in the Component Palette, Delphi added the appropriate component to the dead center of the form. Move your **GroupBox** to the top left-hand corner of the form and try adding any component to the form by double-clicking.

3 Notice how the component didn't appear in the middle of the form, but rather in the dead center of the selected container, the **GroupBox**? Now try moving the **GroupBox** and watch the component retain its position relative to the container.

4 Try moving the component out of the **GroupBox** and you'll get some strange results:

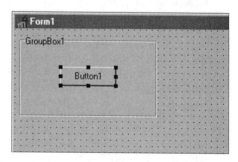

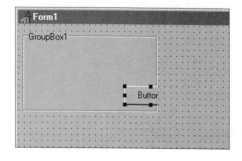

As the **GroupBox** is essentially a cut-down window, trying to drag the button off the edge of the box makes a portion of it disappear.

So What Happened Before?

Now how come the RadioButtons we added earlier all belong to the GroupBox when we made no special efforts to ensure this happened? Well, if we try to add a component to an object that is a container, that component will automatically be assigned to it. If the currently selected object isn't a container object, the component is automatically assigned to that object's parent.

In our example, we added the RadioButtons when the GroupBox was selected, so the first RadioButton was declared as a child of the GroupBox. However, when the second RadioButton was added, the GroupBox wasn't selected - the focus had passed to the first RadioButton, but Delphi still coped. As the current component wasn't a container, the new RadioButton was associated with the parent of the GroupBox, just as we wanted.

As we saw earlier, one of the advantages of the GroupBox is that it provides Delphi with some logical method for grouping controls which have a common function. In the case of RadioButtons, you can only ever have one button in a group selected and pressed down at any one time. The GroupBox component enables you to specify which buttons belong to which group - very handy.

There's another type of GroupBox that we haven't covered yet - the RadioGroup component. Why? Because it has a number of properties that allow you to work with string lists, and for those you'll have to wait until Chapter 4. Check out Chapter 5 for a working example of the RadioGroup.

As you should be able to see by now, container components like GroupBoxes can be very useful. However, outside the context of a real application, it's hard to get a decent feel for them. For that reason, now you understand what they do and how they do it, you'll be able to appreciate the examples in the rest of the book, many of which make extensive use of these powerful components.

Back to the melee. The story so far - stored on your hard disk is the project **Stage1.dpr**, and the form unit **Edit1u.pas**. Their design complete, they only lack the code to finish the application.

Try It Out - Adding the Code

What shall we to do in terms of code? The only thing that we have to code up is the Change button's OnClick event handler. So let's get to it.

1 Open up the project that we saved as **stage1.dpr**.

2 Select the Change button on the form and press *F11* to bring up the Object Inspector if you can't see it on screen.

3 Change to the Events page and double-click on the OnClick event - note that you must double-click on the right hand side of the Object Inspector for this to work. Delphi will generate a default name for the event handler and bring up the code window displaying the new event handler.

4 Add the following lines of code:

```
procedure TEditingForm.cmdChangeClick(Sender: TObject);
begin
    if optDisable.Checked = True then
        txtMainEntry.Enabled := False
    else if optInVisible.Checked = True then
        txtMainEntry.Visible := False
    else if optReEnable.Checked = True then
    begin
        txtMainEntry.Visible := True;
        txtMainEntry.Enabled := True;
        txtMainEntry.SetFocus;
    end;
end;
```

5 Run the program and check out what you can do now.

Using the Application

As soon as the application loads up, you'll be able to key text into the Edit box. Try clicking on the Disable button, then on the Change button. Notice how the text in the Edit box grays out once it becomes disabled - try to change the text; Delphi won't even let you put the cursor in the box!

Now click on the Hide radio button and then on the Change button; two things happen. First, as soon as you clicked on the Hide radio button, the Disable radio button clears out. This is the default behavior of RadioButtons grouped together in a container - we don't have to add any extra code to achieve this functionality! The second thing that happens is more obvious - the Edit box disappears.

If you then select the Re-edit text option and click on the Change button, the Edit box reappears. You should also notice that Delphi allows you to edit the contents - our code assumes that if you want to see the Edit box, you might want to change its contents!

Stop the program running by clicking on the Quit button and we'll explain the code.

How It Works - Understanding the Code

As you can see, the code we have used in this event handler is quite easy to follow - thanks to how Pascal closely resembles real world English. We do three checks, one for each of the RadioButtons, and perform a set of actions depending on which check succeeds.

Most of these actions are straightforward - by setting the Boolean properties of Enabled and Visible to an appropriate value, we simply make the Edit box either visible or invisible, enabled or disabled, depending on which checks succeed.

However, the most interesting line of code is the one I added to the end of this event handler. I know it doesn't look much, but it's quite fun and can be quite useful:

```
txtMainEntry.SetFocus;
```

This line actually gets Delphi to move the focus to the component specified, in this case, **txtMainEntry**. You can call this method at any time in your code, for any components in your application. It's a great way to control your user - it makes them focus on certain controls at critical moments. In our application, as soon as the Edit box is made visible, it is also given the focus.

You might be thinking that you need to call this method in the **FormCreate** event so that the focus begins on the control that you want. However, you might like to know about something that Delphi calls the **Tab Order**. This is a static list of all the components that you add to a form, as long as they can accept the focus - components that can't accept the focus include TLabel, TImage and TBevel.

Delphi normally uses this list to control where the focus travels around the form when the user presses the *Tab* key, but to do this, it must also know where the focus starts. So, when an application begins, Delphi automatically places the focus with the component that appears first in this list.

To have a look at this listing, select
Edit | Tab Order... :

As you can see, we have two Buttons, one Edit and a GroupBox component on our form. The Edit box will receive the focus when the application is loaded. If you want to change this order, you'll need to highlight a component and move it up and down the list until you have the components in the order that you want.

Now that you know about this tool, you should be able to see that SetFocus only comes into its own when you want to do something a little different, such as give a newly visible control the focus. In all other occasions, it's best to let the Tab Order sort out where the focus moves next.

Optimizing this Code

Even though code optimization is a subject that you'd usually leave until you were happy about the language as a whole - after all, a working application is much more important that an optimized broken one - I'm going to talk about it because, believe it or not, you already know a lot and by talking about it, you should firm up your understanding a little more.

In this event handler, we have used an extended **If** statement to get the required results. However, we have used a new **If** statement on each **else** statement, so we could rewrite this code as three independent **If** statements:

```
procedure TEditingForm.cmdChangeClick(Sender: TObject);
begin
    if optDisable.Checked = True then txtMainEntry.Enabled := False;
    if optInVisible.Checked = True then txtMainEntry.Visible := False;
    if optReEnable.Checked = True then
    begin
        txtMainEntry.Visible := True;
        txtMainEntry.Enabled := True;
        txtMainEntry.SetFocus;
    end;
end;
```

You could try out any of the code optimization stages by simply replacing the current event handler with the new code. This is because we aren't changing the meaning of the code, we are just improving on it - there is usually more than one way to skin a cat when you're coding. However, I've put this section in for you to simply read through. I've included the finished optimized code in the event handler for you (commented out, of course), so you can quickly try out the final solution, but I thought I'd just mention what I was doing!

Nothing too complicated there. In fact, rather than using an extended **If** statement when you write your own code, this might be how you first think about putting the tests together. I hope you found that step easy because the next one is a little more complex. Take the first line:

```
if optDisable.Checked = True then txtMainEntry.Enabled := False;
```

If you check out help for reference to the word **Checked**, Delphi will happily tell you that this is a property that returns a Boolean value - good job as that's what code checks are for!

I hope you remember that math lesson where you covered logic - that's what a Boolean value is all about. If it was all too long ago, just remember that the **not** operator switches a **True** value to **False**, and vice versa.

Now, think about what we are asking Delphi to check with this code - 'If the RadioButton is checked, make the Edit box disabled'. Another way to say this is 'Change the state of the Edit box's **Enabled** property to the opposite of the RadioButton's **Checked** property', hence:

```
txtMainEntry.Enabled := not(optDisable.Checked);
```

You might notice that I've covered more options than I need to with this code - if the RadioButton isn't checked, this code will make the Edit box enabled - but I'll come to that in a moment.

In a similar way, you can rewrite the second **If** statement, so our event handler should now look like this:

```
procedure TEditingForm.cmdChangeClick(Sender: TObject);
begin
    txtMainEntry.Enabled := not(optDisable.Checked);
    txtMainEntry.Visible := not(optInVisible.Checked);
    if optReEnable.Checked = True then
    begin
        txtMainEntry.Visible := True;
        txtMainEntry.Enabled := True;
        txtMainEntry.SetFocus;
    end;
end;
```

Now comes the interesting bit. Remember that really neat feature of a set of RadioButtons - only one is checked at any one time? This means that if **optReEnable** is checked, **optDisable** and `optInVisible` aren't. If you combine this with the results of changing the code for the first two **if** statements, you can see that we are actually repeating ourselves when we set the **Visible** and **Enabled** properties of the Edit box when **optReEnabled** is checked. We could save some typing (and that second set of calls to change the Edit box's properties) and delete those two lines:

```
if optReEnable.Checked = True then
    begin
        txtMainEntry.Visible := True;
        txtMainEntry.Enabled := True;
        txtMainEntry.SetFocus;
    end;
```

Now we can simply tidy up that final **If** statement and we have got a truly tight, well-optimized event handler:

```
procedure TEditingForm.cmdChangeClick(Sender: TObject);
begin
    txtMainEntry.Enabled := not(optDisable.Checked);
    txtMainEntry.Visible := not(optInVisible.Checked);
    if optReEnable.Checked = True then txtMainEntry.SetFocus;
end;
```

By optimizing this code, we have looked into how it is possible to use the features of an **If** statement without actual using the statement itself - a feat made possible because we used a Boolean values in our conditional checks. Look out for this opportunity - it'll earn you Brownie points if another programmer (your boss?) looks at your code.

The Edit Box

We have already seen the Edit box in action briefly. Now it's time to look at it in a little more depth. The primary function of the Edit box is, of course, to give the user a place on screen where they can enter and edit text. However, it does much more than this, allowing users to select portions of text, cut and paste using the clipboard and so on, all without any need for intervention from you, the programmer.

Of course, the Edit box would be of no use to anyone if it didn't provide any means for the program to get at the data it contains while it is running. After all, you may want to store the information entered somewhere, use it to control the flow of the program, and much more besides.

The way that you can do all this is through the **Text** property. Let's write a little code.

Try It Out - Dealing with Edit Boxes

1 Open up Delphi and load in the last project, **stage2.dpr**.

2 Add a new Button to the form and change its caption to Edit Selected Text (note that you have to put the ampersand (&) directly before the S in Selected to get the underline in the right place), its name to cmdBrkDownText.

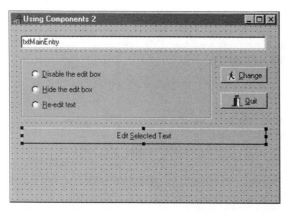

3 Now, let's add a little code to the Button so that a message about the contents of the Edit box is displayed when it is clicked. Double-click on the button to bring up the code window and change the code displayed so that it looks like this:

```
procedure TEditingForm.cmdBrkDownTextClick(Sender : Tobject);
begin
    ShowMessage('You entered :   ' + txtMainEntry.Text);
end;
```

4 Run the application and see what happens when you type something into the Edit box and click the button.

How It Works

This is just a small addition to our project, but already we have introduced two new items of interest - the **ShowMessage** command and the Edit box's **Text** property. This property is quite straightforward - if you query it (as we do in the example), Delphi will return the contents of the Edit box.

The **ShowMessage** command is not that much more complex. In fact, it does just what it says - it shows a message on the screen for the user to see. **ShowMessage** is just one of number of ways of getting dialogs up in front of the user and is something we cover in a lot more detail a little later in the book. For now, just remember that **ShowMessage** is a great way of outputting some string of data onto the screen right in front of the user.

Dealing with Selected Text

The **Text** property associated with Edit boxes is not the only useful property they possess. Quite often, you may need to write code to deal with just the highlighted text in an Edit box. For this, we can make use of the **Sel-** properties (**SelStart**, **SelText** and **SelLength**).

To illustrate these properties, we're going to adapt our project to take advantage of them. On the following page, you can see a screenshot of the finished application.

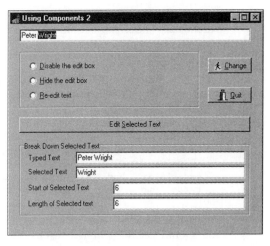

In the example shown, my surname is highlighted. **SelStart**, which is an integer that represents the start position of the selected portion of text, would be set to **6**, meaning that the selection begins with the 6th character in the Edit box.

SelLength is another integer which defines the number of characters actually selected in the Edit box, so as my surname is 6 characters long, this would also be set to **6**. The value of **SelText** would be Wright, since that is the text selected.

Note that the **Sel-** properties work totally independently of the normal **Edit** box properties. Just because **SelText** in this example holds some data, it doesn't mean that you can no longer access any data in the **Edit** box.

Try It Out - Breaking up Text

Okay, let's do it. To save time, you can load up **stage3.dpr** from the disk and go from there, but unless you got in a real mess, I suggest you keep building on the last project and replace the code behind the Edit Selected Text button - you can start to see why we called it that now!

1 Before we get to the button, add a GroupBox and place four Labels and four Edit boxes on it (remember that you must have it selected when you add the components). Make the usual changes to these components to match the shot below:

You also need to change the Names of the Edit components to, starting at the top, txtEchoText, txtSelText, txtSelStart and txtSelLength.

2 Now select the GroupBox again and set its Enabled property to False - more on this later.

3 Code time! Bring up the Edit Selected Text's OnClick event handler and delete (or comment it out as I did) the **ShowMessage** line, replacing it with these new lines:

```
procedure TEditingForm.cmdBrkDownTextClick(Sender: TObject);
begin
    //ShowMessage('You entered :  ' + txtMainEntry.Text);
    txtEchoText.Text  := txtMainEntry.Text;
    txtSelText.Text   := txtMainEntry.SelText;
    txtSelStart.Text  := IntToStr(txtMainEntry.SelStart);
    txtSelLength.Text := IntToStr(txtMainEntry.SelLength);
end;
```

4 Run the application, enter my name, highlight my surname and hit the button and hopefully you should get the required results.

How It Works

The first thing we do is to disable the GroupBox. Again, one of the features of this component is that anything you do to the container is passed through to the components contained in it - by disabling the GroupBox, we have disabled all of the labels and Edit boxes contained in it.

FYI Did you remember that you can change the value of some entries in the Object Inspector by double-clicking on them? All the Boolean properties fall into this category, as do the properties with a fixed number of choices, such as our **Button's Cursor** property. If you double-click on this property, it will scroll through the possible shapes that the cursor will have when the application is run and the user places the cursor over it.

We've done this because we don't want the user to be able to be able to alter the contents of the new Edit boxes, which will contain the values of the **Text**, **Selstart**, **SelLength** and **SelText** properties, when the application is running - any altered values wouldn't cascade back to the contents of the Edit box - the integrity of the display would have been broken.

The first two lines of code that I've added to the event handler are straightforward assignments - the first line copies the content of the Edit box to a display (i.e. disabled) Edit box, while the second performs a similar task except that it focuses on the highlighted portion of the Edit box's content.

But hold on. What's going on in the final two lines? What's this **IntToStr** thing? Well, if you remember, I said that both **SelStart** and **SelLength** are integers that represent the start position or the length of the highlighted text.

This is all well and good, but Edit boxes display text, not integers, so we need to convert from one to the other. Fortunately, Delphi provides us with **IntToStr** for exactly this purpose.

FYI This may seem a little confusing at the moment, but when we cover data and data types in the next chapter, all should become crystal clear.

Therefore, you can see that we convert the integer values given by the two properties to their text equivalent and pass these new values to be displayed in the disabled Edit boxes.

One point of interest. If you enter a couple of words into the top Edit box and select the first one, you'll see that `SelStart` is actually set to 0. Delphi always treats the first element of something you select as being numbered 0. If you have a string of 8 letters, these letters are numbered 0, 1, 2 and so on up to 7. If this bugs you, then add one to the `txtMainEntry.SelStart` in the relevant line of code, making sure it's within the bracket, so it's still regarded as a number.

Common Edit Box Events

Using properties to get at the values in an Edit box is great for many applications, but occasionally you want an even greater level of control. Just as you have added code to tell the button what to do when it is clicked, you can also add code to tell the Edit box what to do when certain events occur.

If you bring up the Object Inspector's Events page and select one of the Edit boxes, you'll see a whole host of events that you can code up for the Edit boxes to bring them to life at run time.

For example, you can write code for:

> The **OnChange** event that will run every time the text in the Edit box is changed.

> The **OnEnter** event to do something every time the user selects the text box to start entering data.

> The **OnExit** event to deal with the user leaving the component and selecting a new one.

In addition, you could even write code to do something every time the user presses a key. These events give you a great deal of flexibility in your code, and also give the text box a great deal of power.

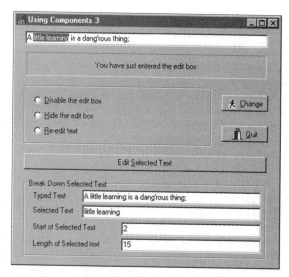

We'll now extend our program so that it updates the caption of a Panel component each time the OnEnter, OnExit and OnKeyPress events occur in that Edit box. The Panel component is really nothing more than a powerful label - you set its caption at run time to provide the user with important feedback on what they are doing and on what the application is up to.

All we do through the code is to set the caption property up in the same way as we did for the text properties in the Edit box examples earlier on.

Try It Out - Showing Edit Box Events in the Panel

1 Load up our example project and insert a Panel onto the form so that it mirrors the above screenshot. Change its Name to pnlStatus and its BevelInner property to bvLowered.

2 Now move to the Object Inspector, select txtMainEntry from the drop down list box to choose your component, swap to the Events page and double-click on the OnEnter event. Delphi creates the event handler for you to which you should add the following code:

```
procedure TEditingForm.txtMainEntryEnter(Sender : TObject);
begin
    pnlStatus.Caption := 'You have just entered the Edit box';
end;
```

3 Repeat the previous step for the OnExit event - the only difference is in the **Caption** that the application should display - you might use 'You have just left the Edit box'.

4 The final event that we need to add a handler to is the OnKeyPress event:

```
procedure TEditingForm.txtMainEntryKeyPress(Sender : TObject; var Key: Char);
begin
    pnlStatus.Caption := 'Key just pressed : ' + Key;
end;
```

5 Run the application and try entering some text into the Edit box. Also notice what happens to the Panel's Caption when you click on one of the RadioButtons and then return to the Edit box.

How It Works

Again, this iteration of the project isn't that complicated - as with a lot of Delphi programming, just by adding a few simple lines of code in the right place can give you a lot of functionality. In this example, only one of the three event handlers has anything new happening in it - I'm taking it for granted that you understand that a Panel's Caption works in exactly the same way as a Label's.

The event handler to focus in on is OnKeyPress and the new feature is the word **Key**. This parameter (more on this later) simply holds the value of the last key pressed, so our event handler simply tacks this value on the end of our prefix sentence using our text concatenation operator (+).

Buttons

Almost every Delphi application that you will ever write, with the exception of some multimedia type apps, will make use of Delphi's Button components. There are actually three (the final one being the SpeedButton - we've already seen the other two), but before you go...

Caption

Although it's a very powerful component, the Button is also one of the simplest to deal with; it has only three useful properties and just one useful event. Let's look at the properties first.

The most important property is, of course, Caption. The text you put in here defines the text that will appear on the button's face. Although you can set this through the Object Inspector, it's also possible to set it through code. For example, the Caption can change when a certain event occurs, informing the user that this has happened. At the risk of being flippant, you can change the caption of **cmdChange** from Change to Changed once you've clicked it, simply by adding to your existing code:

```
procedure TEditingForm.cmdChangeClick(Sender: TObject);
begin
  ...
    {Change button''s caption}
    cmdChange.Caption := '&Changed';
end;
```

Default and Cancel Buttons

During your travels through the realm of Windows applications, you will have become very familiar with the OK and Cancel button dynamic duo. However, have you noticed that they have default actions? When you are faced with these buttons, you can normally press *Enter* to accept the current selection (the same as clicking the OK button) or *Esc* to cancel (you've guessed it - the Cancel button action!).

Delphi lets you set up this kind of functionality using just two button properties; Default and Cancel. If you set the Cancel property of a Button to True, you are telling Delphi that should the user press *Esc*, it should trigger this Button's OnClick code. Conversely, if you set the Default property to True, Delphi will run this Button's OnClick code if the user press *Enter*.

Try It Out - Default and Cancel Buttons

We'll illustrate button properties with the first two we created on our form - Change will be our default and Quit our cancel.

1 Working with our example project again, double-click on the Change button and add this **ShowMessage** line to the event handler:

```
procedure TEditingForm.cmdChangeClick(Sender: TObject);
begin
    if optDisable.Checked = True then
        txtMainEntry.Enabled := False
    else if optInVisible.Checked = True then
        txtMainEntry.Visible := False
    else if optReEnable.Checked = True then
        begin
            txtMainEntry.Visible := True;
            txtMainEntry.Enabled := True;
        end;
    {Change button''s caption}
    cmdChange.Caption := '&Changed';
    ShowMessage('You voted for Change');
end;
```

2 Now do the same for the Quit button, adding this **ShowMessage** line in:

```
procedure TEditingForm.cmdQuitClick(Sender: TObject);
begin
    ShowMessage('You pressed Quit. TTFN');
end;
```

3 Finally, set the Cancel property of your Quit button and the Default property of your Change button to True.

If you now run your program and press either *Enter* or *Esc*, you'll see the code behind the appropriate button come to life, all without a single wave of the mouse:

 FYI One thing that you might have noticed that is quite interesting - you don't override the **Quit SpeedButton**'s inherent functionality by adding code to the component's **OnClick** event - the two features work in harmony.

Little touches like these which take little or no effort to put into your Delphi programs, can improve the user's life tremendously by allowing them more flexibility. They can then run your application with their left hand while drinking a cup of tea in the right.

Adding Tabs

The last component we'll cover in this chapter is the PageControl component from the Win95 page of the Component Palette. It has several close relatives: TabControl, TabSet and TabbedNotebook; the first is also a Win95 component, while the other two are for Win 3.1 applications. The difference between the two types of component is rather subtle.

With PageControl and TabbedNotebook, the page associated with the tab is ready for you to select and use. With their siblings, though, any links between tabs and what is shown on the form has to be written in your code. We'll use the more developed components at present.

Adding a new tab couldn't be easier: just right-click on the PageControl and select New Page a few times. You can then select the different pages of the control by clicking on the tabs at design time. Having selected a page, you can click below the tabbed region to access the TabSheet that forms the selected page.

This sheet is just like the other container components that we have already looked at - you can drop components on to it which are then considered as its children - except that this container is designed so that you can only see the controls on a given page - the other controls are hidden until the appropriate tab is selected!

This design issue means that it's good to name the tabs of the **PageControl** with a useful and descriptive term - I'm not saying that users need all the help that they can get, but...

Why would you want to use a PageControl? Well, mainly to save space, especially when your application has some quite disparate elements, as in the example we've been using in this chapter. As it now stands, the example centers around the txtMainEntry Edit box, and each Try It Out has added some feature which has no interrelation - for example, we could put the RadioButtons on a separate tab from the text breakdown sections and the Panel on yet another.

Using the PageControl

As with all of the other container components, it's kind of difficult to add them in as an afterthought. You can do it, but you have to remove the old components from the form, add the container, replace the old components with new versions and change all the Object Inspector based property settings to reflect the originals - a little too much work, if you ask me.

So, cut me a little slack and imagine that we had built the user interface with the PageControl right fram the start - load up **Stage6.dpr** and no-one will ever know! If you run the application, you'll see that the application is just the same except for the reorganization of the components onto the PageControl:

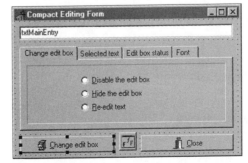

The easiest way to check out the changes I've made to this form's layout is to look at what Delphi calls <u>V</u>iew as Text. You can take a look at the form in this view by right-clicking anywhere on the form and selecting <u>V</u>iew as Text from the resulting menu:

```
object CompactForm: TCompactForm
  Left = 201
  Top = 133
  Width = 371
  Height = 237
  Caption = 'Compact Editing Form'
  OnCreate = FormCreate
  object PageControl1: TPageControl
    Left = 8
    Top = 40
    object TabSheet1: TTabSheet
      Caption = 'Change Edit box'
```

As you can see, this is a way of looking at the graphical user interface using text. This method has the advantage of displaying not only the visual attributes of the form, but also all the properties that you have set in the Object Inspector, all together in one place.

Note that any changes that you make here will be reflected in the visual representation of this structure when you return by right-clicking again and selecting <u>V</u>iew as Form. You can also quickly swap between both of these views using the *Alt+F12*.

In fact, the only change is to the code where we have combined the code to change the Edit box and analyze the text. Double-click the <u>C</u>hange edit box button and you'll see a giant **If...then...else** statement that works out which tab is uppermost (giving the ActivePage property of the PageControl statement) and then performs the relevant code.

Okay, fair enough, you've got me - I did sneak a new component onto the form: the Font dialog which I put between the buttons. If the user selects the Font tab and clicks on Change, the Font dialog executes. If the user selects a font (remember the Open dialog in Chapter 1), the code continues:

```
procedure TCompactForm.cmdChangeClick(Sender: TObject);
begin
...
      else if PageControl1.ActivePage = TabSheet4 then
      {Or could use ...ActivePage.Caption = 'Font'...}
      begin
        if FontDialog1.Execute then
        begin
          txtFont.Text          := FontDialog1.Font.Name;
          txtFontDisplay.Font := FontDialog1.Font;
          txtFontDisplay.Text := txtMainEntry.Text;
        end;
      end;
  end;
```

When the Font dialog executes, it returns a Font object, which contains information on the font name, style, size, color and so on. To see exact what the Font object rules over, click on the Font property in the Object Inspector, and the various 'subproperties' will be shown:

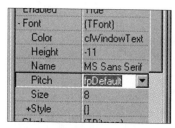

So, getting back to the code, we display the selected font in **txtFont** and rewrite the contents of **txtMainEntry** to **txtFontDisplay** using the selected font. Because the Edit box has its AutoSize property set to True by default, the box's height will automatically grow to show all text, no matter which font you use.

This option can be very useful when you allow the user to select a font size as well - no matter how big the font, Delphi will resize the display to cope, but this can get a little out of hand. While performing this task, Delphi pays no attention to the components that it encounters when it resizes the display - fortunately, Delphi does put the resized component behind all the others so you can't cover up the Quit button for example, but it can lead to a horrible screen layout.

Just as other Windows programs, you can create a multi-line dialog box with rows of tabs, just by setting the **PageControl's Multiline** property to True. This property comes complete with the disconcerting shuffling of the rows when you select a tab at the back.

Other Components

One of the true beauties of a development package like Delphi is that it can be extended through the use of third party components. Since the release of Visual Basic, there has been a growing market of software manufacturers able to supply add-in components which you can simply slot into your development environment to extend your design possibilities. There are two main sorts of add-in components supported by Delphi:

> VCL
>
> OCX

To the standard Visual Component Library (VCL) on the Component Palette, we can add new Delphi components, either as their Pascal source files, or in their ***.dcu** compiled format. It's quite possible to write new components yourself within Delphi - we refer you to other books for more on this.

There's another benefit of a truly integrated development environment, you can use the same environment to program and to extend the environment. Spooky!

Try It Out - Adding a Third Party Component

1 Close the current project.

2 Select the Component | Install... option and then after clicking on the Add... button, browse to find the target component - you are looking for a file called **tredit.dcu**, so remember to change the Add Module dialog's filter to Unit File (*.DCU):

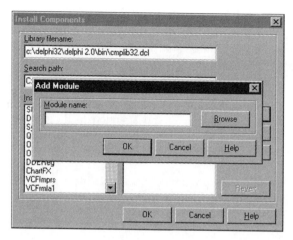

3 When you press OK, the Delphi compiler recompiles the components that are listed here - it treats the whole Component Palette as an application (you can see on the compiler progress that it calls the Palette **cmplib32.dpr**). Finally, after a long wait on some systems, the new Palette is displayed, with the new tab - Dr. Bob.

4 If you check this new tab out, you'll see that it contains only one component, TREdit. You can use this component in just the same way as you would use a normal Edit component - the only difference between the two is that this component will right justify any text it has to deal with, as opposed to the normal Edit box's left justification.

Microsoft's OCX Standard

Microsoft decided that the idea of component-based programming was a good idea a long time before Delphi hit the streets. To back up this decision, they announced the **OCX** (the **OLE** Control Extension) specification. This specification followed on the heels of the more restrictive and rambling VBX specification and also opened up the arena to 32-bit developers.

Essentially, this specification outlined how generic controls could be written in such a way as to allow other programming languages trouble free access to the functionality that they embodied through the use of OLE.

To take advantage of this technology, Delphi makes you work really hard - not! You simply follow the same steps as when installing a third party VCL component, except that you click on the OC**X**... button rather than the **A**dd... button. You then select the registered OCX that you wish to include in your IDE and Delphi does all of the hard work (writing the OCX wrapper) for you.

Check out the documentation that comes along with the OCX for more information on registering the OCX. Note that any OCXs that come along with other software will, more than likely, be registered by the parent's installation.

Summary

We have covered a lot of ground in this chapter, so it's time for a break. Just to recap though, we have covered:

- Drawing components on forms
- Using the Object Inspector to look at properties
- Setting and reading properties through code
- Writing event handling code
- The most common component properties
- How to use RadioButtons, Edits, Panels and GroupBoxes
- How to create default buttons on forms
- How to use the grid to make your designing life easier

What we haven't covered are most of the more advanced controls. Over the coming chapters, as your experience with Delphi code grows, we'll embark on bigger, more adventurous projects and also learn a great deal about what these additional components are and how to use them.

For now, though, give yourself a pat on the back - you have learnt a lot and acquired a foundation that will stick with you throughout your time with Delphi.

Writing Code

So far, you've just been dabbling your toes in the ocean that is Pascal, and perhaps you're a little cold, perhaps a little scared on the beach there. Time to take the plunge and recklessly throw yourself into the murky waters. Go on, you never know, you might enjoy it...!

In this and the next chapter, we examine the basics of Delphi Pascal - the delightful dialect of Pascal that allows you to make your application jump through hoops. These chapters cover basic code structure, while Chapter 5 covers the added power provided by object orientation. You might also be interested in Chapter 7 where I cover some of the ways to deal with the errors that hapless users can cause in an application.

But before I get to all that, let's get down to writing some code. In this chapter you'll learn:

- What the weird stuff that Delphi puts into your code windows actually means
- How to break your programs down into smaller, manageable groups of code
- What variables are and how to set them up
- How to make the most of numbers and Booleans
- How to get Delphi to make decisions

Talking in Code

The power of any computer language is really governed by two things: its core language (the support it gives to testing conditions, looping, procedures, and such like) and its ability to deal with **run-time data**, the nuggets of information that we're all interested in.

 Don't confuse the subject of data with that of databases: the two subjects are very different. Database applications store information in disk files for permanent access. What we look at in this chapter is nothing more than the different types of data that Delphi lets you deal with, and the components it provides to present this data.

So, just what do we mean when we say 'writing code'? The phrase goes back to ancient times, when programmers were scientists and programming meant twiddling large switches on the front of huge steel cases.

In those days, developers would create their masterpieces by entering numbers into computers. Each number would instruct the computer to do something, like add, subtract, store, and so on, and together, they would resemble some sort of code. A bank of switches on the front of a mainframe computer would enable the developer to key in numbers as a series of 1s and 0s. If all went well, some time later, the program would run. If it didn't, the developers would try again, attempting to avoid the mistake that caused the problem the first time round.

Today, for most developers it's quite a different story. Entering code means entering phrases similar to English that tell the computer what we want it to do. Of course, no computer is intelligent enough yet to understand straight English, and, often, the way we use English to explain what we want is less than clear. So there are various highly defined forms of pidgin English, known as programming languages. In Delphi's case, that programming language that we use to write code is called Pascal.

Pascal was invented back in the 70s as a specialized language meant to train new developers in programming theory and structure. Over time, more trendy languages, such as C, came along and were adopted by the commercial developer community, relegating Pascal very much to the classroom.

Back in the 80s, Borland went a little out on a limb, though, releasing a PC-based Pascal system that could easily rival a C equivalent in terms of power and how easy it was to use. Turbo Pascal quickly became the development system of choice for many, and has, over time, evolved to become what you now have on your computer - Delphi 2.0.

Before we get to the code proper, which I know you're just itching for, we need to know a little more about its setting - that is, the structure of a Delphi application.

Deciphering the Source Code Layout

You've already seen from the previous chapters that the projects you create in Delphi, which eventually become stand-alone applications, consist of a number of separate files. If you've already taken a wander around the code window, you'll have noticed that there's a great deal more to the source code than the event handlers that we've been playing with so far.

Some of the technicalities must wait for Chapter 5 when we look at those strange concepts - objects. At this stage, though, it's worth explaining a little bit about them to satisfy your curiosity, assuming, of course, that you do have some!

Units

Let's start off with our old friend, the unit, that place where all the event handlers hang out and so where all the action happens.

Try It Out - What's in a Unit?

1 Select File | New Application from the menu. Up comes a new project, and you're given a blank form with a partially completed code window. Quite a cute trick really - we select one menu option and Delphi creates loads of stuff for us.

2 Take a look at the code window. Here's what you should see:

```
unit Unit1;

interface

uses
  Windows, Messages, SysUtils, Classes, Graphics, Controls, Forms, Dialogs;

type
  TForm1 = class(TForm)
  private
    { Private declarations }
  public
    { Public declarations }
  end;

var
  Form1: TForm1;

implementation

{$R *.DFM}

end.
```

It's all a little confusing to start with, but let's take a look at what happens when we add some components to the form - perhaps that will help us understand what's going on.

3 Add an edit box, a label and a button to the form and label it like this:

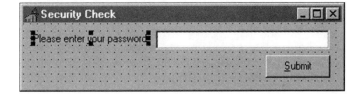

Change the name of the button to cmdSubmit, the label to lbPlease and the edit box to txtPassword using the Object Inspector. While we're here, add an OnClick event handler to the code by, as usual, double-clicking on the button.

4 Now return to the code window, maximize it and scroll up the window so that you can see exactly what has changed in the unit as a whole:

```
unit Unit1;

...

type
  TForm1 = class(TForm)
    txtPassword: TEdit;
    cmdSubmit: TButton;
    lbPlease: TLabel;
    procedure cmdSubmitClick(Sender : TObject);
  private
```

73

```
    { Private declarations }

...

implementation

{$R *.DFM}

procedure TForm1.cmdSubmitClick(Sender: TObject);
begin

end;

end.
```

Notice that I've used the normal convention of three dots (an ellipsis) to indicate some missing code - it's not that this code is unimportant, I'm just trying to save some trees here by focusing on the interesting parts of the unit!

5 Now change the name of the form to **frmPassword** and see what Delphi automatically changes in the code window:

```
unit Unit1;

...

type
    TfrmPassword = class(TForm)
        txtPassword: TEdit;

...

var
    frmPassword: TfrmPassword;

implementation

{$R *.DFM}

procedure TfrmPassword.cmdSubmitClick(Sender: TObject);
begin

end;

end.
```

6 Save the unit as **pwordu.pas**, and the project as **password.dpr**. Take a look at the code window now - see that the name of the unit has changed to reflect this new name:

```
unit pwordu;

interface

uses
    Windows, Messages, SysUtils, Classes, Graphics, Controls, Forms, Dialogs;
```

How It Works

What we've just done is to lay down the basic structure of a password program (the guts of which I'll return to in a moment), but what's really interesting is what happened when we performed these simple actions. When we simply add some components to the form, or just double-click on them, Delphi understands what we want and automatically generates faultless code to support the demands. Is that cool, or what?

Just think about it a while - here we have a tool that helps you to use a complex programming language by implementing a 'fill in the gaps' approach. Remember how those multiple choice questions back in school were a lot easier to handle than the essays - when the structure's already there, you can concentrate on solving the problem at hand.

As you've just seen, Delphi also takes charge of maintaining the code that it creates. If you change the name of the form, Delphi changes any references that it made to the form to reflect this alteration. Now that's what I call changing the names to protect the innocent!

However, problems can occur when you start to consider writing your own code, or if you start to manually alter the code that Delphi has created, but by understanding how the unit's structure works, we can, hopefully, avoid these problems. So let's take a much more detailed look at the unit's structure, starting with the **header**.

Header

Funnily enough, the unit's header appears at the head of the unit, and is, in fact, the first line of code in the unit. Don't try and put any code before this statement, the compiler will get in a little bit of a tizzy!

Actually, as inconsequential as it might at first appear, this line of code is vital for a successful compile. Delphi uses it to denote exactly what type of file it is (there are several options, one of which, **program**, I'm saving until later!), and what the file's contents is called.

Fortunately, in normal everyday Delphi programming, you should never have to touch this line of code. Delphi automatically creates the line when you first ask for a new unit, and it keeps the name of the unit updated to reflect the name of the unit's file. In fact, the name of the unit is the same as the name of the file that you can find on your hard disk but without the **.pas** extension.

Essentially, Delphi will take every line of code that it finds between this header and the terminating **end.** to be the contents of the unit - any code after **end.** will be regarded by the compiler as a comment, and won't be included in the resulting executable.

Interface

The **interface** section is where Delphi declares its intentions for the coming unit - just like an election manifesto, only slightly more reliable! Everything that the unit wants the world at large to know about will be declared here.

For example, in our Password project, Delphi declares that there is such a thing as TfrmPassword, which is like a blank form, except that it has three components on it, a label called lbPlease, an edit box, called txtPasssword, and a button, called cmdSubmit. This class (I'll come back to explain this term in a while) also knows how to handle the user clicking on the button because it has a procedure to run, called cmdSubmitClick, when this event occurs:

```
type
  TfrmPassword = class(TForm)
    lbPlease: TLabel;
    txtPassword: TEdit;
    cmdSubmit: TButton;
    procedure cmdSubmitClick(Sender: TObject);
  private
    { Private declarations }
  public
    { Public declarations }
  end;
```

If you compare the code snippet here to your code, you might notice that the component declarations, `lbPlease: TLabel` and so on, are in a different order. This is because of the order that you dropped the components onto the form in the first place. In my code, I put the label on first, followed it with the edit box and finally the button, but if you did it differently, they'll be in a different order! Delphi doesn't care about the order, so you shouldn't either!

In the very next line, Delphi goes on to declare that there is, in fact, a form lurking around that closely resembles this class, and that it answers to the name of frmPassword:

```
var
  frmPassword: TfrmPassword;
```

This is an important concept to understand when you are programming in Delphi. If you're going to ask someone to draw a circle with a stencil, you must first describe the correct stencil that they are to use. In the same way, you must tell Delphi what kind of form you want before you can ask it to create one. I'll come back to this idea in Chapter 5 when I explain more about objects, classes and instantation.

The **interface** section of a unit is really the outer descriptive shell of the unit. This is where you should look if you want to know what the unit can do, what goodies it has to offer and what mechanisms it uses to do what is has to do. Again, looking at our password example, this unit offers a form, called frmPassword. It can handle the user clicking on the Submit button on that form and it uses a whole load of other units to help it do this job:

```
uses
  Windows, Messages, SysUtils, Classes, Graphics, Controls, Forms, Dialogs,
  StdCtrls;
```

This is the part of the **interface** section to which the compiler will look to find the names of all the other units that the code contained relies on. Normally, the units named here will be part of Delphi's own class library (the **VCL** or **Visual Component Library**). This is where the Borland programmers have put all the code that enables a short line of code like,

```
ShowMessage('Hello');
```

to display a message on the screen. Obviously, this line of code means nothing to the compiler, but by comparing it to the descriptions given in the VCL, the compiler can come up with the appropriate results.

If you have the VCL source code, you can go and take a look at what's happening in these supporting units. I suggest, though, that you wait until after Chapter 5 where I explain a little bit more about OOP.

Don't worry if you don't quite follow all this stuff at the moment. This section touches on topics that we've not yet properly covered. Hopefully, it will provide food for a revelatory "Ah! That's what it means..." later on.

Implementation

Remember, I said that the **interface** section is where all of the unit's goodies are listed, as well as the events that it can handle and the supporting units that it uses? Well, the **implementation** section is where we actually describe what these goodies really are, and exactly what happens when an event occurs. It's where the hype of the **interface** section becomes reality.

Why things are organized this way is one of the subjects of Chapter 5 - all I can say here is that we're stuck with it , so let's start getting used to it! Let's take a closer look at what's going on so that when I start describing the techie bits in Chapter 5, you already understand what I'm talking about, at least from a practical point of view!

When you examine the **implementation** section of any unit, you'll see two distinct ways that Delphi refers to how an event is to be handled, or what a goodie actually looks like. On the one hand, you've got the event handlers:

```
procedure TfrmPassword.cmdSubmitClick(Sender: TObject);
begin

end;
```

These sections of code are where we can place the lines of Pascal that describe how our application should react when an event occurs - you should be quite happy with these fellows by now, as we've been using them for the past two chapters!

One the other hand, you've got this:

```
{$R *.DFM}
```

This is what's known in the trade as a **compiler directive** - it looks like a comment doesn't it? Don't be deceived - this is actually an instruction to the compiler to include the file called **pwordu.dfm**. You can tell it's not a comment because the first symbol after the opening comment marker is a dollar (**$**) symbol - the capital **R** is the actually compiler directive that tells the compiler that you want something special to happen to...the appropriate **.DFM** files.

This file, **pwordu.dfm**, has important information about the layout of our form. If you think back to the **interface** section, we saw a type declaration describe the contents of our form, but tell us nothing about how the components on it were actually organized.

FYI

A type declaration - new terminology, I think! A data type, as you'll see later in the chapter, is just a set of predefined terms which you can assign to your variables - don't worry about this now, the important thing is that you remember that Delphi considers forms in the same way as it considers data types, at least in terms of their declarations (okay, a form is more complex, but the concept is the same). All these declarations come under the type keyword and indicate to Delphi that if you declare a variable, it can be assigned to this new type of data structure.

In other words **frmMyForm : TRedForm** means that the form called **frmMyForm** is based upon the type declaration called **TRedForm**. If this type declaration includes a reference to two labels, four buttons and an edit box, then, as **frmMyForm** is based upon this type declaration, this variable will have two labels, four buttons and an edit box when it's created.

This is where this file and compiler directive come in. If you check out the directory that contains our password example, you'll see that there are several files in there. The two to focus on both have the same name, but different extensions: **pwordu.pas** and **pwordu.dfm**.

FYI

Note that you don't have to explicitly save a **.dfm** file. Delphi automatically handles this for you if the **.pas** file includes the **{$R *.DFM}** compiler directive. It also carries out any further maintenance required to keep the files in sync - the automatic renaming of components is one example of this maintenance.

These two files work hand in hand, one describing the content of the form (**.PAS**) and the way in which it handles any events associated with it, and one documenting the actual layout of the components on the form (**.DFM**).

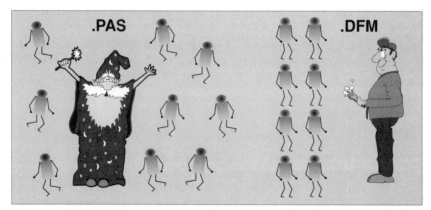

.PAS   .DFM

Remember that we saw the textual version of our form back in Chapter 2? This is a translated version of the **.dfm** file - translated because the native format for the contents of this file is binary ones and zeros.

And that's all there is to a generic Delphi unit. But hang on a moment. When we save our application, Delphi asks us for the name of our project file as well as our unit! What's a project file for and what does it look like?

Project Files

The easiest way to think of a project file is as the organizer of the group. The project file lists all the units of code that we've written for our application, both by title and file name. It documents how the application should be initialized and fired off, and also offers you the opportunity to run some code before the application itself begins.

Are you thinking about those natty little splash screens you see on all those commerical applications? I am! I've included one into the final application, so you'll have to wait until the final chapter to see how you can make use of this part of your project file!

Let's take a look at what that makes up the project file's source code. You can see this code at any time as you develop your unit by simply selecting the View | Project Source option:

```
program password;

uses
  Forms,
  pwordu in 'pwordu.pas' {frmPassword};

{$R *.RES}

begin
  Application.Initialize;
  Application.CreateForm(TfrmPassword, frmPassword);
  Application.Run;
end.
```

At first glance, it looks quite similar to a normal unit, but you might notice that there aren't any explicit **interface** or **implementation** sections. This is because it's all part of the **implementation** section - there isn't an **interface** section! Obviously, as this file organizes all the others, it should be dedicated to this job - it shouldn't contain any code that any other unit might need to reference.

The other fairly obvious difference that you should have spotted is that this file isn't called a **unit**. It's actually called a **program**. By convention, Delphi denotes the master file with this entry at the start of its code, and because there can only ever be one master, Delphi demands that there is only ever one **program** file in a project.

When you compile your project, the compiler reads through the contents of this file to understand what should happen:

```
{$R *.RES}

begin
  Application.Initialize;
  Application.CreateForm(TfrmPassword, frmPassword);
  Application.Run;
end.
```

The first thing to do is initialize the application - I'll come back to this later on in Chapter 5. Then you create the main form of the application, in this case, **frmPassword**. The compiler knows how to create this form because it looks for a type definition called **TfrmPassword** in the units listed in the **uses** clause - in this case, it will find it in **pwordu.pas**, as the comment indicates:

```
program password;

uses
  Forms,
  pwordu in 'pwordu.pas' {frmPassword};

{$R *.RES}
```

Once Delphi has created this form and added it to the application, the application runs and the form is loaded onto the screen. Delphi then runs the code that appears in the form's OnCreate event handler.

The only other item of interest is that compiler directive:

```
pwordu in 'pwordu.pas' {frmPassword};

{$R *.RES}

begin
```

To conclude this section, I'd just like to say that, most of the time, you shouldn't need to change any of the code in this file. Delphi does an expert job of maintaining these lines, so why throw a potential spanner in the works when you could be concentrating on something much more interesting?

Summing Up - What is a Delphi Project?

To end this section, let's just take a little time out to go over what I've just explained. If you're a little uncertain of what's going on with Delphi's file structure, you'll find objects, classes, and so on easy to understand, but quite hard to implement.

When you create a new application, Delphi creates a number of files for you, based on a number of assumptions. The first of these is that you're actually going to compile and run your work, so you get a project file which documents exactly how the compiler should achieve this.

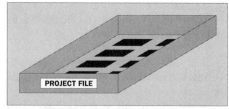

Next, you get a unit file in which you can describe the structure of a variety of things, including your forms, any new data types you need and a number of event handlers, so that once the application is running, it can respond to certain events.

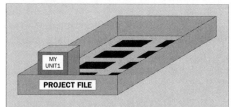

To fully describe the layout of the form, Delphi then creates a form file which records the number, size and position (among other things) of the components that you have placed on the form.

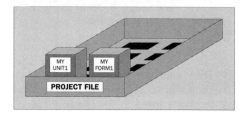

Most of the time, you can forget about the contents of the project and form unit files, Delphi automatically handles them for you - when you change a property in the Object Inspector, Delphi will record it in the form unit file, the project file, or, sometimes, in the unit file itself.

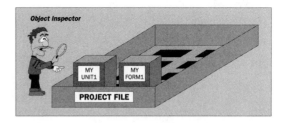

If you decide to create some code to handle an event, Delphi will automatically create and maintain the basic structure of the event handler - all you have to create is the code that will be executed when the event occurs.

Essentially, if you're using Delphi to create an executable application, most of the time you can let it do all the hard work - what an easy life being a Delphi developer is! However, if you really want to put Delphi through its paces, you do need to start adding your own code to the structures that it generates. The first thing to think about is how you're going to transport your data round your application. So without further ado...

Variables

A **variable** is a container for an item of data that the compiler allows you to change at any point in your executable - hence the name! Just as in the case of a form, before you can create a variable, you must do a few things before you're ready to rumble:

- Define your data type
- Create an instance of the data type
- Initialize it

Let's take a quick look at one way in which you can prepare a variable to use in your code:

```
unit Unit1;

interface

uses
   Windows, Messages, SysUtils, Classes, Graphics, Controls, Forms, Dialogs;

type
   TForm1 = class(TForm)
      procedure FormCreate(Sender: TObject);
   private
      { Private declarations }
   public
      { Public declarations }
   end;
   MyColors = (black, white, red, blue, green);

var
   Form1: TForm1;
   WhatColorIsIt : MyColors;
```

```
implementation

{$R *.DFM}

procedure TForm1.FormCreate(Sender: TObject);
begin
    WhatColorIsIt := black;
end;

end.
```

The first line of code indicates where I've defined the type of data that I'm going to work with. I've chosen to create my own data type which allows me to select one of five colors. You can negate this step if you want to use one of Delphi's predefined data types, but I'll come to those in a moment.

The next line declares a variable called **WhatColorIsIt** and defines it as a container that can hold one of the five values that make up the data type. The final stage is to initialize the variable, as we do in the form's OnCreate event handler. If you attempt to assign a value to a variable that doesn't belong to the variable's data type, the compiler will complain - you've been warned!

That's all there is to declaring variables. The problem comes when you start messing around with when the variable is available (that's called the variable's **scope**), or the data type that the variable is based upon - you might not always want to select a value from a list of five colors!

FYI When you become a Delphi guru, you might want to return to the subject of variables and data types, as you can improve your application's performance by making your selections with a little more care. However, for us, the aim is to produce code that achieves what we want, so I won't go into the subjects of memory allocation, short strings or your choice of Real (a numeric data type, as you'll see in a moment) here.

Now that you understand the basic principles behind the preparation of a variable, let's look a little closer at the problem of data types. Delphi provides you with a wide variety of predefined data types, and also allows you to create your own, so how do you choose the right one?

Data Types

When you're considering what data type to use, you should really be thinking about what type of data the variable will store. However, before you can make a decent choice, you really need to understand the various data types that Delphi has to offer.

Delphi offers three major groups:

▶ Sets that contain a known number of fixed elements

▶ Numerical ranges with varying degrees of accuracy, say two decimal places

▶ Data types designed to hold a group of related facts in one place

I'm going to cover the first two of these groups in this chapter, leaving the other till later on - you don't want to learn everything at the same time do you? So, let's move on and tackle the first of these groups - sets.

Sets

To answer your first question, a **set** is a group of related items. Although all the items they contain are connected, the order in which they appear in the set is completely arbitrary.

To give you a better idea of what these unordered groups of items can be used for, take a look at the following example.

Try It Out - Dynamically Creating Your Own Message Boxes

You may know (have you been playing with Delphi's help files?) that Delphi provides you with a function call, **MessageDlg**, that allows you to quickly throw up a dialog on screen, with various buttons, a small graphic and some custom text. I'm going to use this example to show you how to use sets to dynamically change the buttons that will appear in that dialog at run time.

1 Start up a new application and save it as **setsu.pas** and **usesets.dpr**.

2 Drop a label, three check boxes and a button onto the form and rename them with ckNo for checkbox1, ckHelp for checkbox2, ckAbort for checkbox3 and cmdDisplay for button1. While you're here, change the name of the form to frmSets. Arrange the components as shown below, changing their captions to match my example:

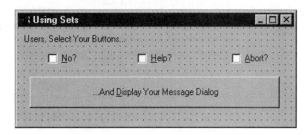

3 Add the following line of code to the OnClick event handler of the button:

```
procedure TfrmSets.cmdDisplayClick(Sender: TObject);
begin
    MessageDlg('You have chosen the following buttons for your dialog:',
            mtInformation, [mbYes], 0);
end;
```

Notice that this function uses two different types of brackets - normal parentheses (**(   )**) to surround the function's parameters and square brackets (**[   ]**) to surround **mbYes**. Now I've pointed that out to you, run the project - click on the button and Delphi will provide you with the dialog shown here:

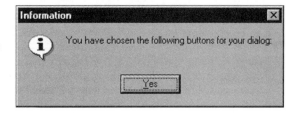

4 Okay, so far so good, but what about the run-time dynamics? Add the following lines of code to the **interface** section of the unit:

```
type
  TfrmSets = class(TForm)
    ckNo: TCheckBox;
```

```
...
    public
      { Public declarations }
    end;
    TMyButtons = set of TMsgDlgBtn;
var
    frmSets: TfrmSets;
    MyButtons TMyButtons;
    MyDialogText : String;
implementation
```

5 Now go back to the button's OnClick event handler, delete the existing **MessageDlg** function and add this new code:

```
procedure TfrmSets.cmdDisplayClick(Sender: TObject);
begin
     MyButtons := [mbYes];
     If ckNo.checked then
        MyButtons := MyButtons + [mbNo];
     If ckHelp.checked then
        MyButtons := MyButtons + [mbHelp];
     If ckAbort.checked then
        MyButtons := MyButtons + [mbAbort];
     MessageDlg(MyDialogText, mtInformation, MyButtons, 0);
end;
```

6 The final step of this Try It Out is to initialize the new string variable that we've just declared. Switch back to the form, double-click on it and add the following line of code to the form's OnCreate event handler:

```
procedure TfrmSets.FormCreate(Sender: TObject);
begin
     MyDialogText := 'You have chosen the following buttons for your dialog:';
end;
```

And that's it! Run the project and select a couple of the check boxes. If you hit the button, a message box springs up with a number of buttons reflecting the check boxes you selected. Now click any of the message box buttons, de-select one of the check boxes on the main form and generate the message box again. Notice that you've now got one less button on your message box! Dynamic buttons... neat!

How It Works

The first thing we should do is explain the real engine of this code, the **MessageDlg** function. The easiest way to do this is to guide you through what Delphi has to say on the matter, so go ahead and dial up the online help for **MessageDlg** - the easiest way to do this is by highlighting it in the code window and pressing *F1*.

As you can see, this function takes four parameters:

▶ A string that contains the text that you want to appear on your dialog.

▶ One member of the TMsgDlgType enumerated type which Delphi uses to decide which graphic to place in the dialog.

- One or more members of the TMsgDlgBtn set, the focus of our example, which Delphi uses to decide which buttons to add to the dialog.

- A help context value which Delphi uses to determine which help page to display when the user cries for more information.

Most of these entries are straightforward, so I'm not going to go into too much detail here. In fact, I'm only going to say that you can see the five options for the TMsgDlgType on the **MessageDlg** help page. As we haven't covered help yet, set the help context value to 0. Of course, you're free to type in any text that you like for the first parameter.

The only parameter I'm interested in here is TMsgDlgBtn. As you can see from the help file, Delphi offers you a number of predefined constant values in this set, each one representing a particular button that it can add to the dialog:

```
TMsgDlgBtn = (mbYes, mbNo, mbOK, mbCancel, mbAbort, mbRetry, mbIgnore, mbAll,
mbHelp);
```

In our code, we've created a set from this enumerated data type with the following line of code:

```
TMyButtons = set of TMsgDlgBtn;
```

We've then declared a variable of this new type called **MyButtons**:

```
var
   frmSets: TfrmSets;
   MyButtons : TMyButtons;
   MyDialogText : String;
implementation
```

Then we've initialized the value of this set by checking which options the user has selected via the check boxes, and built up the contents of the variable in the first part of the button's OnClick event handler:

```
procedure TfrmSets.cmdDisplayClick(Sender: TObject);
begin
     MyButtons := [mbYes];
     If ckNo.checked then
        MyButtons := MyButtons + [mbNo];
     If ckHelp.checked then
        MyButtons := MyButtons + [mbHelp];
     If ckAbort.checked then
        MyButtons := MyButtons + [mbAbort];
     MessageDlg(MyDialogText, mtInformation, MyButtons, 0);
end;
```

All we do here is start off the contents of a variable with the Yes button (it's not a good idea to throw up a dialog without any buttons at all!) and then check the value of each check box. If it's checked, we add the appropriate button to our variable.

Once we've completely built our set, we can pass it directly to the **MessageDlg** function. As you'll see when we look at procedures and functions in more detail later on in the chapter, when you pass values to parameters, you can actually pass physical values to the function (as in our first **MessageDlg** call) or you can pass variables (as in the case of this example). Of course,

85

passing a variable does mean that you have that extra flexibility to manipulate its value before you come to use it in the function call (this is what gives us dynamic creation in our example), as opposed to hard-coding (boo!! hiss!!) your options into the unit.

You may also notice that I've replaced the physical string in the **MessageDlg** with a variable. This is usually a good idea for two reasons, the first of which is purely aesthetic. You'll usually find that a variable name is shorter than the string that you want on the dialog, so by using the variable, you can limit the code to one line - I hate code that spreads over a number of lines, it kills Pascal's readability!

The second reason is that you may want to use this line of text somewhere else in your application. By making the string into a variable, you can quickly reference the line of text, without needing to type it again and run the risk of introducing typos. It also has the added benefit that if you want to change the text later on, you only have to change it in one place and all references are updated automatically throughout the application. You don't have to plow through the whole application looking for each and every reference (missing half of them, if you're like me) and change them by hand.

As you can see, a set can be a very useful type, but you can get a lot more functionality from a related type called **ordinal**, so without further ado, let's take a look.

Ordinal Data Types

What a title! Well, that's what they're called in Delphi's online help. Each data type is a set who's elements appear in a particular order, thus allowing you to refer to the predecessor and successor of the value that's currently selected. The data value's relative position in the set is determined by its ordinality, a fixed numerical value. An obvious example is that of the **Integer** data type where the elements in the set share the same value as their ordinality.

So what? Well, we've introduced them here because they tie up a few loose ends from the past few chapters, while preparing the ground for all that follows.

You see, both the Booleans and the **Integer**s that we used in the previous chapter are members of an ordinal data type. The set of Boolean has just two elements - True and False. In contrast, the set of integers includes all the whole numbers in the range from negative to plus 2 billion (approx.). The elements of both sets also have an ordinality - the Boolean False has an ordinality of 0; True has an ordinality of 1. The ordinality of **Integer**'s elements is the same as their value - clever use of resources, huh?

If you remember, I mentioned that an ordinal type is a set whose elements have a predefined order. This allows us to perform some quite interesting feats with only a little code. By choosing the correct data type, we can actually cut down on the coding that we must perform:

Try It Out - Using an Ordinal Data Type's Built-in Functions

1 Start a new application and save it as **ordinalu.pas** and **ordfuncs.dpr**.

2 Drop a group box onto the form, and add three radio buttons and an edit box to it. Also add an edit box and two buttons to the form outside the group box. Arrange them like this:

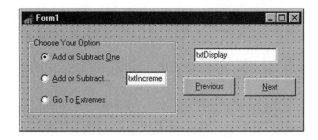

While we're here, change the names of the components as follows: GroupBox1 (grpMovement), RadioButton1 (rdoAddSubOne), RadioButton2 (rdoIncrement), RadioButton3 (rdoExtreme), Edit1 (txtIncrement - note that this should be the edit box inside the groupbox), Button1 (cmdPrevious), Button2 (cmdNext) and Edit2 (txtDisplay). You could also take the opportunity to rename the form to frmOrdinal.

3 Change the Captions of the various components on the form to correspond to this textual description of my form:

```
object frmOrdinal: TfrmOrdinal
    Caption = 'Moving Around In An Ordinal Data Type'
  object cmdNext: TButton
    Caption = '&Next'
    OnClick = cmdNextClick
  end
  object cmdPrevious: TButton
    Caption = '&Previous'
    OnClick = cmdPreviousClick
  end
  object grpMovement: TGroupBox
    Caption = 'Choose Your Option'
    object rdoAddSubOne: TRadioButton
      Caption = 'Add or Subtract &One'
      Checked = True
      OnClick = rdoAddSubOneClick
    end
    object rdoIncrement: TRadioButton
      Caption = '&Add or Subtract...'
      OnClick = rdoIncrementClick
    end
    object txtIncrement: TEdit
      Enabled = False
    end
    object rdoExtreme: TRadioButton
      Caption = 'Go To &Extremes'
      OnClick = rdoExtremeClick
    end
  end
end
```

Just as in the case of a form declaration, the order in which you placed the components on the form will affect the order of the component's visual information. Don't worry if your listing doesn't appear exactly like mine, because you probably build your form in a different order to me - and I've cut out a lot of the descriptive information to save even more trees!

Note that I've also set **rdoAddSubOne** to be checked and **txtIncrement** to be disabled when the form is created and I've included the event handlers for you to see what's going to happen next.

4 The next step is to declare the variable of the ordinal data type and initialize it:

```
var
   frmOrdinal: TfrmOrdinal;
   Counter : Integer;
implementation

{$R *.DFM}

procedure TfrmOrdinal.FormCreate(Sender: TObject);
begin
      Counter := 10;
      txtDisplay.Text := '10';
      txtIncrement.Text := '1';
end;
```

As you can see, we initialize our counter in the form's **OnCreate** event handler (double-click on the form to get it!), and while we're here, we also initialize the contents of the two edit boxes. Remember that once you're looking at an event handler, you can get to the rest of the unit (say, to declare a new variable!) simply by scrolling up the page - maximize the code window to maximize the effect.

5 Let's now get the two buttons working. Add the following code to **cmdPreviousClick**:

```
procedure TfrmOrdinal.cmdPreviousClick(Sender: TObject);
begin
      if rdoAddSubOne.checked then
          Counter := Pred(Counter)
      else if rdoIncrement.Checked then
           dec(Counter, StrToInt(txtIncrement.Text))
      else
          Counter := Low(Counter);
      txtDisplay.Text := IntToStr(Counter);
end;
```

and the following code to **cmdNextClick**:

```
procedure TfrmOrdinal.cmdNextClick(Sender: TObject);
begin
      if rdoAddSubOne.checked then
          Counter := Succ(Counter)
      else if rdoIncrement.Checked then
          inc(Counter, StrToInt(txtIncrement.Text))
      else
          Counter := High(Counter);
      txtDisplay.Text := IntToStr(Counter);
end;
```

6 The final additions to the code are purely aesthetic. Add the following three event handlers to control the workings of **txtIncrement** - note that you will need to double-click on each of the radio buttons to get the appropriate event handler:

```
procedure TfrmOrdinal.rdoAddSubOneClick(Sender: TObject);
begin
    txtIncrement.Enabled := False;
end;

procedure TfrmOrdinal.rdoIncrementClick(Sender: TObject);
begin
    txtIncrement.Enabled := True;
    txtIncrement.SetFocus;
end;

procedure TfrmOrdinal.rdoExtremeClick(Sender: TObject);
begin
    txtIncrement.Enabled := False;
end;
```

Run the application and try out the Next and Previous buttons. Watch what happens to the value displayed in the edit box. You should also try changing the selected option in the group box and see what effect this has on the buttons and the contents of the edit box.

How It Works

Because we're using an ordinal data type, in this case **Integer**, Delphi allows us to use six predefined procedures or functions to change the current value of our variable to another member of the ordinal data type. The options that Delphi allows you to choose from are:

- **Pred** and **Succ**
- **Inc** and **Dec**
- **High** and **Low**

The easiest way to explain what these options do is to examine what happens when we use them. We've set up this example so that if the first radio button is selected, we're using **Pred** and **Succ** on the current value of **counter**, based on whether the user clicks on Previous or Next.

Quite simply, **Succ** will move the variable through the data type, one value at a time, adding one to the current value's ordinality to get the next value, while **Pred** does exactly the same thing except that it subtracts instead of adding. If the variable current holds a value of 10, and the user clicks on the Next button, Delphi uses **Succ** to move to the next value in the data type, which as we're using **Integer** is 11.

Inc and **Dec** perform a very similar task except that they allow you specify the number to add or subtract from the current ordinality - we've used an edit box to allow the user to choose this value.

If the user selects the last option in the group box, Delphi reads the button clicks as instructions to move to the extremes of the data type - we'll look at what these ranges are in more detail later on.

You might have noticed the terms **StrToInt** and **IntToStr** in this code, and after sweeping **IntToStr** under the table back in the last chapter, now would be a good time to talk about them. From what you've learned in this chapter already, it should be fairly obvious what they do. To summarize:

- Delphi is data-type mad, with a very strict compiler.

- Strings hold a string of characters - more on them in the next chapter.

- **Integer** stores just whole numbers.

- You'd like to view the number in the edit box, so you need to take the number, and convert it to a string - each digit becomes a character.

- Delphi provides you with yet more functions to help you do this.

It couldn't be simpler - **StrToInt** allows us to convert a **String** to an **Integer** (in our example, the value the user keys into the edit box), while **IntToStr** allows us to go the other way (we convert the new value of our counter so that we can display it in our edit box).

The only other thing to mention about the code is those final three aesthetic event handlers. I only included them to remind you that it's a good idea to give the user as many visual clues on how to use your application as possible. In this case, the only time that you'd need to use the edit box is when you want to use your own increment. So, when you're using **Succ**, **Pred**, **High** or **Low**, why should you make the edit box available?

I've also made use of the **SetFocus** method again, as yet another suggestion to the user. If they select the **Inc/Dec** option, it's more than likely that they'll want to change the value in the edit box, so let's draw their attention to it by automatically moving the focus - my motto is 'Why let my users make a decision when I can make it for them!'.

Other Ordinal Data Types

I picked **Integer** as a good example of an ordinal data type because it's one of the ones that you'll be using quite a lot throughout your future programs. However, it's not the only one by a long way. The ordinal group actually contains all the following data types:

- Boolean
- Char
- Enumerated types
- Subranges
- Specialized forms of Integer

I'm not going to go into detail on these other data types as you'll see enough of them in the future chapters, but there are a couple of things that are worth mentioning about some of them. We've already covered Booleans in quite some detail, so I'll leave those with no more comment. I'm also not going to mention Char in any great detail. Why? Because they're really easy to understand - it's the characters that make up the ASCII character set, and each character has a well documented ordinality (check out a general computer book, or take a look at the application on disk called **ascii.dpr**) - it follows all the rules of the ordinal group and characters are the building blocks of strings, one of the subjects of the next chapter.

Having explained why I'm not going to cover Booleans and Chars, you'll be glad to know that I am going to cover enumerated types, so here goes...

Enumerated Types

An enumerated type is really a set with ordinality which, as I've explained, means that you can move from one element to another using all of those neat functions. I've included an example on the disk called **enum.dpr** which illustrates this quite nicely.

If you open the project, you can see that I've defined a new type called **Stages**:

```
TStages = (st1, st2, st3, st4, st5, st6);
```

If you run the application, you'll see that by pressing the appropriate button, you can scroll backwards and forwards through evolution, checking out some of its landmark events:

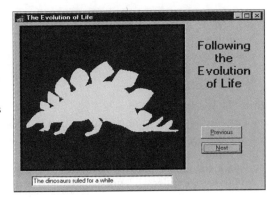

You should note that this is different from using a predefined ordinal data type, as you can pick and choose the exact values that are included, as opposed to being lumbered with all the integers or characters. Fortunately, Delphi comes replete with data types, and one of them is particularly suitable for reducing the large predefined data types down to size.

Subrange Types

A subrange data type is exactly that - a subset of another data type that runs from a start point to an end point. Some examples of a subrange data type might be:

```
TTopTen    : 1..10;
TGrades    : a..g;
TPrimates  : st4..st6;
```

You can see an example of this data type by amending the previous example:

Try It Out - Using a Subrange Data Type

1 Open up **enum2.dpr**.

2 Add the following line of code to the **interface** section of the unit:

```
type
  TfrmEnum = class(TForm)
    cmdNext: TButton;

...

  end;
  TStages = (st1, st2, st3, st4, st5, st6);
  TPrimates = st4..st6;
  procedure DisplayYearInfo(eCurrentStage : TStages; imgMyImage : TImage;
                    txtMyEdit : TEdit);
```

91

3 Place the cursor at the beginning of the definition of **TPrimates** and select the <u>S</u>earch | <u>R</u>eplace menu option. Type in TStages in <u>T</u>ext to find:, TPrimates in <u>R</u>eplace with:, deselect the <u>P</u>rompt on Replace check box and hit OK:

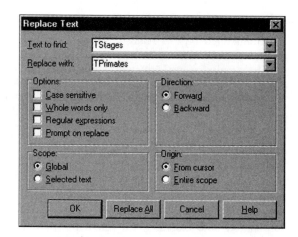

If you now run the application, you'll see that we've restricted the range of the data type down so the application only covers the evolution of primates!

How It Works

This example is really based around the use of Delphi's **Search and Replace** facility. By replacing all the occurrences of the term **TStages** with its child, **TPrimates**, we've instructed the compiler to create an application that uses **TPrimates** not **TStages**. Note that we have to place the cursor after the definition of **TStages**, otherwise that occurrence will also be replaced and the compiler will not understand what data type **TPrimates** is based upon.

You should also note that all the rest of the code works even when we do something as controversial as change the data type. This is because all the functions that we used in this example apply to the ordinal data types as a whole, and as **TPrimates** is derived directly from **TStages** (which is an ordinal), the compiler knows what to do.

Working the Numbers Game

As you've already seen, Delphi supports a data type called **Integer**, that allows us to work with numbers in our applications. However, you might be interested to know that Delphi supports a whole host of other numerical data types for several reasons.

The first of these reasons is the range that the data type supports. Under Delphi 2.0, **Integer** is a 32-bit number (it runs from -2^{16} to $+2^{16} -1$), but to support it, Delphi needs to allocate 4 bytes of memory to store it. For a variable, that's quite a lot of memory, let me tell you!

To optimize your memory usage, Delphi offers you the following set of **Integer**-related data types that have a varying impact on your memory:

Data Type	Size	Range	Description
Shortint	1 byte (8 bits)	-128 to 127	A small, signed whole number.
Byte	1 byte	0 to 255	A small, unsigned whole number.
Smallint	2 bytes (16 bits)	-32768 to 32768	Medium size whole numbers (signed).

Table Continued on Following Page

Data Type	Size	Range	Description
Word	2 bytes	0 to 65535	Medium size whole numbers (unsigned).
Longint	4 byte (32 bits)	-2147483648 to 2147483647	A big whole number.

The reserved word, **Integer**, which you'll usually use in your programs, takes a value that depends on the environment in which you're programming. In Delphi 2.0, a 32-bit program, **Integer**s are equivalent to **longint**, while in Delphi 1.0, they were identical to **smallint**. This may be important if you have to recompile a Delphi 1.0 program in Delphi 2.0, and strange things start to happen...

After all of that, for most of the time, we can get away with using **Integer** as our numerical data type. The others are really only provided for purposes of optimization, but I had to mention them, didn't I?

If you're interested in **Integer**s, you might well be encouraged to know that Delphi comes with a selection of components that have been specifically designed to help users work with numbers. I've included a couple of examples on our web site that you should take a look at, **trackbar.dpr** and **scroll.dpr**, which deal with the TTrackBar and TScrollBar components.

Some things to note when you examine these projects include:

> TTrackBar's lack of an OnScroll event.

> The use of the Max, Min and Position properties to denote the range and current position of the component's marker.

> The use of the OnChange event to handle user interaction.

> TScrollBar's MinChange and LargeChange properties.

> The use of TScrollBar's ScrollPos parameter to eliminate the need for the Position.

Floating Numbers

No, you can't go yet, there are some more numerical data types to talk about! These data types allow for decimal places - and tremendous accuracy. The currency type also allows accurate monetary calculations, if you're into that sort of thing, and the Borland help confidently asserts that there are no resultant rounding errors. Shall we get out the scientist's skepticism, or is the world really that rosy?

The problem with these numbers is that it's difficult to divorce them from math or account calculations. These are either important to you, or they're not. So here, we'll just look at the different data types Delphi provides and a few of the functions you may need to deal with them:

Data Type	Size (Bytes)	Description
Comp	8	Holds big whole numbers.
Single	4	Holds small decimal numbers.

Table Continued on Following Page

Data Type	Size (Bytes)	Description
Real	6	Holds medium decimal numbers.
Double	8	Big decimal numbers.
Extended	10	Immense decimal numbers
Currency	8	Decimal money values. Designed to deal with numbers representing amounts of money. In the UK and US for example this means a number with two fixed decimal places.

A word to the wise - don't use `Real` unless you have to. It's there for backwards compatibility with Pascal and Delphi 1.0. The other real numbers work faster, as they latch into native data formats used by the Intel chips you're probably using.

You've already seen how you sometimes need to convert one type of variable to another to get the results you want - remember the **Integer**/**String** conversion a few pages back? Well the same thing applies to these numerical data types... sometimes.

Take a look at this:

```
procedure TForm1.FormCreate(Sender: TObject);
var
   nRealAge : double;
   nIntAge  : integer;
begin
    nIntAge  := 25;
    nRealAge := nIntAge;
end;
```

If you were to key this code in and run the program, everything would be fine. The code sets up two variables: an **Integer** (for whole numbers) and a **Real** (for decimals). It then sets the **Integer** variable to 25 and copies the integer into the **Real** value.

What actually happens is that the **Integer** variable, **nIntAge**, is set up with the value 25. By setting **nRealAge** to equal **nIntAge** Delphi sets **nIntAge** up as 25.0 - a decimal number.

If you were to change the code around, though, so that it read like this,

```
procedure TForm1.FormCreate(Sender: TObject);
var
   nRealAge : double;
   nIntAge  : integer;
begin
    nRealAge := 25;
    nIntAge  := nRealAge;
end;
```

it wouldn't work and you would get a compile error telling you something about 'incompatible types'. Why?

As far as Delphi is concerned, the first line of code sets **nRealAge** to hold 25.0. It could just as well be 0.123124, for all the compiler cares. The second line says copy this (possible) decimal value into an **Integer** variable and that's where the problem lies. If the decimal variable did contain 0.123124, Delphi wouldn't know what to do with it. Do you want to truncate the number to 0, round it up, or what? For that reason, Delphi includes a number of commands which enable you to convert between numeric data types, or more specifically, to convert non-integer values to integers.

Method	Description
`Trunc(Real)  :  Longint`	**Trunc** takes a **Real** (decimal) number as the parameter and throws out an integer value. This is the decimal number with the digits to the right of the decimal point removed. So 1.232 becomes 1, 50.5 becomes 50 and so on.
`Round(Real)  :  Longint`	**Round** take a **Real** (decimal) number as the parameter and throws out an integer value. This is the decimal number rounded to the nearest whole number. So 5.7 become 6 and 5.2 becomes 5.
`Frac(Real)  :  Real`	Strange one this. It takes a **Real** number and returns the digits after the decimal point as another **Real** number. For example **Frac(50.834)** returns 0.834. You could then multiply this result by, say 1000, to get a number which you could convert to an integer.
`Int(Real)  :  Real`	Another weird one. It takes a **Real** value, removes anything after the decimal point and returns another **Real**.

Depending on which function you use, you should find it easy to convert any **Real** number to an integer, or to play around with the contents of your **Real**s. But what about converting to **String**s, the counterpart of **IntToStr**? In this case, you can use **FloatToStr** or **FloatToStrF**. For example, whereas we would previously have written,

```
Edit1.Text := IntToStr(Trunc(50.84324));
```

which would set the **text** property of an edit control to 50, we would instead write,

```
Edit1.Text := FloatToStr(50.84324);
```

which is altogether different - in fact it displays 50.84324!

Now the **FloatToStrF** function allows us to see more of the structure of the floating-point numbers. If we specified,

```
Edit1.Text := FloatToStrF(50.84324, ffExponent, 5, 1);
```

where the final two parameters specify the precision and the number of digits respectively, their meaning depends on the format you choose. The format **ffExponent**, chosen, I admit, solely for effect, is one of several possible options; the others allow for general, fixed, currency and comma-divided number formats. This format allows you to display information in scientific notation (3.046E+9) to represent large numbers (in this case, 3,046,000,000), while the following two parameters allow you to define the number of digits before and after the E respectively - they effectively control the precision of the format.

 Check out Delphi's help for more information on these numerical formats.

And with that explanation of floats, I've finally finished off the data types for this chapter. Do you think they're really dead? Well, even if they are, you've got some of their pals, the structured data types to look forward to in the next chapter, but for now, let's take a look at what really makes up procedures and functions.

Procedures and Functions

As you already know, much of the code that you write handles events that occur while your application is running. Obviously, Delphi needs some way of relating each bit of code to that event and, if necessary, the particular part of the application to which that event occurred - say a user clicking on a button. It does this by breaking the code down into blocks known as **procedures** or **functions**.

A procedure is a block of code that can be called at any time. When it is called, it executes the Pascal code contained within it, one line at a time. A function is nothing more than a procedure that returns a result, usually based upon some specific input values, or any number of the global variables (variables, global or otherwise, are described in detail in a moment) that you have used in your application.

Let's take a look at an example to get a feel of how they work.

Try It Out - Experience My Power

1 Start a new application and save it as **poweru.pas** and **proc_fn.dpr**.

2 Drop one button and two edit boxes, labels and UpDown buttons (check out the Win95 page of the Component Palette) onto the form. The form should look something like this:

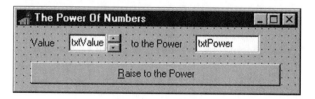

3 Rename the form as frmPower, the edit boxes as shown above, the UpDowns as udValue and udPower and the button as cmdPower.

4 While we're playing with properties in the Object Inspector, select udValue and set its Associate property txtValue - this should cause udValue to snap to the right-hand side of the edit box and change the box's text to the value of udValue's Position property. You should also set the Min and Max properties of this component to 1 and 10 respectively. Do the same for udPower, except that this time select txtPower, and set the Min and Max properties to 1 and 9 respectively.

4 In the button's OnClick event handler, type in the following code:

```
procedure TfrmPower.cmdPowerClick(Sender: TObject);
var
    RaisedToPower: double;
begin
    RaisedToPower := Power(StrToInt(txtValue.Text),StrToInt(txtPower.Text));
    MessageDlg('Result = ' + IntToStr(Round(RaisedToPower)),
               mtInformation, [mbOK], 0);
end;
```

5 Just below the **implementation** section, add in the following variable declarations:

```
implementation

var
  nValue, nPower : Integer;

{$R *.DFM}
```

6 Now it's time to create our own function, to calculate the new result of **nValue** raised to the power **nPower**. Add the following new function just below the compiler declaration in the **implementation** section of your unit:

```
{$R *.DFM}

function TfrmPower.Power(const nValue, nPower: integer) : double;
begin
    Result := exp(nPower * ln(nValue));
end;
```

7 Lastly, you must add a declaration of the form, which we've said belongs to **TfrmPower**, to the type declaration of the form. Because we don't want the function to be publicly available, we put it in the **private** subsection of the type declaration:

```
type
  TfrmPower = class(TForm)
    txtValue: TEdit;
    cmdPower: TButton;
    txtPower: TEdit;
    UDValue: TUpDown;
    UDPower: TUpDown;
    Label1: TLabel;
    Label2: TLabel;
    procedure cmdPowerClick(Sender: TObject);
  private
    function Power(const nValue, nPower: integer) : double;
    { Private declarations }
  public
    { Public declarations }
  end;
```

How It Works

Run the application and you can choose any base value from 1 to 10 and any power from 1 to 9. When you click on the Raise to the Power button, the program will go off to think about it for a while before displaying the appropriate result in a message dialog.

These numbers were chosen so that the 2 billion limit on Delphi's Integer data type wasn't exceeded.

Let's look at the important bit of the program first - the function we coded from scratch. It's just like the procedures that Delphi has been coding for us:

> There's the heading, with the word **function** to alert the compiler that what follows is, in fact, a function. Then there's the function's name - necessary to distinguish it from the thousands of others you've just written.

> The bit in brackets is a list of parameters, data that must be given to the function so that it can do its stuff. In this case, we need to give **Power** two integers, the second being the power to which the first should be raised.

> After a colon, the word **double** tells the compiler that the result of the function will be a type of **Real** number (which can include decimal values) known as a **double**.

> Last of all, we have the obligatory semicolon to finish off the heading.

After the heading, the **begin...end** pair enclose the code which belongs to the function. In this case, it's just one line. The code in a function is unusual, only in so far as the last line must set either the name of the function (**Power**), or the word **Result**, equal to the value the function will return. Procedures are coded just like functions, except they need no return value, or type declarations.

In most cases, we need to declare functions and procedures before we use them, although, as always, there's an exception which we'll look at later on. So, once we have written the function, we put its header in the form's type declaration. You'll have to wait until your read Chapter 5 to find out why we put it in the **private** section.

Now for another look at those parameters that we introduced earlier. The list consists of a word (**var** or **const**), followed by a comma-separated list of parameters of the same type (here it's **Integer**), then a colon, and finally that type. Any other types of parameter you need to declare follow the same rigmarole after a semicolon:

```
function <Function owner>.<Function name>
    (const <Parameter1>,  <Parameter2> : <Type1>;
     var <Parameter3> : <Type2>; <Parameter4> : <Type3>)
    : <Return Type>;
```

In this case, we've used the **const** definition because we don't want the function to change the value of **nValue** and **nPower**. The **const** word guarantees that the compiler won't let the value be changed by an inadvertent mistake in our code - OK, we'll come clean - if you make a mistake.

Another advantage of this keyword is that the code the compiler generates is also a little more efficient.

The final comment to make on this code concerns the contents of the **MessageDlg** parameter list. As the **Power** function has to return a **Double**, we need to convert it to an **Integer** before we can convert it to a **String** using **IntToStr**. Note that we could use **FloatToStr** as we recommended before, but if you try this, you'll see that for some unknown reason, you'll get some slightly different results (try 10 to the power of 9 which should be 1000000000, not 99999999.99999!).

This is one of those cases where you can't rely on the computer to give you the right result - it's a good idea to check out how your application works with a few test entries before you ship it!

All about Scope

It's something I've been promising you for a long while now, so here goes the first installment.

As you've already seen, procedures and functions allow you to break your application into small re-useable chunks. **Scope** enables you to control which units in your application can use which methods and functions, and which procedures and functions can use which variables.

Basically, there are two types of scope when you're considering variables: **local** and **global**.

Local Scope

Obviously, a variable called **sName** needs to be declared somewhere, but does it make sense to declare it in such a way that it can be used by all the procedures in the unit? Or does it make more sense to declare it so that it can only be used by the one block of code?

In the example below, we use both to show the consequences of using two variables with the same name, but different scope.

Try It Out - Scoping

1 Start up a new Delphi application and save it as **localu.pas** and **scoping.dpr**.

2 Bring up the code window and, beneath the **implementation** section of **localu.pas**, add the following variable declaration:

```
Implementation

{$R *.DFM}

var
    sName : String   ;
```

3 Drop two buttons on the form and rename them **cmdLocal** and **cmdLocalToUnit**. While you're renaming stuff, change the name of the form to **frmScope**. Recaption the form and the buttons as shown here:

4 The form's OnCreate event handler is used to set the variable's content:

```
procedure TfrmScope.FormCreate(Sender: TObject);
begin
    sName := 'To be';
end;
```

5 In the OnClick event of the Unit Wide button, add the following code to show what is held in the variable, **sName**.

```
procedure TfrmScope.cmdLocalToUnitClick(Sender: TObject);
begin
    Display(sName);
end;
```

6 Now add the following code to the Local button's OnClick event handler:

```
procedure TfrmScope.cmdLocalClick(Sender: TObject);
var
    sName : string;
begin
    sName := 'or not to be:';
    Display(sName);
end;
```

7 Finally, add this procedure to your unit. Note that it's vitally important to add the procedure so that it appears first in the unit's **implementation** section:

```
implementation

{$R *.DFM}

var
  sName : String;

procedure Display(sName : String);
begin
    ShowMessage('Current contents of string are  : ' + sName);
end;

procedure TfrmScope.FormCreate(Sender: TObject);
```

When you run this example, you are greeted by an unspectacular form with just two buttons. Even when you click on them, the responses that you get aren't that astounding. However, if you consider that both dialogs are created with the exact same line of code (our **Display** procedure), the results can suddenly take on another light.

How It Works

The first **sName** variable, declared within the **implementation** section, is local to the unit and may be used by any code within that section.

The second variable, with the value 'Or not to be:', is declared within a procedure, so it's limited to use within that procedure. Going out of the block destroys the second variable. This new value effectively overrides the first **sName** variable declared at the head of the unit, while it is within the **cmdLocalClick** procedure - that is, while it's 'within scope'. The variable which is local to the unit hasn't been destroyed, though. It still exists, but is just hidden from view by this new local variable.

Note that we didn't have to declare `Display` in the `interface` section of the unit. If you define the implementation of a function or a procedure before it's used in a unit, you can get away without a declaration, which in turn has the effect of limiting it's scope to just this unit. This means that any procedure or function in this unit can call it! Cool!

To summarize, scope defines not only the visibility of a variable, but also its life span.

Scope of Functions

Now you remember the **Power** function we used earlier? If we wanted, we could declare that function within the **cmdPowerClick** event handler, making it local to that event handler. And let's face it, we're not likely to need it anywhere else. So let's quickly update that:

Try It Out - Keeping Function Local

1 Load up **proc_fn.dpr**. Change to the code window and select File |Save As... to save the unit as **power2u.pas**. Now select File | Save Project As... to save the project as **proc_fn2.dpr**.

2 Delete the function declaration from the **private** section of the **frmPower** type declaration.

3 Now cut the function from the **implementation** section and paste it between the **OnClick** procedure and the previous **var** declaration. The only change that you need to make is to remove the **TfrmPower.** before the function name:

```
procedure TfrmPower.cmdPowerClick(Sender: TObject);

function Power(const nValue, nPower: integer) : double;
begin
    Result := exp(nPower * ln(nValue));
end;

var
   RaisedToPower: double;
begin
    RaisedToPower := Power(StrToInt(txtValue.Text),StrToInt(txtPower.Text));
    MessageDlg('Result = ' + FloatToStr(RaisedToPower),
               mtInformation, [mbOK], 0);
end;
```

If you run the program, everything seems to run as before! However, if you drop a new button onto the form and add the following line of code to its **OnClick** event handler,

```
procedure TfrmPower.Button1Click(Sender:TObject);
begin
    ShowMessage('The answer to 2 raised to the power of 2 is ' +
            FloatToStr(Power(2,2)));
end;
```

and if you try and compile the project now, Delphi will complain:

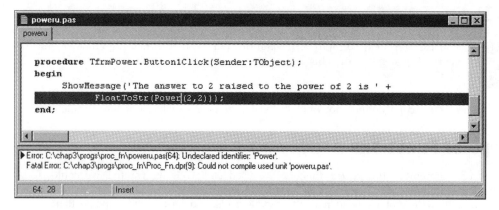

The new event handler can't find the specialized conversion function, **Power**, because it is declared as a local function to the **cmdPowerClick** event handler. As you can see, scope can have a very dramatic effect on the workings of your application, and may even stop it from compiling!

The final type of variable scope is **global**, a variable that is accessible by any and all units within the application.

Global Variables

We've seen in the previous sections how to declare variables so that they are within scope to all the procedures and functions of a unit, and so that they are local to just one procedure or function.

Now we look at **global** scope - when the variable is not only visible to its unit, but also to any other unit that references the unit in its **uses** clause. We create variables with global scope by declaring the variable in the **interface**, rather than the **implementation** section. As we saw earlier, the **interface** section is the public face of the unit.

In the following example, we're going to use two forms to illustrate global scope. Fasten your seat belts...

Try It Out - Global Scope

1 Start a new application and save it as **globalu.pas** and **gscope.dpr**.

2 Change the name of the form to frmGlobal1 and its
caption to In The Beginning:

3 Add a button to the form, changing its Name to cmdDiscover and its Caption to Discover,
and then add the following code to its OnClick event handler:

```
procedure TfrmGlobal1.cmdDiscoverClick(Sender: TObject);
begin
     frmGlobal2.ShowModal;
     ShowMessage('You typed the phrase ' + sName + ' into the other form');
end;
```

4 This code obviously refers to two items that we've not yet declared, so let's do that next.
Add the following global variable declaration to the **interface** section and a reference to a
second unit in the **implementation** section:

```
var
   frmGlobal1: TfrmGlobal1;
   sName : String;
implementation

uses global2u;

{$R *.DFM}
```

That should satisfy the compiler - you must declare before you use - and leads us to the
next step - creating a second form!

5 Select the File | New Form
menu option and Delphi will
provide you with a new form
and its associated unit:

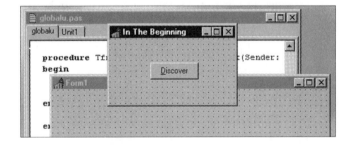

Save this new unit as **global2u.pas**.

6 Change the Name of the form to frmGlobal2
and its Caption to There Were Two Forms.
Add two bitmap buttons (BitBtn) and an edit
box to the form and arrange them like this:

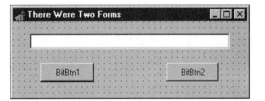

103

7 Change the Names of the buttons to cmdOK and cmdCancel, respectively, and change their Kind properties to match - i.e. select bkOK and bkCancel from the properties drop-down list. Add the following code to the cmdOK's OnClick event handler:

```
procedure TfrmGlobal2.cmdOKClick(Sender: TObject);
begin
    if txtEntry.Text = '' then
        sName := 'You didn''t type anything in the other form'
    else
        sName := 'You typed the phrase ''' + txtEntry.Text +
            ''' into the other form';
end;
```

and this code to the cmdCancel's OnClick event handler:

```
procedure TfrmGlobal2.cmdCancelClick(Sender: TObject);
begin
    sName := 'The user canceled the other form';
end;
```

Note the use of two or three apostrophes in the assignment of values to the string variable **sName**. If you want to use an apostrophe in a string, you need to explicitly tell Delphi it's not an apostrophe, otherwise it'll read it as an end of string marker. Therefore, two apostrophes mean 'this is an apostrophe', while three means that 'this is an apostrophe and it's at the end of the string'.

8 Now change the Name of the edit box to txtEntry and delete the contents of its Text property.

9 Make sure that the txtEntry edit box appears first in the tab order - when you're looking at the form, use the Edit | Tab Order... menu option to bring up the Tab Order dialog and move the edit box to the top of the list:

10 The final step is to add the following line of code to the **implementation** section of the unit:

```
implementation
```

```
uses globalu;
```

```
{$R *.DFM}
```

How It Works

The most important thing to notice about this example is that the key variable in our application, **sName**, is declared in one unit and assigned a value in another. To see where it's displayed, we must return to the first unit - quite a circular trip really! You might not think that this is a particularly big thing, but when you consider the lengths I went to at the beginning of the chapter to describe the idea of a unit, its interface and implementation sections, and the ideas of an outer skin and hidden away internals (it wasn't for my health you know!), you might start to see a significance.

All the way through the book so far, we've been using one unit to hold all of our code. This is for one simple reason: when you consider that the code in a unit's **implementation** section is shielded from the prying eyes of the outside world, you have to work quite hard to get at it from another unit!

However, like all good bureaucratic systems, there's a good reason for the structure, and if you follow the rules, anything (within reason) is possible. Let's look at our example in more detail for some clues.

If you run the application, the first thing that happens is that a plain form appears, complete with a button. If you take the hint (or lack of it) and click on the button, Delphi throws up another form! Now depending on what you do with this form, it will eventually disappear and be replaced by a dialog telling you exactly what you did to the second form. However, I didn't use any conditional checks (such as a composite **If** statement) or any other jiggery-pokery to get this context sensitive dialog to appear. I simply made a call to **ShowMessage**, passing one single parameter, a variable called **sName**.

"How did you do that?" I hear you cry. The answer is, of course, with a global variable. This variable sits outside all of the unit's protective shielding, observing the goings on with an unbiased eye, occasionally being collared by a passing unit for the purposes of value interrogation. These passing units even can reset the variable's value, if they feel that way inclined!

Even though this is quite a good way of picturing a global variable, it's not entirely accurate. After all, we all know that code can't exist outside of a unit - there's not enough air out there! In fact, the global variable lives inside a unit's **interface** section, the unit's lobby, if you want. Anyone can come in for a visit or a chat, but you can't get past the reception without a credit card!

Anyway, back to Pascal. If you define a variable in a unit's **interface** section (outside of a type declaration), the variable is considered as global and any unit can reference it. However, if a unit does want to reference it, it must be made aware of the presence of another unit in the scheme of things.

Consider the following diagram:

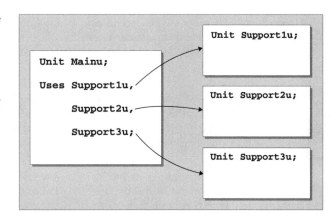

If you make a reference to another unit (or an element in that unit, like a global variable), you must specify it in a **uses** clauses somewhere in the calling unit. However, you might encounter problems, depending on which section you choose - the **interface** or the **implementation** section.

So far (before this last example), we've only seen one place where the **uses** clause appears - it's the first line of code after the **interface** heading. When the compiler starts up, the first thing it wants to know is how big the job at hand really is. To find this out, it needs to identify all of the units that are referenced within your project. The compiler begins the hunt with your project's primary unit, that is, the unit that contains your project's main form. It locates the **uses** clause in the **interface** section and uses the list it finds as the basis for the next step in the hunt. It takes the first unit in the list, opens it up, and locates its **interface uses** clause. It repeats this process until it finds a unit that doesn't have an **interface uses** clause. When this happens, the compiler moves up a level, looks for the second unit in the **uses** clause and repeats the process. In this manner, the compiler logically sorts through each and every **uses** clause that it finds in the **interface** section of the units that make up your project. You can think of this structure as a kind of root system, growing from that first **uses** clause:

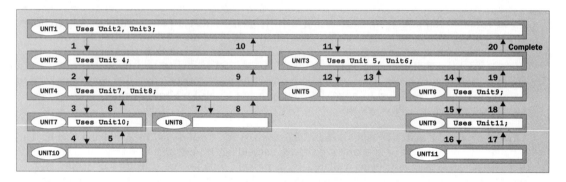

Now think what might happen if **unit1** referenced **unit2** and **unit2** referenced **unit1**. The compiler would start off okay, by opening **unit1** and then opening **unit2**, but then it would all go horribly wrong. The compiler would spot that **unit1** was referenced by **unit2** and so would open that up again and see **unit2** referenced and round it would go, time after time after time. This is what is called a **circular reference** (someone had a difficult time thinking that one up!) and fortunately, the compiler does give up after a while and complain at you to fix the problem.

However, what happens when, as in our example, both units need to refer to each other? **Global2u** needs access to **sName** to set its value, and **Globalu** needs to be able to refer to **frmGlobal2** (the form defined in **Global2u**) in order to pass the instruction to show it modally.

By the way, if you want to throw up a form that the user must respond to, if you use **ShowModal** rather than **Show**, Delphi will stop all user interaction with the rest of the application until that form is closed down. You should note that **ShowMessage** automatically creates a modal dialog box for you.

Well, fortunately, the solution to the circular reference problem is simple. You short-circuit the problem by not referring to the units in the **interface uses** clause. Instead, you create a **uses** clause in the **implementation** section of each unit and make your reference there.

This solution avoids the circular reference problem because the **implementation** section's **uses** clause isn't included in the compiler's job hunt, which leads us to the following suggestion:

FYI

The VCL has been created so that by including all of its units in the same **uses** clause, you still can't create a circular reference, therefore use the **interface uses** clause to reference these units. If you create two or more units for use in the same project, make all your **uses** clause references in the appropriate unit's **implementation** section.

In this section, I didn't explain that much about the actual steps that we followed in the Try It Out, as most, if not all, of the techniques and components that I used we've already covered in quite some detail. If you are still confused about what happened in the actually code itself, why don't you check out the actual code listing on the accompanying disk? This listing comes complete with a full set of comments that outline exactly what I did and what effects each particular line of code will have on the application as a whole.

A Case of Mistaken Identity

Do you remember the example that we looked at in the last chapter? We had a whole load of functions that dealt with the text stored in an edit box and a variety of additional components such as the FontDialog that allowed us to manipulate what we found. You might remember that when you pressed the space bar, or even worse, you deleted a character, the application didn't handle it too well.

We could have dealt with this problem with a series of **If** statements, but Delphi provides us with a much better decision making tool - the **Case** statement. Let's see how it works:

Try It Out - Extending the Panel

1 Right, load up the project from Chapter 2, **stage6.dpr**, and get ready to change the Panel **pnlStatus**'s **KeyPress** event:

```
procedure TCompactForm.txtMainEntryKeyPress(Sender: TObject;
  var Key: Char);
begin
    pnlStatus.Caption := 'Key just pressed :  ' + Key;
end;
```

2 Now add the code:

```
procedure TCompactForm.txtMainEntryKeyPress(Sender: TObject;
  var Key: Char);
begin
    case Ord(Key) of
       32 : pnlStatus.Caption := 'Space Bar hit' ;
        8 : pnlStatus.Caption := 'Character deleted';
    else
            pnlStatus.Caption := 'Key just pressed :  ' + Key;
    end;
end;
```

How It Works

As well as any character keys that have been pressed, the panel now shows whether the space bar (a keyboard character that has an ordinality of 32) or the backspace key (another keyboard character, this time with an ordinality of 8) were pressed. The variable **Key** passed to the event handler is of the ordinal data type **Char**, so either the character or its numerical value may be used to differentiate between different cases.

> The **Case** statement demands that you use an ordinal data type as its check condition. Remember that you can always create your own enumerated data type if none of the others fit your application, and you can still use this statement!

We chose the numerical value (which we deduced by printing **IntToStr(Ord(Key))**), rather than **Key** in the old version of the program to see if it could be done! You should note that the ordinal values of the **Key** parameter correspond to the ASCII codes that normally represent the characters. However, there are some keys that don't have an associated ASCII code, such as the arrow keys, the *Del* key, and the number pad keys, so you can't detect them using the OnKeyPress event.

Instead, if you want to extend the keys that you can identify, you should use the OnKeyDown or OnKeyUp event handlers. These event handlers deal with a **Key** parameter aimed at the **Virtual Key Codes**, which includes all the keys on the keyboard. For more information, check out Delphi's help under (surprise!) Virtual Key Codes.

Remembering the Password

One of the most useful features of a computer is its ability to make rudimentary decisions based on the data that it receives. A security system, for example, needs to look at the name and password entered by a user and use this information to decide whether to allow a given user access to the system, or whether to throw them out on his or her ear!

All this can be accomplished with the **If** statement we've seen already seen in action over the last few chapters, so if just to keep your hand in, why don't you give it a go? You never know, I might have mentioned something new!

Try It Out - Making a Decision

1 Load up **password.dpr**, the project we used at the start of the chapter. You've already designed the form, but we left out the code until now.

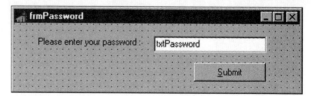

2 The first step to powering up this form as a password entry screen is to set txtPassword's PasswordChar property - change the property to &. Now delete the contents of the edit box's Text property and finally set cmdSubmit's Default property to True. These steps simply create a more user-friendly (and security-conscious) form.

3 Now we're ready to add the all important code. To start with, let's add the following lines to cmdSubmit's OnClick event handler:

```
procedure TfrmPassword.cmdSubmitClick(Sender; TObject);
begin
    if txtPassword.Text = 'SuperUser' then
        MessageDlg(sSuper, mtInformation, [mbOK], 0)
    else if txtPassword.Text = 'GroupLeader' then
        MessageDlg(sGroup, mtInformation, [mbOK], 0)
    else if txtPassword.Text = 'User' then
        MessageDlg(sUser, mtInformation, [mbOK], 0)
    else if txtPassword.Text = 'Master' then
        MessageDlg(sMaster, mtInformation, [mbOK], 0)
    else
        MessageDlg(sFail, mtInformation, [mbOK], 0);
    close;
end;
```

4 You may have noticed that I've used variables to indicate the strings that should appear in the dialog that is presented once the password check has been made. Let's define and initialize those variables next - add the following code to the form's OnCreate event handler:

```
procedure TfrmPassword.FormCreate(Sender: TObject);
begin
    sNewline  := #13 + #10;
    sCheckOut := 'Password Checks Out';

    sSuper  := sCheckout + sNewline + 'Welcome Super User';
    sGroup  := sCheckout + sNewline + 'Welcome Group Leader';
    sUser   := sCheckout + sNewline + 'Welcome User';
    sMaster := 'Welcome Master' + sNewline + 'The Back Door Is Open';
    sFail   := 'Your Password Is Not Recognised' + sNewline +
               'Please Leave The System' + sNewline +
               'Security Has Been Alerted!';
end;
```

5 Following on from the golden rule - always declare before using - add these declarations to the **implementation** section:

```
implementation

var
    sSuper, sGroup, sUser, sMaster, sFail, sNewline, sCheckOut : String;

{$R *.DFM}
```

6 Just one last comment before you run the application. For the purposes of testing, you might find it useful to comment the final line of the **cmdSubmitClick** event handler. This will stop the application stopping down every time you hit the Submit button - it's just a suggestion, but you might find it useful to get an idea of what's going on:

```
    else
        MessageDlg(sFail, mtInformation, [mbOK], 0);
```

```
      //close;
   end;
```

Try running the application and try to get access to the system, i.e. get one of the favorable dialogs. If you're having problems, try using the 'back door' password of **Master**. You should also note that all the passwords are case-sensitive, so if you're still having problems....

How It Works

Okay, I admit, it wasn't as strenuous as the rest of the chapter, but then again, as you've done so well, I thought you should have a little rest and stretch your memory a little, rather than your brain cells.

Having said all that, did you notice some of the things that I sneaked in? How about the use of the new type of message dialog, **mtWarning**? What do you mean that stuff in the form's OnCreate event handler?

Okay, okay, you've got me. I've tried to simplify the **MessageDlg** parameters by swapping the actual strings with variables that I've built up before the cmdSubmit is clicked. In this way, I've added a little more readability to the code, and made it easier to maintain by only having one instance of a repeated string of text, replacing it with a variable instead. Just as in the set example, this will cut down any problems that I might face if I decide to change the text in any way, shape or form.

FYI Note the combination of #13 and #10 (the way that you represent ASCII character codes directly in your Pascal code), referred to as a carriage return and a line feed, has the effect of moving the following text on to the next line of the dialog box. This is the only way to break the text over more than one line in a dialog - if you don't use it, the dialog will grow wider to accommodate the string.

Code Layout and the Semicolon

Let's start with a huge generalization and then qualify it:

▶ All statements in Delphi need to end with a semicolon.

You might have noticed that the composite **If** statement used in the password program's **cmdSubmitClick** event handler had eleven lines of code before you encountered the first semicolon, if you discount the first line, of course. What's going on here? Well, if you read that last sentence again, it immediately becomes obvious. Those eleven lines of code do, in fact, make up one statement.

Actually, Delphi has a number of statements that look like they should have semicolons halfway through: think about the case statement, for example. Not a semicolon in sight until the very end of the last condition!

Another problem that beginners to Pascal usually complain about is these **begin...end** blocks. What's happening with them? Well, if you take the **If** statement, for example, it has been designed to allow you to do one thing (stress the *one* here!) based on each result of the condition. We've already seen how you can create composite **If** statements by getting Delphi to run another **If** statement based on a negative result of the first check, so you should be quite happy with that idea now.

But where does that help us with these **begin...end** blocks? We'll, if you think of a **begin...end** block as a way to fool Delphi into thinking that several statements are in fact one, you are half way to understanding where to put the semicolons. However, the catch comes when you think about the statements inside the **begin...end** block - they are stand-alone statements, so they need semicolons!

Have a look at the following example:

```
if txtTest.Text = 'Test' then
    {Do a statement - no semicolon}
else {No semicolon}
    {Do another statement - add a semicolon, it's the end of the if statement}
```

By following the ideas of the semicolon at the end of a statement and the single line ruse, you could quite happily type in this similar example and not put a semicolon out of place.

```
if txtTest.Text = 'Test' then
    begin {No semicolon}
        {Do a statement - add a semicolon it's the end of a statement}
        {Do another statement - add a semicolon it's the end of a statement}
    end    {No semicolon}
else       {No semicolon}
    begin {No semicolon}
        {Do a statement - add a semicolon it's the end of a statement}
        {Do another statement - add a semicolon it's the end of a statement}
    end;   {Add a semicolon, it's the end of the if statement}
```

There's one other point to make about semicolons when you've only got one line of code in a procedure or function. Look at this procedure - it will compile if you've made the appropriate declarations:

```
procedure TForm1.Button1Click(Sender: TObject);
begin
    txtGreeting.text := 'Hello' {Note the lack of semicolon}
end;
```

This 'feature' is one that is directly attributable to backwards compatibility and the bad old days. In my opinion, it's not a very good idea to take advantage of this feature, as you will invariably run into trouble when you add another line of code and forget to add the semicolon onto this original line, a demand that the compiler will now make!

Add this to the fact that adding the semicolon to this line makes no difference to the compiler, I would suggest that you include it every time - the extra key press avoids the hassle of having to add it in later when a compile has just failed! There's a guy speaking from experience!

By following these guidelines and suggestions, you shouldn't come up against the dreaded ';' expected... compiler error too often.

Formatting Your Code

You may have noticed by now that much of my example code is nicely formatted. Tabs indent lines within blocks of code and carriage returns are used to break up long lines of code.

You shouldn't worry too much if your code doesn't look very much like mine in terms of layout. Delphi doesn't really care about it, it's just a bit of a standard among programmers that code in blocks and unfinished lines of code should be indented. It makes the code a lot easier to read at a glance - you can quickly find the blocks and generally get a glance-overview of the structure of your program. As you start to nest blocks of code within others, indents make matching up those annoying **begin** and **end** lines a whole lot easier.

Format your code however you see fit, but you will find that if you read a lot of example code from books or sources in the public domain, the code formatting style I use here is pretty common. Get used to it now and it will save you a great deal of headache later on in your Delphi career.

Summary

So, there you have it! You should now be able to understand why you and Delphi have placed the code from the last three chapters in the places you have, you should understand the ideas behind procedures and functions and their parameters a little more, and you should be quite a home with simple data types.

In the next chapter, I'm going to go on with data types, taking a look at the most structured data types that Delphi has to offer. I'll be looking at how to create an application to perform the same task a number of times, and I might even have chance to cover how you can use Delphi to graph a list of data.

I urge you to keep going. You've already got half of the basic tools necessary to start writing useful programs, programs that actually do something. At last, you're definitely on your way towards Delphi Guru status!

Advanced Code

In the last chapter, I introduced you to some of the ideas behind Delphi Pascal, including those ideas behind procedures and functions, how scope comes into play in a unit and some basic code structures and data types. By now, you should be quite happy with the layout of the code that makes up your Delphi application, though your imagination should now be starting to kick into action. If you are asking questions like 'Okay, so I can do this if I put that there, but how do I make it do that?' then this chapter will be right up your street.

In the next few pages, I'm going to introduce you to a number of new powerful techniques including:

- Indexed Loops
- Constants
- Arrays
- Strings
- Indefinite Loops

All these topics will start to answer your new questions, allowing you to achieve more interesting and flexible solutions, and produce top quality Delphi apps. As you will see, we've based a lot of this chapter's examples on those from previous chapters, showing you how to improve and adapt your code to take advantage of all these new tools.

Without any further ado, let's start looping round and round and round...

Indexed Loops

One of the worst points of most programming languages is the complex 'technical' terms in use, and the importance that authors of books like this tend to attach to them. Guilty as charged, your honor. In my defense, though, introducing these terms does make it easier for you to find the topic in the online help hereafter.

Indexed loops is a phrase that instantly rings alarm bells for beginners who think we're on to something really complex. Well, we're not. An **indexed loop** is nothing more than a section of code which runs for a preset number of times.

The word **indexed** comes from the fact that the code needs to keep track of how many times it needs to run, and how many times it has run already. It's nothing more than a number; if you like, a counter of the number of times the code has run in this session.

Load up the **Forloops.dpr** project and we'll take a look at these things in action:

If you run the program, you'll find yourself presented with a black form. Click on the button, though, and the background color of the form fades from black to an attractive shade of red. What's happening here is that the code is changing the background color of the form (the form's **Color** property) to a different value over and over, a set number of times.

Stop the program by clicking on the close icon at the top right of the window and double-click on the command button to bring up its **Click** event handler:

```
procedure TForm1.Button1Click(Sender: TObject);
var
    nIndex : integer;
begin
    for nIndex := 0 to 255 do
    begin
        Application.ProcessMessages;
        Form1.Color := nIndex;
    end;
end;
```

The first two lines declare **nIndex** as an integer - we met integer data types and variable declaration in the last chapter. And from those ideas of scope also introduced in the last chapter, we see that the value of **nIndex** is valid (i.e. within scope) only within the procedure - it's a local variable. As for its name - it declares itself as a number by the prefix **n**, and its name tells us that it will represent some kind of index. That's elementary enough, isn't it, my dear Watson…

To recap, a variable is a place where we can store temporary items of data, in this case, a number.

Take a look at the code itself:

```
begin
    For nIndex := 0 to 255 do
    begin
        Application.ProcessMessages;
        Form1.Color := nIndex;
    end;
end;
```

This is where the loop itself lives and, as you can see, the reason for its name, the **For** loop, is quite obvious. If you have ever looked at C or Basic programs, you will probably have come across the **For** loop already, though in a slightly different format.

The format is quite simple: having set up a variable to act as a counter for the loop, you just need to write,

For *<variable name>* **:=** *< startnumber >* **to** *<endnumber>* **do**

substituting the name of your variable for **<variable name>**, and the start and end values for the loop for **<startnumber>** and **<endnumber>**. For example, set the start and end up for **1** and **10**, and the loop will count from 1 to 10. You finish the **For** command with the word **do**. Delphi then runs the line, or block, of code that follows the set number of times.

Going back to our example, the **For** loop runs a block of code 256 times (0 to 255 is 256):

```
begin
    For nIndex := 0 to 255 do
    begin
        Application.ProcessMessages;
        Form1.Color := nIndex;
    end;
end;
```

On each pass through the loop, the form's **Color** property is set to the current value of **nIndex**. You'll learn a lot more about the **Color** property and color numbers later in the book. For now though, just take it as read (Boom! Boom!) that 0 means black and 255 means red.

You might notice that the help files refer to the colors by their hexadecimal representation, i.e. Red is $000000FF. If you're a bit rusty, dig out that old math book or just remember that hexadecimal is another name for base 16, so $17 is (1*16) + 7 = 23 and $FF (Red) is (15*16) + 15 = 255.

That **Application.ProcessMessages;** line looks slightly daunting, but it does illustrate an important point of Windows 95 development. You see, what can happen with small loops like the one above is that they will run through so fast that, by the time Windows gets round to redrawing the display, the loop has finished. For our example, this would mean that when you click the button on the form you would see the black form, then a red one, but nothing in between. Try commenting this line out and running the application again.

Application.ProcessMessages; gets round this. It basically says to Windows "Hey, I've done something that you might want to deal with - so deal with it". Windows can then go away and mull over any recent events, received as **messages**, such as the order to redraw (paint) the form. The result is that the color is changed, the form is redrawn, the color is changed, the form is redrawn..., and so on.

This also illustrates an important difference between Windows 3.xx and Windows 95, and the way they handle mutiple simultaneous tasks.

117

FYI

In Windows 3.xx, a loop running within an application could lock up Windows for a time if it didn't yield control back to Windows and allow the handling of other events. Thus, you needed `ProcessMessages` so that you could continue to interact with the application while the tricky loop was being processed.

By comparison, Windows 95 is a true 32-bit multitasking operating system, which in English means that it can do more than one thing at a time. So, instead of hogging Windows, we're left with the problem that a program won't wait for Windows to catch up with it. Which do you prefer?

Controlling the Code in a Loop

Loops are great for running a block of code a number of times, but what if you only need to run some code on certain passes? The logical way to deal with this would be to stick a few **If** tests in the block of code and break it up into smaller chunks. However, Delphi also provides you with a couple of alternatives: the **break** and **continue** commands.

Try It Out - Breaking Out of Loops

1 Load up **forloops.dpr** again. From the Standard page of the Component Palette, find the Panel component and drop it onto the form. Your form should now look like this:

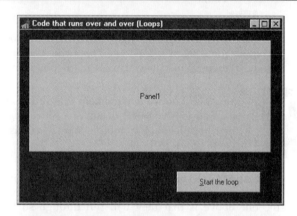

2 Use the Object Inspector to remove the Panel's Caption and then drop a CheckBox onto the bottom of the form:

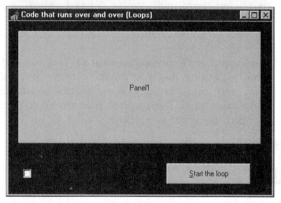

3 Problem: the text next to the CheckBox is black so, of course, it instantly vanishes when you drop it onto the form. Find the CheckBox's Color property in the Object Inspector and double-click it to bring the color dialog into view. Select a nice yellow (clYellow) and click the OK button. The CheckBox and its caption (which you could change to Panel?) will now be significantly more visible than before!

4 Double-click the command button to bring up its OnClick event handler ready for the change.

5 Now we can add a couple of lines beneath the line which determines the form's color:

```
begin
      Application.ProcessMessages;
      Form1.Color := nIndex;
      If Checkbox1.State = cbUnChecked then continue;
      Panel1.Color := nIndex;
end;
```

6 Once you've typed in the code, save both the unit (use File | Save As...) and the project (use File | Save Project As...) in a new directory. This means that when you run the application (*F9*), Delphi won't automatically copy your changes over the original application:

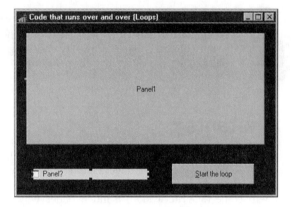

7 Let's make one more change to the code. How about quitting the loop when the code reaches a certain value (say 150) when the CheckBox is checked? Stop the program by closing the form down in the normal way and bring up the command button's click code again. Change the code in that **For** loop now so that it looks like this.

```
for nIndex := 0 to 255 do
    begin
        Application.ProcessMessages;
        Form1.Color := nIndex;
        if Checkbox1.State = cbUnChecked then continue;
        Panel1.Color := nIndex;
        if nIndex = 150 then break;
    end;
```

8 Now try running the application!

How It Works

The first **If** statement is really quite easy to follow. If the **State** property of the CheckBox is equal to the built-in Delphi value **cbUnChecked** (which, of course, means that the CheckBox hasn't yet been checked), then the **continue** command runs. **continue** tells Delphi to ignore the rest of the code in the block and 'continue' to the next pass of the loop. In this case, if the condition is fulfilled, the first loop sets the form's color, skips the rest of the code and starts on the next loop.

Conversely, if the CheckBox is checked, the **continue** command will not be called and Delphi will fall through to the line that sets up the panel's color.

Now for the second **If** statement. As before, if the CheckBox is set, we want the command to run - this time to 'break' out of the loop when the index of the loop reaches 150. The **break** command tells Delphi to ignore the rest of the loop.

If you run this code and check the CheckBox, you will see that the background color doesn't get quite as bright because the loop finishes sooner. Uncheck the CheckBox, and run the program again. The panel retains its off-red color, while the form returns to its previous full red - very tasteful.

Due to the way Windows works, and because we've included a **ProcessMessages** command in our code, we can control how the panel changes colour while the form's color change is happening. Try checking and unchecking the CheckBox after you have clicked on the <u>S</u>tart the loop button.

Constants

If variables are things that can change (hence their name), then **constants** are things that can't. For example, you might have a game where you need to repeatedly refer, in a loop, to the maximum number of aliens visible on the screen. Rather than typing in the number each time you come to write a loop, a much better way to do things is to declare a constant and use that in the loop instead.

By writing an application that needs to continually refer to some set value using a constant, you can easily change all the loops and conditions that use that value simply by changing a single line of code. Plus, your code is slightly more readable if a loop's upper bound is the constant **ALIENS**, rather than an obscure number, the meaning of which you won't quite remember in six months time.

You declare a constant in a similar way that you declare a variable with the obvious difference that you use **const** instead of **var** as the keyword.

There are actually two ways to declare constants, as typed and as untyped. Untyped constants, as their name suggests, do not have their type defined in the code. Instead, the value you assign to the constant when it's defined determines the constant's type when the compiler gets hold of it. Typed constants have their type defined with their value. We'll use this in the next section.

Wizards and Warlocks

Load up **wizards.dpr** and run it - click on the form itself when the program is running to see what it does.

As you can see, the program draws wizards (unfortunately, warlocks are rather thin on the ground these days) at random positions all over the form. The number of wizards that are drawn with each mouse click is held in a constant. A loop is used to draw that number of wizards, and this needs a variable to keep track of what it's doing. It's an ideal program to look at right now!

Stop the program running, bring up the Object Inspector and take a look at the events that have been coded for this form:

Only one event is handled - the form's **Click** event. If you double-click this in the Object Inspector, the code window will come into view, showing you the code for that event:

```
procedure TForm1.FormClick(Sender: TObject);
const
   NUMWIZARDS    : integer = 10;
var
   nIndex        : integer;
   Wizard        : TBitmap;
begin
   Wizard := TBitmap.Create;
   Wizard.LoadFromFile('wiz.bmp');

   randomize;

   For nIndex := 1 to NUMWIZARDS do
      Form1.Canvas.Draw( Random( Form1.Width  ), Random (form1.Height), Wizard);

   Wizard.Free;
end;
```

As it was running, the program looked almost impressive! If we take a peek at the code, though, we see surprisingly little. From our point of view, it's the section that declares the constant that's most interesting:

```
const
    NUMWIZARDS  : integer = 10;
```

As you can see, this sets up a typed constant, called **NUMWIZARDS**. It's pretty much a standard to name constants only with capital letters, rather than the mix of capital and lower case letters that you will see for variables. When you're looking at the code of an application, this makes it easy for you to see which bits are dealing with variables and which are dealing with constants.

In much the same way that you might declare a variable, the type of data that the constant holds is written following a full colon. The main difference between a variable and a typed constant declaration, though, is that you must also give the constant a value, which you can see here is **10**.

In older versions of Pascal and in Delphi 1.0, typed constants could be thought of as initialised variables, and their values changed later in the code block, but those days are gone - a constant's constant, not a misnomer.

Delphi 2.0 does, however, allow backwards compatability through the use of so-called compiler directives. Writing the statement {$J+} at the top of the program code tells the compiler that you want to allow the value of a typed constant to be changed, if necessary. There are quite a few other compiler directives available in Delphi - you can see your current project's settings by pressing *Ctrl+O+O* when you're looking at some code.

That's really all there is to know about constants, other than the fact that you can't change the value of a constant while a program is running. For example, this code would never work:

```
Procedure A_Procedure;
const
    Age : integer = 24;
begin
    Age := 12;
end;
```

Odd Variables and Other Trivia

As a point of interest, the code following the constant declaration defines a couple of variables:

```
var
    nIndex       : integer;
    Wizard       : TBitmap;
```

The first **nIndex** is nothing new, but **Wizard** is a rather special variable. As well as telling Delphi what type of data a variable can hold, you can also declare variables to hold entire objects, such as components or forms, and so on. In this case, we have set up the **Wizard** variable and told Delphi that this is going to hold bitmap-type objects (**TBitmap**). Why? Because the wizards that the program draws all come from a bitmap file (a file whose name ends in **.bmp**) on the book's disk.

And as you've seen when we looked at the structure of Delphi Pascal source files, even **Form1** is declared as a variable of type **TForm1** in the interface section. Don't miss Chapter 5's exciting explanation of this strange code device.

At this point, you can move on to the next section to find out about collections of data, but if you have an urge to find out what the rest of the program does, read on:

```
begin
    Wizard := TBitmap.Create;
    Wizard.LoadFromFile('wiz.bmp');

    randomize;

    for nIndex := 1 to NUMWIZARDS do
        Form1.Canvas.Draw( Random( Form1.Width  ), Random (form1.Height), Wizard);

    Wizard.Free;
end;
```

The first two lines place something into our **Wizard** variable. (From now on we'll ignore **begin** - it should be clear to you at this stage what that does.) The first line tells Delphi that we want to create a new object of type **TBitmap** and that it needs to be stored in the **Wizard** variable. The **Create** method is just about the most important object method there is - we go into this again in the next chapter. So, it's not enough just to declare **Wizard** as a variable of the type **TBitmap**, we need also to create it in code.

Bitmap objects come with a number of special methods of their own, **LoadFromFile** being one of them. In the case of a bitmap (graphic) object, this loads a graphic file from the disk and attaches it to the bitmap variable you specify. We saw something similar when we programmed the bitmap viewer in the first chapter, way back when. The only difference here is that we specify the full path for **wiz.bmp**, rather than looking at the **Filename** property of **OpenDialog1**.

As you saw when you ran the program earlier, the wizards are drawn onto the form at random positions. The **Randomize** method on the third line tells Delphi to go away and think of a whole stack of random numbers, with the starting point based on some cunning calculation using the system time. If you don't use the system clock to initialize the **Randomize** method, the chances are that every time you run the program the wizards will appear in the same locations because each 'random' set of numbers would have the same start point (or seed).

The fourth and fifth lines actually do the drawing, using a **For** loop:

```
for nIndex := 1 to NUMWIZARDS do
    Form1.Canvas.Draw(Random(Form1.Width), Random(Form1.Height), Wizard);
```

As you can see, the loop counts from **1** to the value stored in our **NUMWIZARDS** constant, in this case **10**. The code that follows tells Delphi to draw a bitmap on the **canvas** of **Form1** at the specified (random) x and y coordinates. Delphi graphics methods are covered in more detail in Chapter 6.

In our case, we tell Delphi that the x coordinate should be a random number no bigger than the width of the form, and the y coordinate should be a random number no bigger than the height of the form. The final parameter is the name of the bitmap object that we want to draw.

123

FYI   This example augments one that can be found in the help by searching for the `Randomize` procedure. There, `Randomize` provides for random coordinates at which to paint **Boo!**, using the `Canvas.TextOut` method. Just thought you might like to know.

The last line of code gets rid of the **Wizard** object:

```
Wizard.Free;
```

Since object variables can consume vast amounts of memory, it's a good idea to tell Delphi to free it up when you've finished dealing with the objects.

Arrays - Collections of Data

Quite often, you'll find that you need to deal with lists of data. The data is of the same type, but you need to handle lots of it simultaneously. As examples: in a game, you might need a list of the screen coordinates of all the aliens; in a database application, you might need a list of strings, one for each of the different staff titles used in your company. The best way to get what you need is to use something called an **array**.

So, what exactly is an array? Take a look at this:

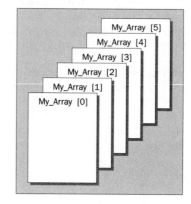

An array is a collection of variables, all of the same type, but each with a unique index number that lets you identify each element of the array in your code. Declaring an array is really quite easy. You define the variable just as you would normally, except between the data type and the full colon you write,

<variable name> **: array[***m..n***] of** *<data type>***;**

and replace the ***m*** and ***n*** with the number of the array's first and last elements.

For example, in the diagram above, we set up an array called **My_Array** which is used to hold up to 6 string values, each element numbered from 0 to 5. Arrays are the first of the so-called structured types, which we're now looking at, and will continue with in the next chapter.

Let's play with some math to see how it all works for real. In the following example, we use a 2D array to store the results of a calculation of the function sin(X)/X, chosen mainly because it gives a pretty picture when you graph it. Not for nothing do we study all that math...

Charting Arrays

Okay, so we want to chart some numbers. We've really got two separate tasks to perform: prepare the numbers for the graph and the actual painting of the graph itself. Well, first things first, let's take a look at the finished application. Load in **charting.dpr**.

Before you can run the application, I should tell you about a small problem with this OCX. As with all new components that you add to a form, you need to add an entry to your **uses** clause - normally Delphi will handle this automatically for you, but with this OCX, for some unknown reason, it only adds one of the necessary unit references, in this case **ChartFX**. The other unit reference, **CFXOCX2**, is completely ignored, and this causes the compilation to crash and burn.

As you can see from our code, we have added this unit reference to our **uses** clause, but this still doesn't solve the problem. When you place a reference in the **uses** clause, you are in fact asking the compiler to look in all of the normal places for the source code for these components. For some unknown reason, Borland didn't include the source code file for this unit in your **Delphi/Lib** directory - this means that Delphi can't find it and so the compilation crashes and burns again!

The solution to this problem can take one of two forms. The simplest is to copy the **cfxocx2.pas** file to **Delphi/Lib**, but this does break down the logical layout of the Delphi file structure. The other solution is to make use of Delphi's project options to inform the compiler of where to look for this source file. If you decide on this course of action, you'll need to locate the Directories/Conditionals page of the Project | Options... dialog. Simply type the full path to the OCX's files into Search path:... On my system, I had to type in **C:\Delphi 2.0\OCX\ChartFX** to get the project to compile.

Choose your solution and run the application:

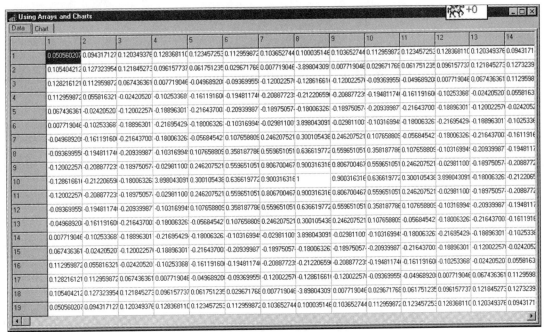

As you can see, when the application starts up, you're presented with a grid of numbers which you can see charted by switching tabs on the notebook.

So what can we deduce from this? Well, we need to set up the grid and populate it with the figures right at the start, but we can leave the chart until the user changes pages. So let's take a look at the **FormCreate** event handler.

```
procedure TfrmShowArray.FormCreate(Sender: TObject);
begin
      {Columns give the X count, rows the Y count}
      StringGrid1.ColCount := CountX + 1;
      StringGrid1.RowCount := CountY + 1;

      for nIndeX := 1 to CountX do
      begin
         fXval := (nIndex/4 - 2)*Pi;
         StringGrid1.Cols[nIndex].Add(IntToStr(nIndex));

         for nIndeY := 1 to CountY do
         begin
            fYval := (nIndeY/4 - 2.5)*Pi;
            fZval := Sqrt(fXval*fXval + fYval*fYval);
            if (fZval <> 0) then
              arnResult[nIndeX, nIndeY] := sin(fZval)/fZval
            else
              arnResult[nIndeX, nIndeY] := 1;

            StringGrid1.Rows[nIndeY].Add(IntToStr(nIndeY));
            StringGrid1.Cells[nIndeX, nIndeY] :=
                    FloatToStr(arnResult[nIndeX, nIndeY]);
         end;
      end;
      ChartFX1.View3D    := TRUE;
      ChartFX1.Angles3D  := MAKELONG(30,330);
end;
```

As you can see, this code sets up the grid and populates it. I've highlighted the relevant code, including the lines that set up the number of columns and rows that we'll need and then label those columns and rows with titles.

We make use of a new Delphi component in this example - the StringGrid. This control is designed to look exactly like a spreadsheet, so it's perfect for displaying the tabular data that we're using to plot our chart. As you can see, the component is very easy to use - simply set up the size of the component by setting ColCount and RowCount to appropriate values and then pass values directly to the component's cells, referenced by their (x, y) coordinates.

The component also comes with its own column and row headers. I've made use of these to display the values of X used in the calculation of SinX/X using the following syntax:

```
StringGrid1.Rows[nIndeY].Add(IntToStr(nIndeY));
```

You should note that this line of code only works because of its position within a **For** loop (**nIndeY** is the **For** loop counter variable) and it only applies to labeling the row headers. As you can see further up the code, to label the columns, all you need to do is replace this line of code with a near identical version, just swapping the term **Rows** for **Cols**. Of course, we also need to use the other **For** loop counter variable to scroll across the columns, as opposed to dropping down the rows.

To set up the grid, we make use of a number of constants and variables - you can see their declarations in the **implementation** section of this unit:

```
implementation

  const
    CountX = 21;
    CountY = 19;
  var
    nIndeX, nIndeY       : integer;
    {Actual values of x, y axes and their circular combination}
    fXval, fYval, fZval : double;
    {Array of result of calculation, for display
      This is equivalent to array[1..CountX, 1..CountY] of double}
    arnResult            : array[1..CountX] of array[1..CountY] of double;
```

```
{$R *.DFM}
```

The constants are used as the upper limit of the loop counters **nIndeX** and **nIndeY**, and give the number of entries to the array. We use untyped constants so that we can use them in the array variable declaration - Delphi doesn't allow you to use typed constants in your array declarations.

The rest of the code is based on the equation that we use to create the figures we need for our chart, including a little error handling (we check to see if the divisor is 0, and neatly avoid a divide-by-zero situation), with the final line of the inner **For** loop actually populating the grid with the numbers:

```
StringGrid1.Cells[nIndeX,nIndeY] := FloatToStr(arnResult[nIndeX,nIndeY]);
```

Note the use of two **For** loops, one nested inside the other to get the required movement through the grid - we cycle down the grid, moving across a column as we complete the previous one.

The final two lines of the procedure just set up two of the chart's properties that allow you to view the result in three dimensions. The first line turns the feature on and the second sets up the point-of-view. Check out the OCX's help file for more information on these properties.

Animating the Application

So we've got an application that presents us with a grid full of numbers ready for charting, but we still haven't sorted out the chart. Fortunately, by using the ChartFX OCX, we don't have to worry about any of the details of how the charting works, we just need to pass the data to the OCX and let it work its magic.

To organize this magic, we need to write two more event handlers, one to actually handle the OCX, while the other is more of a housekeeping feature. Let's talk about this one first, as it's easier to deal with!

```
procedure TfrmShowArray.FormResize(Sender: TObject);
begin
    ChartFX1.BoundsRect := TabSheet2.ClientRect;
end;
```

In the simplest terms, all this code does is to make the rectangle that is the chart the same size as the rectangle that is the tabsheet when the form is resized. This property, combined with the fact that the PageControl's Align property is set to alClient, means that no matter what the user does to the window, the chart will always fill the tabsheet.

Normally, you wouldn't need this **BoundsRect/ClientRect** line of code, but unfortunately, the OCX doesn't come with an **Align** property.

Here, we have used two new properties, **BoundsRect** and **ClientRect**, both of which operate with TRect data structures. A TRect data structure is simply a set of four values, the first two giving the top-left coordinate, the final two giving the bottom-right coordinate. What rectangle you get depends on which property you query. **BoundsRect** deals with the boundary of the associated object, while **ClientRect** deals with the client area of that object.

These two rectangles are quite often confused, so it's important to understand the distinction between them. If we consider a form, its boundary rectangle encompasses the whole form, whereas its client area is the boundary rectangle minus the space taken up by the borders, the title bar and the menu.

The final event handler that we must consider is the one that handles the painting of the chart itself, which we've decided to do when the user selects the appropriate page of the notebook.

```
procedure TfrmShowArray.PageControl1Change(Sender: TObject);
begin
    if PageControl1.ActivePage = TabSheet2 then
    begin
        {Open data exchange, to set CountX series of data, with CountY
         elements in each 'serie', and the data representing the data Value}
        ChartFX1.OpenDataEx(COD_VALUES,CountX,CountY);
        {Chart type is 3D, and of the type area}
        ChartFX1.Type_   := area or CT_3D;

        for nIndex := 1 to CountX do
        begin
            {Set current 'serie' - a zero-based index}
            ChartFX1.ThisSerie := nIndex - 1;
            {Set serie legend}
            ChartFX1.SerLeg[nIndeX - 1] := IntToStr(nIndeX);
            for nIndey := 1 to CountY do
            begin
              {Set value to value of array element - again allowing for a
               zero-based array}
              ChartFX1.Value[nIndeY - 1]  := arnResult[nIndeX, nIndeY];
              {Add Key legend}
              ChartFX1.KeyLeg[nIndeX-1] := IntToStr(nIndeX);
            end;
        end;
        {Set gap between Value-axis markers - using the Administration property}
```

```
ChartFX1.Adm[CSA_Gap] := 0.1;
{Set Value-axis maximum}
ChartFX1.Adm[CSA_MAX] := 1;
{Close data}
ChartFx1.CloseData(COD_VALUES);
{Call the Resize procedure to match the size of the chart to the size of
 the tabsheet, otherwise we will have to wait until the user resizes the
 form}
frmShowArray.Resize;
    end;
  end;
```

As you can see, this event handler is a little more complex than the ones we've dealt with before, but again, it's dealing with two separate tasks: loading in the data to the chart (see the highlighted code) and reformatting the chart so it looks brill! I'm going to leave you to research the formatting features of the OCX, except to say that the Type property is quite important.

What I'm going to cover is the method of passing the data to the chart, a potentially simple task that the OCX seems to make unnecessarily complex. Basically, you need to follow four steps:

- Open a channel to the chart
- Select a series and pass the necessary data to fill the series
- Repeat the last step for each series
- Close the channel to the chart

The first of these steps is quite easy - you simply call the **OpenDataEx** method of the chart and pass through a few parameters that deal with the amount and type of data you wish to graph.

The next two steps could be quite difficult if we hadn't already got the data in a table-like format - I knew that that StringGrid would come in useful! All we have to do is select a series and read the data from the StringGrid directly into the channel, changing the series each time we move across a column. We even copy the layout of the code used to populate the StringGrid, i.e. two nested **For** loops, to control the series choice and the passing of the data.

Finally, we close down the channel using a simply call to **CloseData** and we're finished. Setting up an array of numbers and then charting them couldn't be easier. Well....

Strings and Text

Now after that long haul, we arrive at strings. Declared by the **string** reserved word, they are made up of a series of characters strung together, usually taken from the extended ASCII set. You've been using them since Chapter 1, so they're no big deal. The next few sections just look a little more at the ways Delphi handles them, at the different types of strings and eventually introduce string lists (arrays of strings).

As regards string-handling, you're in luck, because Borland have made significant changes in Delphi 2.0 compared to Delphi 1.0. These were made possible chiefly by the improved memory management provided by Windows 95 and NT. Declare a string and (depending on your system resources) you have up to 2GB-worth of characters (each taking a byte) at your disposal, which should be enough even for the most loquacious.

FYI all the dirty work of finding room for the string in memory is done automatically. All the program does is remember the address of the string and runs to look it up as required. The fact you've been using strings without fuss for four chapters is a testament to how easy they are to use.

Historically, this is a slightly convoluted subject, muddled by Borland's attempt to keep compatibility with previous versions of Turbo Pascal and Delphi, and to cater for the C-style strings required by Windows.

As a demonstration of string handling, let's round off an old example:

Try It Out - Dealing with String Properties

1 Load up last chapter's **case** statement example, **stage7.dpr**. This is the final modification to the epic program you wrote in Chapter 2.

2 Under the **implementation** section, add in the following variable declaration:

```
var
  sLastWord : string;
```

3 In the edit box's **KeyPress** event handler, where we added the **case** statement in the last chapter, change the text to the following:

```
procedure TCompactForm.txtMainEntryKeyPress(Sender: TObject;
  var Key: Char);
begin
    case Ord(Key) of
      32 : begin
              pnlStatus.Caption := 'Last word typed was :  ' + sLastWord
                              + ' and it was ' + IntToStr(Length(sLastWord))
                              + ' characters long.';
              sLastWord := '';
            end;
       8 : pnlStatus.Caption := 'Character deleted';
    else
            begin
              sLastWord := sLastWord + Key;
              pnlStatus.Caption := 'Key just pressed :  ' + Key;
            end;
    end;
end;
```

How It Works

To restate the obvious, and give it a fancy name, you see the **pnlStatus.Caption** which is set equal to a whole load of stuff, including several strings and a couple of plus signs - that's **string concatenation**. To make a larger string by combining two strings - just 'add' them up.

The **sLastWord** string is declared beneath the **implementation** section so that it's in scope for the whole unit. Its current value remains intact when we leave the **txtMainEntry.KeyPress** procedure. Every character that we type is added to the **sLastWord** string. If the key press is space, though, the panel's caption displays the contents of **sLastWord**, which hopefully is some sort of word, and then resets the string to the empty string represented by two single quotes.

At the same time, it also displays the number of characters in that string, calculated using the standard function **Length**. As usual, the integer returned by **Length** must be converted to a string format using yet another standard function, **IntToStr**. The only problem with the program is that **Length** gets confused when you press *Enter* while entering text.

As we have seen before, you need to take special care to surround any explicit bits of text that you write into your code with single quotes; the single quotes tell Delphi that this is indeed a string and not another variable name, procedure name or a simple spelling mistake. It's quite common practice to prefix string variable names with a small **s**, just another of those naming conventions that we will review in Appendix A.

Short Strings

There's a second sort of string (from Pascal proper) known in Delphi 2.0 as the **ShortString**. Such strings are treated as **arrays** of characters, with the first (zeroth) element of the array giving the length of the string. These arrays have a maximum of 256 elements, and can therefore hold 255 characters, taking that length byte into account. Now Shakespeare's best, at its shortest, couldn't fit into this. Why bother with such a limiting form? Well, these strings have a very distinguished lineage that goes right back to 8-bit computing.

Now we're going to take a quick look at short strings, and their similarity to arrays. They're the default in Delphi 1.0, and, if you're going to program for 16-bit Windows, you'll need to know something about them. In Delphi 2.0, you can declare a short string, either by using a string variable with a predefined length, less than 255 characters, or by setting the **$H** compiler switch to **{$H-}**:

```
var
   sShortSentence : string[255];
```

An important thing to remember about short strings is that they are, in essence, identical to arrays of characters. The above declaration of a 255 character string, is effectively the same as:

```
var
   sShortSentence : array[0..255] of char;
```

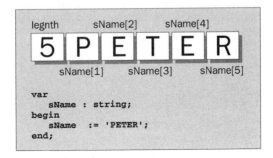

```
var
   sName : string;
begin
   sName := 'PETER';
end;
```

As you can see from the diagram, you can access each character in the string in the same way that you might access the elements of an array. For example,

```
MessageDlg( sShortSentence[4], mtInformation, [mbOK],0);
```

would print out the fourth character of the string in a message box at run time.

When you're dealing with strings in this way, though, be careful. If you declare a string to be only, say, 10 characters in length and then try to write to the 11th character, strange things can happen. Unless you tell Delphi that you want it to catch these kinds of errors, it won't, the result being that you'll start to write information in memory which may already be in use by other things. Doing this, you might crash your own program, but you're far more likely to crash another program, maybe even Windows itself.

Catching the Problems

You can tell Delphi to keep an eye out for this kind of problem by using the Project | Options dialog:

If you check out the Compiler page, you're looking for the Range checking option. By selecting this option, you're asking Delphi to keep an eye on anything you do with strings and arrays and to tell you at run time if you do something nasty.

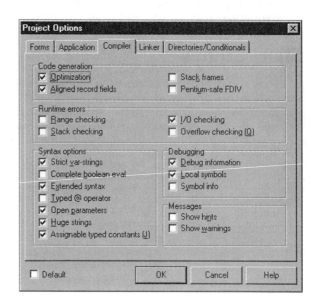

The downside of this safety net, though, is that your application will run a little slower than normal. It's a good idea to use all the help the compiler gives during the development of your application, and once the compiler is entirely happy, switch options like range-checking off, prior to a final compilation.

Indefinite Loops

No, I don't mean that I'm not sure whether they'll loop - only that they'll run without end, until, or while, some specific condition is met. Someday, you'll need them. In both cases, the **For** loop we saw in the last section isn't quite the ticket, because the number of times it loops is preset in the program

On the flip side of the coin, the **Repeat** and **While** loops are free and wild, looping until you say stop. As we're getting near the end of the chapter, let's go out with a bang, by constructing a truly useful application in three sections.

The While Loop

The **While** loop works 'while' the condition is met. We're going to use it to read data from the file and write it into the memo box (a multiline edit box) while there's still data left to be read.

The syntax is simply,

while *<Condition is True>* **do**

where **<Condition>** is some Boolean comparison, the truth of which allows the loop to continue, as in:

```
While it's raining do take an umbrella with you;
```

Try It Out - While We're on the Subject...

1 Start a new Delphi application and save it as **showfile.dpr** and the form unit as **whileu.pas**.

2 Drop two buttons - one standard, the other a BitBtn onto the form - and from the Component Palette's Standard page, select the Memo component. Size and caption them as shown in the following diagram:

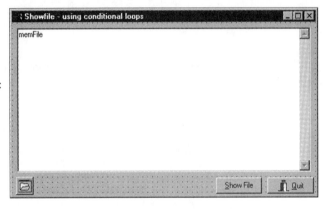

Change the BitBtn's Kind property to bkClose. Finally, add an OpenDialog component, change its Name to cmdShow, the form to frmShowFile and the Memo to memFile.

3 Bring up the cmdShow button's **Click** event handler and start the way you mean to go on by declaring a few variables: the first variable is a string called **sTheData**, the second is a **TextFile** variable called **TheFile**. This gives you the event handler:

```
procedure TfrmShowFile.cmdShowClick(Sender: TObject);
var
    TheFile:  TextFile;
    {Variable to let us deal with a text file}
    sTheData:  string;
    {Variable to hold the information we pull in}
begin

end;
```

4 Moving to within the code block, we open an **if...then...else** block with the condition straight from Chapter 1, **OpenDialog1.Execute**. In the **else** statement, type in, as a reprimand:

```
If OpenDialog.Execute then
    begin
        {We're coming to this part of the code next}
    end
```

```
        else
            MessageDlg('No file was selected', mtInformation, [mbOK], 0);
```

Note that you can add a **begin...end** block to both active parts of the **If** statement, i.e. the **then** and **else** statements, but we've only added one to the **then** statement as I know we're only going to add one statement after **else**.

5 Now for the missing **begin...end** block. Add the following code to our event handler to handle the file manipulations:

```
    If OpenDialog.Execute then
    begin
        AssignFile(TheFile, OpenDialog.Filename);
        Reset(TheFile);


        CloseFile(TheFile);
    end
```

6 After this struggle, we get to the **while** loop which gives the unit its name:

```
    Reset(TheFile);

    While not EOF(TheFile) do
    begin
        readln(TheFile, sTheData);
        memFile.Lines.Add(sTheData);
    end;

    CloseFile(TheFile);
```

7 Finally, in the Form's **Create** event, we add the line:

```
procedure TfrmShowFile.FormCreate(Sender: TObject);
begin
    memFile.Clear;
end;
```

I know - it looks like a bit of a nightmare. As always, though, it's not as nasty as it first appears. Also, if you take a look at the code on the disk, you'll see that it has more commented text to help you follow what's going on.

The program is pretty simple on the surface. You click on the Show File button and up pops a File Open dialog. As soon as you select a text file, its contents are displayed in the Memo box that takes up the majority of the form.

Most of the program code is taken up with dealing with the selected text file, so that's our first port of call in our explanation. Though we're ostensibly covering **While** loops, it won't hurt to use realistic code while we're here.

How It Works - Working with Files

Of our two variables, **TheFile** is set up to handle **TextFile** type data. Whenever you deal with files in Delphi code, you need to store information about those files as variables. Declaring a variable as a **TextFile** lets Delphi know that, when we open the file, we want to treat it as a text file.

Assuming that the user actually selects a file, the file handling code starts:

```
AssignFile(TheFile, OpenDialog.Filename);
Reset(TheFile);

While not EOF(TheFile) do
begin
    readln(TheFile, sTheData);
    memFile.Lines.Add(sTheData);
end;

CloseFile(TheFile);
```

AssignFile tells Delphi that we want to start dealing with a file on the disk. It takes two parameters: the first being the **TheFile** variable we set up, the second being the name of the file that the user selected in the **OpenFile** dialog. The **TheFile** variable is necessary since you could use any number of files simultaneously within a Delphi program. Each file variable you declare is then given a unique **number** by **AssignFile** so that Delphi can keep track of which one is being used.

The next step is to **reset** the file, a step which makes Delphi move to the start of the file ready to begin reading the information. All you need to do is throw the newly assigned integer value of **TheFile** at the **Reset** method.

```
Reset(TheFile);
```

Then, preliminaries over, the **While** loop kicks in. The **While** loop needs to run, reading data from the file for as long as there' still data to be read.

The **EOF** (**End Of File**) method that Delphi provides for use with files will return True if the end of the file has been reached, and False otherwise. So, the line,

```
while not EOF(TheFile) do
```

tells Delphi that we want the loop to run until we get to the end of the file. As before, you need to use the **TheFile** value in **EOF** in order that it works on the correct file.

> The While loop is very much like the For loop in terms of its structure. It expects either a single line of code to run over and over, after the word **do**, or a block of code, signified by the **begin** and **end;** pair that we've seen so often before.

Within the loop, the code is really simple:

```
readln(TheFile, sTheData);
memFile.Lines.Add(sTheData);
```

The **readln** procedure reads a line of data from the specified file and dumps it into the variable you pass it as the second parameter, the first appearance of the string we defined earlier.

We then use the **Add** method to append the data to the bottom of the list displayed by the Memo box. Again, don't worry too much about what means what here. We cover the Memo component and their Lines property in more details later on.

All that remains is to tell Delphi that we're done with the file:

```
CloseFile(TheFile);
```

As for the lonely line of code in the **Create** event handler, it calls the **Clear** method of the Memo box to clear the memo of all its data - at start-up this is usually just the Memo's name, but you never know!

And there you have it - a complete working example of a **While** loop in action, and also a complete application for you to take a look round and get familiar with. Given the ground we've covered in the last few chapters, as you load it off the disk, there's nothing in the application that should be too confusing.

The Repeat Loop

Time to use a **Repeat** loop to see how that works. **Repeat** works in the opposite way to a **While** loop, but performs basically the same purpose. Instead of testing a condition before running a block of code, **Repeat** runs the block of code first, then tests a condition to see if it needs to carry on.

It has the syntax:

repeat

until <Condition is True>;

We'll cover the differences later. For now, we're going to change the **showfile.dpr** application to use a **Repeat** instead of a **While** loop, which allows us to show off the Delphi Project Manager.

Try It Out - Modifying the Project

1 Start by closing the previous project, **showfile.dpr**. Then open the **whileu.pas** file, by pressing the Open file speed button. Change the name of the form to **frmShowFile2**, and then save the unit as **repeatu.pas**.

2 Reopen the **showfile.dpr** application and select View | Project Manager from the menu. Next press the Add unit button (the folder with a green plus) and select **Repeatu.pas**.

3 Next remove the **whileu.pas** unit file from the application by selecting it and pressing the Remove unit button (the folder with a red minus sign). The **showfile.dpr** is now ready for the **Repeat** loop alternative.

4 Find the **While** loop within the **cmdShowClick** event handler. Replace the **While** statement with the lines below:

```
Repeat
begin
    readln(TheFile, TheData);
    memFile.Lines.Add(TheData);
end;
Until EOF(TheFile);
```

5 The code will now run. But there's no need for the **begin...end;** block within the **Repeat...until** loop. The loop performs all the code between the **Repeat** and the **until** keywords, as, in essence, it's waiting for the **until** statement. If you're feeling mischievous, try taking these statements out.

How It Works - Subtle Differences

Firstly, the **Repeat** command is not officially finished until the end of the **until** statement, so we must wait until after that statement to add the semicolon. Also, notice how the code logic has changed. We want the code to run **until** the end of the file is read, not **while** the end of the file has not been reached. For this reason,

```
While not EOF(TheFile)
```

becomes:

```
Until EOF(TheFile)
```

Logic problems like this can be a real pain if you don't keep your wits about you. Be sure of what you want to do, then decide which kind of loop you want to use.

 An important point to note here is that the code in a **While** loop may not necessarily run. Because the check is done before the loop code, if the condition fails first time through the **While** line, then the code may not run. With a **Repeat** loop, though, the code in the loop will always run at least once.

And so to all that nonsense with the Project Manager. This tool allows you to control the content of your Delphi project, while maintaining the integrity of the code - note how the project source file is changed to reflect the new unit. This is yet another way in which Delphi makes your life impossibly easy. Using the Project Manager to swap the units, you automatically tie the new unit into your application and, since the component references are correct, the new project is ready for compilation.

String Lists - Arrays of Strings

Quite often, you will need to deal with an array of strings, for example the individual lines in a text file. However, considering what we know already about text files, loading them into an array has an obvious problem. Until you actually start to load the data in, you have no idea how many elements in the array you will need. The solution is something known to Delphi as a **string list**.

String lists crop up all over the place in Delphi. The ListBox, StringGrid, ComboBox and Memo components all store their data in string lists. And they can all exchange this information because the string list is a generic object - the same format is used by them all. Borland have just made your life so much easier. After a build-up like that, this is probably a good time to take a look at some of these components!

Try It Out - Perfecting the Example

1 Load up **showfile.dpr**. Save the various parts of this project as **memo_eg.dpr** and **memou.pas** for the project and unit files respectively. This allows us to mess around with this new project without altering **showfile.dpr** - remember that Delphi automatically saves a projects source code when you ask it to compile.

2 Drop on three new buttons. Change their captions to match the above diagram and change their names to **cmdAdd**, **cmdEdit** and **cmdDelete**.

3 Double-click the **cmdAdd** button and add the following code:

```
procedure TfrmShowFile.cmdAddClick(Sender: TObject);
var
    sLine  : string;
    nLine  : integer;
begin
    sLine := InputBox('Add line', 'Enter the data to add', '');

    if sLine <> '' then
    begin
      nLine := memFile.Lines.Add( sLine );
      MessageDlg('The line you added was numbered ' + IntToStr(nLine),
                 mtInformation, [mbOK], 0);
    end;
end;
```

4 Now get the copy and paste going to get the code behind the cmdEdit and cmdDelete buttons sorted:

```
procedure TfrmShowFile.cmdEditClick(Sender: TObject);
var
    sLine : string;
    nLine : integer;
begin
    sLine := InputBox('Select line', 'Edit which line ?', '');
    if sLine <> '' then
    begin
```

```
        nLine := StrToInt(sLine);
        sLine := InputBox('Edit line', 'Edit the data and click OK',
            memFile.Lines[nLine] );
        memFile.Lines[nLine] := sLine;
    end;
end;

procedure TfrmShowFile.cmdDeleteClick(Sender: TObject);
var
   sLine : string;
begin
    sLine := InputBox( 'Delete Line',
        'Which line number to delete?', '');
    if sLine <> '' then
        memFile.Lines.Delete( StrToInt(sLine) );
end;
```

5 Now we're ready, so run the project and see how it works:

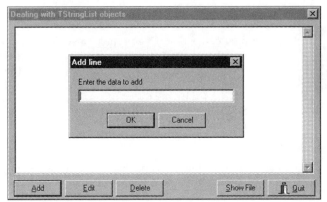

Using the Application

As soon as you click on the Add button, an InputBox appears (so called because it provides an area for you to input information). If you type something into this dialog box and then click on the OK button, the data appears in the memo component on the form and a message box appears telling you the line number of the data that you just added.

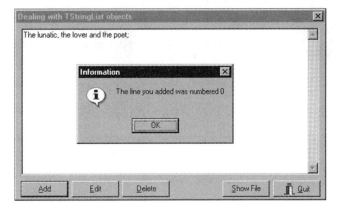

Click on the OK button to get rid of this message box, then hit the Edit button. Another InputBox appears, this time asking you which line you want to edit. The last message that appeared told you that you entered line number 0, so type in 0 and press OK.

The InputBox should come back, this time with the line of data that you previously entered on display. Make some changes if you like and click on the OK button to put those changes back into the memo box.

Now click on the Delete button. Again an InputBox asks you for a line number, this time the number of the line that you want to delete.

Enter 0 (the number of the line that we've been playing around with so far) and click on the OK button - the line you entered previously will now vanish from the memo box.

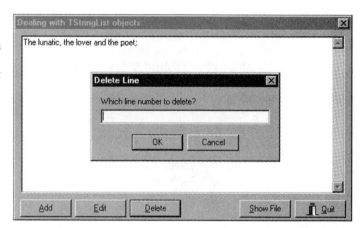

FYI

You may notice that if you type in a string value when the **InputBox** is asking for a line number, the `StrToInt` function can't work - it returns an `EConvertError`, and stops your program. You can handle these problems internally within your application, a task that we cover in Chapter 11. In essense, the programmer must try to predict the loopholes that the user will inadvertently find and cope with them in the code.

How It Works

The code behind all this functionality is really quite simple to understand and makes use of the fact that the Memo component has a **Lines** property which is a TStringList object. TStringLists aren't simple arrays of strings. Like any other object in Delphi, they have their own properties and methods which you can use in code to add functionality to your application and remove some of the programming burden.

FYI

We'll talk more about objects and objects within objects in the next chapter.

The first line in the code block uses a new statement that you won't have seen before; InputBox. This has nothing to do with TStringLists, but, just as with any problem, you need to set it up before you can solve it. It's just a general dialog box that you can use in your code to obtain a string of information from the user. As you can see, it takes three parameters, the first being the title to display in the dialog, the second being a piece of text to display above the InputBox's edit area and the third being the value to feed into the edit area as default:

```
sLine := InputBox('Add line', 'Enter the data to add', '');
```

With this example code we want an InputBox to appear on the screen with Add Line as the title of the dialog, and Enter the data to add to appear above the data entry area. The third parameter in this case tells Delphi that the entry area should be entered when the dialog appears:

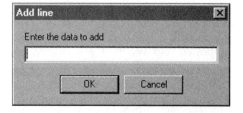

The **InputBox** function always returns a string, so in our example we pass the result into a string variable **sLine** which we declared earlier for this exact purpose. If the user clicks on the Cancel button in the InputBox dialog, the result is an empty string (**''**).

The **If** condition on the next line checks for this empty string. In Delphi, 'not equal' is represented by **<>**:

```
if sLine <> '' then
```

Providing that the user did actually enter some data, the code block runs, and it's here that we can start to deal with the **Lines** object of the Memo component:

```
nLine := memFile.Lines.Add( sLine );
MessageDlg('The line you added was numbered ' + IntToStr(nLine),
        mtInformation, [mbOK], 0);
```

All TStringList objects have a number of methods attached to them which you can call to simplify string manipulations - **Add** is one of them. Look at this fragment of code for a second:

```
var
    MyStrings : TStringList;
begin
    MyStrings.Add('Hi There');
end;
```

This declares a variable to be a TStringList and then uses its **Add** method to add a value into the list. The variable itself handles all the details of where to store the string, and so on. All we need to do is to tell it to **Add** the given string to the list.

That's exactly what the code does in the example program:

```
nLine := memFile.Lines.Add(sLine);
```

It calls the **Add** method of the **Lines** object attached to the Memo component on the form, and passes it the string that the user previously entered, to add to the list. As you can see from the code, the **Add** method returns a value, an integer in fact. **nLine** is set to the line number where the string was added to the list.

The example program uses this value to display a message box telling the user where the string was added. It's important to note that the strings in a TStringList object are numbered from 0, that is, the first element of the TStringList is number **0**. In Delphi, unless we explicitly state otherwise, all arrays are zero-based.

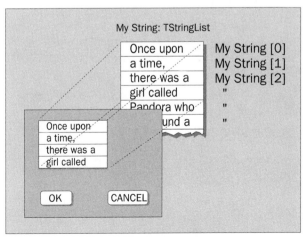

141

Having added values into a TStringList object, though, you're probably going to need to get at those values some time. That's just what the code behind the Edit button demonstrates. The easiest way to do this is with an InputBox again.

But remember what I said earlier: InputBoxes return string values. So how can we use an InputBox to ask the user the number of the string that they want to edit? Imagine, for example, that the user entered 10 as the line number. Instead of the routine kicking out 10 it actually kicks out '10' - a string containing the digits 1 and 0. Just as we can convert a number into a string (using the **IntToStr** function), we can also convert a string into a number, using **StrToInt**.

After we've checked that the user has actually entered some data, that's exactly what happens:

```
if sLine <> '' then
begin
   nLine := StrToInt(sLine);
```

Summary

That wraps up our survey of Delphi Pascal code. We built upon the Pascal (and the examples!) we saw in the last chapter, adding more insight into its murky depths, while introducing the following ideas and concepts:

- Loops, both indexed and indefinite
- Constants and what you use them for
- General arrays and the more specific string list
- How to use an OCX and how to chart some numerical data

However, before you settle down to the rest of the chapters, thinking that all the hard work is over and there's just the playgrounds of graphics, multimedia and the like to skip through, there's one more essential stop on your itinerary - that which deals with Delphi's object-oriented principles. They underpin everything in Delphi, and you can't afford to miss it, so settle down for the next chapter and get ready to look at ideas such as encapsulation, inheritance and good old polymorphism.

Object-oriented Pascal

Traditionally, a programmer approaching a new problem starts to think in terms of data and code. What kind of data do we need in this application to emulate the real-world data? What code will we need in the application to maintain this data? What kind of user interface will we need to handle data access? The original problem has to be reformulated in terms of a number of new problems that the computer program can solve...

In contrast, **object-oriented** techniques free programmers to think about their program solution in the same terms as the real-world objects. This is a huge claim, one which I'll try to justify in this chapter. You have a problem: you break it up into a number of attributes (or properties) and then add in any operations (or methods) that need to be performed on these attributes, to deal with the data. This is best illustrated by example.

A sales entry system would be so much easier to write if you had a product object which could maintain itself. It might have such properties as product name, code, description, and, most important, price. When someone places an order, you could tell the product to dispatch itself. You could pass across the delivery address and let the object worry about the intricacies of producing the invoice, printing the dispatch note, decreasing the amount of itself in stock, and so on. All this could be as simple as calling the product object's order method, in much the same way that you might call the show method of a form object.

"Seems obvious!", you cry, which surely marks it out as a great idea!

Such ideas are very much in vogue and there are quite a number of object-oriented development environments on the market. But Delphi provides one of the most comprehensive, easy-to-use versions available to developers today - yes, it's that good!

In this chapter, you're going to learn everything there is to know about creating and dealing with objects in your own code. You will learn:

- All about the record, a structured data type
- How a class improves on a record - encapsulation
- What inheritance is all about
- How to create and destroy an object
- About weird terms like *polymorphism*
- What scope means to a class

By the end of this chapter, OOP will hold no fears for you, and your ideas about development will be much improved for it. "Mmmm! A jedi of programmers someday you will be!" And it won't take 900 years....

Concepts

At first glance, the world of OOP can be a daunting place, filled with strange terms and ideas that are difficult to relate to. Rather than diving into code, this section, which may turn it into something of a vocabulary lesson, is going to introduce you to some of those concepts. Some of them you will have already come across in the previous chapters, but they are probably still as clear as mud.

Last of the Structured Data Types

First, let's take a look at **records**. They're another structured data type, rather like the arrays, files and sets that we met in the last couple of chapters.

To cut a long story short, a record enables you to store a number of different data types in a group and assign them a generic name (a collective noun). They are like cousins to arrays, except you can combine different types to give you a personalized record. Once you have given it a name, the record itself becomes a data type, much like **integer** or **string**. Once you've defined a record type, you can then create record variables from it.

Now for the surprise: you can think of all these variables as objects. Well, okay not true objects. Let's just say objects that aren't quite fully fledged. The following example defines a new record type called **TEmployee**:

```
type
   TEmployee = record
       Surname  : string;
       Initials : string;
       Age      : integer;
   end;
```

Once we've defined the **TEmployee** type, we use it to create variables of the type, using exactly the same syntax as any other data type, custom or not. Then we can assign data to the individual data elements of the record in much the same way that you might assign something to a property of a form:

```
Procedure  TForm1.Button1Click(Sender:  TObject);
var
   Employee : TEmployee;
begin
    Employee.Surname  := 'Wright';
    Employee.Initials := 'P';
    Employee.Age := 99;
end;
```

Real Objects

Records, and the other variables we discussed in the last two chapters, are not true objects in the sense of object-oriented programming. However, dealing with them is really very similar. Declaring a record allows you to define a new data type which can hold nothing but data.

The true object, though, has both its own data (like the record) and code to deal with that data. Just as with records, sets and enumerated types, you must first make a **type** declaration before you can create the object. For true objects, that type is called a **class**.

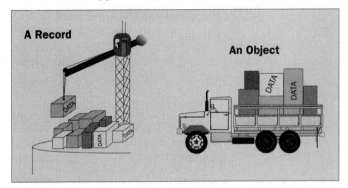

Think of class and record definitions as cookie cutters. The cutter defines the shape and appearance of an object, but until you actually apply the cutter to some dough, you don't have a cookie. Take a look at this:

```
Type
  TOldEmployee = class
      Surname  : string;
      Initials : string;
      Age      : integer;
      procedure Print_Payslip;
      procedure Sack_Employee( sReason : string );
  end;
```

This is how you might define a very simple class. Notice how, as well as data elements inside the class, I actually have what look like procedures in here as well. I don't write any code to support them, I just tell the class that any objects created from this declaration will have two procedures attached to them, in this case **Print_Payslip** and **Sack_Employee**. They just tell Delphi of the existence of some procedures but don't actually define them - that will be done elsewhere:

```
implementation
```

```
procedure TEmployee.Print_Payslip;
begin

end;
```

Does it look familiar - it should do! This is how the event handlers attached to forms are written. The event handlers are really nothing more than procedures incorporated within the form object, as we saw in Chapter 3.

So, to summarize:

> A **record** is a type that allows you to define the format of an object that will just hold data.

> A **class** is a type that allows you to define the format of an object that will hold both data and code.

Some more terms for you:

> Member properties are data belonging to a type, be it a class or record.

> Member methods are procedures and functions belonging to a class.

As you'll already have guessed, all the components and forms that you have dealt with so far in this book have been objects. The properties and methods you've been dealing with are almost the same as the concepts we're using in the declaration of our classes, bar a few differences which have to do with the Object Inspector.

What Makes a Class Good?

Using classes makes it easy for you to reuse your code, one of the many benefits this type has over its user-defined cousins. Having defined a decent class, you should then be able to reuse that class in other projects with very little effort. In multideveloper projects, classes let you give a whole set of prewritten functionality to the other developers. Delphi itself is built on these principles - the components and forms all testify to the advantages of this way of programming.

FYI
If at any time throughout this chapter you have the screaming heebie-jeebies about all this abstract techno-babble, you should think about the ideas we're trying to get across in terms of the Delphi components you're using. If you have the VCL source code, you should feel privileged to be able to see almost all the principles of OOP in action. And the poster of the VCL hierarchy that comes with Delphi 2.0 gives you the flavor of what OOP can achieve.

Encapsulation

Now for another of the copy-writer's buzzwords - OOP allows **encapsulation**. Using the methods and properties of the class, or rather the objects created from such type declarations, other developers can then deal with your code as a black box. They know what the object should do, how to make it do that and who to blame if it doesn't work. What goes on inside the class is none of their business, nor should it concern them unduly.

In geek-speak, this translates to 'the object hides the implementation of its data handling from the user'. The user, in this case, is any other developer making use of the object and, for this, they should only need the class declaration to see the properties and the methods (procedures and functions) and the required parameters that are on offer.

Inheritance

So, when you've done your homework and defined your problem in terms of a few basic classes, OOP allows you to extend these base classes to more specific (usually more complicated) cases as the problem solution develops, perhaps even generating the answers to as yet totally unforeseen problems. This is known as **inheritance** and enables developers to incorporate the basic structure of one class into their own.

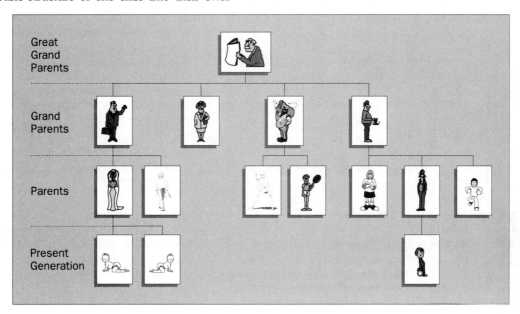

Polymorphism

By inheriting that cunningly contrived base class you just created, when you make a new, more specific class, you save yourself the bother of re-implementing all of those common properties and methods. Yet another feature, **polymorphism**, lets you override some of the code in these base classes with your own.

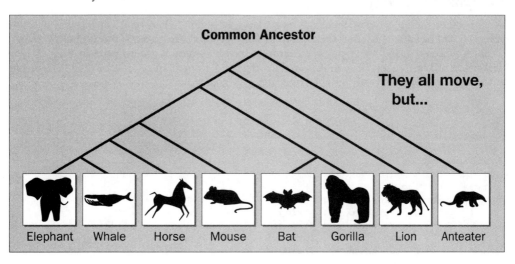

All in all, objects and classes are very powerful things. However, before I get completely bogged down, let's move on to consider some practical record examples and see how classes can sometimes make our lives a little easier.

Records

Let's now fill in the details of records with a couple of practical examples.

```
type
   <Record Name> = record
      ...
      {Declare the member data types here}
      ...
   end;
```

The first step in setting up a new record type is to specify the new name for the type, followed by **= record**. No, this isn't a typo. Although in code you use the **:=** sign to assign something, when you set up classes and records, you use the **=** sign to tell Delphi what kind of type you are declaring.

Note that this syntax holds true for all type declarations, not just classes and records. It's one of those things that usually trips up the unsuspecting programmer for the first fifty times they declare a new type. After a while, though, the compiler's nagging will take over and it starts to sink in. Save yourself some heartache and notice that type declarations are semicolon-less.

Notice also that the record declaration finishes with an **end;**. You don't have to **end;** the type section itself - that happens as soon as Delphi finds the start of a new section. You do, though, have to **end;** the record declaration, otherwise Delphi can get confused as to where it actually stops.

A New Type's Visibility

As with other variable types, there are two places in a unit where you can declare a record type: the **interface** and the **implementation** sections. This affects the visibility of any variables declared using the type. For example, if you declare a record type in the **implementation** section of a unit, variables declared from it may only be declared in the same unit - they are like the local variables we met in Chapter 3:

```
unit Unit2;

interface

implementation

type
   TEmployee = record
               sSurname    : String;
               sForename   : String;
               sAge        : integer;
               sDepartment : String;
   end;

end.
```

The alternative is to declare the record type in the **interface** section of the unit:

```
unit Unit2;

interface

type
    TEmployee = record
                sSurname    : String;
                sForename   : String;
                sAge        : integer;
                sDepartment : String;
        end;

implementation


end.
```

In this case, I've made a **global type declaration**. Variables can be declared using the **TEmployee** type in any other unit in the project that makes use of this unit.

You may remember from earlier on in the chapter that we can access the member fields of a record in the same way that we might access the properties of a component or any other object in Delphi.

Try It Out - Criminal Records

1 Start up a new application. Bring up the code window and beneath the **implementation** section type in the following:

```
implementation

{$R *.DFM}
```

```
type
    TEmployee = record
                sSurname   : String;
                sForename  : String;
                sDepartment: String;
        end;

var
    Employee : TEmployee;
```

2 Now add a button, a bitmap button, a group box, three labels, three edit boxes and a string list to the form, to get something like this:

3 To the <u>S</u>et Record button's OnClick event handler, add the following code:

```
procedure TfrmRecords.cmdSetClick(Sender: TObject);
begin
    Employee.sSurname    := txtSurname.text;
    Employee.sForename   := txtForename.text;
    Employee.sDepartment := txtDepartment.text;
end;
```

4 To the <u>V</u>iew Record button's OnClick event handler:

```
procedure TfrmRecords.cmdViewClick(Sender: TObject);
begin
    memRecord.Lines.Clear;
    memRecord.Lines.Add('Surname : ' + Employee.sSurname);
    memRecord.Lines.Add('Forename : ' + Employee.sForename);
    memRecord.Lines.Add('Department : ' + Employee.sDepartment);
end;
```

5 Now run the application and see what you can see.

How It Works

When you run the program, you enter an employee's details into the three edit boxes on the form and then click on the <u>S</u>et Record button. This runs code which updates the members of a record to the present contents of the text boxes. Clicking on the <u>V</u>iew Record button prints the contents of each member of the record to the memo **memRecord**:

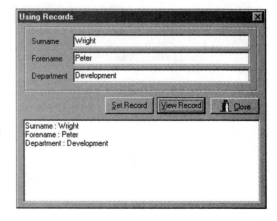

The record type is declared in the **implementation** section of the unit making it a local type declaration to this unit. A variable of the type **TEmployee** is also declared here, making it available to all the code in this unit. This is the variable that we use throughout the program.

The code that handles the Set Record button's OnClick event puts data into the members of a record in just the same way as we would set a property of an object equal to some data, such as a form or a component.

You can retrieve data from a record just as easily. In this example, we use a **TStringList** type object - the **Lines** property of a memo - to display that data once we have cleared it of any previous information it contained. Each line we add to the memo is a concatenation of a string literal and the contents of a member of the record.

Nesting Records

The simplicity of a record belies its power. For example, by nesting records you can soon build up some very powerful structures, essentially inheriting one record within another. In fact, this is the basis of inheritance, which we'll cover when we look at classes and objects in a short while.

As an example, suppose I needed to deal with job types and link an employee to such a type? We could add the following type declaration beneath the one we added in the last example:

```
type
    TEmployee = record
                sSurname    : String;
                sForename   : String;
                sDepartment : String;
    end;

    TJob = record
                Employee : TEmployee;
                sTitle   : string;
                nSalary  : real;
    end;
```

In this code, we have declared two record types, one to hold employee details and another to hold job information to which an employee is linked. In code, you can access the **Employee** member of **TJob** type records just like a normal member. For example:

```
var
    Director : Tjob;
begin
    Director.Employee.sSurname    := 'Bloggs';
    Director.Employee.sForename   := 'Joe';
    Director.Employee.sDepartment := 'Development';
    Director.sTitle  := 'Director';
    Director.nSalary := 10000.00;
end;
```

Note that, because the first member of **Job** is itself a record, we also have to reference the individual data members of that record. That's why you now have to insert two identifiers separated by full stops:

```
<Job Record>.<Employee Record>.<Employee Data>
```

Pretty neat, wouldn't you say? In fact, like a jigsaw, the whole concept fits together with classes and objects, so let's take a look at them now.

Classes

Classes are the life blood of object-oriented programming, enabling you to create object templates which later help you to add a great deal of functionality to your application with very little effort. Despite the recent hype, object-oriented programming is really nothing new. It was first introduced in the 70s in a little known language, Simula, and then in Xerox Parc's SmallTalk.

However, it wasn't until Bjarne Stroustrup came along with his object extensions to C (so giving birth to C++) that it really became popular. It's worth noting, though, that around the time that C++ really started to catch on (1986 or so), that the US Air Force stated that they wouldn't consider weapons or flight control systems written in an object-oriented language like C++. Their reason was that if one base class contained a bug, it could cause a cascade effect throughout the entire system. A little inconvenient to say the least!

Fortunately, such attitudes have now changed following the increased manageability that an object-oriented language such as C++ or Delphi brings to large scale application development. This manageability far outweighs the possibility of a cascading bug, especially when you consider that you can fix one bug and improve the functionality of a whole system by ten-fold!

Before we go any further, it's worth clearing up a big area of confusion. Many programmers use the terms *class* and *object* interchangeably. This problem is quite common among Delphi programmers who have moved across from previous versions of Borland's Object Pascal, because there they used the keyword **Object** to define a class. In this book, though, **class** refers to an object type declaration, while **object** refers to a specific instance of that class type, one of those cookies, not the cookie cutter.

FYI When you create an object based upon an class declaration, you could say that that object is an *instance* of that class. Remember a class is really nothing more than a user-defined type. In the same way that **integer** and **string** are useless unless they declare a variable, classes are useless unless you use them to declare objects.

Designing a class, though, is a little different to designing your average record. Classes should mimic the real-world objects that you are trying to code into the system.

Think about that **TEmployee** record again. What would an **Employee** object need to do in a payroll system? Printing its own pay-slip would be a good start (if only that were the case in the real world), as would the ability to print its pay details for the current financial year. Take a look at this:

```
type
    TEmployee = class
        { Member variables / properties }
        sSurname    : string;
```

```
        sForename    : string;
        sDepartment  : string;
        nSalary      : Real;

        { Member methods }
        procedure Print_Payslip;
        procedure Print_PaySummary;
    end;
```

Looks familiar, doesn't it! Other than the fact that the type is declared as a class and includes references to two procedures, the code is really no different to how I declared our record type earlier. The procedure references tell Delphi that objects derived from this class will have two member procedures attached to them - methods, in other words.

 Just as in Chapter 3 where I covered declaring and implementing a form, a class also follows this model, obeying the same rules of scope. The form is nothing more than a glorified class definition.

You can actually define the procedures. The code that goes in them is like this:

```
procedure TEmployee.Print_Payslip;
begin

end;

procedure TEmployee.Print_Summary;
begin

end;
```

You declare the procedures as you would for any other procedure or function in your code, the difference here being that you need to prefix the name of the procedure with the name of the class that it belongs to. Why? Because you could have a number of routines all with the same name but each performing different things, depending on the class to which they are attached. You need to tell Delphi which method lives in which class. I'll look at this idea in more detail later when I consider a new class called TVehicle.

Asteroids - A Class Game

Time to put the theory into practice. Think about Asteroids - the game not the galactic objects. We could turn the asteroids themselves into objects, each of which would have its own *x* and *y* coordinates on the screen and methods to draw it and erase it.

Load up the **asteroid.dpr** project and take a look at the source code behind the main form. If you take a look at the **implementation** section, you'll see an appropriate class declaration. We are going to spend a little time working on this together to make it a whole lot better and introduce you to all the concepts behind classes and objects in the process:

```
implementation

{$R *.DFM}
```

```
type
    TAsteroid = class
        { Properties }
        X : integer;
        Y : integer;

        { Methods }
        procedure Draw (TheForm : TForm);
        procedure Erase (TheForm : TForm);
    end;
```

At first glance, it seems okay. The class includes properties to determine the asteroid's **X** and **Y** position on the form and includes methods to draw and erase the asteroid. The idea is that we should be able to draw and erase the asteroid while changing the **X** and **Y** coordinates to give the impression that it's moving.

 FYI Don't worry too much about the graphical concepts in the program; we take a look at graphics in detail in the next chapter. Remember that the idea here is to introduce you to the concepts behind object-oriented programming, not graphics

So, what can we do to make this class better? Well, if you take a look at both the **Draw** or **Erase** methods, you should see one thing immediately:

```
procedure TAsteroid.Draw( TheForm : TForm );
begin
    With TheForm.Canvas do
    begin
        Pen.Color := clBlue;

        MoveTo( -10 + X, 5 + Y );
        LineTo( -10 + X, 9 + Y );
        LineTo( -5 + X, 11 + Y);
        LineTo( X, Y + 14);
        LineTo( 10 + X, 13 + Y);
        LineTo( 16 + X, Y);
        LineTo( 10 + X, -2 + Y);
        LineTo( 7+ X, -10 + Y);
        LineTo( 1 + X, -9 + Y);
        LineTo( -5 + X, -5 + Y);
        LineTo( -10 + X, -2 + Y);
        LineTo( -10 + X, 5 + Y);
    end;

end;
```

With the exception of the line that sets the **Pen** color (the color that the asteroid will be drawn in) both routines are exactly the same. In addition, both routines contain a lot of code that doesn't really have to be there; the routines draw straight lines from one point to another until the shape of the asteroid has been defined.

156

Wouldn't it be so much nicer if the **Draw** and **Erase** methods called a **private** routine to draw the shape and passed it the color to draw in? Of course it would!

> By **private** I mean that we want the object to have a routine all to itself to handle the drawing - it shouldn't be a method that the user can call since we want to keep things simple.
>
> Hand in hand with this keyword goes **public**, which declares public members of a class, those that the programmer can use in their own code. The declarations we have been making so far have all been **public**, which is the default visibility for members of a class.

To do this, we need to add a new routine to the object and tell Delphi which parts are **public** (available to code using the object) and which are **private** (only available to code within the object itself).

Try It Out - Improving Your Class

1 Load up the **asteroid.dpr** project. Change the **TAsteroid** class declaration so that it looks like this:

```
implementation

{$R *.DFM}

type
    TAsteroid = class
    Public
        { Properties }
        X : integer;
        Y : integer;

        { Methods }
        procedure Draw (TheForm : TForm);
        procedure Erase (TheForm : TForm);
    Private
        procedure Plot_Shape ( TheForm : TForm; nColor : integer);
    end;
```

2 So, having told Delphi that we have a **private Plot_Shape** method, it's probably a good idea to write that method's code. We can do this quite easily - all we need to do is first declare the procedure:

```
procedure TAsteroid.Plot_Shape ( TheForm : TForm ; nColor : integer );
begin

end;
```

3 Then we need to copy the code from either the **Draw** or the **Erase** methods into this new **Plot_Shape** method:

```
procedure TAsteroid.Plot_Shape ( TheForm : TForm ; nColor : integer );
begin
      With TheForm.Canvas do
      begin
            Pen.Color := nColor;

            MoveTo( -10 + X, 5 + Y );
            LineTo( -10 + X, 9 + Y );
            LineTo( -5 + X, 11 + Y);
            LineTo( X, Y + 14);
            LineTo( 10 + X, 13 + Y);
            LineTo( 16 + X, Y);
            LineTo( 10 + X, -2 + Y);
            LineTo( 7+ X, -10 + Y);
            LineTo( 1 + X, -9 + Y);
            LineTo( -5 + X, -5 + Y);
            LineTo( -10 + X, -2 + Y);
            LineTo( -10 + X, 5 + Y);
      end;
end;
```

Don't forget to the change the **Pen.Color :=** line so that it copies the **nColor** parameter over, instead of the **clBlack** or **clBlue** constants that the **Draw** and **Erase** methods use.

4 Now we're ready to simplify the code in **Draw** and **Erase** themselves. Change the routines so that they look like this:

```
procedure TAsteroid.Draw( TheForm : TForm );
begin
      Plot_Shape(TheForm, clBlue);
end;

procedure TAsteroid.Erase( TheForm : TForm);
begin
      Plot_Shape(TheForm, clBlack);
end;
```

Now the class is beginning to look a little more efficient and really quite useful.

However, the program still does nothing. Remember, a class is nothing more than a template. To make use of its methods and properties in code, we need to apply this template to an object.

5 Use the Object Inspector to bring the form's OnClick event into view. When the user clicks on the form, we want to move an asteroid across it. The first thing we need to do is add an object to the routine using the **TAsteroid** class:

```
procedure TForm1.FormClick(Sender: TObject);
var
   Asteroid : TAsteroid ;
```

6 Add another variable that we'll use to keep track of where the asteroid should be:

```
procedure TForm1.FormClick(Sender: TObject);
var
    Asteroid : TAsteroid;
    nXCoord  : integer;
```

7 Finally, we can add some code to the event to make the asteroid move:

```
procedure TForm1.FormClick(Sender: TObject);
var
    Asteroid : TAsteroid;
    nXCoord  : integer;
begin
    Asteroid := TAsteroid.Create;

    Asteroid.Y := 100;
    ASteroid.X := 100;
    For nXCoord := 20 to Form1.ClientWidth do
    begin
        Asteroid.Erase (Form1);
        Asteroid.X := nXCoord;
        Asteroid.Draw (Form1);
    end;

    Asteroid.Free;
end;
```

At this point, you can at last run the program. If you have coded everything properly, you'll find that, as soon as you click on the form, an asteroid will whiz across it:

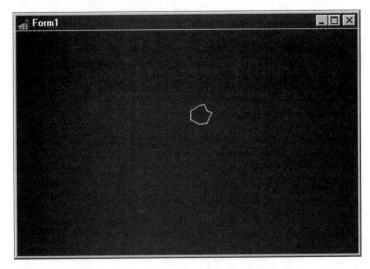

Just in case you figured that writing all that code would be too much for you, you can find the completed program on the disk in the **moverock.dpr** project!

How It Works

Once you have created an object from the class (more of this in the next section), getting at its properties and methods is just the same as dealing with a component, record or indeed any other kind of object that you are likely to come across in Delphi.

The first lines set up the asteroid's initial **X** and **Y** coordinates. Then a loop changes the **X** coordinate of the asteroid, effectively moving it across the screen by first erasing the previous image, then changing the horizontal position and drawing it again.

The asteroid class can draw and erase itself within your own application's code just by calling the following two methods:

```
Asteroid.Draw( <Form> );
Asteroid.Erase( <Form> );
```

That's the power of objects and classes. Once you've spent the time defining the class, your users can then use it over and over without ever having to know how it does what it does. All you need to remember are the methods and properties that you need to control objects created with the class. If we were really working on a new version of the Asteroids game, we could pass this asteroids object over to the project's AI developer to add a little life to it.

From the tutorial point of view, though, there are still one or two gray areas that need to be cleared up.

Creating an Object

You might be thinking, "What's this heading on about, we've just created an object...?" Well, not true - you've designed a class. Now we need to create an object from this declaration. Did you notice how the first line of actual code in the event handler calls a **Create** method of the asteroid? We never wrote a **Create** method, so where is it coming from?

Create is a method that Delphi automatically inherits from TObject. It handles the allocation of memory to store any objects derived from the class and must be called before you can actually use them. The **Create** method instantiates the object from the class definition.

So, declaring an object variable like this,

```
var
    Asteroid : TAsteroid;
```

isn't quite enough to actually start working with the object. We must explicitly create the object using the **Create** method before we can get down to it:

```
Asteroid := TAsteroid.Create;
```

 Remember that we had this problem with the wizard **TBitmap** object in Chapter 4.

Likewise, before your code ends, you need to free up the space in memory that the object took up. You can do this with the **Free** method which, again, Delphi automatically inherits from TObject:

```
Asteroid.Free;
```

What a palaver!

Summary

As it stands, the program illustrates the basic concepts of objects and classes quite nicely. You have seen how to:

▶ Create a class

▶ Use that class to create an object

▶ Segment the code into **public** and **private** areas.

However, it could do so much more. As it stands, it's really nothing more than a well-designed collection of variables and subroutines.

Class Struggle

To turn this into a truly useful real-world class, we should have it do a number of things itself. When the class is created, for example, it should set up an array of points so that the drawing code can be simplified. It should also set up its initial **X** and **Y** coordinates and the speed that it will travel around the screen. We should then be able to add a **Move** method to the class to lose that nasty drawing loop.

In the next project, I've committed the cardinal error of changing loads of things at once. Let's split up the discussion into a few sections.

Controlling Creation and Destruction

There are two very special procedures that you can add into a class. Called **constructor**s and **destructor**s, these routines are automatically run by Delphi every time you create an object from the class, allowing you to initialize the data in an object once it has been created.

If you load up **rockplot.dpr** and select View | Project Manager from the menu bar, double-clicking on AstObj3u will show the **TAsteroid** class type as it is now:

```
type
    TAsteroid = class
        Public
            { Methods }
            procedure Draw;
            procedure Erase;
            procedure Move ;

            constructor Create(Form : TForm);
            destructor Destroy;
```

161

```
        Private
            TheForm                 : TForm;
            Scale                   : integer;
            X                       : integer;
            Y                       : integer;
            XSpeed                  : integer;
            YSpeed                  : integer;
            ShapeXPoints            : array[0..10] of integer;
            ShapeYPoints            : array[0..10] of integer;
            procedure Plot_Shape (nColor : integer);
    end;
```

Most important here is the declaration of the **constructor** and **destructor**. To declare a **constructor** method simply write:

constructor *<Class type>.<method name> <parameters>;*

Similarly for the **destructor** method. It's really the same as you would declare any other method in the class, but with the obvious difference that, instead of using the **procedure** or **function** keywords to define the method, we now use **constructor**. Note that you must specify the owner of the method - the class type within which the method is declared.

Notice also how the **constructor** method also has a parameter declaration. In the previous example, whenever we wanted to draw or erase the asteroid, we needed to pass across a parameter to tell the method on what form to do the drawing. With this class, we only need to do that when we first create an object from the class. The **constructor** method stores the parameter in a **private** field within the class which the other methods can use to check which form to deal with.

Here's the code that follows in the unit's **implementation** section:

```
constructor TAsteroid.Create(Form : TForm);
begin

    TheForm := Form;

    { Randomly calculate the starting position for the asteroid }
    X := Random(TheForm.ClientWidth-20)+ 10;
    Y := Random(TheForm.ClientHeight-20)+ 10;

    Scale := 4;

    { Randomly calculate the speed of travel in the horizontal and
      vertical axis }
    XSpeed := Random(10) - 5;
    YSpeed := Random(10) - 5;

    { Finally set up the X and Y coordinates of each point in the
      asteroid's shape, filling the arrays ShapeXPoints and
      ShapeYPoints }

    {I've not put the drawing code in here because I like trees!}
end;
```

```
destructor TAsteroid.Destroy;
begin

end;
```

There's no special code when the asteroid object is destroyed (there could be if you wanted to score some points!), but each asteroid does need some serious initialization code. The **constructor** is passed the calling form as a parameter. This allows the **astobj3u.pas** unit to be used with any form, in any project, without you having to change the code. Next up, initial coordinates and asteroid speeds are randomly selected, the **randomize** command having been called in the calling form (here it's **frmAsteroids** in the **astplot.pas**) before the asteroid is created.

Even if we do add in a constructor or destructor, there's no obligation to actually write any code. Leaving a constructor or destructor blank doesn't interfere with the normal operation of an object's Create and Free methods. Note that any new objects that inherit this Asteroid class automatically inherit its constructor and destructor methods and can add to or completely overwrite them if they wish.

When the form is created, it uses a simple **for** loop to create an array of objects of the TAsteroid type. The form is passed across as a parameter of the **Create** method so that the asteroid can be drawn on its **Canvas**. Delphi then goes away, allocates memory to store the object, runs the **constructor** method (passing it the parameter specified) and stores the resulting object in the **Asteroid** object array:

```
procedure TfrmAsteroids.FormCreate(Sender: TObject);
var
    nIndex : integer;
begin
    Randomize;
    for nIndex := 1 to 5 do
        Asteroids[nIndex] := TAsteroid.Create(frmAsteroids);
end;
```

While we're here, we'll just take a peek at the form's OnDestroy event handler which frees the five asteroids that we've just created:

```
procedure TfrmAsteroids.FormDestroy(Sender: TObject);
var
    nIndex : integer;
begin
    for nIndex := 1 to 5 do
        Asteroids[nIndex].Free;
end;
```

Just as before, when the form is destroyed we also need to free up any objects we've created. If we have a declared **destructor**, **Free** automatically runs this code first, before it de-allocates the memory associated with the object. If, as is the case in our new TAsteroid class, the **destructor** is empty, nothing special happens. I've only included this **destructor** ready for a later version of the code that handles the asteroid's screen meltdown.

Other Changes

Now to the rest of the code. The **draw** and **erase** methods have changed only in that the **Plot_Shape** method has changed its parameter calls. It no longer needs the form to be passed and the draw mechanism uses the coordinate arrays set up in the object's **constructor**.

The **Move** method, new to this example, uses the asteroid's speeds to calculate its new position and also handles what happens when the asteroid hits the edge of the screen. In our example, I've made the asteroid appear on the opposite side of the screen to where it left - true Asteroids fashion:

```
procedure TAsteroid.Move;
begin
    Erase;

    X := X + XSpeed;
    Y := Y + YSpeed;

    if X > TheForm.ClientWidth then
        X := X - TheForm.ClientWidth
    else if X < 0 then
        X := TheForm.ClientWidth + X;

    if Y > TheForm.ClientHeight then
        Y := Y - TheForm.ClientHeight
    else if Y < 0 then
        Y := TheForm.ClientHeight + Y;

    Draw;
end;
```

If you run the program, you'll see that it moves five asteroids around the screen in the usual manner. However, because this is using a much more powerful asteroid class (which has its own **constructor** and **destructor**) the form itself contains just three event handlers, each with only two lines of code.

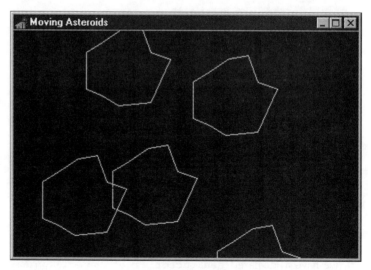

By adding a **constructor** and **destructor** to a class, as well as getting a more self sufficient data type, you also get the ability to create some very powerful applications with a very little effort. With just six lines of code in this program, we have five asteroids capable of drawing and erasing themselves, moving themselves around the form and making sure that if they go off any edge of the form they come back.

Don't worry too much about what the bulk of the code does. The point here is that we have a totally independent object with a **constructor** and **destructor**, as well as three other methods that we can call in code. The data relating to the control of the class (in this case, the asteroid's position on screen, how fast it travels, and so on) is all held in the **private** section of the class. The **public** section of the object, its methods and properties (but there are none in our example), are what programmers can use when they create an object from your class type.

Coupling

When you're designing your objects, one of the most important things for you to consider is **coupling**. This dictates just how attached an object is to your application. One of the benefits of object-oriented development is the ability to reuse a great deal of your code in other projects. If the object is tightly coupled to your application, it will be difficult for you to use it again because it might rely on certain forms being present in your application, or on certain global variables being defined.

The ideal situation is to end up with a loosely coupled object, one which depends on nothing from the application in which it lives other than the parameters passed to its methods. An important step towards a loosely coupled object is placing it and all its methods inside their own unit. Adding the object to another project should then involve little more than adding that unit to the new project.

You can see this in the **rockplot.dpr** project we saw in the last example - TAsteroid is defined in its own unit. In addition, when objects are declared from a class, they need to be told on which form they should draw themselves. The properties of that form are then used to determine the dimensions of the drawing area, and so on.

When you put a class declaration into an external unit, you must move the class declaration from the **implementation** section of the unit (where we have previously put it) to the **interface** section. It's that old chestnut - scope - again, where using a class type in another unit requires that its scope be **public**, i.e. you must put the type declaration in its unit's interface. As always, the code itself lives in the **implementation** section; after all, it does constitute the implementation of the class.

In addition, though, you need to change the **uses** clause of any unit which contains objects derived from the class. Load up **rockplot.dpr** again check this out. If you take a look at the asteroids unit, you can see what I mean about the class declaration:

```
interface

uses Forms, Graphics;

type
    TAsteroid = class
        Public
            :
        Private
            :
    end;
```

I have also added a **uses** clause to the head of the unit. TAsteroid makes use of a number of other classes which are included with Delphi. For example, we have a **Form** type object in the class to determine where the asteroid should draw itself, so, as TForm is defined in Delphi's **Form** unit, we need to place that in the **uses** clause. Also, the drawing code makes use of color constants (**clBlack** and **clBlue**) which are defined in Delphi's **Graphics** unit. That is also added to the **uses** clause.

When you're designing your own objects, check what Delphi units you need to use by looking at the online help for the relevant Delphi functions. The unit in which they reside is usually mentioned at the top.

If you now take a look at the **uses** clause of the application's main form, you'll see that I have also added the TAsteroid unit (**AstObj3u**) to its **uses** clause. Why? Because the form unit contains code which defines objects derived from this unit. It's what we saw in Chapter 3 when we talked about circular reference.

```
uses
    Windows, Messages, SysUtils, Classes, Graphics, Controls, Forms, Dialogs,
    ExtCtrls, AstObj3u;
```

Inheritance

Earlier on, you saw how you could **embed** one record type inside another. It was a bit clumsy though - you end up with code looking like this, or worse:

record.subrecord.field := *<value>*

When you're using classes, you can make use of something much neater called **inheritance**. What does it mean? Well, many of the objects that you will deal with in your applications are based around similar classes.

For example, if you were writing an application to deal with vehicles, you could find yourself writing a truck, car and bus class all with some very similar fields and methods.

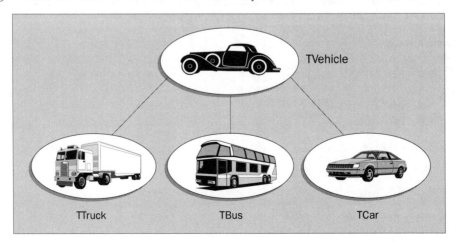

With inheritance, you can define a base class and then produce (**derive** or **descend**) new classes that inherit the base class' functionality.

 These new classes are said to descend or be derived from the base class... and you can get quite a complicated family tree. Thank goodness it's not confused by multiple inheritance, where you can inherit from several classes at once, as happens in C++.

```
Type
    TVehicle = class
        nNumWheels : integer;
        procedure Drive_To( sLocation : string );
    end;
```

Here we have a class, called **TVehicle**, which defines some of the common bits and bobs that most people would agree constitute a vehicle. A car is more than a generic vehicle because it can hold passengers. A truck, on the other hand, can carry cargo. We can extend the vehicle class to give two new classes:

```
    TCar = class( TVehicle )
        nNumPassengers : integer;
        procedure Pick_Up ( nPassengers : integer );
    end;

    TTruck = class( TVehicle )
        nCapacity : integer;
        procedure Load_Up ( nUnits : integer );
    end;
```

Instead of just defining two new types of class, this block of code defines two new TVehicle type classes. The methods and fields in the classes are added to the base class, so you could write code like this:

```
    var
        Car : TCar;
    begin
        Car = TCar.Create;
        Car.NumWheels := 4;
        Car.DriveTo( 'MyHouse' );
        Car.Pick_Up( 2 );
        Car.Free;
    end;
```

The members of the base class are not embedded inside the new class and its objects, they are actually part of them. The TCar and TTruck classes are comprised of all the code from the TVehicle class and that which is added directly into their definitions.

With inheritance goes that other weird OOP term - **polymorphism**.

Polymorphism

Poly who? Designers love coming up with strange names for their hard won concepts. Usually they're logical, but they don't exactly roll off the tongue!

Polymorphism, from the Greek, means literally *to have many manifestations under the same basic form*. In an object-oriented programming language, polymorphism relates to the language's ability to give a method in a derived class the same name as the method in its base (or ancestor) class, but to use different code in each implementation. Call the method using the same name and you'll get a different effect, depending on the calling object.

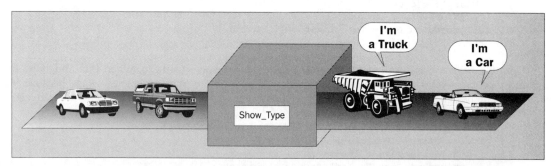

The decision as to which set of code to run is made at run time on the basis of which class type the object belongs to. The fact that the program can't always unambiguously say which method it needs to use before the program runs causes the compiler a bit of trouble. It gets round this problem using something called late binding. It's this solution that generates the keyword `virtual`.

If you want to know more about this subject (which is all about the internal workings of compilers and not Delphi), I suggest that you take a look at a book that cover the subject of compiler writing.

We're going to see these concepts in action as we construct a unit file for the TCar and TVehicle classes. You can add this to the **cars.dpr** project on the disk to give the final working application.

Try It Out - Playing Cars

1 Select File | New... to bring up the New Items window and double-click on the Unit icon. This brings up just the code window. Save it as **classcar.pas**.

2 In the unit's **interface** section add the following **uses** clause:

```
unit ClassCar;

interface

uses Dialogs;
```

3 Continue with the **TVehicle** class type declaration:

```
interface

uses Dialogs;
```

```
type
    { Create the generic vehicle class }
    TVehicle = class
      public
          nNumWheels : integer;
          nMaxSpeed  : integer;
          nNumSeats  : integer;

          constructor Create ;
          procedure Show_Type ; virtual;
    end;
```

4 And the **TCar** class type declaration:

```
          procedure Show_Type ; virtual;
    end;
```

```
TCar = class(TVehicle)
      public
          constructor Create;
          procedure Set_Type( sType : String ) ;
          procedure Show_Type ; override;
      private
          sVehicleType : string;
    end;
```

5 Now to the **implementation** section and the code proper. First, we deal with the **TVehicle**'s **constructor** code:

```
implementation
```

```
constructor TVehicle.Create;
begin
    nNumWheels := 0;
    nMaxSpeed := 0;
    nNumSeats := 0;

    MessageDlg('Vehicle created.', mtInformation, [mbOK], 0);
end;
```

6 Now for the **TCar**'s **constructor** code, which is very similar to what you've just written. We've highlighted the major differences below, but you'll need to type it all into the unit:

```
constructor TCar.Create;
begin
    inherited;

    nMaxSpeed := 150;
```

```
        sVehicleType := 'A Very Fast Car';

        MessageDlg('Brand new car created', mtInformation, [mbOK], 0);
   end;
```

7 Now to fill in the **TVehicle**'s **Show_Type** procedure:

```
MessageDlg('Brand new car created', mtInformation, [mbOK], 0);
   end;

procedure TVehicle.Show_Type;
{ TVehicle method to show that the TVehicle class has no details
  Attack is the best form of defense }
begin
     MessageDlg('Dunno what you are looking at here. Must be foreign!',
                    mtInformation, [mbOK],0 );
end;

procedure TCar.Set_Type( sType : string ) ;
{ General TCar method for use by the programmer to set up the car type private
  field using the Carsu unit's choice of car }
begin
     sVehicleType := sType;
end;

procedure TCar.Show_Type;
{ Displays a message box telling the user that they're looking at a car. Also
  displays the car's type. }
begin
     MessageDlg('You''re totally looking at a car...dude... It''s a ' +
                sVehicleType, mtInformation, [mbOK],0);
end;

end.
```

8 Save all these changes. Load up **cars.dpr**. Press the Add file to project speed button and add in the class unit you've just spent so long creating. The Project Manager (selected, as before, from the View menu) should now look like this:

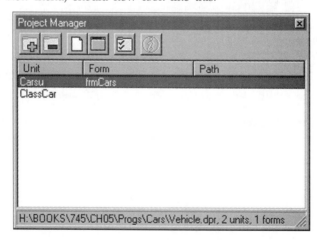

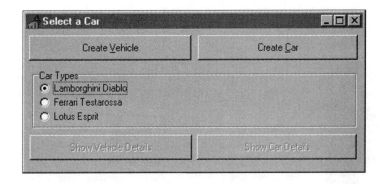

Finally, you can run the
application:

How It Works

It's a pretty simple application, but as you'll see in a minute, it does make use of both
inheritance and polymorphism. The program itself contains two classes: TVehicle and TCar. The
TVehicle class defines the basic format of a vehicle - you know, something with wheels, etc. The
TCar class builds on it with the addition of a **private VehicleType** field.

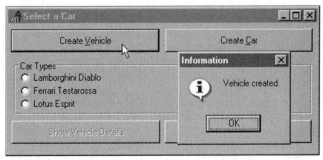

Take a look at the program running.
If you click on the Create Vehicle
button, the code underneath creates an
object from the TVehicle class, its
Create method which displays a
message to show just what's going on:

If you then go on to click the Show vehicle details button, a method of the class runs telling
you that this is just a generic vehicle object - it doesn't have any details as such.

Let's start off by looking at the two class types we've defined. We see that the TVehicle class
defines your average vehicle, while TCar adds in its own properties and methods. Both classes
have a **Show_Type** method, but both have different keywords at the end of their declarations.

This is the practical side of polymorphism. You must define methods you think may be used
differently in descendent classes using either of the keywords **virtual** or **dynamic**. These
prepare Delphi for the late-binding we mentioned earlier. In terms of program execution, there's
a little more overhead to having **virtual** methods, but these are the problems you'll have to
face if you're serious about getting the most out of your class families.

Suppose, for example, that you wanted to derive your own class of buttons that allow animation
on the button's face. In this case, you could derive a new button from Delphi's TButton
component class, TAnimButton, override the inherited TButton's **Focused** method and add your
functionality in the **Focused** method local to the class.

Any overridden classes must have identical parameter lists to their **virtual** ancestors (slightly
strange wording that!). As far as other programmers are concerned, the TCar class is derived
from the TVehicle class, so **Show_Type**, although it might act differently, should be called in
just the same way, whether you're using TVehicle or any of its descendents.

In the descendent classes themselves, if you want to replace the previously declared **virtual** method, you use the keyword **override**, to 'override' the old code with the new.

Notice that, even though the method is declared with the **virtual** keyword tacked on the end, this is only necessary in the class declaration. The implementation code doesn't really care either way.

Similarly, for procedures declared in the **interface** section, you can remove the parameter lists from the procedure header which implements the code later in the unit. In fact, all you need for method headers in the **implementation** section is either the keyword **procedure** or **function**, the class type and the name of the method.

As for inheritance, TCar is descended from TVehicle. This is important in TCar's **constructor**, because if we define a **constructor** in a descendent class, it will just replace the base class's **constructor**. However, you may not want this to happen, so, just by adding the statement **inherited;** to the first line of **constructor**, you can get the base class' **constructor** to run before the native code.

This explains why the message dialog 'Vehicle Created' appears before 'Brand new car created', when you create a new car. If you don't want to completely replace the code in any overridden class, if you just want to add extra functionality, you must use the **inherited** keyword and, to be safe, follow it with the name of the ancestor's method.

If you want, set a breakpoint at the start of the **Create Car** button's **OnClick** event handler. You do this by double-clicking to the far left of the code window at the correct line. A red bar and stop sign should appear. Now run the code: the program will run and, when you press the button, the execution will stop. Now press either the **Trace Into** or **Step Over** speed buttons and the code will run a step at a time. When A_Car is created, the trace line will leap to the **ClassCar** unit, go to the **TCar.Create** constructor and then immediately up to the **TVehicle.Create constructor**.

This is a useful way for you to trace through your code when things go awry. The program is still running, just a line or a procedure at a time. So, once a procedure is finished or a dialog box displayed, you'll need to provide input to the application just as if you were using it, say, by clicking the relevant button.

In TCar's **Set_Type** method, the string parameter, **sType**, passes the selected car type string to the code within the class method, where the **private sVehicleType** string variable is set equal to its value.

How do we get that value, though? In the **Carsu** unit, we finally get to use a radio group to let the user select their car. RadioGroups have an **Items** property which is a **StringList** object, just like the **Lines** property of a Memo. By adding items to this array in the unit's **FormCreate** event handler, I'm instructing the RadioGroup to create a new radio button with the given string as its label:

```
procedure TfrmCars.FormCreate(Sender: TObject);
begin
     rdoCarType.Items.Add('Lamborghini Diablo');
     rdoCarType.Items.Add('Ferrari Testarossa');
     rdoCarType.Items.Add('Lotus Esprit');
end;
```

The RadioGroup has a very useful property - **ItemIndex** - which returns the currently selected item in the list (starting at zero), or **-1** if no item is selected. This should go some way to explaining the use of the large **if...then...else** loop in the **cmdCarCreateClick** event handler.

All being well, an **A_Car** object is created from the TCar class and the type of car set by a call to the new object's **Set_Type** method. The **ItemIndex** property of the RadioGroup forms the ordinal data for the decision-making **case** statement.

```
procedure TfrmCars.cmdCarCreateClick(Sender: TObject);
begin
     if rdoCarType.ItemIndex <> -1 then
     begin
       {Create a TCar object}
       A_Car := TCar.Create;

       {Input user's selection of car to Set_Type method}
       case rdoCarType.ItemIndex of
           0 : A_Car.Set_Type('Lamborghini Diablo');
           1 : A_Car.Set_Type('Ferrari Testarossa');
           2 : A_Car.Set_Type('Lotus Esprit');
       end;

       {Change buttons enabled, a car having been created}
       cmdCarCreate.Enabled := False;
       cmdShowCar.Enabled := True;
     end
     else
        MessageDlg('Go on, select a car type...', mtInformation, [mbOK], 0);
end;
```

You should note that all of the buttons on the form use the OnClick event handler (**cmdShowVehClick**). They all want to perform similar functions but they all use different criteria. So how does the code identify which button has been clicked to work out which set of criteria to use?

Well, we use the **Sender** parameter that's been included for free in the event handler. **Sender**, which can be any object (since it's declared to be of type **TObject**), identifies the source of the event message. By making use of this extra information, we can code the event handler to respond in different ways, depending on the source of the event. If it's the **cmdShowVeh** button, we call the **TVehicle.Show_Type** method and for **cmdShowCar**, we call its method:

```
procedure TfrmCars.cmdShowVehClick(Sender: TObject);
begin
     if Sender = cmdShowVeh then
       begin
         A_Vehicle.Show_Type;
         cmdVehCreate.Enabled := True;
```

```
                    cmdShowVeh.Enabled    := False;
                end
            else if Sender = cmdShowCar then
                begin
                    A_Car.Show_Type;
                    cmdCarCreate.Enabled := True;
                    cmdShowCar.Enabled   := False;
                end;
        end;
```

In the code above, as in the event handlers for each of the buttons, we disable the button once it has been pressed and enable its complement - thus hopefully guiding the user to press the other button.

The **TVehicle's** **Show_Type** method shows the type of vehicle we're looking at. In the case of **TVehicle**, though, as the **TVehicle** class has no vehicle type property, it could be anything - so a message is displayed telling the user something to that effect.

The Object Repository

When we created the new unit, we used the New Items window. This allows you access to the **Object Repository**, new to Delphi 2.0. The Object Repository is just that, a place where you can store useful objects, forms, projects, units, etc., for further use.

For starters, it makes it easier for you to find those files that you want to reuse. But it goes further than that. With units and forms, you can not only *copy* but also *inherit* the original file. What's the difference? The main use of form inheritance is that any changes to the original form (hopefully improving it) are automatically passed down to the inherited form.

Any units you need across the spectrum of your application development are ideal candidates for addition to the repository. You can do this by right-clicking on the form and selecting Add To Repository..., or, if you want to add a whole project to the repository, select Project | Add To Repository.... The current project is also available in the New Items box for you to work with.

Designing a Class Hierarchy

This is all rather subtle, so let's recap.

You can create a base class and inherit its properties and methods in any number of descendent classes. So, the first task of solving a problem in an object-oriented way is to try and extract those common features of the various objects in your system. Just start with a few.

Because of inheritance, if you find you later need to declare a new property or method which is generally applicable, you can add it to the base class and have all the base class's descendents automatically inherit that new functionality. No longer are you constrained to solve the problem on paper before you start coding. While you still need to plan the project, all of your effort should be thrown into understanding the problem - the solution will be dictated by the requirements of the actual coding, as you go. You've no excuse - start today!

An ideal base class, therefore, does everything it can, but also predicts what methods are likely to need changing in its descendent classes. A rule of thumb - if the method definitely won't change, leave it that way. It will be subject to early binding. However, if a method is likely to need modifying or extending, bite the bullet, face up to the extra overhead and make it **virtual**.

> If **virtual** is too painful in terms of memory requirements, use the alternative, **dynamic**, which generates less code but executes slightly slower. Otherwise, from our point of view, they're identical.

Don't feel that having **virtual** methods limits the code you can add to the base class. Because you can inherit the code if you need to, save yourself typing and put it in the base class.

If you can't be bothered with implementing the code for the method you just rashly declared, but you feel sure you'll need it later in a descendent class, after **virtual** or **dynamic**, you can use the **abstract** keyword. This requires that the method be overridden in the descendent and the code included there. It all depends on the amount of future planning you can do. If we were feeling daft, we could define an **abstract** method, **Hover**, in the TVehicle method that we can use in the future when anti-matter drives come as standard. But in each of the other more conventional vehicles, we would need to put some code to this effect:

```
procedure TCar.Hover;
begin
     ShowMessage('Not a chance, mate!');
end;
```

As long as you do your housekeeping and provide at least the **interface** section of your class units, any other developer can derive new classes from yours and add their code leitmotif.

The Protection Racket

We've already seen **public** and **private** in action in class definitions. However, they have a baby brother - **protected** - that can help segment the functionality and data inside a class.

Let's go over what **public** and **private** actually do.

The properties and methods that you declare in the **public** section of the class represent the interface to the class. Programmers deriving objects from your class use the **public** properties and methods to bring it to life.

However, the properties and methods that you declare in the **private** section of a class are quite strange. Programmers using objects declared from the class can't touch these **private** sections at run time. Instead, they need to use **public** methods to access the object's **private** section. Usually, the **private** properties and methods are used for the object's internal calculations - encapsulation at work. That's why TCar's **sVehicleType** property is stored in the **private** section where it may only be accessed by the **public** methods, **Set_Type(sType)** and **Show_Type**.

It's directly due to class scope that you couldn't write the following and get a successful compile:

```
A_Car.sVehicleType := 'A very, very fast car indeed';
```

It may appear a somewhat roundabout way to get at data, but it ensures that users can't set data to anything other than what your class can handle.

FYI If you inherit the class, the new descendent class can access the **private** areas of its ancestor. Programmers declaring descendent classes in a different unit, though, can't. This is great if you're producing a unit consisting of nothing more than a class and its descendents which you're then going to hand to another programmer or use in other units in your application. As long as code using these classes lives in a different unit, you can rest assured that elements in your **private** section are safe.

Protected is a new section that we haven't seen before - it's a cross between **public** and **private**. Like **private**, the methods and fields in the **protected** section of a class can't be accessed by users of objects created from the class. However, anyone creating a descendent class anywhere in the project can still get at the **protected** areas. So, why use **protected** blocks at all? They seem to be nothing more than insecure **private** sections.

Think back to the asteroid class from earlier. There, we have a **Plot_Shape** routine declared in the **private** section of the class. Why? Because we want users of objects derived form the TAsteroid class to use **Move**, **Draw** and **Erase** to change where the asteroid appears and do all the drawing.

However, if a developer were to create a new descendent of the TAsteroid class in a different unit, she wouldn't be able to write methods that call the **Plot_Shape** routine. Now, if the **Plot_Shape** routine was in a **protected** rather than a **private** block, it wouldn't be a problem. For example:

```
type
    TAsteroid = class
        public
                { Methods }
                procedure Draw;
                procedure Move ;
                procedure Erase;
                constructor Create(Form : TForm);
                destructor Destroy;
        private
                TheForm              : TForm;
                Scale                : integer;
                X                    : integer;
                Y                    : integer;
                XSpeed               : integer;
                YSpeed               : integer;
                ShapeXPoints         : array[0..10] of integer;
                ShapeYPoints         : array[0..10] of integer;
        protected
                procedure Plot_Shape (nColor : integer);
    end;
```

Anyone deriving new classes from here can write methods which directly call the **Plot_Shape** procedure. This greatly increases the opportunities to reuse the class.

Say I wanted to draw each asteroid differently - I could combine this technique with **virtual** methods:

```
type
    TAsteroid = class
        public
                { Methods }
                procedure Draw; virtual;
                procedure Move ; virtual;
                procedure Erase; virtual;

                constructor Create(Form : TForm); virtual;
                destructor Destroy; virtual;
                :
        protected
                procedure Plot_Shape (nColor : integer);
```

Now any developer deriving new classes from this one can not only still get at the **Plot_Shape** procedure, but can also totally redefine the way the class works by overriding the **Draw, Move** and **Erase** methods and by overriding the default **constructor** and **destructor**.

We can further extend the asteroid example by using inheritance. The base class will be inherited to form a new class **TSmallRock** which will draw a smaller asteroid. It gets closer to the game every time!

Try It Out - Little Asteroids

1 Load up **rockplot.dpr**. Save it as **rocku.pas**, **baserock.pas** and **minirock.dpr**. With this new project, select File | New... and choose Unit in the New Items window. Do it again. You now have two new units.

2 Make a copy of the contents of **baserock.pas**, the asteroid class definition unit. Paste the code into the two units.

3 Change the base class declaration in **baserock.pas** to:

```
type
    TAsteroid = class
        public
            { Methods }
            procedure Draw; virtual; abstract;
            procedure Erase;
            procedure Move ;
            constructor Create(Form : TForm); virtual;
            destructor Destroy;

        protected
            TheForm             : TForm;
            Scale               : integer;
            X                   : integer;
```

```
        Y                          : integer;
        XSpeed                     : integer;
        YSpeed                     : integer;
        ShapeXPoints               : array[0..10] of integer;
        ShapeYPoints               : array[0..10] of integer;
        procedure Plot_Shape (nColor : integer);
    end;
```

4 Cut the **ShapeXPoints** and **ShapeYPoints** array initialization from the **TAsteroid.Create constructor**. Also cut out the **TAsteroid.Draw** method.

5 In **rock1.pas**, we'll create the **TBigAsteroid** class descended from the **TAsteroid** class:

```
interface
  uses Forms, Graphics, baserock;

type
    TBigAsteroid = class(TAsteroid)
        Public
                procedure Draw; override;
                constructor Create(Form : TForm); override;
    end;
```

6 Below that, in the **implementation** section, modify the **constructor** and remove the other methods except for the **Draw** method, which is now renamed to belong to **TBigAsteroid**:

```
implementation
```

```
{ The BigAsteroid's constructor }
constructor TBigAsteroid.Create(Form : TForm);
begin
    inherited;

    { Now set up the X and Y coordinates of each point in the
      asteroid's shape }
    ShapeXPoints[0] := -10;
    ShapeXPoints[1] := -10;
        :
    ShapeYPoints[0] := 5;
    ShapeYPoints[1] := 9;
end;
```

```
{ The BigAsteroid's draw method }
procedure TBigAsteroid.Draw;
begin
    Plot_Shape(clBlue);
end;
```

In the **uses** clause, add in a reference to **baserock.pas**.

7 Turning to **rock2.pas**, we do a similar thing, except we make the **Plot_Shape** color **clYellow** and alter the asteroid vertices.

8 In **rocku.pas**, add the three class units to the **uses** clause. Then change the drawing, moving and erasing code so that five of each type of asteroids feature when the program runs. For example:

```
var
    BigAsteroids   : array[1..5] of TBigAsteroid;
    SmallAsteroids : array[1..5] of TSmallAsteroid;

procedure TfrmAsteroids.FormCreate(Sender: TObject);
var
    nIndex : integer;
begin
    Randomize;
    for nIndex := 1 to 5 do
    begin
        BigAsteroids[nIndex]   := TBigAsteroid.Create(frmAsteroids);
        SmallAsteroids[nIndex] :=
                            TSmallAsteroid.Create(frmAsteroids);
    end;
end;
```

Run the application and the form will maximize to display ten moving asteroids which, unfortunately, are oblivious to each other.

How It Works

This example ties up all the theory we've just met.

The base TAsteroid class needs to have its **private** section redeclared as **protected**, so that the other units in the project can use these properties and methods in the derived asteroid classes.

The **virtual** and **abstract** method declarations enable us to put in specific code for the two sorts of asteroid. The **inherited** word in the two **constructor**s makes use of the base class **constructor** too, which still sets up the random positions and speeds.

The **Draw** method may not be the most efficient. The same code could be put in the base class and a color property set by the **constructor** instead, but I wanted to show off the form of an **abstract** method declaration.

True Properties

Although we don't cover them in this book, Delphi allows you to create your own components, derived from the components in Delphi's Visual Component Library (VCL). Components are defined in class types and are just like any other class... except for some subtle differences that are needed to allow the component to be designed into the application's form.

FYI If you're interested in trying out your hand at Delphi component writing, why not take a look at *Instant Delphi Components*, ISBN 1-861000-20-0, from Wrox Press.

There's another optional section in the class declaration: **published**. Properties declared in this section are like those in the **public** section, except for some special run-time information it provides to the application. Usually the **published** section holds the properties you see in the Object Inspector at design time.

Hang on, though, what's that we said about keeping data in the **private** section, to keep it beyond the reach of prying programmers? There's nothing like paranoia for stimulating inventiveness! The properties declared in the **published** section are 'dummies'. They read their value from **private** data fields (the properties we've been using up to now, by another name), and call methods to write any changes to that data set in the Object Inspector.

Seems complicated? Well it's allowing design-time use of objects that does it. So, if you ever graduate to writing your own components, remember - **published** properties access data held in **private** fields. And if you want to have a sane conversation with a C++ programmer, properties are the nouns of an object, methods the verbs.

Summary

In this chapter, you've been introduced to the big wide world of OOP. We hope you've enjoyed the tour. The idea is so obviously sensible, you wonder why we ever bothered with anything else, but attaining true wisdom is not so easy a task. Implementing objects well takes practice.

In the next chapter, I move on to a more restrained subject: graphics. Nothing like a visual chapter to perk up your reader after an OOP fest. In fact, as I began to illustrate in the asteroids class, objects come into their own in graphics programming, so you will be putting into practice some of the theory that you've covered here.

So, without much further ado, onward and upward towards the realms of animation, graphics and the world of the artist - I hope you can draw!

Graphics

It's been a bit of a hard slog so far, with most of the previous chapters devoted to building up a necessary programming foundation for the rest of the book. Now it's time for a break, time to have a bit of fun.

One of the more fun areas of programming, though none the less demanding for it, has to be creating graphics and animation. Whether you intend to write the next Wing Commander, or just a quick data charting application, Delphi's power, flexibility and speed can help you a great deal. Programming graphics is no exception. Delphi makes it easy to create animation, as well as static art (of sorts) through code, but those guys at Borland have even thrown in a few graphic components to enable you to draw simple art at design time.

In this chapter, we'll explore some of the graphics facilities in Delphi. You will learn:

- How to use the graphical components
- What coordinate systems are and how to use them
- How to draw graphics at run time
- How to display and animate pictures

Aside from this, though, you'll also see nearly all of the stuff we learnt in previous chapters (loops, variables, functions and procedures) put into action.

The Graphical Components

Delphi includes two components which you can drop onto a form at run time to spice up how it looks and feels; the Shape component and the Image component. The Shape component has very little functionality that you can make use of at run time, and exists mainly to give you a way to add a little variation to your forms, or even to produce very simple drawings.

On the other hand, the Image component provides a complete set of methods and properties to load images off the disk and display them, move the images around and even make them respond to user interaction, such as moving or clicking the mouse.

Let's keep it simple to start off with, though, and look at the Shape component.

The Shape Component

The Shape component (to be found on the Additional page of the Component Palette) gives you the ability to create a variety of static shapes, from lines and boxes to circles and ellipses, all in one component. As you might guess, using the Shape component is really easy; just drop it onto a form and then use the Object Inspector to get at the properties that control the shape and colors of the object. Let's try it out.

Try It Out - Testing Out the Shape Component

In this Try It Out, we're not going to create anything, we're just going to put this component through its paces and see what happens. Hopefully, this should spark off some ideas for how you can use Shape within your own applications.

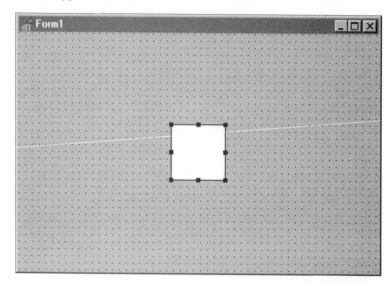

1 Start a new application and drop a Shape component onto the form by double-clicking on the icon in the Component Palette:

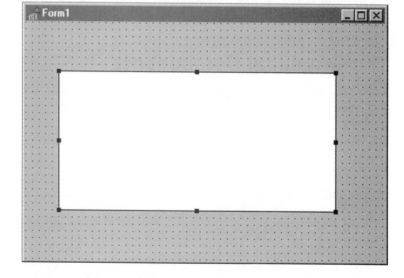

By default, the Shape starts off life as a square. Just like any other component, you can easily change its size and shape using the resize handles:

2 Take a look at the Object Inspector. As I said earlier, TShape has a number of properties that allow you to change its appearance, including Brush, Pen and Shape itself. You can use all of these to define the physical shape of the component, as well as the color and style of the border and interior.

For example, you can quickly change the shape by double-clicking on its Shape property:

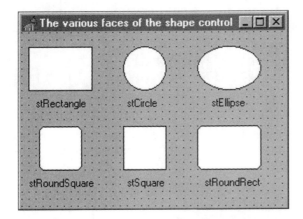

The figure on the left shows you all the possible settings for this component's Shape property.

3 An interesting point - you can use the Shape control to draw lines, rather then geometric shapes, but you have to be a little sneaky. You might have noticed that there isn't a stLine setting for the Shape property. Change the height of the shape that you have on your form - you'll find that Delphi will let you resize it down to just one pixel. When you release the mouse button, you'll see that you have drawn a line on the form:

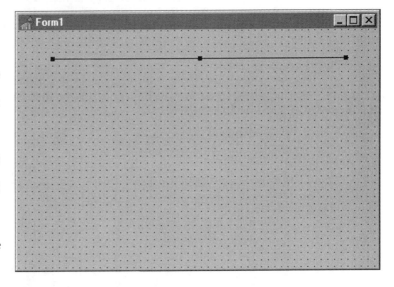

FYI You might notice that this feature isn't that powerful because you can't use it to get Delphi to create a diagonal line - you are restricted to horizontal and vertical. I wonder why Borland didn't provide a Line component?

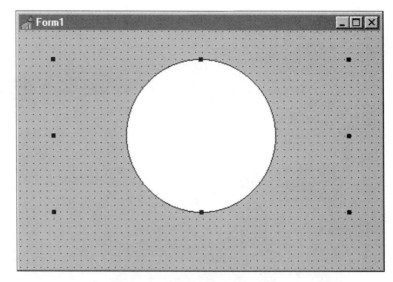

4 Change the shape back into a large rectangle, then try changing the **Shape** property to something else, like stCircle. Straight away, the shape on the form changes to match your selection:

An interesting point here is that if you select a true shape like a square or a circle, the shape won't necessarily fill the dimensions of the component when you resize it using the resize handles.

5 Through all that shape drawing, you probably noticed that the shape actually has two colors. One for the border around the shape and one for inside the shape. To determine these, the **Shape** component has two objects attached to it: the **TPen** object and the **TBrush** object. By manipulating the **TPen** object's properties, you can set up the border's color, style, width and something known as the **draw mode** (more on this later). The **TBrush** object works in a similar way and governs the 'brush' used to paint the interior of the shape.

If you bring up the Object Inspector again and find the **Pen** and **Brush** properties, you can see that they are in fact objects contained within the **Shape** component - you can tell this because of the small plus sign to the left of the property name which unfolds to display the properties of this internal object:

Find the Brush property and double-click it to see the entire object (a staggering two properties!). Now try double-clicking the Color property of the TBrush object and up pops a Color dialog allowing you to change the color inside the shape:

6 Follow the same procedure to reveal the TPen object's properties. The first one to consider is called Style.

On the whole, each of these styles should be self explanatory; psSolid draws a solid border, psClear removes the border, psDash draws a dashed border, and so on. Try selecting some of these; if you still have a circle selected, you might want to change the Style property of the shape itself to stRectangle to makes it easier to see the change in the Pen's Style.

7 One other property worth mentioning is called Width, a property which governs how thick the border is. Try setting it to 10.

Wow - that made a difference. The problem with choosing a thick border is that it effectively negates the Pen's Style setting. A thick border like this is so thick that the gaps in a dashed border vanish - a little annoying I know, but now you know, it shouldn't cause you any problems.

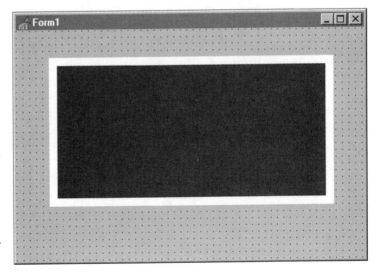

187

That's all there is to the Shape component - told you it would be easy. We haven't look at the Pen's Mode property, but it's easier to demonstrate that later on in the chapter when we take a look at the graphics drawing methods that are available to you.

For now, though, let's move on to some real graphics.

The Image Component

The Image component is a very powerful component allowing you to load image files off your computer's hard disk and display them on the form. However, because it is a component, you can play around with its properties at run time to produce some interesting effects, such as simple animation, a moving image (around the screen at least), and so on.

Let's take a look at how you will normally set up the Image component when you want to use it.

Try It Out - Preparing the Image Component

1 Create a new application, change to the Additional page of the Component Palette and drop an Image component onto your form so that it looks just like this:

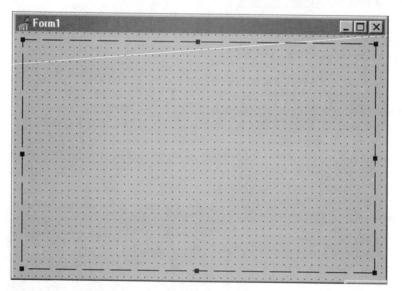

2 Using the Object Inspector, load in a graphic with the help of the Picture property. Locate this property and hit the ellipsis to call up the Picture Editor:

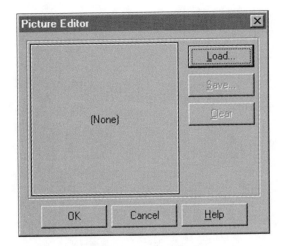

3 Click on the Load... button to bring up the usual File Open dialog with which you can select the appropriate file - I suggest the **wizard.bmp** image that we have supplied on disk. Notice how, as soon as you select an image to display, the Picture Editor dialog changes to show you a preview of the selected image:

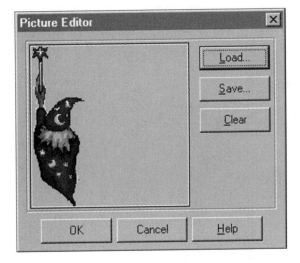

4 All that remains is to click on the OK button to see the picture appear inside the Image component on the form, as shown over the page.

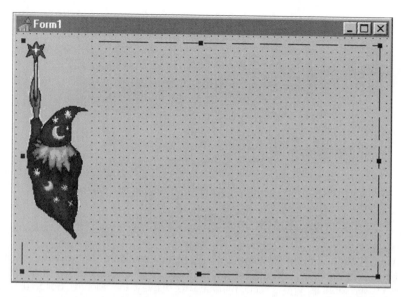

5 Finally, change the AutoSize property to True and we've finished preparing the component:

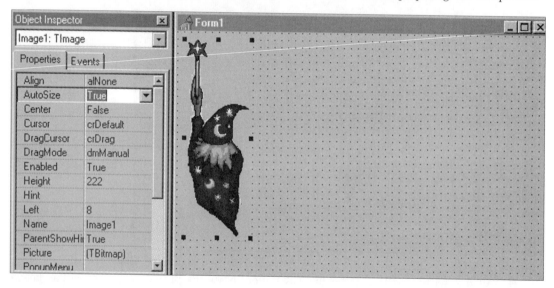

How It Works

As soon as you drop this component onto the form, you'll notice something a little different about it - the only visual clue that this component is there is a thin dotted line marking its outline. That's all it's there to do - the Image component is essentially invisible. It has been designed to display a graphic and that's all - it doesn't have a visible frame or any other 'solid' feature.

To this end, I always find it useful to load in a dummy graphic during design time, or at least to initialize it with its first contents. However, one of the problems with graphics is that they don't necessarily fit the dimensions of our component. The easiest way around this is to set the AutoSize property of the component to True - this makes the component the same size as the graphic and so saves our screen real estate.

One alternative to AutoSize is Stretch. I discussed this property back in Chapter 1, but just as a reminder, it resizes the graphic to fit the current dimensions of the component. Another alternative is to set the Center property to True - this makes the graphic occupy the center of the component at its original dimensions:

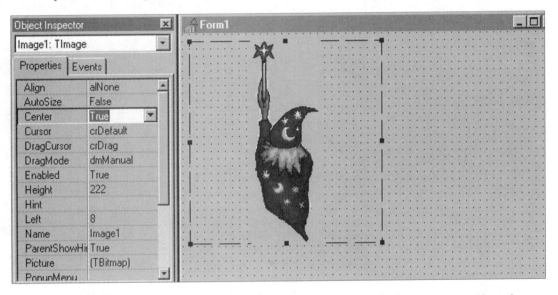

The only other interesting property is Align. This allows you to lock the image control to the top, bottom, left or right-hand edge of the form. At run time, if the user resizes the form, the control will move with the form to remain locked to wherever you aligned it:

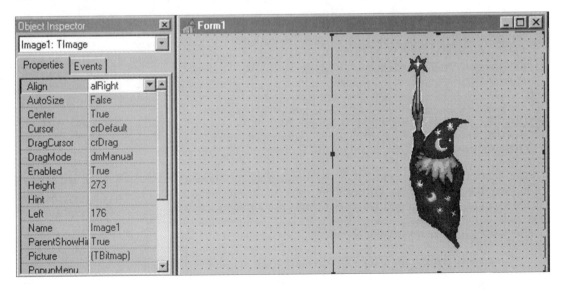

You can also set the Align property to alClient, which causes the control to resize itself to take over the whole of the form. As with the other alignment settings, the control will remain locked and resize itself should the user decide to resize the form at run time.

Anyway, enough of this idle banter - let's see the component at work.

Bringing the Component to Life

I mentioned earlier that you can use the component to create animation. There are two ways to do this (well, three actually if you combine these two, but let's not split hairs).

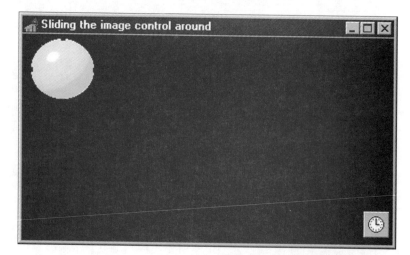

The first is to slide the component around the form at run time using a simple loop or a rather neat Timer component. Load up **slide.dpr** to see what I mean:

The form in this project has just two components on the form; the Image component containing the picture that will slide around at run time and a weird clock symbol in the bottom right.

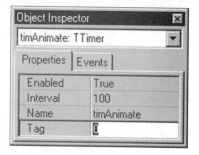

The clock symbol is the Timer component I've just mentioned. The Timer component is rather useful - it triggers an event after a preset amount of time has elapsed. Let's take a closer look:

The Timer component has fewer properties than most, the most important being the Name property and an Interval property which defines the length of time that must elapse between each event.

The Interval property is actually a number referring to thousandths of a second. If we put 1000 in here, the timer will fire an event off every second or so. With a value of 100, as we have in the example, the event will fire every tenth of a second.

But what event are we talking about? Double-click the Timer component:

```
procedure TfrmSliding.timAnimateTimer(Sender: TObject);
var
   nRightEdge : integer;
   nBottomEdge : integer;
```

```
begin
    nRightEdge := frmSliding.ClientWidth - imgBall.Width;
    nBottomEdge := frmSliding.ClientHeight - imgBall.Height;

    if (imgBall.Left + nXSpeed > nRightEdge) or (imgBall.Left + nXSpeed < 0) then
        nXSpeed := 0 - nXSpeed;

    if (imgBall.Top + nYSpeed > nBottomEdge) or (imgBall.Top + nYSpeed < 0 ) then
        nYSpeed := 0 - nYSpeed;

    imgBall.Left := imgBall.Left + nXSpeed;
    imgBall.Top := imgBall.Top + nYSpeed;
end;
```

This code runs every tenth of a second and is really quite simple to decode. The general gist is this: Delphi checks to see where the ball is currently located and thus decides whether to change the direction that it is traveling. After this check, the ball is moved, based on the previous decision. However, this technique would fall apart if we didn't have a way of updating the ball's position on the form.

As you might remember, back in Chapter 2 we used two properties to define exactly where our components should appear; these two properties are Top and Left. Fortunately, Delphi allows us to reset those properties at run time simply by passing them new values - the plot thickens!

This is quite easy, but what values should we pass, and how does Delphi know where to put the component? Well, think back to that math lesson where you were first introduced to graph paper and the idea of coordinates - you remember, the x axis, the y axis, (0, 0) is the origin, and so on. Borland have extended that idea and mapped this coordinate system onto your form. This is what allows us to define two values and so position a component at a given point.

Based on these simple ideas, everything should be fine and dandy, but due to some historical blunder, Delphi has the system origin in the wrong place. Thinking back to that math lesson again, you would expect to have the origin in the bottom left-hand corner. However, Delphi has it in the top left-hand corner. It still counts the x axis correctly but the y axis is positive down the page, so really it just a twisted version of what we all learned in school.

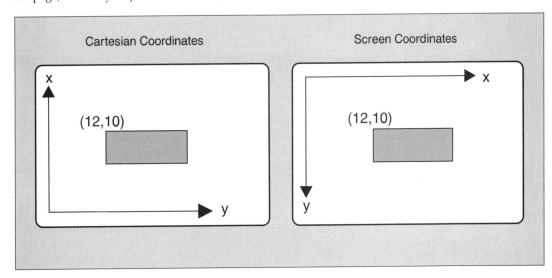

193

After that little lot, let's get back to the code. We've figured out how to locate where the component is and we know we can move it based on some criteria, but what makes up these criteria? Now we could get complex here and start talking about the current angle of travel or the speed of the object, but why bother? We're programmers, so we're supposed to simplify problems, not make them more complex and this venture into trigonometry wouldn't help matters at all.

It's a lot easier to simply break up the problem to ask how far left and how far down we want to move the image. For this reason, I've set up two global variables that contain nothing more than these calculated values:

```
procedure TfrmSliding.FormCreate(Sender: TObject);
begin
    Randomize;
    {Choose a random speed between -10 and 10 for the X
        and Y coordinates of our image}
    nXSpeed := Random(20) - 10;
    nYSpeed := Random(20) - 10;
end;
```

These values are randomly generated between -10 and 10 to give the user a different path each time they run the application. The only change that occurs to these values is during the Timer event when the signs of the variables can be reversed, depending on whether the ball is about to disappear off screen or not - remember that these variables are used to work out where the ball will move to next, so swapping the sign essentially makes the ball 'bounce' off the edge of the screen:

```
    if (imgBall.Left + nXSpeed > nRightEdge) or (imgBall.Left + nXSpeed < 0) then
        nXSpeed := 0 - nXSpeed;

    if (imgBall.Top + nYSpeed > nBottomEdge) or (imgBall.Top + nYSpeed < 0 ) then
        nYSpeed := 0 - nYSpeed;
```

The rest of the code really falls into two separate camps. **nRightEdge** and **nBottomEdge** are two variables which have been declared just for this event handler (**local** variables) and are used to simplify the task of determining the form's boundaries.

```
    nBottomEdge : integer;
begin
    nRightEdge := frmSliding.ClientWidth - imgBall.Width;
    nBottomEdge := frmSliding.ClientHeight - imgBall.Height;

    if (imgBall.Left + nXSpeed > nRightEdge) or (imgBall.Left + nXSpeed < 0) then
        nXSpeed := 0 - nXSpeed;
```

You must remember that our reference to the position of the ball is based upon the location of the top left-hand corner of the Image - if we simply checked to make sure that this point remained on the form, we could have the Image all but disappearing from the screen. In fact, what we have to check is that the whole ball remains on screen, so we have to artificially restrict this square:

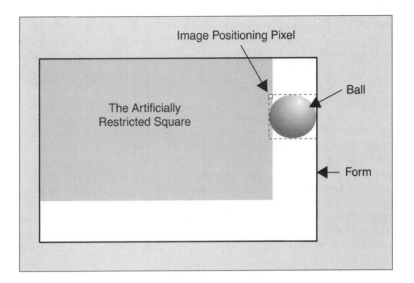

In an attempt to make these conditions slightly more manageable, all these calculations are performed before the conditional part of the **If** statements using properties of the Image component and the form itself. The Image properties are straightforward - we use the Width and Height properties to outline the size of the component - but we must use **ClientWidth** and **ClientHeight** when we talk about the form's dimensions. This is because we only want the ball to move over the normal drawing area of our window, known as the **client area**, and the form could be resized by the user. These two properties refer to this area and are dynamically updated as the form changes shape.

So, the furthest position to the right that the ball can travel is the width of the client area minus the width of the ball image itself. Likewise, the lowest that the ball can travel is the height of the client area minus the height of the ball image.

The second camp details the code that actually moves the Image:

```
if (imgBall.Top + nYSpeed > nBottomEdge) or (imgBall.Top + nYSpeed < 0 ) then
    nYSpeed := 0 - nYSpeed;

    imgBall.Left := imgBall.Left + nXSpeed;
    imgBall.Top := imgBall.Top + nYSpeed;
end;
```

Quite simply, this code simply reassigns the Image component with a new position, based on the old position and the direction and speed of the ball. That's all there is to it!

It's important to notice the order of this code - I checked the position of the image before actually moving it. If I hadn't done this, the ball would occasionally go beyond the form's edge, before being pulled away from the abyss. Not a very good effect, particularly when you consider that Delphi doesn't complain, it just throws up some scroll bars.

Now we come to the crunch - run the program and watch the ball. Two things should strike you. Firstly, the ball is moving quite slow and jerkily - you can change this by reducing the Timer's Interval, the result being that the ball moves faster and the motion appears a little smoother. The second point is that the ball flashes as it moves - a real nasty headache-inducing, low budget kind of flicker.

How do we stop it? Unfortunately, we can't! One of the inherent problems of dealing with the Image component is that it's not the fastest way to display and move graphics around a form. You can get much better results with the TGraphic object that we'll look at in a little while. If it's slick graphic movement you are after, avoid the Image component! It's great for static graphics and displaying pictures at run time, but not that cool when it comes to high performance graphics.

However, we can still play with it a little more to explore the second method of animating an object - changing the graphic on the fly.

Changing the Graphic on the Fly

There are two ways you can change the image on the fly. The first is to use the **LoadPicture** method to load in an image from the disk. Let's leave that till later. The second is to actually copy the image out of another Image component, making use of the component's TPicture object, a member of the fabled TGraphic's family.

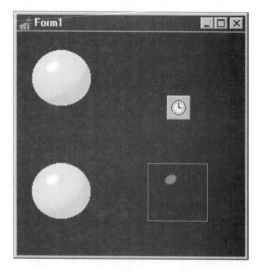

Load up **animate2.dpr** and take a look at what I've done:

This time, we have one Timer and three Image components, one to display the current bitmap and two for storing the resources for the animation. By making the two resource components invisible (both component's Visible properties are set to False), we can hide them away from the user while still having the bitmaps close to hand when we need them. I'm just using the Timer to regulate the switch between the resource bitmaps held in the two hidden components and the display Image.

If you run the program, you can see this image flipping taking place, with the ball periodically changing from the blue *on* image to the black *off* image. If you stop the program running and double-click on the Timer component, you can see the simplicity of the code for yourself:

```
procedure TForm1.timAnimateTimer(Sender: TObject);
begin
    if bImage then
        imgAnimate.Picture := imgOn.Picture
    else
        imgAnimate.Picture := imgOff.Picture;

    bImage := NOT bImage;

end;
```

bImage is a global variable declared elsewhere in the code. As you can see from the **b** prefix, it's a Boolean variable, so will only ever be True or False, which makes any **If** clauses that deal with it quite simple, as we saw in Chapter 1.

The code checks **bImage**. If the value is True, the picture in **imgOn** is copied to the visible Image component, **imgAnimate**. If it's False, the picture in **imgOff** is copied over. This is really easy to do, and involves nothing more than copying the **Picture** property from one component to another.

```
imgAnimate.Picture := imgOff.Picture;
```

As you may already have guessed, though, the **Picture** property is really an object with its own methods and properties. This object, in fact, encapsulates a TGraphic object under the disguise of its own Graphic property which allows you to store any of the usual types of graphic in your Image component, i.e. bitmaps, metafiles or icons. However, by just asking Delphi to copy one **Picture** over another, we are really implying that Delphi should copy the graphic contained in the TGraphic object from one to another - we don't have to be explicit in our request.

You might be wondering why we need a **TPicture** object between **TImage** and **TGraphic** if **TGraphic** does all the hard work. Well, in true OOP style, **TPicture** brings its own functionality to the party in terms of methods and properties that allow the **TImage** component not only to deal with the usual types of graphic held on disk, but also to handle them if they are being stored on the Clipboard. Check out Delphi's help under **Picture** for more details.

The final line of code sets **bImage** to whatever it is not; if it's True, it becomes False, if it's False, it becomes True.

Of course, this is a very simple example - it only deals with animating between two frames. With only a small increase in the complexity of the code, we could have the animation run over any number of frames, although playing with more than three Image components can not only be bad for your health, it can also greatly increase the memory footprint of your application.

However, one of the biggest problems with this type of animation is redrawing the screen. To illustrate this, I've included one more example of using the Image component for animation. Load up **tlights.dpr** and run it.

As you can see, this is a common or garden traffic light. Choose your country and click on the Start button to see the light in action. You should see that when the lights are turned off, you get a flicker as the screen tries to keep up with the demands of the CPU.

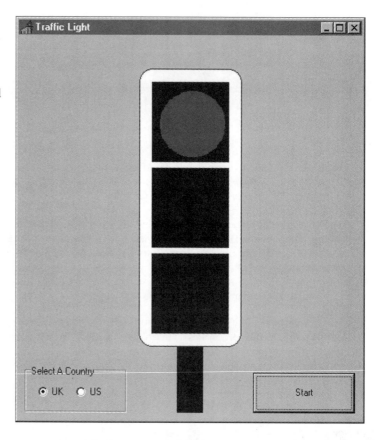

It wasn't my intention to describe the code behind this application, but a quick guided tour might be quite useful - take a look at the source code for a more detailed discussion.

I've used two global variables, **bStop** and **iCounter**. **bStop** is used to indicate which end of the Traffic Light we are currently working at, while **iCounter** is used to decide which lights should be illuminated - note that we use the value of **bStop** to decide whether **iCounter** should be increased or decreased when a timer event is generated.

To actually control the lights, I've used one *on* image for each light and a generic mask to act as an *off* image. To turn a light on we use the same technique as before - we simply copy the *on* image onto the display image component. To turn it off again, simply apply the mask in the same way.

I've used a **Case** statement to decide which set of lights should be turned on and which should be turned off, and just to add another level of difficulty, I've included a country selection GroupBox so you have more control over the Traffic Light. The **Case** statement also deals with this selection, using a number of **If** statements to check a variety of conditions and illuminate or extinguish the appropriate lights.

However, all this clever code doesn't get around the fact that the underlying technique isn't that great. As we'll see, it's much better to use TGraphic objects.

Using the TGraphic Object

The TGraphic object provides your application with all the functionality that you can find inside the Image component, but without the overhead of the component itself. Unlike the component, you can create arrays of graphics (ideal for dealing with frames of animation); you can paint the images anywhere on the form;. you can produce copies of the graphic on the form without having to create additional components, and much, much more. As an extra, but none the less important, bonus, this object also works a lot faster than the Image component. All in all, it's just a whole lot smarter to work with TGraphic objects rather than Image components.

Think back to the previous chapter on objects, classes and such like. TGraphic is nothing more than a foundation class for some other kinds of graphic object. Most Windows applications know how to deal with three kinds of graphic data; icons, bitmaps and metafiles. It makes sense then that the general functionality of the TGraphic class (which allows you to load and save pictures from disk, and so on) should be inherited by specific classes designed to deal with each specific data type.

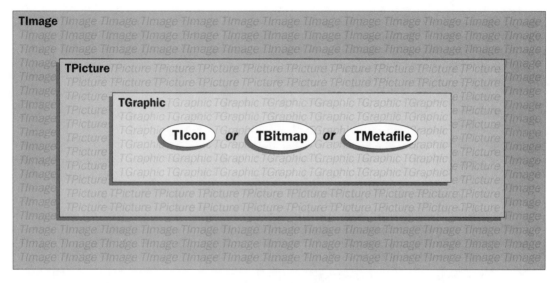

When you use any of the higher level TGraphic-based objects to work with graphics, you are essentially using the same set of methods and properties - those provided by TGraphic. To make life a little simpler, and because of this similarity, I'm only going to take a look at TBitmap objects and the generic properties and methods they provide.

Some of the more advanced animation-related topics, such as the complexities of changing a graphics palette, and so on, are a little beyond the scope of this book, so if you intend to do some really heavy graphics work, you really should take a look at *Beginning Delphi Games* **from Wrox Press.**

So, without further ado, let's look at a much nicer version of our bouncing ball program, this time using the faster, slicker TBitmap object.

Try It Out - Bouncing with a TBitmap Object

1 Save (using File | Save Project As...) the project that you currently have open (if any) and start a new application. Save this project as **bounce2u.pas** and **bounce2.dpr**.

2 Drop a Timer component (System page of the Component Palette) onto your form, change its Name to timAnimate and its Interval to 1.

3 Now complete the user interface by renaming the form as frmBounce2, its Caption to A much nicer bounce (using TBitmap) and its Color to clBlack. Finally, change the WindowState property to wsMaximized so that the window maximizes when the application is created. Now for the code!

4 We'll need five local variables to handle our animation, two to define the current position, two to define the image's speed and one to define the image itself. Add these lines to your unit:

```
implementation

{$R *.DFM}
```

```
var
    nXCoord : integer;      { Holds the graphics X coordinate  (Left) }
    nYCoord : integer;      { Holds the graphics Y coordinate  (Top)  }
    nXSpeed : integer;      { Holds the X speed }
    nYSpeed : integer;      { Holds the Y speed }
    Ball    : TBitmap;      { The graphic object itself - create before use}
```

5 Now for the rest of the code that makes use of these variables. First things first - we need to initialize these variables, and what better place than in the OnCreate event of the form. Double-click on the form and add the following lines of code to the form's default event handler:

```
procedure TfrmBounce2.FormCreate(Sender: TObject);
begin
    randomize;

    nXCoord := Abs(Random(ClientWidth) - 75);
    nYCoord := Abs(Random(ClientHeight) - 75);
    nXSpeed := Random(20) - 10 ;
    nYSpeed := Random(20) - 10 ;

    Ball := TBitmap.Create;
    Ball.LoadFromFile('ball.bmp');
end;
```

6 The next task is to organize the code that handles the actual movement of the graphic. All of this code is exactly the same as the previous version of the program, except for the last line which actually handles the drawing of the object on the screen. Double-click on the Timer component and add this code to the component's default event handler:

```
procedure TfrmBounce2.timAnimateTimer(Sender: TObject);
begin
    if ( nXCoord + nXSpeed < 0 ) or
       ( nXCoord + nXSpeed > frmBounce2.ClientWidth - Ball.Width) then
            nXSpeed := 0 - nXSpeed;

    if ( nYCoord + nYSpeed < 0 ) or
       ( nYCoord + nYSpeed > frmBounce2.ClientHeight - Ball.Height) then
            nYSpeed := 0 - nYSpeed;

    nXCoord := nXCoord + nXSpeed;
    nYCoord := nYCoord + nYSpeed;
```

```
        frmBounce2.Canvas.Draw( nXCoord, nYCoord, Ball);
end;
```

7 The final step to this Try It Out is to make sure that the object that we created when we built the form is destroyed when the form is destroyed. Select the form, swap over to the Object Inspector's Events page, double-click on the OnDestroy event and add this code:

```
procedure TfrmBounce2.FormDestroy(Sender: TObject);
begin
     Ball.Free;
end;
```

To get the application to run successfully, you'll need to copy the file supplied on the disk, called **ball.bmp**, into your project's directory. When you do this and run it, you should see something like this:

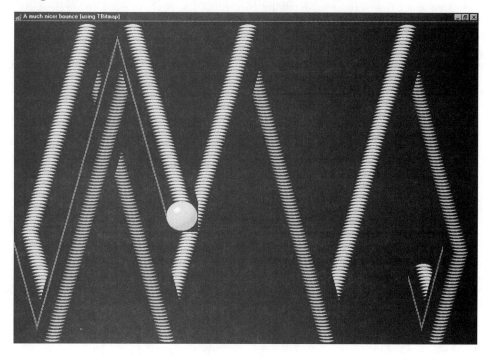

How It Works

There are a couple of important differences between this and the previous bouncing ball program we saw. First of all, the ball in this program leaves a trail behind it. You have to bear in mind that TBitmap objects (or TIcon, TMetafile, or TPicture objects for that matter) are not components. If you use an Image component, you have a single entity on the form that you simply move around to get the impression of animation.

In contrast, TBitmap objects only hold their data in memory - it's not visible on screen. You can make that data (in this case, a bitmap image) visible by calling up the **Draw** method, but all that does is to draw the data on the screen. It still lives in memory - you have just drawn a 'likeness' on the form. Drawing another 'likeness' in a different position gives the impression of two graphic objects - it doesn't automatically remove the first image. The truth, though, is that there are no graphic objects on the form at all, you have just drawn one object twice.

In this program, the image is drawn over and over as it moves around the form. The reason for the trail is simply that I haven't told Delphi to draw a black image to erase the previous visible image. TGraphic objects have a **Draw** method, but a major shortfall in my opinion is that they don't have an **UnDraw** or **MoveImage** method. You'll see how to clear an area of a form in the next section where we talk about using Delphi's graphic methods. For now, though, let's concentrate on the code.

There are only three things that I've got to mention about this code as a lot of it was pillaged from the last example, but each point is really important, explaining a little more of the OOP puzzle.

As we hinted in the code, the first thing to mention is that you need to initialize an object variable just as if it was any other kind of variable. This might seem obvious on the surface, but it's a step that confuses and upsets novices and professional alike. In the implementation section of our code, we have told Delphi that we may want an **TBitmap** object in the future, and when we do, we want it to be called **Ball**.

However, it doesn't actually exist until we actually tell Delphi to create it using the following code:

```
Ball := TBitmap.Create;
```

If you try to run the application with this line commented out, you'll see a spectacular compiler run-time error.

Now that we have created the object, it's a good idea to finish off its initialization by loading the bitmap into it. We do this with the following line of code that should be familiar to you from Chapter 1:

```
Ball.LoadFromFile('ball.bmp');
```

The second point to consider also relates to us manually creating this object - until you actually create the object, it doesn't exist, so you can't refer to it!! Again, this is apparently obvious, but it can cause the unsuspecting programmer a few problems.

For example, because of the way in which we ordered the code, we had to hard code the size of the bitmap into the following lines of code to make sure that all of the ball appears on screen when the form is first created:

```
nXCoord := Abs(Random(ClientWidth) - 75);
nYCoord := Abs(Random(ClientHeight) - 75);
```

Of course, this is quite a bad programming technique, because if the user changes the size of **ball.bmp**, it won't all be displayed unless you change these values in the source code and recompile. Fortunately, it's quite easy to adapt the code to avoid this problem - you simply create the object before initializing these variables and use **Ball.Width** and **Ball.Height** - but I needed a good example of what happens if you create your objects in the wrong order!

You should take on board from the the source code's comments that I had to use the **Abs** function to ensure that the value assigned to these variables was always positive and therefore on the form. You should watch out for this kind of problem when you are performing calculations that include a subtraction in your own programs.

The final point to consider is based around the contents of the form's OnDestroy event handler:

```
procedure TfrmBounce2.FormDestroy(Sender: TObject);
begin
    Ball.Free;
end;
```

When you place a component on a form and run the application, Delphi automatically takes charge of creating and destroying all the objects required by that component. When you start creating objects manually, Delphi doesn't provide this vital service for your objects, so you must destroy any objects that you create.

 Note that Delphi continues to manage its objects, not just the ones that you created manually. You mind your own business and leave Delphi to mind its own.

This is quite an important subject because each time that you create an object, you are allocating a little bit of your computer's memory to deal with it. If you don't destroy this object when you have finished with it, you are essentially condemning that memory to be locked away from your global pool forever - actually it's only until you turn off the computer, but that's not the point.

 This subject is so important that Borland have created a Pascal code structure to ensure that, even if something goes wrong before you have chance to destroy your objects, the task is still completed. The structure is called a **try...finally** block and I cover it in Chapter 7.

You might think that the amount of memory that computers come with today is so large that wasting a little bit until you turn the computer off at the end of the day might not be a problem. However, consider the following circumstances:

▶ Your program is working on a server that is never turned off, never mind about the end of the day.

▶ You are creating an object within a loop or within a popular event handler.

▶ The computer that the completed application will run on isn't as powerful as the one that you are developing on.

▶ Your program has been developed to run on Windows 95 (or NT) which is a system that allows the user to run a lot of applications at the same time, and if they all waste memory every time a new one started up....

Hopefully, all these reasons should make you think twice about introducing a 'memory leak' into your applications and, besides, it's not the tidy way to work - and as you know, software developers are the tidiest people in the world!

203

Drawing on a Form

In the last example, I used an object and a method of that object to get our ball draw at the appropriate position on the form. The object was called **Canvas**, and its method was called **Draw**:

```
frmBounce2.Canvas.Draw( nXCoord, nYCoord, Ball);
```

Quite simply, the **Canvas** is the drawing surface, in this case, of the **frmBounce2** form, upon which our image can be drawn and the **Draw** method is the procedure which actually does all the hard work. The first two parameters passed to the **Draw** method are the x and y coordinates that specify where we want to draw the final parameter, which is name of our **Bitmap** object. Simple enough!

Unfortunately, because Delphi is such a versatile language, you aren't restricted to one method for putting your image onto the canvas - you have to decide exactly how you want the image to look when you paint it - what a pain!

StretchDraw

One of the methods that Delphi offers you is called **StretchDraw**. This method actually allows you to specify the part of a bitmap (or icon, or metafile, or...) that you want to paint, and also to resize that selection however you like. For example, try changing the **Draw** code in our new and improved **Bounce** program so that it looks like this:

```
frmBounce2.Canvas.StretchDraw(rect(nXCoord,  nYCoord,
                              nXCoord + 200, nYCoord + 200),
                              Ball);
```

Now run the application and you should see something like this:

StretchDraw takes just two parameters; a **TRect** parameter which defines the size of the new object, and the object that you want to draw. As you should remember, a **TRect** object is basically a record defining the position and size of a rectangle. The image that you want to draw is resized so that it fits this rectangle precisely, then it's drawn to the screen.

> Obviously, because you have total control over both the source image and the target rectangle, and the method automatically stretches the content of the image to fit the rectangle, the **StretchDraw** method also lets you perform some weird stretch effects on the image.

However, rather than muck about setting up **TRect** variables and filling them in, we can use the coordinates of the top left and bottom right corners of our rectangle in the **Rect** function. This in turn returns a **TRect** value which can be used by **StretchDraw** in place of the explicit **TRect** object it expects.

StretchDraw is an ideal method to use for the inevitable time when you need to write a program where the sizes of graphics on your forms must always be the same, no matter what screen resolution the user is running.

CopyRect

The final method available for drawing a bitmap onto a canvas is the **CopyRect** procedure. Unlike the other two methods, though, this one will let you copy a portion of a bitmap onto a form, ideal for example, if you want to use some rather weird fonts stored in a bitmap, or if you want a load of animation frames stored within a single bitmap. You can even use the **CopyRect** method to write a very simple graphics scroller.

To see what I mean, load up **scroller.dpr** and run it:

The program loads in a large bitmap and then scrolls it from left to right within the form so that you eventually get to see all of it. However, at any one time, the form will only display a small part of it, i.e. the rectangle that you tell **CopyRect** to display.

Take a look at the code behind the Timer component to see what it does:

```
procedure TfrmScroll.timScrollTimer(Sender: TObject);
begin
    if (nXCoord < 0) or (nXCoord + frmScroll.ClientWidth > ScrollGfx.Width) then
        nXSpeed := 0 - nXSpeed;

    nXCoord := nXCoord + nXSpeed;

    frmScroll.Canvas.CopyRect(
        Rect(0, 0, frmScroll.ClientWidth, ScrollGfx.Height),
        ScrollGfx.Canvas,
        Rect(nXCoord, 0, nXCoord + frmScroll.ClientWidth, ScrollGfx.Height));
end;
```

As with our familiar bouncing ball code, we have two global variables. The **X** coordinate is the coordinate within the graphic from which we wish to extract the data, and the **Speed** is the speed of the scroll. Each time this code runs, the **Speed** is added to the **X** coordinate, meaning that we effectively are looking at the bitmap through a moving window.

As you can see from the **CopyRect** line, we need three parameters: the destination rectangle to paint into, the canvas to copy from, and the rectangle within that canvas to copy. In the case of both the source and destination rectangles, the width of the area copied is always the width of the form itself.

Note that I keep the height of the graphic at a constant so that we get a horizontal scroll with no vertical movement.

When I was writing this code, I actually introduced a little bug which has quite a nice effect. **CopyRect** will stretch or squash an image just like **StretchDraw** if the source rectangle and the destination rectangle are different sizes. If, when you specify the source rectangle, you set the bottom right-hand corner of the rectangle to a fixed position, you end up with a stretchy-squashy scroller.

Change the code in our example to reflect this line of code and run the application:

```
frmScroll.Canvas.CopyRect(
          Rect( 0, 0, frmScroll.ClientWidth, ScrollGfx.Height),
          ScrollGfx.Canvas,
          Rect( nXCoord, 0, frmScroll.ClientWidth, ScrollGfx.Height) );
```

It's worth spending a little time playing around with the things you pick up in this chapter - some of them are good fun.

Using TGraphic's Methods

Aside from the graphical objects and the components that Delphi provides to help you deal with this topic, it also has a wide range of built in graphical methods that enable you to create art on the fly, without having to use pre-built images on the computer's hard disk.

Before we dive into a discussion of each of these, though, it's worth taking a look at some of the bigger issues surrounding graphics in Windows.

Coordinates

I've already discussed the coordinate system that Delphi uses, the same coordinate system that is represented by the grid of dots that appears on the form. Some of the tools that Delphi provides are directly related to this system, such as Snap to grid, but you don't have to use this system if you don't want to.

It's possible to make Delphi, or rather Windows, use a coordinate system that doesn't directly relate to the dots you see on the screen, but that really is a little beyond the scope of this book. Let's keep things simple for the time being.

Getting Colorful

Being able to draw graphics is a great thing, but unless you add a little color, your users soon start to get bored. Unfortunately, specifying colors for a computer can be little tricky. Remember, some video cards in PCs are capable of displaying literally millions of colors. We can't refer to a color as being a 'slightly greenish shade of blue' since that isn't accurate enough. On the other hand, we can't give every possible color a unique number, since there is no way that any programmer would be able to deal with that lot effectively. What is needed is some form of easy to use, memorable color numbering system.

If you think back to your first days at school, you may remember the teacher telling you something about primary colors: red, blue and yellow. Using these colors, you're supposed to be able to paint any color you can imagine. Computers work in a very similar way, but their primary colors are red, green and blue.

When you need to tell the PC to draw something in a new color, all you have to do is tell the computer how much red, green and blue to put into the color. It's a little more complex than that, though, in that you need to turn these three values into one all-encompassing number.

Luckily, there's a function built into Windows, called **RGB**, that can help.

Load up **colors.dpr** and run it:

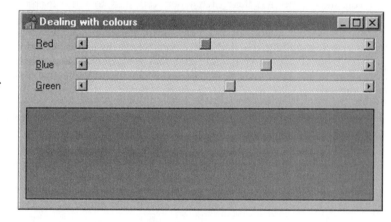

The form includes three ScrollBars, one each for red, green and blue, and a Shape component, the color of which changes in response to the ScrollBar movements. Have a play for a while, then stop the program and bring up the Object Inspector to see the events linked to the ScrollBars.

All the ScrollBars in this program have their OnScroll event linked to a routine called **ScrollbarScroll**. Double-click on the event in the Object Inspector to see the code - just one line of code is all that we need to set up the color of the Shape component.

```
procedure TfrmColours.ScrollbarScroll(Sender: TObject; ScrollCode: TScrollCode;
                                      var ScrollPos: Integer);
begin
   Shape.Brush.Color := RGB(scrRed.Position, scrGreen.Position, scrBlue.Position);
end;
```

To change the color of the shape, you'll recall that you need to change the Shape's Brush Color. This is quite easy - throw the red, green and blue values at the **RGB** function, which returns a number that can be fed into any Color property.

The **RGB** function expects the values you pass it to be between 0 and 255. For example, if you pass 255, 255, 255 to **RGB**, the resulting color number just happens to correspond to bright white. Likewise, if you pass 0, 0, 0, then the resulting number corresponds to black.

 Don't worry if your video card can't handle many colors - Windows automatically handles mapping the color you ask for to the closest color that your card can handle. You can see this matching when you create a custom color in a Color dialog - adjacent pixels are different colors and shades to give the required overall look.

Delphi's Color Constants

Delphi also has a great many built-in color constants which you can specify in your code directly. For example, **clBlack** is the color black, **clWhite** is white, and so on. However, these color constants come into their own when you start to write user-aware applications.

Under Windows 95, users can use the Control Panel to change almost any aspect of Windows look and feel, including the standard colors to use in almost every component of the user interface. What if your user has decided that gray is dull, and so on her machine all buttons appear as purple? Your code really should pick up stuff like this, and these color constants listed below can help:

clBackground	clActiveCaption	clInactiveCaption
clMenu	clWindow	clWindowsFrame
clMenuText	clWindowText	clCaptionText
clActiveBorder	clInactiveBorder	clAppWorkSpace
clHighlight	clHighlightText	clBtnFace
clBtnShadow	clGrayText	clBtnText
clInActiveCaptionText	clBtnHighlight	

Each of these constants returns a color value matching that which the user has chosen using the Windows 95 Control Panel. All these color constants can be fed direct into any Color property you come across.

Writing applications that only use these constants where necessary can be a real pain in the butt. But at the end of the day, it does make for a very friendly application that goes some way to becoming fully Windows compliant. Your users will love you for it!

Drawing Things

On with the show. There are a number of ways to draw things onto a form at run time without resorting to using an Image component or a TGraphic-type object. If you intend to draw on a component, you really need to deal with its TCanvas object. For example, to draw on a form, you must call drawing methods attached to the form's **Canvas**.

The table below lists some of the methods available to you:

Method	Description
MoveTo	Takes an *x* and *y* value (making a coordinate) and moves the drawing pen to the specified position ready to start drawing.
LineTo	Takes an *x* and *y* value (making a coordinate) and draws a line from the pen's current position to the one specified by the coordinates.
Rectangle	Takes two coordinates, which are used to specify the position of the top left and bottom right-hand corner of the rectangle.
RoundRect	Takes two coordinates, which are used to specify first the position of the top left and bottom right-hand corners of the rectangle. The final two parameters are used to round the corners of the rectangle using quarter ellipses. The ellipse is generated using the first parameter as the width and the second as the height.
Ellipse	Takes two coordinates which specify the top left and bottom right corner of a rectangle that could be drawn around the ellipse. The rectangle is not actually drawn, but just defines the shape and size of the ellipse.
Arc	Takes four coordinates to draw the arc. The first two define the bounding rectangle in the same way as an ellipse. If you could draw lines from the third and fourth set to the center of this rectangle, the arc is drawn from the points on these lines where they intercept the ellipse defined by the rectangle.
Pie	Draws a pie chart segment from the four sets of coordinates passed to the routine. The first two define the rectangle which, in turn, defines the shape of the original ellipse. The pie is then determined by the two lines radiating from the center of the ellipse through the points defined by the third and fourth coordinates.

Rather than show you a set of seven programs to demonstrate each routine, let's work through a small example to give you some hands-on experience of how to use the most common methods.

Try It Out - Using the TGraphic's Methods.

1 Create a new project in Delphi, saving the old existing project if you have one - you might want to look at it later.

2 Add the following code to the form's OnClick event handler:

```
procedure TForm1.FormClick(Sender: TObject);
begin
With Form1.Canvas do
   begin
      Pen.Color := clBlack;
```

```
        MoveTo(10,10);
        LineTo(150,150);
    end;
end;
```

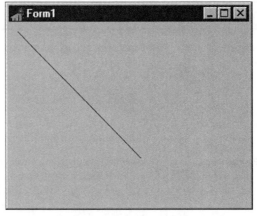

3 Run the application, click on the form and see what you've created:

4 Stop the program running and get back to our event handler. Let's add in a **Rectangle** statement to draw a rectangle on the form:

```
        LineTo(150,150);

        Brush.Color := clBlue;
        Rectangle(150,150, 200, 200);
    end;
```

5 Run the application again and see how our Picasso is going:

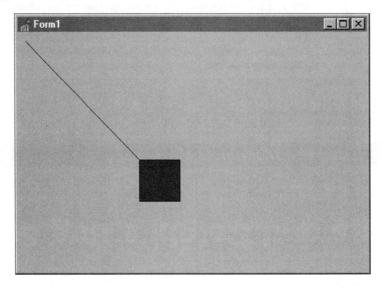

6 Stop the application again and add something else. This time, it's an ellipse:

```
Brush.Color := clBlue;
Rectangle (150, 150, 200, 200);
Ellipse (10, 10, 90, 170);
end;
```

Again run the application, and start spending the millions:

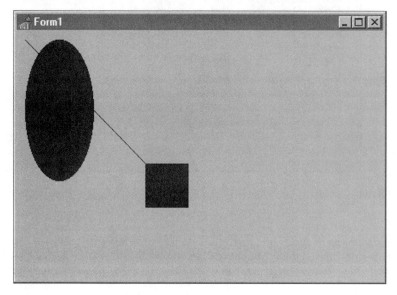

7 Well that completes the basic additions to our masterpiece, but before we call Sotherby's, let's try one more thing. Add the following lines of code:

```
procedure TForm1.FormClick(Sender: TObject);
begin
     With Form1.Canvas do
     begin
          Pen.Color := clBlack;
          MoveTo(10,10);
          LineTo(150,150);

          Brush.Color := clBlue;
          Rectangle(150,150, 200, 200);

          Ellipse(10,10,90,170);

          Pen.Mode := pmXor;
          Ellipse(0, 0, 100, 100);

     end;
end;
```

If you run the code now, you'll see some very weird results.

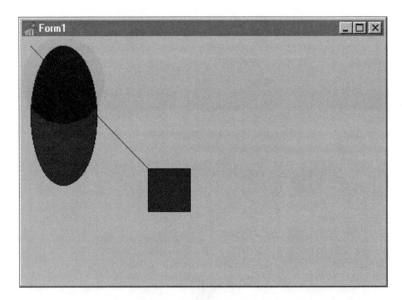

What's going on?

How It Works

All of these graphical methods are pretty straightforward; **MoveTo** moves the pen around the screen without drawing anything, **LineTo** does the same thing, except that this time, a line is drawn between the pen's starting point and that given to the **LineTo** procedure.

Rectangle and **Ellipse** are even simpler - just give Delphi four integers and it will draw the rectangle, while an ellipse is 'best-fitted' into this bounding rectangle. But what, as the question asked, is going on with the last addition to our masterpiece?

Instead of the last ellipse statement simply drawing another circle on the screen, what you actually get is a kind of faded circle appearing on the form, not covering anything that was there before, but almost casting a shadow over it.

This is thanks to the Pen's **Mode** property which determines how the graphics are to be drawn on the canvas. Its default setting is the Delphi constant known as **pmCopy**, which means that any drawing you do is copied directly on to the canvas exactly as you would expect it to appear, hence why we didn't notice anything strange happening with the first shapes.

However, when it comes to this final ellipse, we change the value of this property to **pmXor**, one of the sixteen possible settings for the a Pen's Mode. What **pmXor** does is to tell Delphi to combine the color it is trying to draw with any colors it finds at the drawing location on the canvas. The result is that the colors are mixed.

Obviously, we haven't got room here to go into detail on every one of the possible Pen settings, but they can be quite good fun to play with. Do a search for the word Mode in Delphi's help files to see what other values you have available to you.

Pixels

Aside from the graphical methods I've just covered, you can also get at the individual pixels on an object's canvas. Attached to the canvas is a multi-dimensional array called **Pixels** which you can use to find or set the color of any dot on the canvas. For example, if you wanted to set the top left-hand dot to black, you could write

```
Form1.Canvas.Pixels[0,0] := cmBlack;
```

Likewise, if you wanted to find out the color of the pixel at position (**100,100**), you could write:

```
nColour := Form1.Canvas.Pixels[100,100] ;
```

This is by far the easiest way to get directly at the information contained on a canvas, and it is also one of the fastest for dealing with individual dots in the canvas. Try writing some code of your own to get a feel for how it works. You could revamp the ball bouncing code once again, but this time to bounce dots around the screen. Have fun.

Summary

In this chapter, I've just touched upon some of the techniques that you can use in your Delphi animation projects. This can be a fascinating topic and a lot of fun, and I would recommend that you play around with it for a while - creating your own paint package might not be what you are looking for, but a small animation might make your application stand out from the crowd.

This topic does come up again in Chapter 13 when we discuss multimedia in Delphi, but I would urge you to look out for *Beginning Delphi Games* (also from Wrox Press) if you are interested in taking this subject further.

For now, let's get on to the subject of debugging your applications.

Bugs and Delphi's Bug Spray

No matter how good you are at using Delphi, or how much development experience you have, you'll always find yourself writing buggy code. Thankfully, computers and programming have been around long enough for the brighter sparks to come up with ways of guarding against the bugs, or at least to make it easier for you to track them down and fix them.

In addition to the vast arsenal that I've already discussed, Delphi has a very powerful set of tools specifically designed to not only hunt the bugs down, but also to help prevent them appearing in the first place. The run-time debugger effectively allows you to dissect your application while it's in motion, while the Object Repository helps to reduce bugs by allowing developers to use previously tried and tested libraries of code. Should any problems slip through this net, you can rely on Delphi's exception (error) handling facilities to provide you with a nice safe way to catch any problems and prevent them from doing something nasty to your user's machine at run time.

In this chapter, I'm going to look at the whole process of not only writing bug-free code (or as near to it as we can reasonably expect), but also at each of the tools that Delphi provides to help you out.

You will learn:

▶ Some of the bug reducing theory behind OOP development

▶ How to use the integrated debugger

▶ What conditional compilation is and how to use it

▶ What exception handling is and how to write your own exception handlers

It's worth bearing in mind that, while none of this is essential to achieving the required programming results, an understanding will help you produce really high quality durable code with which your users will feel so much more secure.

Dealing with Exceptions

As the name would suggest, **exceptions** are those nasty times when the code you write doesn't work as you planned. Being budding gurus (like I know you all are), these moments should constitute the exception rather than the rule, but still they can be quite annoying.

Let's take a look at a few lines of code that could prove to be disastrous. If you load up **division.dpr** and take a look around, you'll quickly work out that it was designed as a quick division program. It takes in two integers from the user, divides one number by the other when the user presses the Do The Math button and displays the answer. Take a particularly close look at the code behind the button's OnClick event:

```
procedure TfrmDivision.cmdDivideClick(Sender: TObject);
var
    Number1 : real;
    Number2 : real;
    Result  : real;
    sResult : string;
    ErrorCode : integer;
begin
    val(txtNumber1.text, Number1, ErrorCode);
    val(txtNumber2.text, Number2, ErrorCode);

    Result := Number1 / Number2;

    str(Result, sResult);
    txtResult.Text := sResult;
end;
```

At first glance, it may appear quite innocuous, and indeed, if you hit *Ctrl+F9*, it does compile. If you run the application from Explorer (don't run it in from inside Delphi yet), when you enter some integers into the first two edit boxes and hit the button, it will give you the correct answers. Try it with say, 10 and 5, or 35 and 7. It will even handle decimal results - try 40 and 7:

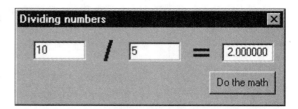

The problem comes when you try to do something naughty, like divide by zero. All the mathematicians out there will have been shaking their heads since they first looked at the code, having noted the potential disaster on the horizon. However, this might come as quite a surprise to the rest of us mere mortals. Ah well, let's try it out anyway. Try out 10, 0 and click the button:

What's happening? We didn't code this message box into our application! Where has it come from? Hopefully, if you've been following my code word for word and letter for letter, you have just experienced your first exception, and indeed, the results of your first exception handler!

What's Going On?

When you are considering Delphi, an exception could be anything from a simple File not found error when you try to open a file, to something much more serious, like an application error that crashes your app, taking Windows with it.

We've just generated an EZeroDivide error which is greeted with horror by Delphi, the operating system and most of the world of mathematics. In fact, the operating system is so unhappy that it throws a wobbly and attempts to crash your application. If you had been using C++, it would have succeeded, but we're using Delphi and things are a little more relaxed over here.

What, in fact, happens is that your application picks up on the fact that the operating system is trying to do unmentionable things to it, and generates a new object to encapsulate the system's requests. It then looks for a way to avoid an unceremonious death by pushing this exception object around in your application until all the code is checked, or an appropriate exception handler is found.

If it can't find an exception handler, the application gives up the ghost and lets the operating system pick up the pieces (or crash itself!). However, if it does, it calms down the operating system and runs some user defined code to recover from this embarrassing state of affairs.

But hang on! We didn't code any exception handling into our app! Why does this message box turn up? Well, the answer to your question is quite simply that your Delphi application comes complete with some basic exception handling already built-in. Ain't this system just great? First, it practically writes the code for you and then helps tidy up any mess that the user makes without you hardly touching the keyboard!

Checking Out the Integrated Debugger

Do you remember that I said that you must run the application from Explorer? You *could* have seen the same results if you had run the application from inside Delphi, but you would have had your first, completely uninvited visit from Delphi's jumpy integrated debugger, a scary thing when you are expecting it, let alone when you've not met it before.

To take a look at this beastie, load up the project into Delphi and hit that Run button!

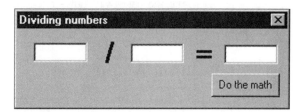

Scared ya!! Remember that the application compiles fine! It's not the compiler that complains - the code is syntactically okay. The problem only comes when you try to do something that the system doesn't like, like divide by zero. Go on, try it, dare ya:

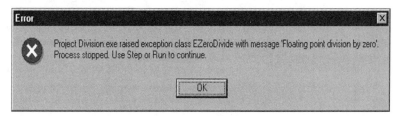

Nice dialog, isn't it? Fortunately, it does indicate a number of things that Delphi's built-in exception handler doesn't:

⏵ It warns of the impending doom.

⏵ It indicates the reason for the problem and the intermediary solution - an EZeroDivide class instantiation.

⏵ It documents the 'in-house' exception handler result - a message along the lines of 'Floating point division by zero'.

⏵ It mentions that the process has been stopped.

⏵ It also mentions what you've got to do next to remedy the situation.

Dealing with the Integrated Debugger

When the integrated debugger detects an exception being raised, it automatically steps in and takes control of the application - in effect, it freezes the application, jumps into the code, locates the trouble and digs around in the exception object to find out why the trouble has occurred in the first place.

It then presents this information to you in a less than pleasant fashion - the dialog - and re-activates the IDE to let you take control of the situation. From here you have two choices - you can either take the debugger's hint and use some of its features to slowly proceed through the rest of the code, or you can select Run | Program Reset (*Ctrl+F2*) to close the application down and return to the design environment.

Note that you can turn off this default behaviour of the integrated debugger if you wish. If you deselect the check mark in the Break on exception option on the Environment Options dialog (Tools | Options..., Preferences tab), you will be able to run and compile your application, type in the fault data and see Delphi's built-in exception handler, without the integrated debugger jumping in and spoiling the show.

For now, let's take the easy way out - after all, we know what the problem is - and go with the latter option. I'll come back to the debugger's options a little later when I investigate a more complex example.

An Exceptional Analogy

Before we take a look at the specifics of dealing with exceptions, it's worth noting that there are really two ways to deal with errors. I call them 'after the fact' and 'before the fact' processing. With 'after the fact' processing, your code gives you an error and, in response, you fire up some prewritten code to deal with it....

There's a famous story of a guy who, as he stands by a river fishing one day, notices a woman drowning. Without thinking, he dives in and rescues her. When he returns to the bank, he sees another woman drowning, so he jumps back in and rescues her, too. To cut a long story short, he's at this rescuing lark all afternoon. This is 'after the fact' exception handling: the guy has noticed a problem and jumps in to stop it getting worse. If he had decided to deal with the error 'before the fact', he would have walked up river, found the guy who was throwing the women into the river and punched him on the nose.

In our example program, 'before the fact' would mean writing code to check the data entered into the text boxes to make sure that (a) it is a number, and (b) the number is always non-zero - *before* we do the division. Exception handling (a.k.a. 'after the fact' error handling) adds a lot of stability to your application, but is no substitute for spending a little time thinking about how you could prevent the exceptions from occurring in the first place.

Creating an Exception Handler

There's only one problem with Delphi's built-in exception handlers - they're not very good! Okay, you get them for free, but like all free stuff, it's never as good as the code you could write yourself. Let's continue with this example of erroneous code and add our own exception handler to the division program. This should have the effect of replacing Delphi's built-in exception handler with our own, so allowing us to prompt the user with a much more informative dialog.

Try It Out - After the Fact

1 Open **division.dpr** and select cmdDivide - the 'power' button in our application.

2 Bring up the **cmdDivideClick** event handler and add the following code to it:

```
procedure TfrmDivision.cmdDivideClick(Sender: TObject);
var
    iNumber1 : real;
    iNumber2 : real;
    iResult  : real;
    sResult : string;
    iErrorCode : integer;
begin
    try
        val(txtNumber1.text, iNumber1, iErrorCode);
        val(txtNumber2.text, iNumber2, iErrorCode);

        iResult := iNumber1 / iNumber2;

        str(iResult, sResult);
        txtResult.Text := sResult;

    except
        On EZeroDivide do
            showmessage('You shouldn''t really try to divide by zero.');
    end;

end;
```

3 That's all there is to it. Compile the application (using *Ctrl + F9*) and, to avoid the integrated debugger's comments, run the application using Explorer.

How It Works

Now when the user attempts to do division with zero, the application will again create the exception object and look for an EZeroDivide exception handler. After a short search, it will find our exception handler and execute the **ShowMessage** statement that it finds:

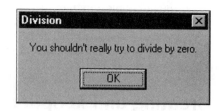

Let's take a closer look at the exception handler to discover how it works. In a Delphi exception handler, there are three sections of interest: the **try** block, the **except** block that includes how the exception object is interpreted, and the code that runs, based on the type of exception object that is generated.

The **try** block is used to surround the code which you want to put under the protection of an exception handler. As you can see from our example, the **try** block is defined from the Delphi keyword **try** to its compatriot **except**:

```
begin
    try
        val(txtNumber1.text, iNumber1, iErrorCode);
        val(txtNumber2.text, iNumber2, iErrorCode);

        iResult := iNumber1 / iNumber2;

        str(iResult, sResult);
        txtResult.Text := sResult;

    except
```

The **except** block runs from the Delphi keyword **except** and to the **end** of the block:

```
        txtResult.Text := sResult;

    except
        On EZeroDivide do
            showmessage('You shouldn''t really try to divide by zero.');
    end;
```

This section contains a list of all the exception objects that the exception handler has been designed to cover. Each of these exception object handlers is provided with its own **on...do** statement, as show in our example:

```
        txtResult.Text := sResult;

    except
        On EZeroDivide do
            showmessage('You shouldn''t really try to divide by zero.');
    end;
```

Your application will execute any code that it finds in the block after the definition of the exception object handler - note that you should use a **begin...end** block after the handler if you wish to run more than one statement based on the type of exception object that has been created:

```
        txtResult.Text := sResult;

    except
        On EZeroDivide do
            showmessage('You shouldn''t really try to divide by zero.');
    end;
```

That's all there is to adding your own exception handler to your code. You might be interested to know that you can add others using the structure that I've just implemented, but without another **try** block.

Finding out the exact type of exception handler to refer to in your **except** statement can be a bit of a pain sometimes. There are two solutions. The first and simplest is just to use Delphi's help files. Do a search on **Exceptions** and you will see an item called **Exceptions Predefined**. Click on this and it will list most of Delphi's predefined exceptions.

The alternative, of course, is to leave the **Break on exception** check box in the **Environment Options** dialog checked. This means that when an error occurs, Delphi will actually tell you which type of exception object was raised, so allowing you to write an appropriate exception handler.

If you're getting into these exception things and some of the situations that might generate them, you might try to enter something other than a number into the edit boxes. If you try to enter a letter into the divisor edit box, Delphi still throws an EZeroDivide exception due to the workings of the **Val** function - it defaults to a zero value if it can't make sense of the source string (see the help files for more information).

Obviously, typing a non-numerical value into the first edit box doesn't generate an error, as everyone knows that 0/X is always 0.

However, the application does read 0/0 as a new problem, generating a different exception object for this situation, namely EInvalidOp:

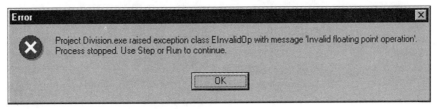

To avoid Delphi's built-in exception handler for this exception, we need to add these lines of code to our example:

```
    except
        on EZeroDivide do
            showmessage('You shouldn''t really try to divide by zero.');
        on EInvalidOp do
            showmessage('I''m not sure what you did, but you can''t do it!' +
                        'Try again!');
    end;
```

Of course, if I wasn't too worried about the exception that I was catching with this exception handler, I could define a generic handler and put it into operation under the guise of a normal **else** clause:

```
except
      on EZeroDivide do
            showmessage('You shouldn''t really try to divide by zero.');
      else
            showmessage('I''m not sure what you did, but you can''t do it!' +
                  'Try again!');
end;
```

Using this exception handler, if anything went wrong in our key five lines of code, the user would be presented with one of the two message dialogs - the first for an EZeroDivide error and a second if it was anything else.

Cascading Exception Objects

One of the most interesting things about exceptions is that the application will try very hard to handle them! Let's examine the following situation, as described in **calling.dpr**. This is essentially the same project as **division.dpr**, except that the potentially troublesome calculation is now performed in a third-party function:

```
procedure TfrmDivision.cmdDivideClick(Sender: TObject);

...

      Result := Divide_Numbers(Number1, Number2);

...

end;

Function Divide_Numbers(Number1 : Real ; Number2 : Real) : Real;
begin
      Divide_Numbers := Number1 / Number2;
end;
```

At run time, the results of the program are the same as before. If you enter a zero into the second text box, then make the program do the calculation, the exception is caught and our message box is displayed. However, this time, the application has had to work a little harder to generate the appropriate response to the problem.

When Delphi encounters the EZeroDivide error in the **Divide_Numbers**, it looks to see whether that function has an exception handler. Since it doesn't, Delphi then looks to see which block of code called the function, and whether it has an active exception handler capable of dealing with this error. In this case, it does, so Delphi uses that one.

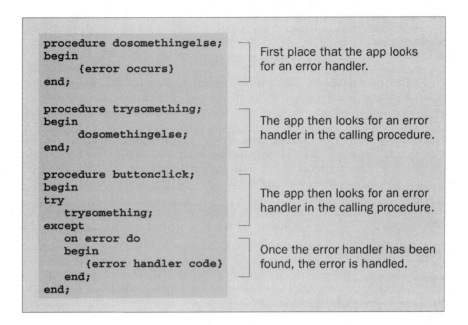

```
procedure dosomethingelse;
begin
      {error occurs}
end;
```
First place that the app looks for an error handler.

```
procedure trysomething;
begin
      dosomethingelse;
end;
```
The app then looks for an error handler in the calling procedure.

```
procedure buttonclick;
begin
try
   trysomething;
except
   on error do
   begin
      {error handler code}
   end;
end;
```
The app then looks for an error handler in the calling procedure.

Once the error handler has been found, the error is handled.

When this happens, both the code in the function and any code following the function call in the OnClick handler is aborted, control transfers to the exception handler in the OnClick event, and the code continues as normal.

Clearing Up the Mess

If you think back to the section on objects, you'll remember all the trees I soaked up talking about the three stages in the life of an object - create, use and free - and how important each stage was to the continuation of life as we know it!

Why am I reminding you of this? Well, what happens when you allocate memory to an object by creating it, only to find yourself with a run-time error? Wouldn't it be neat if we could always force Delphi to execute a chunk of clean-up code, no matter what error occurred? Would it surprise you to hear that we can?

You already know that the **try...except** combination is great for protecting a block of code and assigning an exception handler to that block should things get nasty. However, Delphi also provides another combination that goes around under the guise of a **try...finally** block.

As before, **try** marks the start of a protected block of code, but **finally** marks the start of the wind down block, the cleanup code if you like. Unlike an exception handling block, the code in a **finally** block is always executed, whether an error occurs or not. Take a look at the following:

```
Procedure Draw_Graphic;
var
    Picture : TBitmap;
begin
    Picture := TBitmap.Create(Self);
    Picture.LoadFromFile('c:\test.bmp');
    { Insert some drawing code here }
    Picture.Free;
end;
```

Simple enough. The code creates a TBitmap object and stores it in an appropriately declared variable called **Picture**. It then loads a bitmap file into **Picture** and runs some drawing code, before freeing the object and its associated memory allocation back to the global pool.

What do you think happens if something goes wrong with the load - say the file doesn't exist? Simple, an exception occurs and Delphi displays the exception dialog. That's bad enough at run time, but, in this case, the exception isn't a fatal one, so, as soon as the user clicks on the exception dialog's OK button, the code carries on, drawing god knows what all over the form.

It would be so much nicer to try and load the picture and, in the event of an exception, just drop out of the code and free up the object. That's where **try...finally** comes into play:

```
Procedure Draw_Graphic ;
var
    Picture : TBitmap;
begin
    Picture := TBitmap.Create(Self);
    try
        Picture.LoadFromFile('c:\test.bmp');
        { Insert some drawing code here }
    finally
        Picture.Free;
    end;
end;
```

This time around, the code creates the TBitmap object, then drops into a protected block of code, where it tries to load in the file. If the **LoadFromFile** method generates an exception, the code silently falls into the **finally** block, where it frees the object and exits the procedure. Much nicer!

Handling All-comers - The Try Tag Team

If Delphi made everything so simple, there would be far more programmers in the world. What happens if you want an exception handler and a **finally** block? We want to display our own message box on the screen if there's an error, but still clear up the object without having to write duplicate code either in the exception handler or in the routine itself.

This isn't something that Delphi normally lets you do: you can either have a **try...except** block, or a **try...finally** block, but not both. The solution is to have two blocks together, in much the same way that you might nest one loop inside another. Take a look at **nested.dpr**:

More importantly, though, take a look at the code behind that command button:

```
procedure TfrmNesting.cmdOKClick(Sender: TObject);
var
   Piccie : TBitmap;
begin
    Piccie := TBitmap.Create;
    try
       try
          Piccie.LoadFromFile('whocares.bmp');
          frmNesting.Canvas.Draw( 100,100, Piccie );
       except
          on EFOpenError do
             Showmessage ('The bitmap file could not be opened.');
       end;
    finally
       ShowMessage ('Freeing up the bitmap now');
       Piccie.Free;
    end;
end;
```

In terms of functionality, this code is really quite simple. We want to set up a TBitmap object and load an image into it. If all goes well, the image should get drawn. If something goes wrong, perhaps because the file doesn't exist, an error message needs to be displayed. However, no matter what happens, whether the bitmap is successfully loaded or not, the code must free up the TBitmap object.

As you can see, we can do this by putting the entire exception handler into the **try** block of the **try...finally** statement. If the inner try block fails, the exception handler is triggered causing the message box to be displayed:

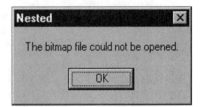

The failure of the inner **try** block causes the failure of the outer **try** block, so the rest of it is dumped and the cleanup code is run, discharging the object and informing the user of what is happening via a message box.

If the inner **try** block is successfully completed, the exception handlers aren't called upon and the inner **try...except** block is completed. This in turn means that the outer **try** block is completed, so the clean code is run just as before, to tidy up the loose ends:

This structure gives us exactly what we want - if an exception occurs, we handle the situation and cut our losses, destroying the TBitmap object as we go. If an exception doesn't occur, the code runs unmolested, with the **finally** block still destroying the TBitmap before the procedure ends.

Producing Your Own Exceptions

Of course, there are times when the predefined exceptions are simply not good enough. In an accounting system of some kind, you might want to have an exception occur that's particular to your problem. In this case, you'll want to make use of the fact that Delphi allows you to define your own exception, as well as the handlers to deal with them. In a game, wouldn't an EEndOfTurn exception be handy?

Declaring a new type of exception object is really quite easy: all you have to do is declare a new type - the **implementation** section of a unit is probably the best place, although, if you really wanted to, you could declare global exception types by placing the declaration into the **interface** section.

Load up **viewer.dpr** and take a look:

The program lets you load in a graphic file using the common file open dialog, and then displays it in an image control attached to the form. If the selected file is corrupted, Delphi kicks out an exception which the code can catch and therefore handle. If you select a file of an unknown format, the code raises its own exception and displays a nice consistent error message.

In this case, I have called the custom exception EInvalidFileType, which has been declared in the **interface** section of the form:

```
interface

uses
    Windows, Messages, SysUtils, Classes, Graphics, Controls, Forms, Dialogs,
    Menus, ExtCtrls;
```

```
type
  EInvalidFileType = class(Exception);
  TfrmViewer = class(TForm)
```

As you can see, declaring a custom exception type is really easy: you just derive your type from Delphi's built-in **Exception** class. If you want, you could then add your own methods and properties to extend the functionality of your custom exception type even further, but I'm not going to go into that here.

The exception is then actually raised in the code behind the File | Open menu option:

```
procedure TfrmViewer.mnuFOpenClick(Sender: TObject);
begin
    try
        if dlgFileOpen.Execute then
        begin
            nPos := 0;
            nPos := nPos + Pos('.bmp' , dlgFileOpen.Filename);
            nPos := nPos + Pos('.dib' , dlgFileOpen.Filename);
            nPos := nPos + Pos('.wmf' , dlgFileOPen.Filename);

            if nPos = 0 then
                raise EInvalidFileType.Create('');

            imgLoadedFile.Picture.LoadFromFile(dlgFileOpen.Filename);
        end;
    except
        On EInvalidFileType do
          ShowMessage('You selected a file type not supported. Try again.');
        On EInvalidGraphic do
          ShowMessage('The image component didn''t like that image at all.' +
                      'Try another one.');
    end;
end;
```

The Delphi **Pos** method is used to search the filename for each of the known file types. **Pos** will return a value greater than zero if it finds any of the file types in the chosen filename. So, by adding the return value of the **Pos** method into a variable, we group three tests into one. Simply call **Pos** three times and, if the end result of all the calls is zero, we know that the filename selected doesn't look like a known graphic file.

At that point, we can raise the exception:

```
            if nPos = 0 then
                raise EInvalidFileType.Create('');
```

Remember that exceptions are really just objects with which the application interacts. So, to raise an exception, you must create it before you can offer it up to the application. Of course, this means a call to the Exception class's **Create** method and, as you can see from the syntax of this example, Delphi will return with an object of type EInvalidFileType.

The parameter that Exception's **Create** method expects is just a string that is placed in the exceptions **Message** property. If you want, you can use this property to display a message to the user in the exception handler:

```
except
    On E : Exception do
       ShowMessage E.Message;
end;
```

What this does is to define a new exception object called **E**, and dump the exception object that caused the error into that, so that we can access its **Message** property.

In the case of the exception handler in the Viewer application, though, we just show a pre-set message:

```
except
        On EInvalidFileType do
            ShowMessage('You selected a file type not supported. Try again.');
        On EInvalidGraphic do
            ShowMessage('The image component didn''t like that image at all.' +
                        'Try another one.');
    end;
```

And that's all there is to it. To deal with custom exceptions, simply define the type, then call **raise** when you feel you need to, while at the same time calling the appropriate **Create** method and passing it the error message to put into the object.

Conditional Compilation

One of the subjects that is often missed out of the discussion of debugging is that of **conditional compilation**. This feature allows you to program aggressively, covering a variety of options all in the same unit.

"Hang on!", I hear you cry, "Isn't that what event-driven programming is all about?!" Well, yes, but conditional compilation is slightly more forceful than event handling. Using conditional compilation, you can force the compiler to only compile certain sections of your code into the final executable!

"Why on earth would I want to do that?" you're asking. Well, consider the following problem:

You've gone to all the effort of developing a class hierarchy that defines the look and feel of your generic applications and then your major customer decides that all of your gorgeous blue forms should be red. Rather than permanently altering your class hierarchy to reflect the demands of your major customer (and so tarring the rest of your customers with red forms), you can use conditional compilation to define what color the forms should be in the final executable.

Let's take an example of how this works. Load up **condish.dpr** and take a look at the code behind the form's OnCreate event:

```
    procedure TfrmTest.FormCreate(Sender: TObject);
begin
    {$IFDEF john}
            frmTest.color := clyellow;
    {$ELSE}
            frmTest.color := clblue;
    {$ENDIF}
end;
```

As you can see, it looks like I have defined the color of the form twice in the same procedure, so the first one will always be overlaid by the second, i.e. the form will always be blue. However, the key to this technique is the comments that surround the property settings, which are in fact compiler directives (note the comment starts with a dollar sign!).

Depending on which conditional symbols are defined, the compiler selects the section of code to include into the final executable. In our example, if I was wanting to compile the application for the major customer, I could 'turn on' the **john** symbol to make my application have a red form.

Add the following line into the form's OnCreate event and run it:

```
procedure TfrmTest.FormCreate(Sender: TObject);
begin
    {SDEFINE john}
    {$IFDEF john}
            frmTest.color := clyellow;
    {$ELSE}
            frmTest.color := clblue;
    {$ENDIF}
end;
```

You should get a really nice, bright yellow form:

I mentioned before that you had to turn on the **john** symbol to get the application to compile with a red form because these symbols work by state. This means that Delphi will remember which symbols are set until you turn it off, even if you delete the line that defines it.

If you want to recompile the application for one of the other customers, you'll need to add the following line to the source code to turn off the symbol so you get a blue form:

```
procedure TfrmTest.FormCreate(Sender: TObject);
begin
    {$DEFINE john}
    {$UNDEF john}
    {$IFDEF john}
            frmTest.color := clyellow;
    {$ELSE}
            frmTest.color := clblue;
    {$ENDIF}
end;
```

If you compile and run the application now, you magically get a blue form instead of the red one:

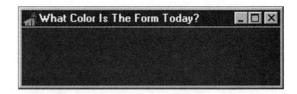

One of the great features of the conditional symbols working to a state is that you can turn the symbols on and off a number of times throughout your unit. Just by using **$DEFINE** and **$UNDEF**, you can select a number of sections of code to be included or left out of the final executable.

Using Conditional Compilation in the Real World

Okay, I admit that this example might not be the greatest use of conditional compilation, but it does illustrate the point that you can radically alter the look and feel of an application just by adding one line of code to your source.

Note that you can also control how an application responds to events by enclosing whole event handlers in conditional compilation blocks.

However, you'll find that conditional compilation comes into its own when you're using API calls in your code. As you'll find out when you go through the later chapter and then start to play around with this subject on your own, each operating system comes with its own set of APIs. Just to make things more interesting, most of the API calls have the same names but will have different parameter lists or acceptable data types.

To get around this problem, if you're targeting a number of systems, you can use conditional compilation to code all the necessary alternatives into your code and simply specify the appropriate conditional symbol to get an executable appropriate to the target.

Note that Delphi comes complete with a list of predefined conditional symbols that you can make use of in your applications. Check out Delphi's help files under **Predefined conditional symbols** for more information.

Of course, this isn't the only time that you might use conditional compilation to achieve the appropriate results, but they are too numerous to mention. However, before you can apply the technique to solve a problem, I had to tell you about it, so there you go.

Using the Delphi Debugger

Okay... you've written your code and laced it full of exception handlers and such like, but it still doesn't work. Don't panic - you haven't done anything that a developer doesn't encounter daily. In fact, there are very few applications out there that don't contain bugs of some kind. The debugging tools in Delphi go a long way towards hunting these bugs down, providing you with a very comprehensive set of tools that essentially allow you to dissect a running application and see what it's up to.

Have a play with **viewer2.dpr** - we're going to use this application to explore the features of the Delphi debugger. For some reason, no matter which kind of file you select, the program won't load them up, although on the surface the code looks almost identical to the previous application.

The first step in debugging an application like this, and in using the debugger in general, is to try and figure out where the bug might be; we have to tell Delphi where to stop the normal execution of the program so that we can start to pull it apart. In **viewer2.dpr**, this isn't that tough, as the bulk of the code lives in the OnClick handler attached to the File | Open menu option.

Run to Cursor

There are two ways that we can stop a program running automatically, both of which live in Delphi's Run. The first is the Run to Cursor item (or *F4*), and you use it by putting your cursor in the line that you want the application to run to and then selecting the option from the menu (or hit the hot key). Why don't you try it out on the **nPos := 0** line in the **mnuFOpenClick** event handler?

Delphi compiles and runs the project as normal, but, as soon as you select a graphic file and click OK, the program is stopped and you find yourself looking at the code window and a highlighted line of code:

```
viewerfrm2.pas                                                    _ □ ×

viewerfrm2

    end;

    procedure TfrmViewer.mnuFOpenClick(Sender: TObject);

    begin
         try
             if dlgFileOpen.Execute then
             begin
                  // We need to check the filename here and trigger an exception
                  // if the extension (.bmp etc) is not known
►                 nPos := 0;
                  nPos := nPos + Pos('.BMP' , dlgFileOpen.Filename);
                  nPos := nPos + Pos('.DIB' , dlgFileOpen.Filename);
                  nPos := nPos + Pos('.WMF' , dlgFileOPen.Filename);

                  // If the supported extensions were not found using the Pos

49: 1              Insert
```

Notice how Delphi has highlighted the line that you were on when you pressed *F4*. Delphi is telling you here that the program is running, but is paused at the highlighted line. Using Run to Cursor, you can only specify one point in the program at which you wish it to stop. Before I look at why you might want to do this, and what you can do when you get here, let's consider the alternative to Run to Cursor - the mysterious breakpoint.

Breakpoints

Before we can set up any breakpoints in our code, we have to rescue the last Run to Cursor operation - do you remember how? Try Run | Program Reset (*Ctrl+F2*).

Now that we're looking at a normal, non- debugger molested code window, we're ready to add some breakpoints. These beasties are incredibly easy to set - simply move over to the left margin of the code window and click in there against the line of code that you wish the application to stop on when it encounters your breakpoint.

Let's run the same experiment, except this time, put a breakpoint on the **nPos := 0** line of the event handler. You should notice that a small red 'No Entry' sign will appear next to the code, which now appears against a red background:

```
viewerfrm2.pas                                                    _ □ X
viewerfrm2

    end;

    procedure TfrmViewer.mnuFOpenClick(Sender: TObject);

    begin
         try
             if dlgFileOpen.Execute then
             begin
                  // We need to check the filename here and trigger an exception
                  // if the extension (.bmp etc) is not known
                  nPos := 0;
                  nPos := nPos + Pos('.BMP' , dlgFileOpen.Filename);
                  nPos := nPos + Pos('.DIB' , dlgFileOpen.Filename);
                  nPos := nPos + Pos('.WMF' , dlgFileOPen.Filename);

                  // If the supported extensions were not found using the Pos

49: 1              Insert
```

FYI If you don't fancy that way of setting a breakpoint, simply put your cursor in the line that you want to break on, then right-click on the code window and select **Toggle Breakpoint**, or press *F5*.

When you have set up the breakpoint, press *F9* to run the program as normal. Once again, as soon as you try and load a file into the application, the integrated debugger will jump in, freezing your application and presenting you with its available debugging tools.

Specialized Breakpoints

One feature that the integrated debugger does support is that of multiple breakpoints in an application, and the ability to add more criteria to the breakpoint than just the application attempting to run a particular line of code.

As an alternative to the options that I've already outlined, if you attempt to add a breakpoint to your code using the <u>R</u>un | Add <u>B</u>reakpoint... menu option, Delphi will present you with the following dialog:

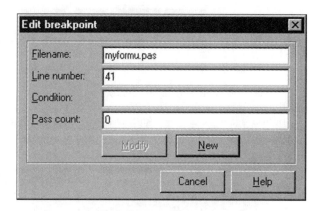

This dialog allows you to specify a number of things about your breakpoint, including its file and the location with which Delphi can identify where the breakpoints are actually set (you can set breakpoints in files that you haven't got open by changing these default entries) and two specialized conditions that can cause the integrated debugger to ignore the breakpoint.

These two conditions allow you to specify exactly when you want the application to break - either on the *n*th time through a loop (the pass condition when *n* is the value entered in the edit box) or when a given condition is met, say **not(dlgFileOpen.Execute)**.

If you want to review or modify any of the breakpoints that you have set, check out the <u>V</u>iew | B<u>r</u>eakpoints menu option that displays the following dialog box:

This displays information on all of the breakpoints that you've set while this project has been loaded into Delphi. By right-clicking on any one of them, you can choose to temporarily disable it, delete it all together, modify it or review the code to which it has been assigned.

Note that breakpoints 'go out of scope' when the project is closed down. If you want to work on a project over a number of sessions and reuse the same breakpoints, you will have to define them at the start of each session.

What Can You Do once the Program Has Been Stopped?

One of the most common things that you'll want to do to a program in this state is to take a peek at the current values of certain properties and variables. For this, Delphi allows you to set watches. These 'spies' sit around and concentrate on one property or variable and relate its current contents back to the Watch List. See the <u>V</u>iew | <u>W</u>atches menu option to get the following dialog:

To see how you set up a watch, return back to our unit and the code window. Double-click on the **nPos** variable so that the entire variable line is highlighted, and then click the right mouse button again. Select the Add Watch At Cursor item (*Ctrl+F5*) and two new windows should appear: the Watch List window itself and the Watch Properties dialog.

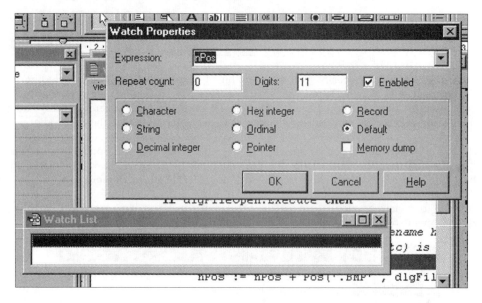

The top of the Watch Properties dialog contains the watch expression, which is normally the name of the variable that you want to keep an eye on. Beneath this you have the Repeat count edit box. If you need to look at an array of some kind, this is where you specify how many elements of the array you want to see in the Watch List. In our example, this isn't important, since we're not dealing with an array.

The Digits edit box is useful for looking at floating point (decimal) numbers and lets you place a limit on the number of digits to the right of the decimal point that you want to look at. As the name would suggest, the Enabled check box lets you enable or disable a watch. Why would you want to?

Well, by disabling watches that aren't relevant to the section of code you're looking at (remember you could have watches set up referring to variables throughout your application, not just in one routine, as in our example), you can actually speed up the debugger and can make it a lot smoother to work with. Finally, the Display As panel lets you tell Delphi how to display the values inside the variables that you're watching.

For now, though, all the settings that Delphi has given you are more than adequate. Click on OK to close the Watch Properties dialog and return control to the main Watch List window. At this point, the watch is currently telling us that it can't tell what the variable's contents is - not surprising really, as our first breakpoint (on the line that initializes the variable) has stopped the application before the declared variable can be initialized.

Playing Doctor

No matter how you stop the application with the integrated debugger, you'll probably want to see how the application was going, change some code or re-evaluate some conditions to check your logic. Watches are a pretty cool feature, but they really come into their own when you start to slowly work your way through the code under the watchful guidance of the debugger.

To transverse the code, Delphi provides you with the Trace into and Step over buttons:

Both buttons perform similar jobs, in that they both execute code one line at a time. The difference between the two is that if you use the Trace into button, when you come to a procedure or function call, the integrated debugger will ferret out the new procedure or function, even if it's in another unit, and proceed to step through that code as well. Step over doesn't bother with all that - it just runs that procedure or function and returns the application to its resting state, at the next line of code after the call.

Okay, let's put this integrated debugger through its paces, using all the tools that I've just gone through.

Try It Out - Testing the Integrated Debugger

1 Close down any testing application that you might have opened during this chapter so far and reload **viewer2.dpr** from fresh, i.e. it hasn't got any breakpoints or watches associated with it.

2 Place a breakpoint on the following line of code, found in **mnuFOpenClick** of the **viewfrm2.pas** (highlight the line and press *F5*):

```
try
    if dlgFileOpen.Execute then
    begin
        nPos := 0;
        nPos := nPos + Pos('.BMP' , dlgFileOpen.Filename);
        nPos := nPos + Pos('.DIB' , dlgFileOpen.Filename);
```

3 Add your first watch to **nPos** (highlight it and press *Ctrl+F5*) and a second to **dlgFileOpen.Filename** just a little ways down the unit in the **LoadFromFile** statement:

```
        if nPos = 0 then
            raise EInvalidFileType.Create( '' );

        // If the code gets this far then all is well.
        imgLoadedFile.Picture.LoadFromFile(dlgFileOpen.Filename);
    end;
except
    On EInvalidFileType do
        ShowMessage('You selected a file type not supported. Try again.');
```

4 Run the application and try to load in the provided bitmap using the File | Open menu option. When the integrated debugger steps in, makes sure that you can see the code window, the Watch List and the IDE's toolbar with the debugger controlling icons on it.

What's Happening?

If you've followed these steps, you should now be looking at a screen something like this:

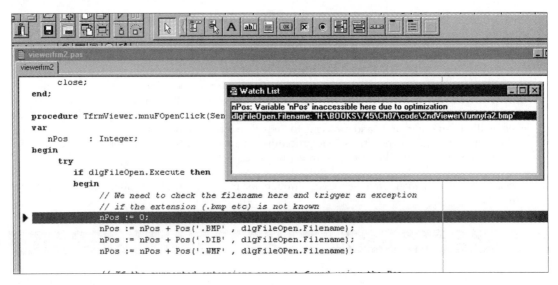

Hit the Trace into button and watch the Watch List and the code window. The highlighted line in the code window should move down to the next statement, and the Watch List should change to reflect the fact that the line of code we just ran put a value into the **nPos** variable.

Continue to step through the code. The lines that we're particularly interested in are those that contain a reference to **nPos**, the integer variable that we're monitoring - after all, as soon as a recognizable file extension is encountered, **nPos** will become non-zero. You might have to arrange your windows so that your Watch List isn't resting on the code window, otherwise every time you move to the next line of code, the Watch List will disappear behind it!

If you get to the line that deals with the **nPos** test, as shown below, and the value of **nPos** still hasn't changed, you should start to get a little puzzled:

```
nPos := nPos + Pos('.DIB' , dlgFileOpen.Filename);
nPos := nPos + Pos('.WMF' , dlgFileOpen.Filename);

if nPos = 0 then
        raise EInvalidFileType.Create('');

    imgLoadedFile.Picture.LoadFromFile(dlgFileOpen.Filename);
end;
```

We've strafed through the code that should have set **nPos** to a greater than zero value. After all, a bitmap has been identified (you can see this by looking at the extension of the value displayed by the **dlgFileOpen.Filename** watch), and still it remains unchanged.

Hang on a minute! It can't be that! It's too obvious!

The value displayed in the watch assigned to **dlgFileOpen.Filename** has a lower case extension, but our **nPos** checks are looking for capitalized extensions!

```
nPos := nPos + Pos('.BMP' , dlgFileOpen.Filename);
nPos := nPos + Pos('.DIB' , dlgFileOpen.Filename);
nPos := nPos + Pos('.WMF' , dlgFileOPen.Filename);
```

Could **Pos** be case-sensitive?

The easiest way to find out is to change the **.BMP Pos** statement to lower case and re-run the application. Let's try it, but let's disable the breakpoint to see the application running smoothly. Hit *Ctrl+F2* to reset the application, bring up the Breakpoint list (View | Breakpoints), right-click on our breakpoint and uncheck the Enabled menu option. Last of all, change the troublesome line of code to:

```
nPos := nPos + Pos('.bmp' , dlgFileOpen.Filename);
```

If you now run the application and try to load in the bitmap, just as before, two things happen. The first is that the integrated debugger doesn't step in when you click on the file open dialog's OK button, and the second is that the file loads into the image component! Success!

So, now that we've identified the problem, we can work on a solution (I'm not going to do that here - think of it as a bit of a challenge), but while we've got a problem at hand, let's just take time out to consider one of Delphi's other tools that works quite closely with the integrated debugger. This tool allows you to manually change the values of properties and variables at run time (under the wing of the integrated debugger) to test out critical values, exceptional conditions and the like.

Re-evaluating Your Variables

Kill the application and drop back down to Delphi's IDE. Re-enable the breakpoint, change the code back to capitals and run the application. Just as before, the application will allow you to select the bitmap of your choice, then the integrated debugger will jump in as you click on the OK button. If you now click on the Trace into button three times until the debugger is looking at the **.WMF nPos** line, and then select Run | Evaluate/Modify... (*Ctrl+F7*), Delphi will present you with this dialog:

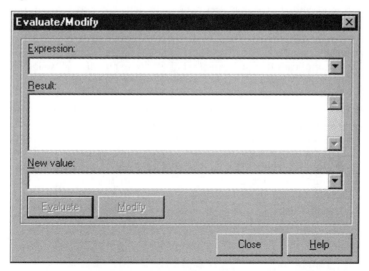

Type the name of the variable you want to evaluate or modify, in our case **nPos**, into the Expression box and click on the Evaluate button. Delphi returns the current value of the variable in the Result box, but more importantly, it now allows you to modify the variable's value.

Type the new value into the New value box and hit the Modify button - you should see both the value in the Result box and the current watch value change to reflect this new entry. If you now Trace into the rest of the code, the new value of **nPos** means that the condition fails, the exception object isn't generated and the bitmap loads into the image component.

This technique is quite useful for testing out sections of code that rely on a variable or property value passing a certain criteria before they run, or for testing out that fail-safe code that you hope you'll never need!

Note that this technique can't be used on local variables - if you find yourself in this situation, you might try temporarily redeclaring the variable as a global to make use of this feature.

Final Thoughts on Bug Reduction

One of my pet hates with tutorial books like this is that they don't focus enough on the real world. It's something I've tried to remedy in this book - I hope I've been successful so far.

Debugging is one area in particular where this lack of real-world focus is most apparent, especially when it comes to the processes that developers need to put into place to reduce the chances of introducing bugs in the first place. In this section, we're not going to do very much in the way of hands on development, but instead I aim to get that brain of yours ticking over. I don't claim to be a guru in the field of writing bug-free code, but I do know a few tricks of the trade that can help.

All about Bugs

As far as a user is concerned, there are really two different kinds of bugs - I call them **functional bugs** and **shortfall bugs**. A functional bug is the most common type you'll come across: having entered incorrect information into an edit box, the user clicks a button and the application crashes in an embarrassing heap. Very distressing, but you can rescue this kind of situation quite easily. Shortfall bugs, on the other hand, are much more serious. These are problems with the application which mean that it doesn't really do what the user needs or wants.

Personal computers and desktop development systems have been with us for a long time now, with many people finding their first introduction to development in the school classroom. However, the development process and the thought processes behind it haven't moved that far forward in over 15 years. Sit most developers in front of an application that crashes and they'll go into debug mode: "Try changing that variable to a global.... how about replacing this block of code with a procedure?" etc., etc. Sit most developers in front of an application that works, but doesn't really do all that the user needs, though, and they look at you with a dazed expression and ask where the problem is.

The fact of the matter is that if an application doesn't do what it's supposed to do, either by design or by developer error, then, in my opinion, it's bugged. A lot of people would contest this, which is strange, especially when you take into account the amount of time and money that it usually takes to fix each kind of bug.

It's a fact that if the system has been shipped and installed, it can take 10-20 times longer and cost 10-20 times more to fix a shortfall bug than it does to fix a functional bug. Tell that to your boss and see which kind of bugs he thinks are more serious! It's also a fact that people who use your application can usually work round many of the functional bugs they find, but shortfall bugs are another matter altogether. They can result in the user dropping your system and resorting to the 'old way' of doing things.

Following on from this idea, debugging isn't simply the process of sitting down with the source code, probing about with a debugger and generally turning into the Indiana Jones of computerdom. Debugging really has to cover the whole development process, including the early design phases. I know, I know… all programmers hate design, but it's an integral part of the process. If you can produce a design, check it, test it out on the users, walk through it with the other members of the team and so on, you're more likely to end up with an accurate blueprint of what your code should look like than if you simply sit down and start hacking (sorry… it's an old computer term which means to chuck out code in a development frenzy, as opposed to gaining illegal entry to a system).

Think about a house builder. His client is the house buyer. The buyer asks for a four-bedroom house with a garden and a garage. She has in mind a three-story affair faced with oak beams. The house builder has in mind a one-story bungalow made of red brick. If the house builder doesn't bother to check the design he comes up with against the requirements of his client, once he has built the house he'll be faced with some expensive re-engineering in terms of both time and money.

Exactly the same principle applies to software development. I think we're the only service and production industry in the world today that can make mistakes on a grand scale and generally get away with it because that is what everyone expects. It doesn't have to be that way!

However, the focus of this book is development: the process of sitting down in front of the Delphi compiler and kicking out code. For that reason, I'm going to assume that you've done your homework and that you have a valid design in front of you that accurately represents what the user wants and needs. How can we reduce the amount of bugs from this point forward?

 Notice I keep saying *reduce*...I know of only one application in the world where a developer actually bet his user base that they couldn't find a bug. Bugs are a nasty fact of life and debugging is more a process of damage limitation than a mature science.

Reducing the Bug Count

The most common way to reduce the number of bugs in an application today is to run tests. We've all been there; you run the program, see if it does what it's supposed to do, and if it does you go "OK... that's done" and move on. WRONG! If that's the way you work, I've got a big shock for you.

In a system like Delphi, this is actually called **unit testing**... you produce a form (which is a unit) test it and then move on. A programming productivity study conducted by Capers Jones in 1986 found that unit testing identifies a maximum of 50% of the bugs in a system. More importantly, on average, it only identifies 25%. Scary, huh?

Some developers get smart to this and say "Ah... but I test my units in a live environment with live data". Great! According to the same study, these guys will find 65% at most, 50% on average. Think about it. If these guys identify and fix 300 bugs in a large application, then they're actually going to ship between 200 and 300 bugs to their users... that's even scarier.

There's no single method available in the world today that can identify all the bugs in an application. Look at Windows 95. It has its fair share of bugs, even though it was tested by almost a million people before it was released - unit and field testing on its grandest scale and it didn't work. However, there are many effective ways to spot bugs which, if combined with unit and field testing, can contribute greatly towards your grand bug quest.

Code Reviews

One of the most boring techniques known to man is the **code review**. Why is it boring? Well, at its simplest level it involves you sitting down with someone prepared to listen and reading the code out to them, explaining what each block of code does, how the flow of control progresses through the code, and so on.

Although it's incredibly boring, a code review is a very good way of spotting bugs, and it can be extremely effective. Combine this technique with unit and field testing and you'll be well on your way to tracking down a large proportion of the bugs in your system.

It works in much the same way as writing a chapter of a book, a letter or a specification. When you are sitting in front of the word-processor, you're normally quite happy that what you've said makes sense, it's all spelt correctly, and so on. It's only when you let someone else take a look at the document that all the mistakes start to show up! (Yep!... Only kidding Peter! Ed.). Unlike a letter or article, though, reading code can be incredibly dull, especially if you wrote it yourself.

If you've ever worked in a development team, you will probably have come across the principles behind a code review before. I've done it so often: I'm sitting down in front of my project, totally unable to figure out why a section of it doesn't work. So, I get up, walk over to a colleague's desk and say "Hey Richard, any ideas why this doesn't work?". Then, as I start to explain the code, it hits me that a variable is being used incorrectly, or a loop is too small, or a block of code is missing. The other guy doesn't really have to say anything - he just has to sit there and listen. It's helpful, though, if they do have a bit of a technical background, as they might spot that technique blunder that has been staring you in the face for the last hour!

The Capers Jones report I mentioned earlier indicates that a code inspection will find around 30% of the bugs in your system at least. However, a well conducted review, using review reports, bug tracking, effective management, and so on, can find up to 70% of the problems.

Let me give you a case study. I had to write an archiving database some time ago for a large multinational company. One of the things the code did was to wait until there were over a million records in a table, then start sucking out the older ones to the separate archiving database.

We tested this first by unit testing. I changed the code so that it would pull out records from the table when there were more than 10 in it. It saved on test data production and, in my opinion, would test the code quite nicely. The code worked and I was convinced that everything would be fine when the product shipped.

My lead developer then asked me (I was but a mere junior at the time) whether I had done a code review. He explained the idea to me and, despite my protestations, I found myself sitting in a small room with two other developers and the lead, reading through the code.

When the records were pulled out to the archiving database, they were given a unique ID which was the date they were archived in year/month/day format, followed by a unique record number. When I started to read through the code, I noticed that the variable I was using to count the records as they were archived could only hold a value of, at most, 65535. This meant that, at archiving time, on a huge database, the system would hit this level and crash, possibly corrupting two databases (both the archiving one and the original one) on the way. With my testing plans, there would have been no way to spot this, but the code review showed it up within minutes.

Unit Testing

It's a common misconception that unit testing in Delphi involves nothing more than running up a form and checking that every component works as it should. This is wrong. When you test your code, you're blind to even the most obvious errors, because subconsciously, you expect it to be perfect.

When you develop your forms, modules, classes, routines, or whatever you develop in, make a list of everything in the code from both a negative and positive point of view. If you have code that runs up a file open dialog, make a note that you need to test that it will let you select a file, but also make a note to test to see what happens if the user opens a file type not supported by the application. In a search routine, you would probably make a note to test the search with a result that you know it can find, and with a result that you know it can't find. What about testing the search routine when there is no data to search at all?

That latter problem is really common, especially in database applications. You sit down, feed in your test data and test your code. The code moves to the first record in the data base, then loops through a search query, displaying all the results. But, if there's no data in the database at all, trying to move to the first record in the database could cause you some nice problems.

Test that your units work, then test to see how easy it is for the user to crash the system.

A New Developmental Approach

There are other testing techniques you can use, but, in general, reading the code at your desk, doing a proper code review, unit testing the components in your project and then doing a proper field test should catch most of the problems. But can you do anything to reduce the bugs being introduced in the first place, or at least make them easier to nail?

Go to your local bookstore and you'll see rows of books telling you that this way to code is cool, that way is foolproof, this way is excellent (and it only costs you X dollars). However, I've found a couple of things which can make life easier.

First… comments. Every programming course that you're ever likely to go on, every programming book that you're ever likely to read will tell you that comments are the bees knees... comment your code, it makes life so much easier.

They have it all wrong, though. NEVER, under any circumstances, comment your code. Instead, *code your comments*.

Confused?

Okay, you need to write a little loop that bounces a picture around the form. Rather than writing code and then adding comments, write your code as comments. Take a look:

```
Procedure Bounce_Picture;
Begin
  // First reset the X and Y coordinates of the picture
  // Work out random values to add to the X and Y coordinates on each movement
  // Start a loop that runs forever
  // Erase the old picture ready to draw the new one
  // Add the values to the X and Y coordinates to update the piccies position
  // If the X coordinate is now off the screen then negate the value you add to it
  // If the Y coordinate is now off the screen then negate the value you add to it
  // Draw the picture
  // Continue the loop
End;
```

Take a look at that. That's the logic of my code as I see it. I can read this easily, I can show this to other programmers and they'll go "Yeah... that should work". It's easy to understand. It works. Now all that remains is to write the code.

When you're writing code in this way, make sure that you limit yourself to no more than four or five lines of code per comment. If you find you have to write more, maybe the solution to your problem isn't clear in your head. Maybe you need to turn the new huge block of code into a procedure or function and call that in your main procedure?

The real beauty of writing code this way is that it lets you focus on the problem. You aren't constantly worrying about which parameters this method needs, or what the syntax of that property was, and so on. Sit down, think about the problem (never think about what you're physically capable of coding - concentrate on the problem), then write out the code as comments. I have developed entire applications like this: sit down, produce a user interface, then whack the comments in. I can then go into a code review, read the comments, explain what I plan to do and get a lot of feedback from the review team. Once everyone is happy that my comments give a precise and concise description of the solution to the problem, I add the code.

So, how does this help to reduce the number of bugs you put in your code? Well, as I said, it lets you focus on the problem. If you have a very clearly defined solution to the problem from an English point of view, the bugs that you put in from that point onward are coding errors - they are probably not logic errors, functionality oversights, or worse still, design flaws (because you reviewed the comments with the team, and perhaps even with the users, right?).

Try it out. Think of a simple program and write it like this. Writing all the comments in can be a bit of a bind at first, but once they're done and the time has come to sit down and write the code, you will be amazed at how much confidence you have. You have a step-by-step guide to writing your code and can switch your focus to Pascal syntax and Delphi's idiosyncrasies. It really does work; it helps you understand the problem more than anything else, and if you understand what you're trying to do, you will be so much more successful than if you were sitting down writing code to solve an unknown problem.

Coding Standards

The next trick is to implement some kind of coding standard. Name your routines, your variables, your components in a consistent manner. Always strive to be consistent in your code layout and content. Appendix A contains a complete summary of my coding standards which you can build on, or simply use as a reference.

Having, and sticking to, a set of standards helps your debugging no end. Because variables are named consistently and named well, you can easily understand what sort of data a variable holds just by looking at its name. Because you are sticking to a standard code layout format, you don't have to waste time matching **end**s up to **begin**s and **end**s. The code simply becomes easier to understand because it looks so similar to the code you write every single day. If you have no consistent standards, you find that the code in one form can look totally different, totally foreign, compared to the code you wrote in all the others.

Another little trick, a very simple trick, is to totally avoid any kind of global variables. These things can really make coding and debugging a nightmare. You set up a value in one routine, but forget that five others overwrite that variable in a slightly different way. When you come to the debugging, you can't figure out who did what and when without stepping through the entire application, one line at a time. Keep your variables local - if you need a separate routine to update a variable, fine - pass it as a parameter to a function and update the variable with the return result. This makes it very easy to look at your code and trace the flow of information within it.

Although it sounds simple, I have to admit that I get a lot of moans and groans about this rule. Programmers in the team say "In an event-driven environment, it's impossible to manage without the odd global". Wrong! If you feel that you must have a global variable of some kind, wrap it up in a nice global object. That way, you can implement the variable as a property and control access to it through the object's methods and functions. With only a tiny amount of code, you can even write code that locks these properties from time to time, to prevent other events from firing and destroying values. Instead of global variables, use objects and the safety features that they bring with them.

Of course, there are many more options open to you, but these are just some of my favorites. In every book I have ever written, I always cite what I consider to be the programmer's bible, and this book is no exception.

If you really want to get a grip on the whole coding process and learn how to write really high quality code then beg, borrow, steal or do what you must to get hold of Steve McConnell's *Code Complete* from Microsoft Press.

This should take pride of place on your bookshelf (next to this book, of course), since it contains some absolute gems in terms of tricks, tips and techniques. Get it, read it, read it again, make your team read it, sleep with it! If you can absorb just a small portion of the tips that it has to offer, you will be a better programmer than many others.

Summary

In this chapter, I have tried to outline some of the basic ideas behind good programming techniques, the differences between 'before the fact' and 'after the fact' error handling and some of the tools that Delphi provides you with to handle these situations.

By now, you should be able to handle the integrated debugger like an old pro, raise an exception like it was a feather and argue the case for 15 different types of testing and review with a boss that wants the project out tomorrow, and occasionally win!

In the next chapter, I'm going to look at the subject of advanced application layout techniques, including the use of menus, MDI parent and child forms and how you can control the Windows common dialogs with the greatest of ease. You shouldn't, though, forget any of the ideas that I've covered here - not while you're reading the next chapter, reading your next book or attending your next seminar - in fact, you'd do well to take these ideas into the next world with you. I'm sure they'll come in handy!

Advanced Components

This chapter is devoted to saving space, so that you can show loads of information in your applications while also keeping all the functionality up your sleeve. Like the 'grown-up' applications you use all the time - Delphi, Office and so on - the main way to save space is to use menus.

We are also going to consider some advanced ways of structuring the layout of your application. Remember the space-saving technique I use back in Chapter 4's charting example? The TPageControl component can be very useful to increase your screen real estate, but what if you wanted to have several pages of information displayed at the same time? To solve this problem, we have to resort to a completely new approach - the **Multiple Document Interface** (**MDI**).

Lastly, I'm also going to consider the subject of common dialogs, those natty little forms without which no application is complete. As part of this chapter's example, a text editor, you'll see the benefits, and quirks, of using these components.

In this chapter you'll learn about:

- Normal and pop-up, context-sensitive menus
- How to create MDI parent and child forms at design time
- How to create MDI child forms at run time
- The methods available to manipulate these child forms at run time
- Menus and toolbars in MDI applications
- How to use the common dialog components

By the end of the chapter, you should have enough experience to start creating your own MDI apps, and thus some very powerful Windows applications. And by way of compensation for your effort, you'll have a working text editor! So, let's go...

Menus

You know what menus are. They lurk beneath a window's title bar, disguised as words. Click them, though, their identity is revealed and a list drops down. Choose an item from the list and take the consequences. To save space on the screen, the menu conveniently hides parts of the application's functionality. It's only fussy users who then insist on having their favorite functions shown as speed buttons, cluttering the window up again... You can't win.

In addition, Windows 95 introduces something of a standard - you should now be able to right-click the mouse on any component or form to bring up a context-sensitive pop-up menu:

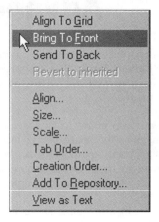

Those clever chaps at Borland have given you two components, so you too can use both these menu types in your applications. Let's try it - you're simply not going to believe how easy it is to create a menu!

Try It Out - Creating a Standard Menu

1 Start a new application. On the far left of the Standard component tab of the Component Palette you'll find the MainMenu component. Double-click on it to drop it onto the form. Doesn't look much like a menu yet, does it?

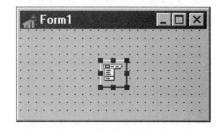

2 Bring up the Object Inspector. Double-click on the **Items** property to bring up the Menu Editor:

248

3 The highlighted square in the top left corner of the Menu Editor window shows you the current menu item that you are editing. Note that the object you're are now inspecting has changed to a blank. Start typing, and the blank object's **Caption** property will change accordingly. Press *Enter* once you've finished, the caption appears in the Menu Editor and provides the name to the object (give or take the '**1**' suffix). You now have a fully fledged menu item:

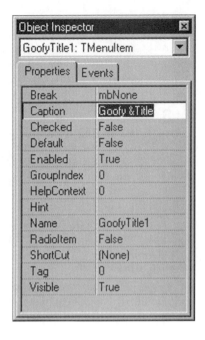

You should, of course, replace the frivolous title above with the more usual and useful &File. The fact it fits in with the standard Windows menu layout should reassure your users - nothing like those good old design standards.

4 The menu item's name is very quaint, but less than useful, so change it to **mnuFile**, following our chosen naming convention.

5 You now have two options: you can either add another menu item to the title bar, or you can go down the first menu you created and add a subsection:

6 Click on the menu item that appeared beneath File and set its caption to **&Open**:

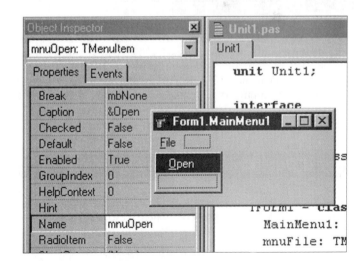

7 Try running the program now - Delphi should ask you to save your project and unit, but then again, you might have hit that groove and have already saved everything, as you should have, at the start of the design. Did you? Ten points if you did, but ten away if you didn't! Click on the File menu item and see it show the Open item. Did you notice that you didn't have to close the Menu Editor to run the application?

8 The Delphi Menu Editor supports drag-and-drop, making it very easy to re-arrange the look of your menu. Let's stop the application and give this a go. Click on the **&Open** item and then drag it to the blank item area to the right of **&File**:

And that's all there is to creating a menu in Delphi - nothing to it, huh?

How It Works

Dropping a Mainmenu component on the form is a bit of an anticlimax. It's just like any other non-visual component. Even its property list is uninspiring. Fortunately, it's not here that a menu's real work is organized.

You see, each menu item is a component in its own right, and its properties, methods and events are just held by a TMenuItem object - MainMenu simple coordinates the accessibility of the menu items, using the Items property to get at the array that indexes each menu item.

At design time, double-clicking this property brings up the TMenuItem property editor. And you can play to your heart's content with the menus for your program; nesting items, specifying hot keys and thinking of whacky captions.

  This property editor forms the only way to set the read-only **Items** property, but you can hardly call that a handicap.

To make life easier, once you have captioned a new menu item, Delphi will always use the caption you enter as a basis for the item's name. Personally, I prefer to change the item names myself to something more obvious - more of these naming conventions in Appendix A. That named menu item is now part of the form's type declaration, and its properties can be accessed any time through the drop-down list at the top of the Object Inspector.

Pop-up menus are just as easy to create - I feel another example coming on...

Try It Out - Creating a Pop-up Menu

1 With the last example application loaded (it's on the accompanying disk as **menu1.dpr**), drop a PopupMenu component onto the form. If you can't see it straight away, it's the component next to the MainMenu component on the Component Palette.

2 As before, all you get is the component icon - nothing spectacular at all. Bring up the Object Inspector, though, and double-click on the Items property of the pop-up menu.

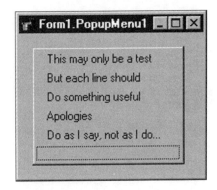

3 That familiar Menu Editor appears, so go on, enter some random thoughts:

4 It's your job to link each pop-up menu you've created to the component or window for which it was designed. Click on the form itself and find the form's PopupMenu property. You face a drop-down list of all the pop-up menus in your application - plenty of choice there. Make that choice, select that pop-up menu.

Now we can run the application. When it appears, right-click on the form to see the pop-up come into view.

How It Works

PopupMenu is very similar to the MainMenu component, except for one slight difference. Since a pop-up menu represents the drop-down list that doesn't have a main heading - after all, it's a free floating list of context-sensitive choices - the Menu Editor for PopupMenu won't let you enter multiple headings.

In addition, pop-up menus don't appear automatically when a program is run. The user needs to right-click the mouse to display the PopupMenu you've associated with that component or form at design time.

What easier way could there be for creating context-sensitive menus, each one individually tailored to meet the needs of the relevant component? Except we still haven't made the menu items do anything, or used the full power of the components provided.

It's time, therefore, to look at some of those other menu component properties.

A Touch of Flair

Take a look at this Delphi menu:

Here, we have a menu with features that we take for granted, such as grayed out, disabled items, items with check marks next to them and lines that divide it up, but, as yet, we don't know how to add them to our Delphi application.

The principle is the same for both menus, so we'll concentrate on the MainMenu component here.

Try It Out - Flash Menus

1 Load up **menu3.dpr**. It's nothing more than a form with a menu attached. Let's spice it up:

2 Select the MainMenu component and bring up the Object Inspector. Double-click on the Items property as before to invoke the Menu Editor. Move to beneath the last item in the menu by clicking on the new item space there.

Find the caption property of the item and enter '-' as the caption. As soon as you press *Enter*, the focus moves down to the next menu item, leaving you with a separator bar in the menu.

3 Now drag the separator bar up to the Exit item. When you let go of the mouse button, the separator bar is inserted above Exit:

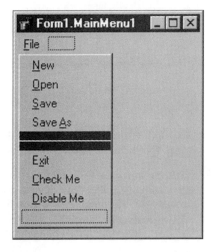

Make another one and drag it onto the Check Me item - the separator bar will appear above it as before.

4 As you saw earlier, you can also make check boxes appear beside menu items. This is handled by the item's Checked property. Select that Check Me item and change the Checked property in the Object Inspector to True:

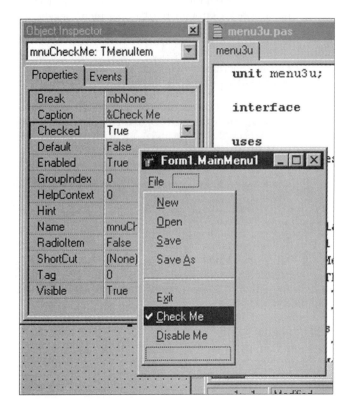

5 Double-click the <u>C</u>heck Me item to bring up the code window. Change the code that you can see there so that it looks like this:

```
procedure TForm1.mnuCheckMeClick(Sender: TObject);
begin
     mnuCheckMe.Checked := not(mnuCheckMe.Checked);
end;
```

Since the Checked property is a Boolean, this new line of code just reverses its current value when the menu item is clicked, as we saw in Chapter 2

6 Now try and run the program. Find the <u>C</u>heck Me menu item and click it. The first time, it appears with a check mark next to it. Once you've clicked it, though, the next time you drop down the menu, you'll see that the check mark has vanished. 'Pah!', you thought, 'That's easy!'. And so it is. There's even a RadioItem property which allows you to replace the little tick that indicates a menu item is checked with a blob. Just set it True or False.

You can do precisely the same with the <u>D</u>isable Me menu item's Enabled property, using the above code with names suitably changed.

7 Now for the shortcut keys. These allow you to access application functionality without having to go through the various menu levels, a sure relief for mouse-wrist.

Bring up the Menu Editor in **menu3.dpr** again. It's quite common in Windows apps for <u>F</u>ile | <u>O</u>pen to have the shortcut *Ctrl+O*, so let's do that. Select the <u>O</u>pen item in the menu and find its Shortcut property in the Object Inspector. If you click the drop-down arrow to the right of the property, a list of possible shortcut keys is displayed. Find *Ctrl+O* and click it.

8 We need to add a little code in here so that we can see the shortcuts in action when the program runs. Drop an OpenDialog onto the form and bring up the Menu Editor and double-click the Open item under the file menu to bring up the code window. Change the code so that it looks like this:

```
procedure TForm1.mnuFOpenClick(Sender: TObject);
begin
     OpenDialog1.Execute;
end;
```

9 Lastly, the Menu Editor has its own speed menu - weird! I mean, how did they set that menu? This tool allows you to create submenus. Just create a menu item, then right-click on the editor. Choose <u>C</u>reate Submenu and you'll see the following:

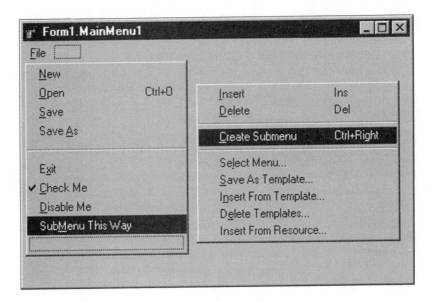

The speed menu also has the ability to save the menu as a template, and insert pret-a-porter Delphi templates. You can even insert menus from other Windows programs if they're stored as resource files.

If you now run the program, you'll find that you almost have a working Open item under the File menu. Click on Open and up pops a standard File Open dialog, just as you might expect. More than this, though, pressing *Ctrl+O* will do just the same. We've been here a matter of minutes, but already the application is beginning to look pukka.

How It Works

So what have we learned?

▶ Even though menu items are themselves objects, embedded within menu objects, they can still respond to events.

▶ Entering '-' as the caption causes Delphi to create a separator bar.

▶ Menu items won't automatically check or uncheck, enable or disable themselves when the user clicks on them. You need to write a little code to deal with that.

▶ Check marks in menus provide you an easy way to get global application settings from the user, and to display those. In Delphi, for example, you can turn the toolbars on and off by checking and unchecking items in the View menu. Obviously, this takes a little more code than we've used, but the point is that you can easily turn on and off two of Delphi's global features with just a single mouse click!

▶ Shortcut keys are different to hot keys (set using the **&** sign in a component's caption). For example, if you set up a menu item called **&Open** within the **&File** menu, you can only press *Alt+O* to access it when the File menu is open. A shortcut key (like *F11* in Delphi) lets you get at the code in the menu's OnClick event handler from anywhere in the application with just a single keypress.

Having introduced menus, we'll now move on to applications that can display windows within windows, in a further attempt to emulate Word, Excel...

MDI? What the Bleep is MDI?

So far, all our Delphi applications have used just one form to interact with the user - if you were lucky, you might have got a couple of dialog boxes to help out, but apart from that you are stuck with this one form - this is known as the Single Document Interface (SDI) approach. The obvious alternative is to use a Multi Document Interface application (MDI). And, yes, Delphi makes it really easy. Read on for the particulars.

FYI
Just a note on why we use the word *document* in both of these terms. In Windows, every application you write deals with a specific kind of data, be it a text file in a word processor, or a sheet of numbers in a spreadsheet. This data is commonly known as the application's document.

With an MDI application, you have a single **parent** form which contains smaller **child** windows, each of which can show different documents, or different views of the same document. This is a much more powerful way for your users to work, as the application (which deals predominantly with just one type of document) can then have many such documents open at the same time. This is why it's also a very common type of Windows application.

To summarize the essentials of an MDI application, let's look at a prime example - Microsoft Word:

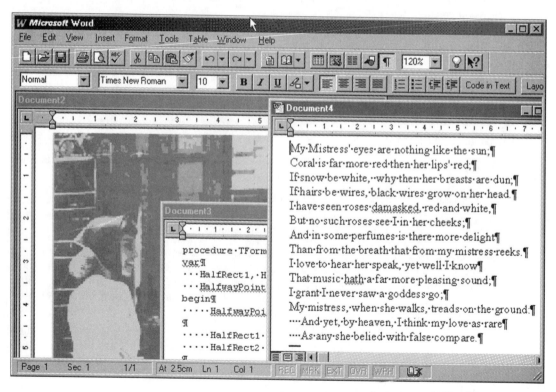

Word has one larger, parent window which holds the application's tool and menu bars at run time. It also acts as the container for the document windows and displays the title of the child window which currently has focus.

To stop Word running, you need to close the MDI parent window (the large container window in the background). Closing an MDI parent window is the same as closing the main form in a traditional SDI application, but with the additional advantages that it will, in turn, close all the open child windows, firing off any code which may live inside their OnClose event handlers.

And the MDI parent form really does contain those child windows, as you can see if you attempt to drag a child window beyond the parent window's boundaries. Just like the group box in Chapter 2, portions of the contained object (in this case a form) that step over the line just vanish. Minimize a child window and, rather than appearing on the desktop, the minimized icon appears within the parent form:

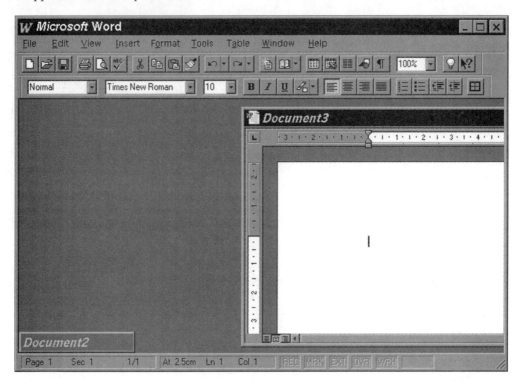

By and large, Windows handles all these features for you automatically. But, it's useful to know about the Delphi properties and methods that enable you to:

- ◗ Create an MDI application
- ◗ Arrange child windows at run time just as you desire
- ◗ Mess around with menus

All these questions, and more, will now be answered.

257

Try It Out - Your Very First MDI Application

1 OK, where to start? The most important thing that you'll need for any MDI application is, of course, an MDI parent form. Without an MDI parent form to contain everything, how on earth can you have an MDI application?

Create a new application in the normal way. Save it as **parentu.pas** and **mdi1.dpr**.

2 We change the blank form that appears into an MDI parent form simply by changing the FormStyle property in the Object Inspector to **fsMDIForm**:

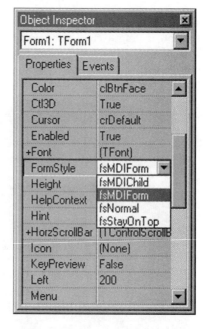

3 Creating an MDI child form is just as easy. Select File | New Form from the menu to add a new form to the project, or use the speed button. Save it as **childu.pas**. Then use the Object Inspector to change the FormStyle property again, this time to **fsMDIChild**. To move easily between the two forms, use the shortcut key *Shift+F12* to show you a list of the project's forms. Select the one you want to see from this list.

4 As yet, the look of the two design-time forms that we have created has not visibly changed. The changes are most evident at run time and, while you're designing, you still have all the usual freedom to do whatever you want to the forms in terms of placing controls and writing code.

So, let's run the application now.

Chapter 8 - Advanced Components

How It Works

When you actually run the code, strange things happen:

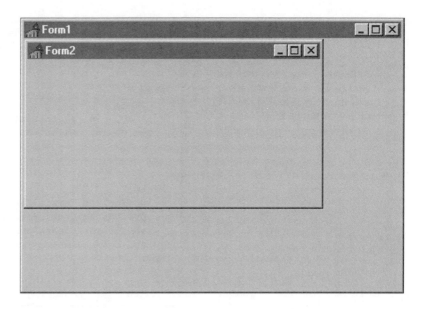

You see, normally, with a Delphi project that has more than one form, only the main form will appear by default when you run the program. Select Project | Options... and then the Forms tab of the Project Options dialog box:

Both forms are listed in the Auto-create list. That's normal in Delphi. Although Form1 is the form that will receive focus when the program is running, and which will also be the first form that the user will have the opportunity to interact with, Delphi lets you specify other forms that you want automatically created when the application runs. All the forms of the project are placed in this list by default:

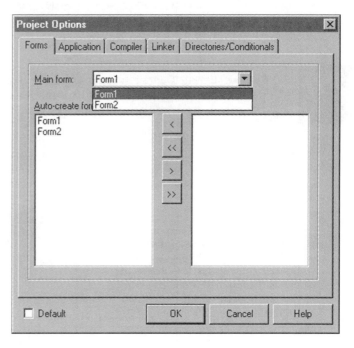

Form1, though, is the main form. Select View | Project Source and you'll see that this means it is created first. It's the form that is first displayed and it effectively marks the start of the program operation:

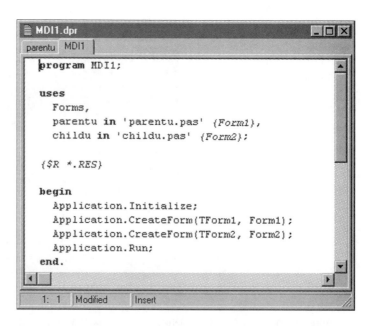

```
program MDI1;

uses
  Forms,
  parentu in 'parentu.pas' {Form1},
  childu in 'childu.pas' {Form2};

{$R *.RES}

begin
  Application.Initialize;
  Application.CreateForm(TForm1, Form1);
  Application.CreateForm(TForm2, Form2);
  Application.Run;
end.
```

Normally, when you create a second form, Delphi will put it together, but won't display it - you've got to do that yourself through code. In the case of an MDI application, things are slightly different. As this type of application is designed specifically to display a number of child windows, Delphi will automatically create and display each new form if it has its FormStyle property set to fsMDIChild.

FYI   A serious **EInvalidOperation** error will occur if you try to set your application's main form to **Form2**. Obviously, you can't have an MDI child floating around without a guiding MDI parent. Try it and see!

You'll also have noticed how the child form has changed size since design time - Delphi appears to have resized it for us. I'll explain why these things happen in a second, but, for now, let's get a feel for how the MDI application actually works.

Try moving that MDI child form outside the parent. You can't, can you? MDI child forms live inside the parent and cannot be dragged outside of the parent form at all. Try minimizing the child window. Notice how it appears inside the MDI parent as an iconized window, but still not outside the parent.

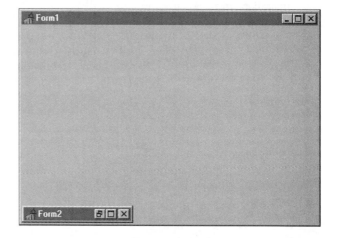

There's another subtle difference between MDI and SDI applications. Think about this for a second. What would happen in a normal application if you could see two forms on the screen, overlapping each other, and you clicked on the one that was partially hidden? The answer, of course, is that the hidden one would come into view and probably obscure the form that was in front. In an MDI application, this works slightly differently.

If you click on the parent form (which is, after all, partially hidden by the child form), you'll see that nothing happens; the MDI parent doesn't snap into view and sit in front of the child. However, if you had two or more child forms within the MDI parent, you would be able to make the overlap and replace each one within the MDI parent in the normal way.

Controlling the Creation Process

As you saw in the previous example, when you first run an MDI application, a couple of things happen:

▶ Any child forms in the application are automatically created and displayed.

▶ These child form are also automatically resized.

At times, you might not be particularly keen on either of these these default features. You might not want your parent window immediately cluttered by a load of children, and you certainly wouldn't want to lose the layout of your child windows, over which you've labored so hard. What can be done?

Try It Out - Controlling Your Children

1 Load up **mdi1.dpr**. We'll develop this example over a number of Try It Outs throughout the chapter. If you made a huge boo boo at any time, you'll find the program at each stage on the disk.

2 You can control which forms are automatically created and which don't by taking another look at the Project Options dialog. Both forms are on the Auto-create Forms list. Select Form2 and press the third speed button (with the single arrow pointing to the right) to move Form2 to the Available Forms list - the list of available, but uncreated forms.

3 OK the choice and call up the project source again. You'll see that only **Form1** is now created. Run it and see.

```
program MDI1;

uses
  Forms,
  parentu in 'parentu.pas' {Form1},
  childu in 'childu.pas' {Form2};

{$R *.RES}

begin
  Application.Initialize;
  Application.CreateForm(TForm1, Form1);
  Application.Run;
end.
```

4 "Hang on a sec!", you say with dawning horror. How are we ever going to display the child form now? Time to add a little code. Stop the program!

Drop a MainMenu component onto Form1 and edit it so that it has the heading File and, within that, New. Set the name properties of them to mnuFile and mnuFNew respectively, just so that the code you are going to write matches mine. I use the capital F in mnuFNew to show that this menu item is nested within the File menu heading.

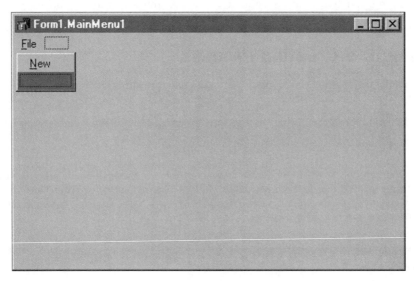

5 On your main form, rather than the Menu Editor, drop down the menu you just created and click on the New item. As if by magic, the code window will appear, ready for you to enter code for the OnClick event handler. Add the following code:

```
procedure TForm1.mnuFNewClick(Sender: TObject);
var
    NewForm : TForm2;
begin
    NewForm := TForm2.Create(Self);
end;
```

6 Try running the program now. You'll find that it won't work:

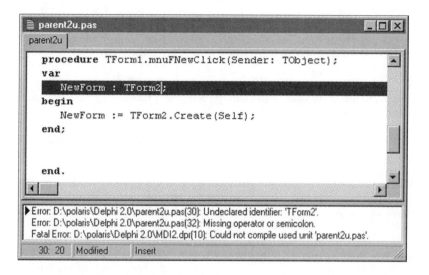

```
procedure TForm1.mnuFNewClick(Sender: TObject);
var
    NewForm : TForm2;
begin
    NewForm := TForm2.Create(Self);
end;


end.
```

Error: D:\polaris\Delphi 2.0\parent2u.pas(30): Undeclared identifier: 'TForm2'.
Error: D:\polaris\Delphi 2.0\parent2u.pas(32): Missing operator or semicolon.
Fatal Error: D:\polaris\Delphi 2.0\MDI2.dpr(10): Could not compile used unit 'parent2u.pas'.

The reason for the error message is that we are calling the **Create** method of a type defined in a different unit. Simply add **childu** to the **uses** clause of the MDI parent form (**parentu.pas**) and all will be well:

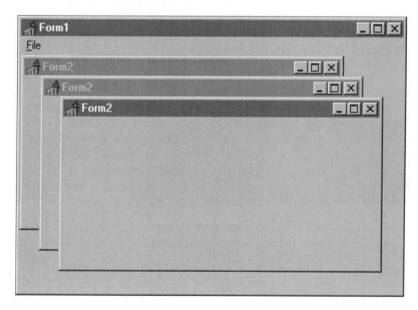

When you have the program running, you can keep on selecting File I New to create more identical child windows. Were this a serious project, each copy of Form2 would have the same components you added at design time, and the same functionality. However, each child window would be capable of displaying a different set of data, or document. Although they are all clones of **TForm2**, each child window is fully independent of other children.

You can find this application among the samples included with the book. It's called **mdi2.dpr**.

How It Works

The first part of the Try It Out makes sure that Form2 (the MDI child form) isn't automatically created when the application starts.

In the second, we see that creating a form at run time is really quite easy. Since all Delphi forms are actually defined as classes in your project, the process of creating a form is no different to that of creating any other kind of object. With normal forms, such as dialogs, you also have to write a tiny bit of code to actually display the form, but with MDI child forms, they automatically display themselves as soon as they are created, which again makes life even easier.

When we finally get round to coding, what we want to do is create a child form - more exactly, a new object of the type **TForm2**. This form type is the product of all our effort (?) with Form2 at design time, and from it we can instantiate as many child forms as we wish - it's just too easy.

The first thing we do in the code is to declare a new object variable, **NewForm**, of type **TForm2**. We then create an instance of the object type by assigning the object returned by **TForm2**'s **Create** method to **NewForm**.

You'll no doubt have noticed how I passed the Delphi keyword **Self** to **TForm2**'s **Create** method. I covered this keyword in quite some detail back in Chapter 5, but, just to jog your memory, here's the streamlined version. When you create an object, you must tell Delphi which object this new addition is related to. For example, when you create an edit box, you must tell it which form it belongs to.

Note that we haven't covered manually creating of components yet - you'll never guess which chapter that's in - but Delphi itself still follows this convention. When you drop a component on a form, Delphi calls the appropriate component's **Create** method and passes the name of the form on which you have just dropped the component. The component is then created and can then be displayed.

In the case of MDI child forms, it's important that we tell the child when it is created that its parent is the MDI parent form. **Self** is a keyword that refers to the object that is currently running the show. So, inside the New menu item's OnClick event, **Self** is set up by Delphi to point to the MDI parent form, **Form1**. Passing **Self** across to the child form's **Create** method is basically the same as saying "Hey, create yourself, but remember - you belong to the MDI parent form currently on display".

Continuing our example from this section, there's still one problem with the program which we haven't yet addressed.

Closing Down

Try running the code and creating a child form or two. When you've done that, try closing one of the child forms down by clicking its close icon:

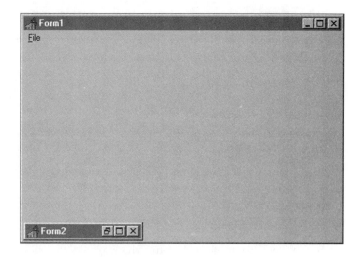

Instead of the window closing, it minimizes itself. This is actually a quirk of Delphi and the way it deals with objects, though it's very easy to look on it as a feature. In a real world application, child windows tend to do nothing but display data and allow it to be edited. If a user accidentally closed the window, they would usually get a "Do you really want to do be that stupid?" dialog to save the day, but not with Delphi.

With Delphi's child forms, you have to write code to explicitly destroy the child form, which, though extreme, does remove the form from view. How do we do that? We can't code **Form2.Close**, since there could be any number of child forms visible, all derived from **Form2**.

Try It Out - Orderly Retreat

1 Load up **mdi2.dpr**. From the Form list (*Shift+F12*) choose Form2. Then, from the Events tab of the Object Inspector, double-click on the OnClose event handler.

2 Add the following code to the code window that pops up:

```
procedure TForm2.FormClose(Sender: TObject; var Action: TCloseAction);
begin
     Action := caFree;
end;
```

How It Works

Though we can't call the form method **Close** to remove a specific form, Delphi provides us with an OnClose event handler which executes between the user closing the form and the form object being freed from memory. It allows you one last chance to perform an orderly shutdown, that is check that the user really wants to shut down and that all data is saved.

As to actually closing the form down, the OnClose event of the child form provides us with a variable parameter (one whose value we can change within the procedure). The **Action** parameter takes one of the four values of the enumerated type TCloseAction. You can feed values into **Action** to tell Delphi what to do when the code in this event is complete.

Value	Description
caNone	Nothing happens - the user can click the close icon as much as they like, but by setting the Action parameter to **caNone**, the form just ignores any attempts to close it down.
caHide	The form is not closed, it's hidden from view instead. Be careful with this one, since although the form may not appear on screen, it's still active and eating memory in your application.
caFree	This is what we want. **caFree** closes the form and frees all memory associated with it, effectively destroying this instance of the form.
caMinimize	The default value for action in an MDI child, the child is minimized rather than closed.

So, to close the form down properly, we need to replace the default **caMinimize** with **caFree** in the **Action** property in the child form's OnClose event. Now if you run the program, create a few child windows and then try to close them, you'll find that they close properly. It makes a lot of sense, though, that in a real world application, you would probably have a lot of other code in the OnClose event so that you can save out any data the user might have been working on, and to check that the user really does want to close the form down.

Controlling the Layout

As you probably already know from your experience of other MDI applications, it's very easy to find yourself running out of screen real estate once you have a few child forms running. It soon becomes a bit of a mouse nightmare as your frantically point and click your way around the application, trying to bring child forms into view, and minimize and close others.

If you have used other Windows programs, though, you'll also be accustomed to certain features being present in an MDI program to help cope with child windows - cascading, tiling and iconizing windows. You can also use the window list to instantly set focus to a specific window and bring it to the front. These features are usually found under a Windows menu heading:

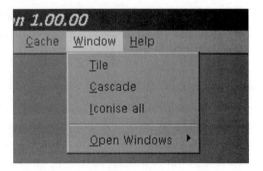

The other important feature is control resizing. It's very common in MDI applications for the components on the child form to move with changes in the child form's size.

The components we're talking about are usually just those needed to represent the document's data - for instance the Memo and StringGrid components. In Word and Excel, for instance, the child windows just display data. The code to manipulate this data is accessed through menus and speed bars, and any process status is reported the form's caption, the bottom panel or other parent form components. The case of a child window influencing the accessible menu items is something that we'll cover in a section or two.

The Resizing Problem

First, what is resizing? Well, there's the obvious mouse drag-and-drop which changes the form's size, but there's also the likelihood that your application will be used under different screen resolutions. What, then, if your components are all aligned to fit on a maximized form? You can even forbid resizing by changing the form's **BorderStyle** property to **bsDialog**, **bsSingle** or **bsNone**. The first reflects the fact that dialogs should never really need resizing as they usually display static information

But the forms in an MDI application tend to benefit from resizing, as they display the application's documents. You can never have a large enough view of some documents, which the user will use to enter and display their information.

Over the years that MDI has been with us, developers have come up with countless blocks of code to handle the resizing problem, and neatly re-arrange the controls on the form. Some write complex code to intercept Windows' resize messages and simply lock forms at preset maximum and minimum sizes so that the resize code is simple. Others dive into complex mathematical formula to resize and replace controls based on their original proportional position on the page.

All sounds a bit much, and even implementing a change in button size based on the **Form**'s **ClientWidth** and **ClientHeight** takes up code. But if you can reduce the components down to one or two, you can use the **Align** property (which can be set for all components at run time, and most at design time) to keep the component's position fixed to one or all of the form's edges as its size changes - remember this from Chapter 2's aligning section?

Try It Out - Alignment

1 With **mdi2.dpr** loaded, add a Memo component to **Form2**. Call it **memFile**.

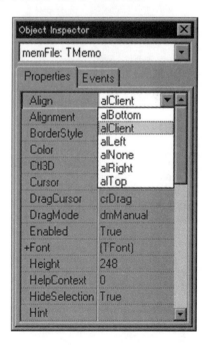

2 Then find the memo's Align property, and set it to alClient:

You can remove the Memo1 caption in the component by double-clicking on the memo's **Lines** property and editing the text in the string list editor provided.

3 Run the application and try resizing the child form. The memo follows suit.

Menus and MDI

How do MDI applications affect menus? Well, any window in any kind of application can have a menu attached. You could have an MDI parent window with a menu, and a child window inside it with its own menu, but what normally happens in this case is that any menus belonging to the child window overwrite the menu of the parent window.

Try It Out - Dealing with Menus in MDI Apps

1 Load up **mdi3.dpr** which we created above. We added a MainMenu component to the parent form a while back to create child windows. Select the component and click on the Items list to bring up the Menu Editor. Add entries for Open and Exit, so the menu looks like the following. Set the menu item names to **mnuFOpen** and **mnuFExit**:

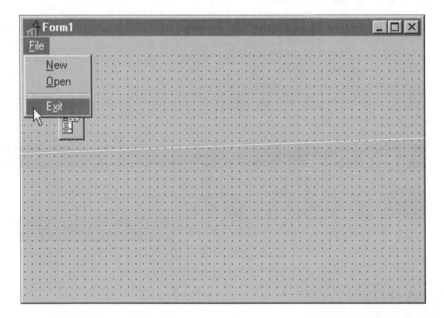

2 Now select the child form, **Form2**, and add a MainMenu component to this form. Call up the Menu Editor and add the following items. Call them **mnuEdit**, **mnuECut**, **mnuECopy** and **mnuEPaste** respectively:

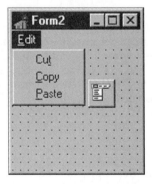

3 Now run the application. Select File | New and you'll see that the Edit menu replaces the File menu:

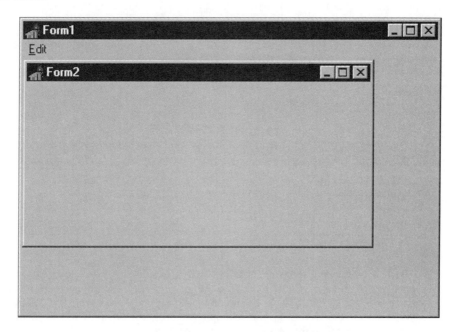

4 Select **Form2** from the Form list and use the Menu Editor to select the menu items. With the Edit menu heading selected, change the GroupIndex property to 2. Then go into the subheadings and change their GroupIndex to 2 as well. The editor will get the idea fairly quickly and do the rest for you.

Repeat this process with **Form1**'s File menu, setting all the menu items' **GroupIndex** to **1**. Now run the application and create a child window and see what happens.

How It Works

If you drop a menu on the child form and set it up as we did at first, the child window's menu takes over the MDI parent menu, overlaying the File menu. The user no longer has access to the File menu and, if this were a real application, would have no way of accessing new data, saving their work or any other such operation.

The reason for this is the GroupIndex property attached to each menu item. By default, this property is set to **0** whenever you create a menu. At run time, Delphi looks at the value of the index and says "It's **0** - I needn't care about any other menus. Yippee!". It then overwrites the parent window's menu with that of the child form.

What you need to do is set the GroupIndex property of each menu heading on the parent menu to a number greater than **0**. You then need to set the GroupIndex properties of the headers on the child window so that they fit in with this numbering system. The relative value of the GroupIndex determines where the heading appears in the parent's list.

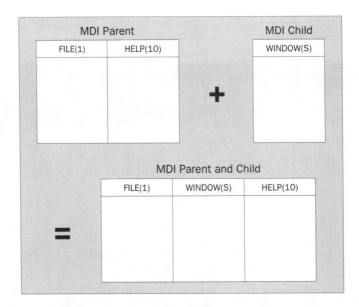

Imagine you have a menu on the parent form with two headings - File and Help. If you set the GroupIndex property of these headings to **1** and **10** respectively, and then create a menu on the child form whose GroupIndex is, say **5**, that menu headings is then inserted between File and Help on the MDI form. And if you set the GroupIndex property on the child form to **11**, the heading would appear to the right of the Help item on the MDI form.

Of course, there's nothing stopping you from simply redefining the File menu on the child window and letting it overwrite the menu on the MDI form, but, in terms of code, you would probably find yourself writing two identical sets of event handlers for the common operations.

Also, if you do need at some point to overwrite a menu on the MDI parent with a menu from a child window, all you need to do is set the child menu items' GroupIndex property to the value of the entry in the parent menu. We'll see this in action with a more fully fledged text editor in a moment.

Arranging the Windows

Most Windows users will expect to find options to Tile, Cascade and Arrange Icons on a menu somewhere in your application. Is this a potential nightmare, or what? Again, Delphi comes to your rescue. It's so easy, you'll think it's a cheat.

Try It Out - Window Dressing

1 Load up **mdi4.dpr**, which is our example up to the last section (plus a few extra lines of code for you to discover). Add a new heading to the parent form's menu, Windows, and fill out the contents so:

2 All you need to do now is to write a single line of code into each menu item's OnClick event handler. Add the following statement to the Next menu item:

```
procedure TfrmMDI.mnuWNextClick(Sender: TObject);
begin
     Next;
end;
```

3 Simple, ain't it? Do the same for the Previous menu item which allows you to move to the previous child window. Instead of calling the **Next** method, though, just call the **Previous** method instead:

```
procedure TfrmMDI.mnuWPreviousClick(Sender: TObject);
begin
     Previous;
end;
```

4 As for the Cascade menu item, it's just boringly simple - just call the parent's **Cascade** method. The **Cascade** method arranges the child windows diagonally down an MDI parent form:

```
procedure TfrmMDI.mnuWCascadeClick(Sender: TObject);
begin
     Cascade;
end;
```

5 Tiling child windows involves a tiny amount more effort, though, since you really should tell the parent how you want to tile the child forms - horizontally or vertically:

```
procedure TfrmMDI.mnuWTileClick(Sender: TObject);
begin
     TileMode := tbVertical;
     Tile;
end;
```

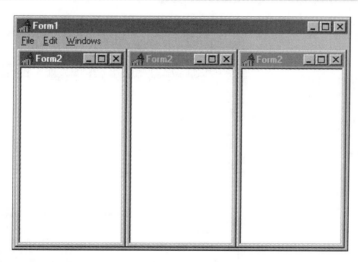

All that you need to do this is to fire a value into the **TileMode** property of the form. It takes just one of two values - **tbVertical** and **tbHorizontal**. After that, just call the **Tile** method to actually make the windows tile. The choice is yours.

6 The final bit of code is the section that neatly arranges the minimized windows, simply call the **ArrangeIcons** method of the MDI parent:

```
procedure TfrmMDI.mnuWArrangeClick(Sender: TObject);
begin
    ArrangeIcons;
end;
```

Minimize all those child windows and make a mess of their icons, before hitting the Arrange Icons menu item.

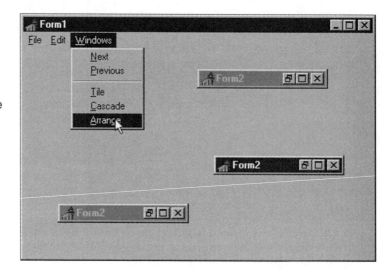

We won't bother explaining these; just rejoice in the unusual number of single word methods doing all the work for you!

An Almost Real-life Example

Now for an apology: your application **mdi5.dpr** is coming along just fine, but we need to show some other features of the parent/child bond. So we have added a few extras to our example, taken out a few extraneous bits, and called it **texedit.dpr**. This application is a very simple MDI text editor that lets you load up, edit and then save text files, with each text file living in its own child window.

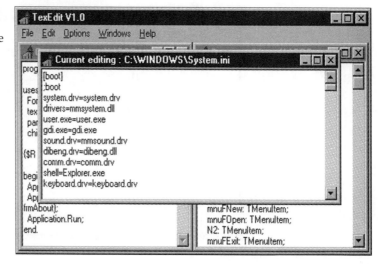

Although the code may look a little complex, TexEdit is actually a very simple program, and demonstrates a lot of MDI features. When I was writing this app, I went through a process of thinking up questions like "What are the child forms going to do?", "What controls do they need?", "How can I make this app as MDI friendly as possible?" Since it's a text editor, the only data the child windows can display is text documents. Obviously, the user needs some way to create new child windows, load up text documents, save them again, close Windows down and quit the application.

The parent form menu relates just to those items of general use - creating a new child window, exiting the application, or arranging windows. The child menus have their own overlay of menu functions to save, edit, or close a particular window.

Select <u>V</u>iew | Project Manager and take a look at the units that make up the project:

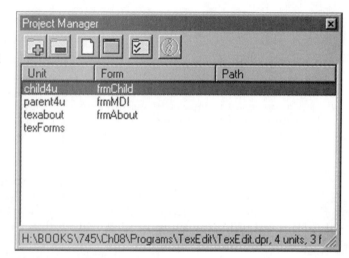

As you can see, the project consists of four units:

- ▶ One About box form (which we can ignore for now)
- ▶ One MDI parent form, **parent4u.pas**
- ▶ One MDI child form, **child4u.pas**
- ▶ A unit called **texforms**.

First an apology, because this is another of those &*@#ing examples which are less than perfect but are meant to show you the best way to go...

TexForms holds all the code to control the creation of the child forms, loading and saving data from these children, and so on. However, it also needs to hold a reference to the MDI parent form somewhere, since in order to create those child forms, it needs to know their parent.

Parent and Child

Wouldn't it be so much easier if the child forms themselves could actually find out the identity of their parent, and vice versa?

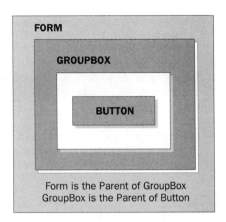

Well, it probably won't come as much of a surprise to learn that they can. There is a collection of objects, almost an array of objects, attached to the MDI parent which you can use to reach its children. Let's take a look at an example:

Form is the Parent of GroupBox
GroupBox is the Parent of Button

Not surprisingly, this is a Windows-based hierarchy (that operating system gets everywhere!). Let me let you into a little secret - Windows is so narrow-minded that it considers everything it sees as a window, even the little controls that it puts onto forms. Once you understand this, you start to understand why you've got a **Parent** property on your components - it indicates which form (or component) the component is associated with. It allows you to traverse the Windows hierarchy in conjunction with **Controls** property, the **Parent** property moving you up the hierarchy, the **Controls** property down.

Try not to confuse the **Parent** property with **Owner** or the **Controls** property with **Components**. **Parent** and **Controls** are Windows-related properties that deal with the parent and child relationship between windows. The **Owner** and **Components** properties deal with a similar relationship between class definitions and instance of a component - a class/object relationship. In this way, a label (no windows handle, so not a window) can be owned by **TForm1** without having a parent. The edit box sitting right next to it, though, would also be owned by **TForm1**, but it *does* have a parent - by coincidence, also **TForm1**.

You can see how I've used this property, **Parent** that is, in the two versions of our text editor.

Checking Out the Application

If you run this application, you will find yourself facing a pretty slick, if not basic word processor. It handles all the basic word processor functions, such as loading in text, saving it again, cutting and pasting from the clipboard and so on. However, all these features, pretty as they are, aren't what we're here to see - we're going to look at the implementation of the code.

The basic structure of the code is shown on the following page:

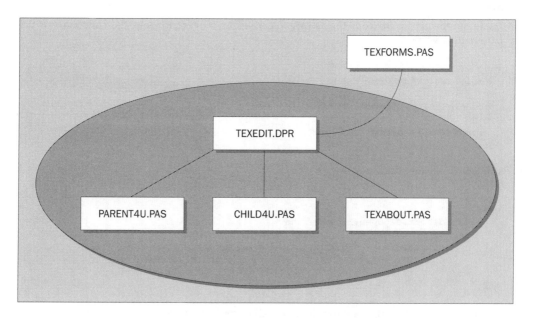

As you can see, I've included a library unit to deal with all the number crunching, but, unfortunately, this doesn't make use of the OOP part of Object Pascal.

Yep, I know, I'd have done it this way as well. You put all of your generic routines in a library and refer to them as and when you need them, but this isn't the OOP way to do stuff. You wrap data and methods into an object and then let objects interact. There's no third party making suitable suggestions about how they should handle a particular situation. Anyway, more on this later, let's get back to the fray.

As you can see from the following code snippet, the main unit deals with the user's interaction with the menus, and in particular, the File | Open menu option by making a call to **Load_File**, a function defined in the library unit, **texforms.pas**:

```
procedure TfrmMDI.mnuFOpenClick(Sender: TObject);
begin
    Load_File;
end;

procedure TfrmChild.mnuFOpenClick(Sender: TObject);
begin
    Load_File;
end;
```

Note how we need two event handlers to cover this event. This is because of the way that menus work in Delphi. We've got one File menu defined in the MDI parent form that allows you to create the first child. When that child is created, the MDI parent form's File menu is replaced by the child's version. As both need to be able to create a new child, we need two event handlers - one for each menu.

This code snippet is taken from the library file itself and refers to how the function call from the parent unit is handled:

```
var
    mdiForm : TfrmMDI;

procedure Init ( AForm : TfrmMDI );
begin
        mdiForm := AForm;
end;

procedure Load_File;
var
    ChildForm : TFrmChild;
begin
        if mdiForm.dlgOpen.Execute then
        begin
                ChildForm := TFrmChild.Create(mdiForm);
                ChildForm.LoadTextFile(mdiForm.dlgOpen.Filename);
        end;
end;
```

Notice all the references in this procedure to **mdiForm**, a variable local to the **texforms** unit. **mdiForm** is an object variable of the parent form type that has to be set up by yet another block of code. We need this variable at run time in order to create new children and access the controls on the parent form.

Since both the MDI parent and child forms need to make use of code in the **texforms** unit, both need a reference to that unit in a **uses** clause in their **implementation** section. In addition, the code in the **texforms** unit needs to know what our MDI parent and child forms are like in order to accept them as parameters to function and procedure calls. To this end, it has a reference to each form inside its **interface** section. Whew! I think we just missed a circular reference.

This is a prime example of a structured approach to application development. It's how you would solve the problem using a non-object-oriented languages like Pascal proper. But Delphi Pascal builds on that by adding in the facility to handle objects. So, though this last example of coding practice is quite okay, and even quite common, it misses out on some of Delphi Pascal's power. The solution looks like this:

Rather than having to make use of a separate code unit which handles interaction between the two forms, we can now cut out the middle man. The bulk of the functionality is written into methods of the child form which can be called by the MDI parent. The MDI child which needs to access the common dialogs on the parent can get at those controls using the **Parent** property, and can also call methods of the MDI parent, such as the **Close** method.

All in all then, the code should adopt a much tidier, more object-oriented approach. Take a look at **texedit2.dpr**. The code for the creation of the child is now contained, as you would expect, in the event handler that deals with the parent MDI forms' File | Open menu option,

```
procedure TfrmMDI.mnuFOpenClick(Sender: TObject);
var
    ChildForm : TFrmChild;
begin
```

```
if frmMDI.dlgOpen.Execute then
    begin
        ChildForm := TfrmChild.Create(Self);
        ChildForm.LoadTextFile(frmMDI.dlgOpen.Filename);
    end;
end;
```

while the code that handles the creation of a new child when one is already open is now one line:

```
procedure TfrmChild.mnuFOpenClick(Sender: TObject);
begin
    (Parent as TFrmMDI).mnuFOpenClick(Self);
end;
```

Rather than cutting and pasting the code from the MDI form into the child form, we have used the **Parent** property to access the actual event handlers on the MDI form.

Parent is an object in itself, so it has methods the same as any other, as well as properties. However, **Parent** is a generic object. As far as Delphi is concerned, it has no form and is just a plain old ordinary object. We need to tell Delphi what kind of object it is.

We can do this by doing something called **typecasting**, which is where the **as** method comes in. By saying,

```
Parent as TFrmMDI
```

we are telling Delphi to use the **Parent** object, and that in this particular piece of code, it should treat the **Parent** object as a **TFrmMDI** derived object. This means that we can start to play with the methods, controls, event handlers and properties of that form. Typecasting makes obvious what you already intuitively know to be true; that the parent of the child window in this case is **TFrmMDI**, for the benefit of a skeptical compiler. (Mind you, I'd be skeptical if I had to deal with some of the code that's written...)

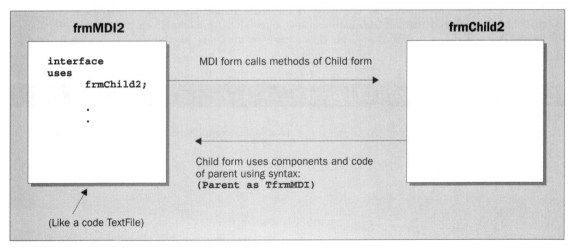

FYI This doesn't mean that typecasting is optional, just that you may often overlook it as being superfluous. Why shouldn't the compiler just know what you know? The thing is, the compiler is completely without class snobbery - it will consider any object to be a suitable parent, it just needs to be told.

Returning to the actual code, we see that, with the typecast object, it's now safe to explicitly call any of the procedures declared in the **TfrmMDI** form:

```
(Parent as TFrmMDI).mnuFOpenClick(Self);
```

The only other point to note is that the Open menu item's OnClick event handler needs to be passed a **Sender** parameter, a TObject. However, as I don't need this value in the code (any old value will do), I'm using the easiest one to reference - **TfrmMDI**.

On the whole, getting at the child forms is easy; the tricky bit depends on exactly when you want to access them. In TexEdit2, for example, the only time that the code in the MDI form ever needs to worry about dealing with a child form is at the child form's conception. Then, the parent has a **private** object variable of a child form type from which the child form is created.

```
procedure TfrmMDI.mnuFNewClick(Sender: TObject);
var
    ChildForm : TFrmChild;
begin
    ChildForm := TFrmChild.Create(Self);
    ChildForm.LoadTextFile('');
end;
```

No problems there then. But, what if you wanted to get back to this new child window from a different event? Well, the simple (but long winded, inelegant and amateurish) way of doing it would be to have an array of these object variables permanently available within the MDI form's unit.

However, a better approach is to use what Delphi has already made available: the **MDIChildCount** and **MDIChildren** properties of an MDI form. We'll use them to modify the **texedit2** project, so that the user can close down or minimize all the child windows in one go?

Try It Out - Dealing with Children

1 Load up **texedit2.dpr**. Double-click the MainMenu component on the MDI form to start up the Menu Editor:

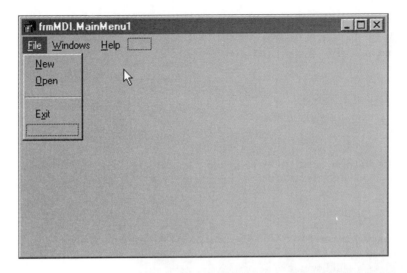

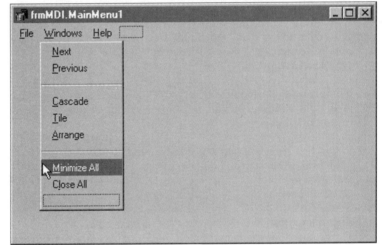

2 Now add to the Window menu so that it looks like the one in the screenshot:

3 Call the new menu items mnuWCloseAll and mnuWMinimizeAll. Make sure their GroupIndex is 3, so that they remain when the child form's menu auto-merges with its parent, as we saw earlier.

4 Time to write some code. Close down the Menu Editor when you have created the new menu, then click on the Close All item on the MDI form to bring up its code window. To close down the child forms, we need to write a loop to go through all the child forms, firing the **Close** method for each. Change the event handler in the code window so that it now looks like this:

```
procedure TfrmMDI.mnuWCloseAllClick(Sender: TObject);
var
    nChild : integer;
begin
    for nChild := 0 to (MDIChildCount-1) do
        MDIChildren[nChild].Close;
end;
```

5 Do the same for the <u>M</u>inimize All menu item and add the same code, but change the **WindowState** property to **wsMinimized**, and add another line to close down the child window with focus:

```
procedure TfrmMDI.mnuWMinimizeAllClick(Sender: TObject);
var
   nChild : Integer;
begin
     for nChild := 0 to (MDIChildCount-1) do
         MDIChildren[nChild].WindowState := wsMinimized;
     frmMDI.ActiveMDIChild.WindowState := wsMinimized;
end;
```

How It Works

The **MDIChildCount** property is quite self-explanatory- it returns the number of child windows currently attached to this form. The **MDIChildren** property is actually an array of objects, each element of which is a child window.

As with all arrays in Delphi, this one is zero-based. So, if you had three child windows open, you could access them individually as **MDIChildren[0]**, **MDIChildren[1]** and **MDIChildren[2]**. This explains why the code you just wrote uses a loop going from **0** to **(MDIChildCount-1)**.

Minimizing the windows at run time is equally easy; instead of calling the **Close** method of each child window, though, you just need to set the **WindowState** property of each child form to **wsMinimized**.

In practice, there's a slight quirk, as Windows appears unwilling to minimize the child window with focus. The active child window is assigned to the parent form's **ActiveMDIChild** property and it is this property that we use to minimize the active window, whatever its place in the **MDIChildren** array.

And there you have it - how to create MDI applications, add in your own menus and provide all the functionality that the user might expect from such an application. One of the final subjects that I've got to cover in this chapter is the common dialogs that the operating system provides for some of the more common requests it will throw at you, such as the File Open dialog. As we've touched on these babies in this last example, let's get to them right away...

Dialogs

As we've already seen, and so had cause for celebration, Windows comes complete with a set of pre-built, fully functional dialog boxes which we can make use of in our Delphi apps. These are known as the Windows **common dialogs**. Common to all applications, they standardize user needs and help integrate the truculent family of Windows applications.

Delphi also makes them phenomenally easy to use. Long live the **execute** method! In this section, we'll add some finishing touches to the dialogs that are at work in the text editor - you can have a sneak preview of them in action if you load and run **texedit3.dpr**.

Using the File Dialogs

We've already coded the File Open and SaveAs dialogs into our application:

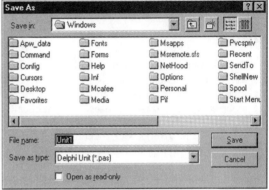

Both dialogs work in an almost identical fashion, the only real difference being that the SaveAs dialog normally gives the user a default filename when the dialog springs into view. This is done by giving the file's current name to the **FileName** property in code.

Both have identical properties as well, most of which are self-explanatory. For instance, the **DefaultExt** property specifies the file extension to be supplied if the user doesn't enter one. The **InitialDir** property gives the initial path to look on - and you can set this to the path that was last used if you've a mind. You can even give the dialog your very own title.

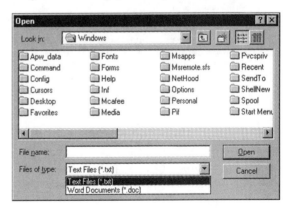

In fact, the trickiest part of the file dialogs has to be dealing with the file filters - this is a hard life isn't it? When you see an Open or Save As dialog box, have you ever noticed a combo box at the bottom left that lets you select the file type that you want to deal with?

You can set these entries using the **Filter** property of the file dialog. The **Filter** property itself expects nothing more than a string. However, this single string can contain any number of different filters which are compared against file extensions. The filter presented to the user initially can be set using the **FilterIndex** property.

Take a look at this:

```
dlgOpen.Filter := 'Text Files (*.txt)|*.txt|Word Documents
                   (*.Doc)|*.doc';
```

This line sets up the filter on an open dialog to show text only documents (files that end in **.txt**) or Word documents (files that end in **.doc**). The format of the data in the string is:

```
'<Description1> | <Filter1> | <Description2> | <Filter2> ...'
```

Color

Just as with the file dialogs, using the color dialog is really simple - just run the **Execute** method. Whichever color is selected in the dialog is passed back to your application via the dialog's **Color** property, and you can get at it by a reference to here. For example, the following code snippet allows the user to dynamically change the memo's color:

```
If dlgColor.Execute then
   memFile.Color := dlgColor.Color;
```

The strangest property to deal with here is the **TStrings** list CustomColors. These are user-defined colors if you like, created using the color editor on the right-hand side of the full dialog. You can set these custom colors up before the dialog appears, and then examine them for any changes added by the user by looking at this list.

Each string in the list defines a color, and you can have up to 16 strings to play with. Chapter 6 explained how to use the Windows **RGB** function to get at a number that represents a color like this. For example:

```
procedure TfrmChild.mnuOColorClick(Sender: TObject);
var
   nsList : TStringList;
begin
      {Instantiate StringList}
      nsList := TStringList.Create;
      nsList.Add('ColorA=000000');
      nsList.Add('ColorB=10A3D4');
      dlgColor.CustomColors.AddStrings(nsList);

      if dlgColor.Execute then
         memFile.Font.Color := dlgColor.Color;
end;
```

You can see the Color dialog in action in the **texedit3.dpr** project again. Take a look at the code behind the Options | Color menu item to see how it all works.

Printing

The Print dialog provides an easy mechanism for controlling printing from your application. However, it doesn't do your printing for you; it just helps you to find out how the user wants to print:

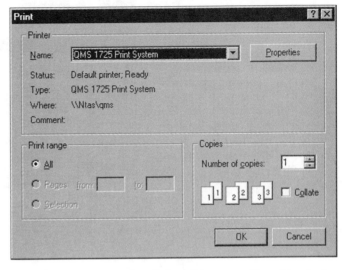

The properties of the dialog are named as they appear on the dialog. Of course, if your code is simply not capable of printing specific pages of a report, or printing to a file and so on, you should disable these options in the dialog through the **Options** set attached to the Print dialog component:

```
procedure TfrmChild.mnuFPrintClick(Sender: TObject);
var
    Line : integer;
    PrintText : System.Text;
begin
    dlgPrint.Options := [poSelection, poPageNums];
    {Uses the Printers unit declared in the uses clause}
    if dlgPrint.Execute then
    begin
        AssignPrn(PrintText);
        Rewrite(PrintText);
        Printer.Canvas.Font := memFile.Font;
        {Prints the file line by line}
        for Line := 0 to (memFile.Lines.Count -1) do
            WriteLn(PrintText, memFile.Lines[Line]);
        System.Close(PrintText);
    end;
end;
```

The Print dialog is what I call a passive dialog. Like the Color and Font dialogs, it does nothing but let the user make choices to which your application should respond.

Print Setup Dialog

The Print Setup dialog is a little different. It provides no useful feedback to your application about what the user has chosen to do inside it; instead, it actively allows them to configure printers and printer settings without any kind of interference from your code. Consequentially, the Print Setup dialog box has no special properties of its own:

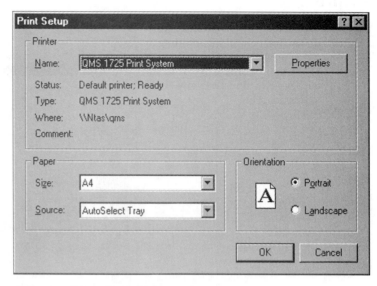

So, all you really need to know about the PrinterSetUpDialog is how to run it, which is as simple as calling its **Execute** method.

```
dlgPrintSetup.Execute;
```

Fonts

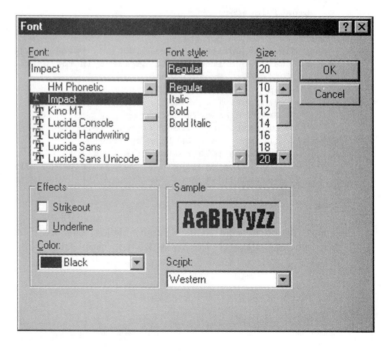

The Font dialog is so passive that it has to provide oodles of feedback on what the user did to the code:

Depending on which options you set up, the Font dialog can return a font name, size, style, color and so on. All these are returned through the **Font** object attached to the component, so you can either assign this object to a component in full, or copy individual properties from it:

```
memFile.Font.Assign(dlgFont.Font);
```

or

```
memFile.Font.Bold := dlgFont.Font.Bold;
memFile.Font.Name := dlgFont.Font.Name;
```

You might also be interested in another Font dialog property, called **Device**. This determines whether your selection affects the screen or the printer or both - check out the help files from more information on this property.

Options

No tour, however whistle-stop, would be complete without giving you a way to waste hours of your free time by tweaking each dialog's **Options** set. The set expects a variable length list of values which are used to change the dialog's operation and appearance. As we saw with **MessageDlg**'s button set, you add values to a set by placing them inside square brackets and separating them with commas:

```
dlgPrint.Options := [poSelection, poPageNums];
```

These options allow you to enable the print dialog's selection and page number options with as little fuss as possible. All of these values are Delphi constants, and you can get a complete list of them by double-clicking the **Options** object in the Object Inspector for each dialog. A breathtaking array awaits...

Summary

Throughout this chapter, I have built upon your existing knowledge of Pascal and the Single Document Interface. I've shown you how to take advantage of the Multiple Document Interface, add menus to your applications and even draw upon Windows common dialogs to give the finished application a little finesse.

Hopefully, you should now be able to produce applications of the quality and usability of the commercial applications such as Word, Excel and even Delphi itself, incorporating these features into your applications so allowing your users the comfort that they are used to.

In the next chapter, I'm moving onto the subject that I know a lot of you have been waiting for - working with databases and creating your first database application.

An Introduction to Databases

Ever since Microsoft released the infamous Visual Basic 3, all the visual development systems that have been aimed at Windows have achieved a reputation for not only allowing rapid application development, but also for providing point-and-click database application development. Delphi is no exception, and with Delphi 2.0 we now have a product that quite literally blows the competition out of the water.

One of the great things about Delphi's database development tools is that they do at last realize the dream of point-and-click application development. By simply dropping components onto a form, filling in just a few properties and then compiling the application, you can have a fully functioning database app. In addition, if you take advantage of the Database Form Expert, you don't even have to drop the components yourself - you can sit back and let Delphi design your form and add functionality to it, while you barely lift a finger.

In this chapter, we'll perform a lot of the groundwork that you'll need to create a database application. We'll cover:

- A few of the terms and titles that make up the database vernacular
- How to use the Database Desktop to create and maintain your databases
- How to create a database application using the Database Form Expert

In the next chapter, we get down and get dirty as we explore the Delphi database components more fully, and also start to link some code into your application.

First, Some Theory

The bulk of this chapter is going to be a real hands-on affair, looking at how we can quickly design a database and then create a Delphi application to interrogate it using the tools that Borland have provided in the Delphi package. However, database development tools (particularly those like Delphi that deal with something known as **relational databases**) come replete with a whole host of weird and wonderful terms and phrases.

If you have worked with relational databases before, you may want to simply flick through this section, or even totally skip it, but if you haven't, grab yourself a coffee, pull up a chair and absorb what follows before you go any further.

Database Terminology

Okay...let's get all those nasty terms out of the way right from the start. Databases in Delphi consist of tables, queries, indexes, records and, of course, the database as a whole. But what do all these weird things mean?

Let's imagine for a second that someone told us we need to move our paper based records system onto computer 'because it's the way of the future'. All this sounded great at the time, but how are we actually going to move, say, all of our employee information currently stored in filing cabinets onto computer? We put them all onto what we call a **database**.

First things first - you wander on down to the Personnel department to take a look at the information itself and, as soon as you walk into the office, you can see their current database. Standing in the corner of the room, adorned by the obligatory potted plant, is the filing cabinet. That filing cabinet holds all the information that the department needs - it is, in effect, their database.

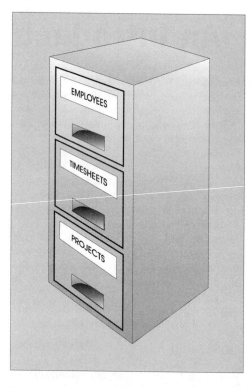

As you move closer to the filing cabinet, you notice that this department is really quite organized. Each drawer is clearly labeled with the type of information it contains, one for Employee information, one for Timesheets and another for Projects. Each drawer is, in effect, a database **table**, a place to store information about a particular subject.

FYI
A database table is simply somewhere to store linked items of information that the database has been designed to accommodate. If you can identify a set of criteria (details of the work that is done in a company) that defines the information to be stored, and you can see relationships between some groups of those criteria (employee details, what they spend their days doing and how their days are broken up between projects), you are already starting to break your data into what a relational database refers to as *tables*.

Opening the Employee drawer reveals a long line of thick cards, each of which has personal information relating to a particular member of the company's staff. Each card relates to a different employee and contains different information, but all the cards have a common format with space to store preset information, such as the employee's name, their home address, and so on. In our Delphi database, these cards will be the **records** in our Employee table.

The structure of these records is completely dependent on the fields in the table. When you define a table in a Delphi database, you are effectively designing the format of the records, the blank cards in the Employee drawer in that filing cabinet. You tell the system what information that table is going to hold, defining what will appear on each and every record contained within the table. Each of these items of information is called a **field.**

You can think of a table in a database as a grid of information, the members of the group laid out along the top and the various items of interest positioned down the side. In this case, each row is a field and each column is a complete record:

		1	2	3	4	5	6	7	8	9	10	11
FIRST	NAME											
	SURNAME											
	ADDRESS											
	COUNTRY											
	PHONE											
	FAX											
	D O B											

EMPLOYEE

Looking at the cards a little closer, you notice some strange little tabs which stick up above the line of cards in the drawer. On each tab, you can identify the employee's surname and personnel number. In a Delphi database, these tabs are referred to as **indexes**, and are used in just the same way as their physical filing cabinet counterparts - a fast way of picking out the card belonging to a particular employee.

As you start to pull the cards out of the drawer, a large piece of paper falls to the floor. You pick it up and notice that at the top it says 'Leavers' and lists a load of employee numbers. These are the employees who have left within the last financial year and provide anyone looking at the Employee drawer with a set of employees that fulfill a given criteria, in this case all those employees who can be removed from the database at the beginning of the next financial year when their details are passed on to another company.

In a Delphi database, this is called a **query**. However, instead of physically linking records in the table to records in the query, we can store a piece of code in a language known as **SQL** (pronounced Sequel and standing for Structured Query Language) in the database. Running the query causes the database engine to scan through the database and return all the records that fit the criteria. For example, the following line of code is a SQL query:

```
Select * from Employee where Left = True
```

Here, I'm asking the database engine to return a set of records from the **Employee** table where the field called **Left** in each of those records has a value of **True**, or, in other words, to tell me which employees have left the company.

So far, so good. Unfortunately, all of the things that I've just described are the common elements of any old database, but, if you remember, I said that Delphi deals with something called a **relational database**. What's the difference between what I've just described and this relational database thing?

Relational Databases

The relational part of the equation is the cool bit. In the bad old days, we had something known as the **flat file database**. A wonderful invention, the flat file database was really nothing more than a single file, more than one if you were really lucky, which held all the data relating to something. This table, as we would now call it, was inherently inefficient.

Getting back to our Employee database example, you would probably want to record which department that employee worked in. In the flat file system, this would typically mean one of two things. Either you store the entire department name in there somewhere, thus duplicating a lot of data within the file itself (since presumably more than one employee would work in most departments), or you would end up with a weird set of numbers and an harassed looking coder wandering around chanting incantations like '1 means personnel, 2 means I.T.' which she would then hard code into her application.

Company	City	Contact	Phone
Wash Co	Paris	John	56742
Tents Ltd	Berlin	Arnold	92744
Argot	New York	Freddy	91287
Ringtons	Montreal	Bruce	31134
M & C's	Rome	Tim	71253
Smiths	Selville	Janice	13843
Wash Co	Paris	Ronald	52342
Wall Inc	Tokyo	Bill	22432
Argot	New York	Nancy	82364

The relational database approach is much nicer, since you would end up with two tables; one for the employee information, and another for the department information. The Employee table would then contain a link in some way to a record in the Department table so that the previously harassed developer need only write a simple query to pull the employee details, and a single snippet of information from the related Department table (the department name).

Company	City	Company ID
Wash Co	Paris	1
Tents Ltd	Berlin	2
Argot	New York	3
Ringtons	Montreal	4
M & C's	Rome	5
Smiths	Selville	6
Wall Inc	Tokyo	7

Company ID	Contact ID	Contact	Phone
1	1	John	56742
2	2	Arnold	92744
3	3	Freddy	91287
4	4	Bruce	31134
5	5	Tim	71253
6	6	Janice	13843
1	7	Ronald	52342
7	8	Bill	22432
3	9	Nancy	82364

In this way, you soon end up with data-driven applications. Rather than writing an application where every little piece of code, indicator and flag of some kind are handwritten into the application, you write an app that links records, that actually uses the data in the database in a logical, independent way. The result is an application that's much easier to understand and debug, and that can be modified in terms of how it presents information by doing nothing more than changing your own view of the information.

To make the trick work, though, requires more than a little thought when you are designing the database itself. To really make the best use of the relational database model, even before you sit down and 'put pen to paper' you should take a long hard look at your data. You should be starting to identify relationships within that data that will cut down on having pieces of information duplicated unnecessarily.

 FYI   If you're interested in learning more about designing your database with respect to the relational model, why not check out *Instant SQL* by Joe Celko, from Wrox Press ISBN 1-874416-508.

Of course, these issues are a little beyond the scope of this book, and there are far more authors out there more qualified to cover the whole area than I. But, even so, throughout the rest of this chapter and the next, I'll still touch on the pitfalls and benefits that you need to keep an eye out for.

Databases in Delphi

Normally, with a visual development tool such as Delphi, you would also need the assistance of another package to help you actually create your database in the first place, before you even think of bolting an application on the front. With those using Visual Basic, for example, it has been a long standing gripe that the only decent tool available to them for dealing with the Access databases is the $200 or more Access package itself.

Borland saw this and included a whole host of database tools with Delphi. Delphi Client/Server edition, for example, has a set of database tools that would rival a dedicated relational database development system, such as Oracle or Informix.

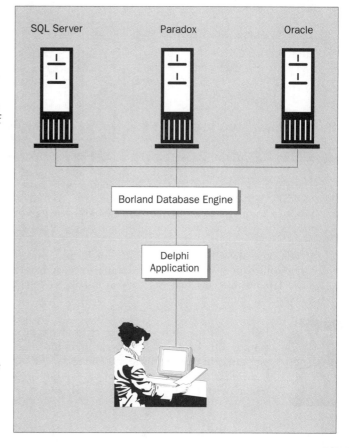

Fortunately, Borland also recognized that everyone might not want to pay for Delphi C/S, but quite a few developers would be interested in database applications, so they chucked a few of the more general database tools into Desktop and Developer as well. The most important of these tools is a little gem known as the **Database Desktop**:

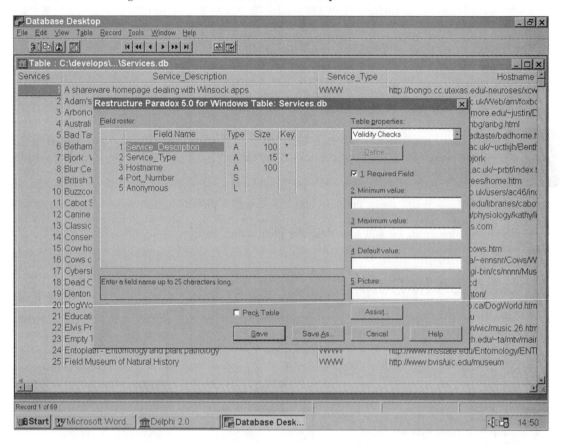

The Database Desktop (just think...someone gets paid to come up with names like that) is basically Borland's equivalent to Paradox for Windows, but without the ability to write code, produce forms or kick out reports. This still leaves you with you with an incredibly powerful tool with which to create and maintain your database, as well as to enter data if you need to.

If you have the Client/Server edition of Delphi, you have even more tools, with weird and wonderful names like Interbase Server and such like. I'm going to ignore these on the whole, since I figure that the majority of you out there don't have such extravagant tastes in your software development tools.

Delphi has the ability to connect to any type of database system - you might have to work a little harder to find the drivers for some of the stranger propriety databases, but you can still connect to them. However, for the rest of this chapter, I'm going to refer to a Delphi database quite a lot - the default type of database that the Database Desktop creates with the Paradox database engine.

A Quick Walkthrough

Time to get to work. We'll spend the rest of the chapter looking at ways to put together a simple contact management system which is obviously going to require some kind of contact management database. If you're really lazy, you can just grab this from the examples on the disk, but you'll learn more by following along. In addition, some of the examples here just can't be put onto the disk because of problems that I will make you aware of later.

Before we set off, if you are going to follow along with these examples, it would be a really good idea to create a directory on your hard disk to hold the database files that we're about to create.

 Relational database suppliers tend to build their wares in one of two ways. On the one hand, you have the Microsoft approach, the 'put all your eggs in a single electronic basket and pray' approach. The Borland approach is much better. A Delphi (or Paradox) database is really nothing more than a directory containing a collection of files, each file containing some of the information that goes towards the database as a whole. This approach means that you can get to the data if the rest of the files have been destroyed - try doing that to a corrupted Access database.

You can open up the Database Desktop by either selecting it from the Borland Delphi group that was created when you installed Delphi, or by selecting Tools | Database Desktop in Delphi itself. Try it now, you're going to need it running in a little while:

Have a play around with the menus for a little while and, even if you have never used Paradox before, you should get the distinct feeling that this is indeed a somewhat crippled version of a bigger product - but that really isn't a bad thing; there's still an incredible amount of power in there.

Preparing the Database Desktop

The first two things you need to set up before you begin working on a database are the **Working** and **Private** directories. The Database Desktop makes great use of these while you work on your databases, storing temporary information, such as the results of queries, and so on in the **Private** directory. The **Working** directory is where the Database Desktop expects to find the tables, their indexes, the queries, in fact any object in the database which you intend to open or save. The **Working** directory is effectively your database.

You should note that the Database Desktop comes complete with default values for these locations, so you could start creating databases straight away. However, just like in Delphi, you would end up mixing together your database files with those of the program itself, which could get messy. For exactly the same reasons as for a Delphi project, I strongly advise you to create your own **Private** and **Working** directories (you don't have to call them that, by the way!).

You can change the settings for both these directories by selecting Working Directory... or Private Directory... from the File menu:

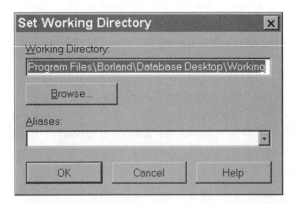

When you click on either of these menu items, up pops a dialog asking you to enter the name of the directory that you wish to use.

Notice that combo box at the bottom of the dialog, labeled Aliases:. Within Paradox, and so also within the Database Desktop, you can assign nicknames to directories (databases) which are known as **aliases**. That way, rather than having to select a directory, or type in a potentially lengthy path by hand, you can just type in the database's alias and use that instead.

Having said that, I'm not going to cover aliases here, since I tend to find them more trouble than they're worth. Why? Because when the time comes to ship the database and application to your end users, you must recreate the aliases on their machines before the application will run, adding yet another step to the installation process. For now, I'm going to forget about these shortcuts and come back to them in the next chapter.

Enough waffle. Set up the Working directory so that it points at the directory I asked you to create earlier, then do the same for the Private directory. Once you've done that, we're ready to get on with the business of creating our database application.

Creating a Contacts Table

Obviously, the first step in building a contact management application and its database is to set up the tables where the information will be stored. We'll only have a single table in this application, a very simply contact table that holds everything.

 Okay, I know I said that we were dealing with a relational database, which meant multiple tables, but this example is so simple that we don't really need more than one. In fact, this kind of example is better suited to a flat-file type of database, but anything they can do...

Let's put this Database Desktop thing through its paces and see what gives.

Try It Out - Creating a Table

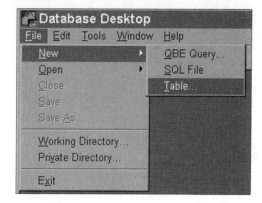

1 To start off, we need to create a basic table structure. To do this, select <u>F</u>ile | <u>N</u>ew | <u>T</u>able...

After a short pause, the **Create Table** dialog will appear. This dialog is asking you to select the type of database table that you wish to create:

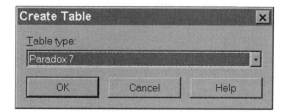

2 As we want to work on the default type of database, a Paradox 7 style, simply click on the OK button. The Database Desktop now goes away, creates the general structure of the database table and returns with it.

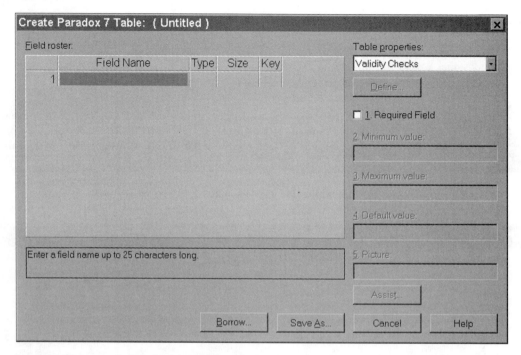

It's here that you define the structure of each of your table's records by informing the Database Desktop of the fields that you wish the records to be based upon, including their name, size and data type. Let's create the first field.

3 When the table editor appears, you'll see that the focus is already waiting for you in the **Field Name** column. We can take a hint - type in the name of out first field Contact_ID (there's more on what this field is used for later on) and hit *Enter*:

As soon as you hit *Enter*, the Database Desktop accepts your **Field Name** and moves the focus into the next column, **Type**.

4 This column is where you tell the Database Desktop what type of information you want to store in this field. As we'll find out in a moment, we want this field to act as a counter, so press +. This marks the field as being of type **AutoIncrement** (more on this later). Hit *Enter* to move to the next field.

5 Hold on, what happened to **Size** - we moved straight to **Key**? Well, as we have set up the field to be a counter, the Database Desktop has decided that it will handle the size of the field, so it jumps straight to the next valid entry field - **Key**. Hit any character key on the keyboard to mark this entry as a key field and hit *Enter* to continue.

6 And now we're onto the next field - that wasn't hard was it? Let's do another - the new field is called **Firstname**:

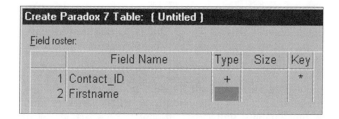

Create Paradox 7 Table: [Untitled]

Field roster:

	Field Name	Type	Size	Key
1	Contact_ID	+		*
2	Firstname			

7 The rest of the field's description is:

Field name	Type	Size	Key
Firstname	A	20	No

Type

Alpha
Number
$ (Money)
Short
Long Integer
(BCD)
Date
Time
@ (Timestamp)
Memo
Formatted Memo
Graphic
OLE
Logical
± (Autoincrement)
Binary
Bytes

This record has a new **Type**. Obviously, a person's surname should be entered as text, so the table editor asks you to specify the data type as AlphaNumeric - **A** for short. When you get to the **Type** entry, press *Space*. The table editor will throw up a list of possible data types for you to select from - you want the one at the top of the list. Notice that the word **Type** isn't a choice, it's a heading for the list.

8 Now enter the rest of the fields into the table editor:

Field name	Type	Size	Key
Surname	A	20	No
Company	A	100	No
Address	M	1	No
City	A	50	No
County	A	50	No
Country	A	50	No
Phone	A	20	No
Fax	A	20	No
Email	A	100	No
Notes	M	1	No

9 When you've completed these field definitions, you will have completed the first stage of designing the table. Save it by clicking on **Save As...** and selecting the appropriate directory from the resulting dialog, saving it with a suitable title, such as **Contacts.db**.

How It Works

In essence, all we have done with this Try It Out is to outline the way a database works; you need to create the structure of a database table before you can begin to add information to the table's records - quite obvious really!

In fact, this is just like programming with Pascal - we have just defined our variables. When we add the records to the database, we'll be initializing these variables and then any further work that we perform on the database will either update these variables or use the values contained in them to make some decisions or create summary statistics.

There are a couple of interesting points about these fields that are worth discussing. First, notice how nearly all the fields have been given a Type of A. Much of the information that we'll store in this database will be quite freeform, so the user should be able to enter anything they want within reason. An AlphaNumeric field provides them with an Edit box's flexibility.

Something else to notice is the two M or Memo fields. Just like Memo components, Memo fields let you store an almost limitless amount of data. The size of the field is not really a size at all, but instead tells the database exactly how much data you want to hold in the database. Anything over this value is dumped out to a separate file. By making these fields have a size of 1, we are effectively saying 'Store all the information about this field outside of the table' - this should allow us to speed up a lot of our queries at the expense of those containing these two fields.

The only other point of interest is the idea of a counter field in the table. Remember I explained that a relational database was a multiple table database that contained a number of links to describe the structure of the database? Well, these counter fields make up part of that system of links.

If you are going to specify a link between two tables, you must specify two fields, one in each table, that contain information of the same type and, more importantly, that the two related records in these tables have the same value in these two fields.

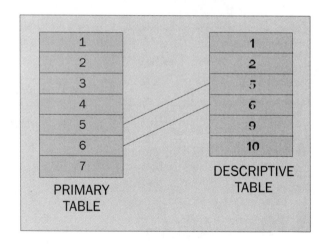

As you can see, this extra field is the overhead which you must pay to be able to gain the advantage of the relational database model. However, if the database engine is to be able to unravel the link system when you query the tables, the values in one of the fields must be unique. To fulfill this requirement, the AutoIncrement Type was introduced. Each time a record is added to the database, the database engine adds one to the counter and assigns it to the new record. In this way, you can guarantee that the link system will work.

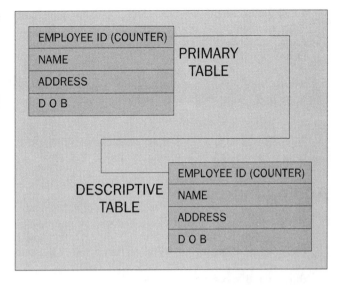

I'll come back to this topic in the next chapter when I focus on creating your own queries and use a multiple-table database to illustrate the example. Until then, I would advise you to include a counter field in all of your primary tables - i.e. those tables that hold root information, not tables that hold information that is used to describe information held in the primary tables.

Adding to the Basic Table

The Database Desktop also allows you to refine the basic table that I've just described. It does this by allowing you to add certain criteria that apply to field level data entry (such as, a number must be between 1 and 100), demand that a field is completed before a new record is accepted into the database, or on the converse, give that field a default value if none is supplied. The Database Desktop also allows you to add to the structure of the table itself by adding security features, secondary indexes (the keyed fields are automatically indexed) and look-up tables.

I won't go into much detail here, as using them can be a little difficult to understand without an example - I'm going to leave them until the next chapter when we have covered the basics and the examples can start to get a little more complex.

However, a lot of these table properties are fairly straightforward, so if you want to have a play, please go ahead - I suggest that you:

> Close down the existing table in the Database Desktop.

> Use Explorer to make a copy of that file and give it a new name.

> Use this copy to experiment on, as we're going to need the original for our simple contacts management system project.

You'll also find the Database Desktop help quite useful - if you get into difficulties and you can't wait until the next chapter, take a look there. It's interesting to note that some of these groups of properties don't actually help us that much when we front-end the database with a Delphi application. The Table Lookup group, for example, is incredibly useful because it allows you to look up values from one table to feed them into the one you are editing, but it only works within the Database Desktop. None of the Delphi database components make use of this most marvelous of features, something I sincerely hope Borland make time to resolve in a future version.

Having said that, we need an example to illustrate the use of these properties, our current project is in need of a secondary index. But why? And how do we apply one? Let's take a look.

Adding Indexes

When you query a database, the database engine has two ways of compiling the set of results you are looking for. It can either look at each record, checking through the fields until it locates the one specified in the search criteria (the SQL statement), before performing the validation to decide whether the record goes into the accept or reject pile. Then it moves to the next record in the list and repeats the process. As you can see, this could be a rather tedious process, but then again, that's what computers are good at.

But why do more work than we need to? By adding an index to a database table, you can effectively short-circuit the work that the database engine has to perform. The appropriate search field is already isolated - the engine doesn't need to look through records to locate the necessary field, it simply does that to the index and starts the validation. Clearly, this saves time and effort, but there is one other advantage to be considered.

When you specify a field to be indexed, the database engine creates the index in a predefined order, depending on the data type - for AlphaNumeric that's alphabetical, numbers first, for Number that's smallest to biggest. Anyway, the key issue here is that they are ordered. If the database engine is looking for numbers less than 10,000 in a Tax field, if the field is indexed, the database engine will know that it's not worth continuing when it finds the first value over 10,000. All the values from there to the end of the table will fail the validation, so why bother to check?

Combining this feature with having the field already isolated can obviously give you some startling speed advantages over searching an unindexed field. When you set a field as a table's key, what you are in fact doing is defining the table's default index. However, due to the nature of this field, it's usually not used as part of normal search criteria.

In fact, this index is primarily used by the database engine to rebuild a full (or partial) record out of the multitude of tables in the database when you execute a query. Without this feature, the speed of the query would drop expontientially as you add more of the database's tables.

Therefore, the Database Desktop allows you to create **secondary indexes** upon the other fields in the table, indexes that will be used exclusively for speeding up our search for information contained within a table. Enough of this theory, let's take a look at how to put an secondary index into place.

Try It Out - Adding Indexes

1 Going back to our **contacts.db** table (you should still have it open in the table editor - if not select File | Open | Table... and select it from the appropriate directory on your hard drive), select Secondary Indexes from the Table properties section on the right:

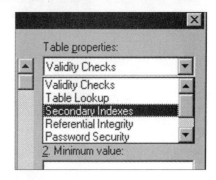

2 As soon as you make the selection, the Database Desktop swaps the table properties to focus upon the current Secondary Indexes. There doesn't appear to be to much going on here, but the really power of this feature is based behind the Define... and Modify... buttons. Click on the Define... button to create a new secondary index:

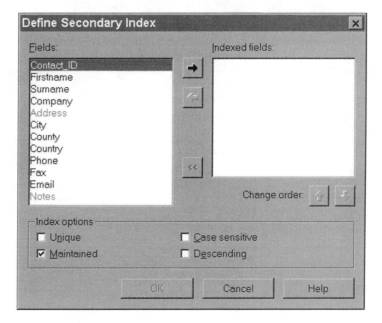

3 One of the most commonly accessed fields in a contact management system is the surname of the contact, so let's add an index to that field. Click on the Surname field in the Fields... column and then the arrow pointing to the Indexed Fields... column. The Database Desktop will put a copy of the Surname field in the right-hand column, indicating that it's part of the new index, and gray out the field in the left-hand column.

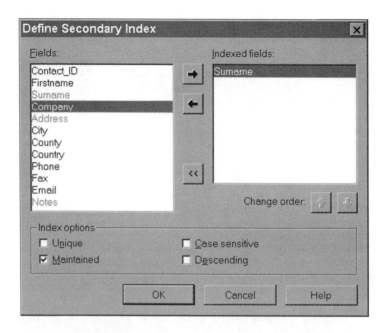

And that's all there is to it!

4 The final stage is to save the index - the Database Desktop throws up a dialog to this effect when you tell it you have finished creating the index by clicking on the OK button. This name will be used in your code a little later, so following a naming convention is a good idea - call the index IDXSurname:

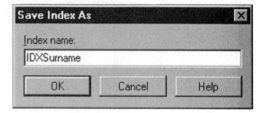

5 The final step to this Try It Out is to complete the other secondary index that we need for our example. This index is exactly the same as IDXSurname, except that it's based on Company rather than Surname. Create this index and save it as IDXCompany:

When you've OKed this dialog, click on the Save button to save your changes to the database table. Now you're ready to look at how to add information to this table.

How It Works

Before we move on to populating the table with information, let's take a closer look at what we've just done. Basically, we have added two simple secondary indexes to the table, but we could have been much more strict with our definitions.

For example, you might have noticed the checkboxes at the bottom of the Define Secondary Index dialog. Each of these options can have quite an effect on the performance of your index and any queries that use it.

Unique allows you to force the user to enter unique information into the fields that make up this index. You should be able to see that this is one of the basic requirements of a key field - behind the scenes, the Database Desktop has selected this option for the index generated by the key field.

 If the user trys to enter duplicate information into a Unique flagged field, the database engine will generate an error that you will have to trap in your code using the techniques explained in the chapter on exception handling.

Maintained is quite a strange option that you might have to think about for a while. The Database Desktop allows you to create an index that isn't automatically updated when you add or remove a record. This has the effect of speeding up data entry - the database engine doesn't have to spend time updating the index when the user changes some of the information in the table, but it does slow down all queries that use this index - the database engine has just postponed the rebuild until the index is used, i.e. a query is run that uses it.

 This option is mainly used to optimize the performance of your database - depending on whether a table's information is updated regularly, or whether the index is frequently used by your queries, you may decide to enable or disable this option. I'll be looking at this technique in more detail in the next chapter.

The final two options are quite closely related. Case sensitive means that the database engine distinguishes between 'Peter' and 'peter', while Descending controls the sort order in which the index is created and maintained. By default, the index is created using an ascending sort order, which means that numbers are listed from smallest to biggest, and alphabetic characters are ordered from A to Z.

However, by selecting Descending, you can reverse this ordering, so 'John' comes before 'Dave'. But what happens when you have 'Peter' and 'peter'? By default, the database engine will add them to the index in the order that they were entered. The Case Sensitive option allows you to take more control, forcing 'Peter' to come before 'peter'.

You can also create indexes based upon more than one field. For example, you may really need to search your tables based on surname and country - 'Find all the Smiths living in England', for example.

However, when you define Secondary Indexes with more than one single field, you must be careful to consider the order that they appear in the Indexed fields: column. Secondary indexes not only provide you with a nice rapid search facility within a database, they also provide a way to access the data in a completely new order. For example, when our index is defined, we'll be able to move through the records, one by one, in Surname order. If we were defining an index that relied on both the Surname and Country fields, and moved the company field across first, the index would sort the records in the database by Country first, then Surname within Country.

This can produce some interested ordering effects which often catches database developers unaware, so bear it in mind.

Adding a Record Using the Database Desktop

Once you have designed your table, once you have integrated it into the overall structure of your database (more on this in the next chapter), once you are satisfied with all the data validation rules and default values (more on this later too!), you're ready to add information to the database.

> **Notice how I've stressed how important it is for you to settle on the design of the table and the database before you start to enter data. Although this isn't a requirement, unless you decide to throw it all away and start again, you might have to perform some really complex data manipulation to restructure a partly filled database.**
>
> **I recommend that you play around with the database structure using some sample data to make sure that it works as it should before you put the database online.**

There are, in fact, two simple ways to manually add data to your table. The first is to create a front-end application that has direct access to the fields in your table, just as I'm going to discuss in a moment, but the second is the method I'm going to discuss now.

Obviously, if you create a front-end application, you have complete control over the way that the data is entered, the order that things happen and, to a large degree, control over what the user enters. The trade off comes when you consider the time and effort that it takes to create the application - admittedly, this isn't as big a problem in Delphi as in other languages, but it's still worth considering. To avoid these disadvantages, why not use the Database Desktop to put the information directly into the database itself?

This is one of the simplest ways of getting information into your database. Let's take a look at how easy it is.

Try It Out - Adding a Record

1 Open the Database Desktop and the table that we've just created using the File | Open | Table... menu:

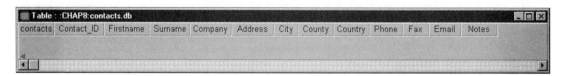

2 As you can see, the Database Desktop opens the table and displays it in a way that we've not seen before. This is called the **Data View** - it enables you to see the data that has already been entered into the table. It looks a little empty at the moment - let's fix that! Select Table | Edit Data:

3 This puts the table in Edit mode, allowing us to enter information directly. Enter the following details into the first record:

Field	Entry
Contact_ID	Don't try to add an entry - it's automatically filled in by the database engine
Firstname	David
Surname	Maclean
Company	Wrox Press Ltd
Address	Unit 16, Sapcote Industrial Estate, 20 James Road, Tyseley
City	Birmingham
County	West Midlands
Country	England
Phone	(+44121) 706 6826
Fax	(+44121) 706 2967
Email	davem@wrox.com
Notes	E-mail is preferred method of communication

4 Notice that as soon as you have finished entering information into the final field, the Desktop Database automatically puts you are the start of the next record:

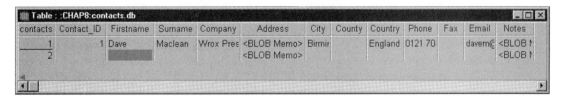

To cement these values in stone, you know need to change back to View mode by selecting Table | View Data or by pressing *F9*.

5 If you wish to review the structure of your table at any time, say you've forgotten the maximum number of characters allowed in an AlphaNumeric field, select Table | Info Structure...

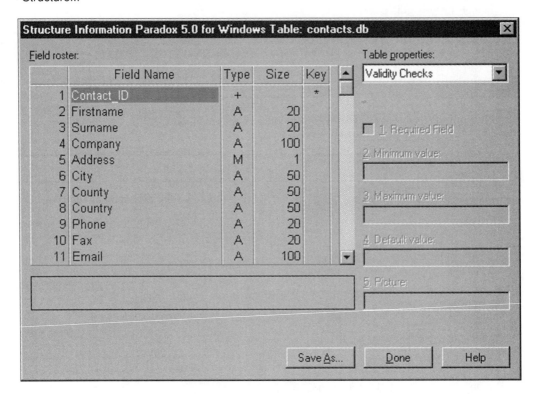

However, if you want to change the structure of the table, select Table | Restructure....

But Hang On

Well, if this method of data entry is so simple, what do we need the Delphi application for? To answer this question, you really need to understand exactly what you are going to give to your users to access the database. You will give them:

- A copy of your Delphi application
- A few database related system files
- Access to a copy of the database

Notice that you don't give them a copy of the Database Desktop, just like you don't give them a copy of Delphi. In fact, you don't need to give your users the tools of the trade that you have come to know and love - they have been designed to produce results that don't need this kind of support.

This method of data entry is really the quick and sloppy way to test out your database structure and to supply the users with a small sample of data to help them understand how to use the database - it's not the method that the user will have to learn.

Bringing it to Life

Although creating tables using the Database Desktop is a big part of developing a database application, and even though you can also enter data into these tables through the Database Desktop, the real power comes when you start 'binding' the tables into Delphi applications.

When Borland created Delphi, one of the keystones of its design was to make the previously complex task of designing a database application as easy as possible. To this end, they included a number of components specifically designed for this job which allow the competent developer to create a functional application in a matter of minutes with little or no code.

In the rest of this chapter, I won't actually be focusing on these components, that discussion is postponed until the next chapter. I'll be focusing on a very useful tool called the **Database Form Expert**. This allows you to create a Delphi database application just by answering a few questions, without knowing anything about TTable or TDBEdit components, or indeed anything about Delphi's method of handling the connection and interrogation of a foreign data source.

I'll be pointing out some of the more important **data-aware** components that the Expert brings into play - it uses the same components that I'll be showing you in the next chapter - but for now, sit back and relax as Delphi takes control.

Using the Database Form Expert

If you want to quickly throw together a data-aware form, or you want to ensure that all of your applications follow a consistent style, without having to create your own forms and store them in the Repository, the Database Form Expert can be an invaluable tool.

Data-aware is simply a term that means something can have access to the information held in a database. A normal Edit component can display information held in a database, but it would involve a few lines of code - it's much better to simply drop a TDBEdit component onto your form and set its DataSource property to the appropriate value.

Let's look at how the Database Form Expert can quickly and easily create a data-aware form that we can use as our Delphi front-end to the database that we've just created - the final part of the database application jigsaw.

Try It Out - Creating a Database Form

1 To start up the beast, select <u>D</u>atabase | <u>F</u>orm Expert...

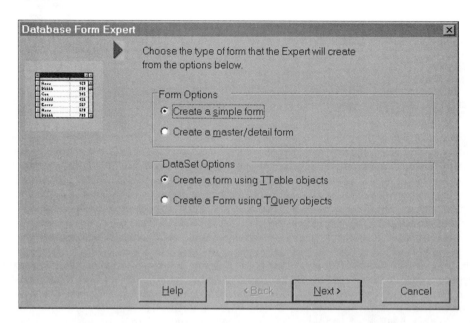

I'm assuming here that you've done the usual steps of closing down the last project, opening a fresh one and saved it to a new directory. If not, click on the Cancel button to stop the Expert, answer Yes to the resulting dialog and then complete the usual project preliminaries.

2 The first thing you are asked is what kind of form you want to create, a simple or a master detail form. For this example, select the option to create a simple form.

3 Just beneath these options is a request for information about the kind of data source you intend to pull the data from - a table or a query. Again, take the default option of TTables. Now move on to the next step using the Next > button (no surprises yet!):

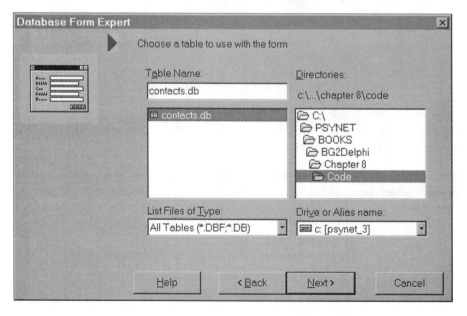

4 At this point, you need to select the table that contains the data you want to see. Use the normal techniques to select the **contacts.db** table that you have just created and then click on the <u>N</u>ext > button again:

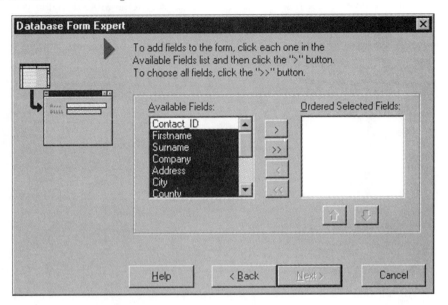

5 Selecting a table causes the Form Expert to have a little think and then show you a list of all the fields within that table for the third step in the form creation process. What you need to do now is to tell the Expert which fields you want to see on the form. Remember, the Contact_ID field we created is really just for internal use by the database engine and doesn't contain any useful user-related data, so let's leave that field out of the selection.

Select all the other fields using either of the normal Windows multiple selection keys, *Shift* and *Ctrl* and click on the single, right-facing arrow button to make your selection:

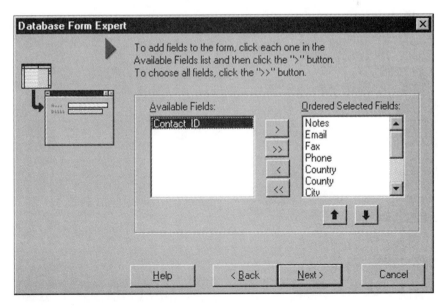

6 Did you notice anything strange about the ordering of the fields when you pulled several over from the left to the right? The Expert has apparently reversed their order. Fortunately, the Expert does allow you to rearrange this ordering, using the arrows under the right column that should now be highlighted. Try moving the fields around in the column until they look in a better order - the arrows affect the position of the selected field in the list.

7 When you are happy with the ordering, click on the Next > button to continue with the questions:

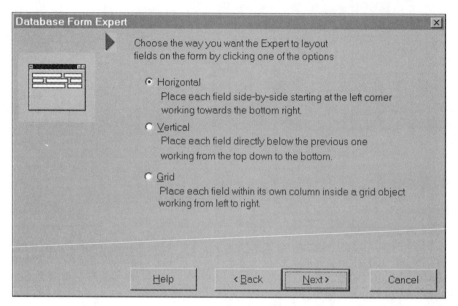

8 This question is simply to ascertain how you want the fields laid out on the form. For our purposes, select the Vertical option (notice how the little graphic changes to illustrate your choice) and click on the Next > button again:

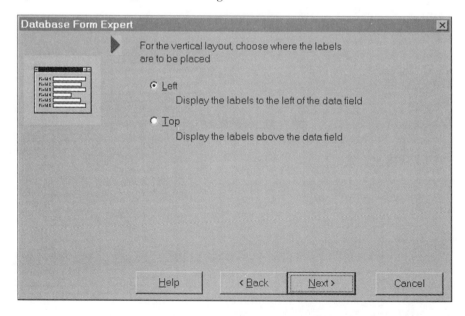

9 This penultimate question simply asks us where we want to place the labels that are associated with the other display controls required on the form. Select the default Left option and proceed to the final confrontation:

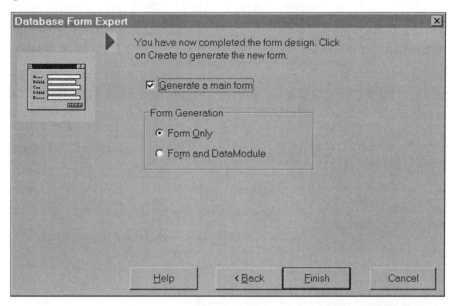

10 This final set of questions deal with the basic structure of the project. The first checkbox enables you to set this form to be the project's main form - go for this option. The radio buttons just below deal with a new feature to Delphi 2.0: the data module. I'll be looking at this feature in more depth in the next chapter, so for now, select the Form Only option. Click on Finish and the Expert will create your new form - just run the project to see the form in action:

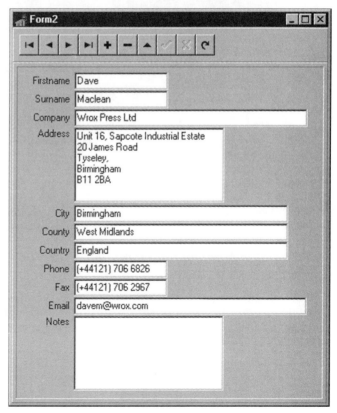

313

Once the Expert has Finished

As you can see, the Expert isn't particularly good at laying out a form - it obviously hasn't read the Microsoft Design Guidelines! Fortunately, the Expert doesn't create anything special, it's just another form, so you can go in and change the layout if you wish.

When you take a look at the design view of the form, you should notice three unusual components on the form, one visual and two non-visual:

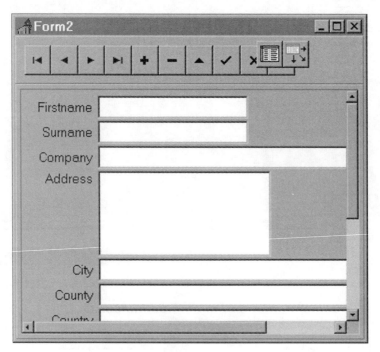

The visual component is called TDBNavigator, which is just a simple tool that allows the user to commit any changes that they make to the database, move around the records in a table and refresh the current view of the database.

The other two components are know as TTable and TDataSource components. In even the most basic Delphi database applications, you will always need a TDataSource and at least one TTable or a TQuery. These components control the flow of information from the database to the form and back again - without them the form would be useless.

I'll be talking about these components and many others in much greater detail in the next chapter.

That's all there is to it - you now have a fully functioning data maintenance form that will quite happily let you add data, delete it, edit it, move through it record-by-record, and so on. Run the program to see how I rearranged and resized the components to make the form look slightly better:

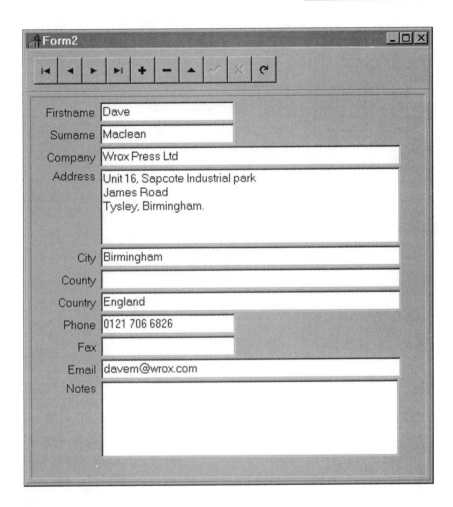

Summary

In this chapter, you have ventured into the underground world of database application development - and survived! Hopefully, you now understand the basic workings of a single table relational database and you know one method for creating a Delphi application that can act as a front-end for the database.

However, what about more complicated, multi-table databases or how about building your own Delphi applications? After all, single table databases aren't that powerful, and the Database Form Expert isn't that flexible - it can come up with a quick database form, but if you want something special, you've got to do it yourself.

So, in the next chapter, I'm going to look at some more database theory, introduce you to the various VCL components that deal with database access and how the information is displayed, and set off down the database reporting path. I'm also going to look at taking more control over the Delphi application (and therefore the database) using Pascal - you'll be surprised by what a few lines of Pascal can do for your application!

Database Coding

In the last chapter, I introduced you to the wonderful world of databases. You saw how to create a database using the Database Desktop, learned some very important terms and then rounded off the whole deal by using the Database Form expert to create a database maintenance form without having to write a single line of code or drop a single component yourself. Now we can get down to some serious work.

If you take a look at Delphi's Component Palette, you'll see that you've got two whole tabs dedicated to database development. You have the **Data Access** tab containing the controls which provide access to the databases you create and, of course, the data inside them. You also have the **Data Controls** tab which provides you with some very powerful controls for actually displaying and editing that data.

In this chapter, we're going to explore the components on both of these tabs. Along the way, you'll see:

- How to use and configure the data access components
- What the various data controls are, and how to use them
- How to add data into the tables in your database
- How to delete records
- How to perform both simple and complex searches on your data
- What the Structure Query Language (SQL) is and how to use it in Delphi
- What data modules are and why they are so useful

Assuming you've read the previous chapter, by the end of this one you will have everything you need to start writing complete database applications yourself. In the next chapter, we look at how to get that data out in the form of reports, equipping you with all the knowledge to start creating some very useful and professional applications.

Dropping the Components by Hand

Although you can use the Database Form expert to create stand-alone maintenance forms in their own right, you're more likely to use it as a quick-start tool for your own projects. The database components available from within Delphi aren't at all hard to use, but setting them up can be a little tedious, especially on complex forms.

For this reason, many developers use the Database Form expert to drop a selection of controls on the form, so avoiding the drudgery of property bindings and being able to concentrate on the issues behind the form's layout, adding further functionality, and so on.

However, there will be occasions when you'll want to drop the controls on the form yourself. Whether you use the Database Form expert or not, there will also undoubtedly be times when you wish you knew what all those components and properties do so that you could have total control over tailoring the form.

Controlling Your Data-aware Components

Creating data-aware forms and applications by hand is a two stage process. The first stage is to drop Table or Query components onto a form and expose the data in them using a DataSource component. The second stage is to either link data components, like bound edit boxes, to the data source, so providing data maintenance and browsing facilities without the need for one line of code, or write code to manually control the Table, Query and DataSource components, say to perform searches or bulk updates.

Enough theory - this stuff is easier to visualize if we actually get down to writing some code and drawing some forms. Before we carry on, though, make sure that you have Delphi loaded and that you have a blank project ready to start work.

Try It Out - Your First Database Application

1 First things first - drop a Table component onto your form and use the Object Inspector to change its name to tblMain.

2 Now, looking at the Table's DatabaseName property, type in the full path to the location of the table to which you want to connect. In this case, that's **contacts.db** in the database directory. If you've followed the setup instructions for the disk, this path should be **c:\begdelf\database**.

3 Now select the actual table you want to connect to by choosing the appropriate entry from the newly populated drop-down list to fill in the Table property. This completes the set up of the Table component.

4 The next stage is to drop a DataSource component on your form, changing its name to dsMain and setting its DataSet property to tblMain. Setting the property is easy - select the drop-down list which, by default, contains the entire selection of Table components that appear on the form.

Now you've finished exposing the information held in an external database table to your application's data-aware components.

5 To take advantage of this exposure, we need to add some of these data-aware components. You can find them all in the Data Controls tab of the Component Palette. The particular one we're interested in is called DBGrid. Find it and drop one onto your form, so it should now look like this:

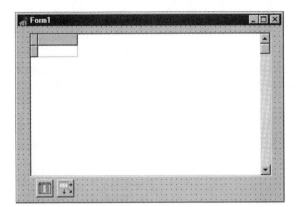

Notice that it doesn't matter where you've dropped the Table and DataSource components. Both of these components are non-visual, so the fact that they are on top of the DBGrid shouldn't make a difference to how the user interface looks.

6 The next step is to hook this new component up to the data access components, allowing the data to be displayed. Set the DataSource property to dsMain (the only entry in the drop-down list). While you're there change the name of the component to grdDisplay.

7 Everything's connected up, so where's the data? By default, the Table component's floodgates are kept securely locked, so holding back the data from your application. You can release these gates by changing the Table component's Active property to True. When you do, the DBGrid component will spring into life:

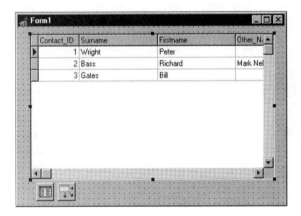

How It Works

Explaining this example is really quite simple. The internal workings of a database application are really easy to follow once you understand the component parts.

First of all, you have the database controller, the Table component that handles all the data retrieval. It identifies which is the current record in the table's set and, at the end of the day, it's this component that controls whether information flows between your database application and the database table. If you just drop a component on the form, set its DatabaseName and TableName properties to identify the location of the appropriate table and finally set the Active property to True, the data will flow straight into your application.

The second type of component that our application uses are the data-aware components found on the Data Access tab of the Component Palette, in this case, the DBGrid. This component specializes in taking the data delivered by a DataSource component and displaying it on a form. In our application, the DBGrid is, in turn, a specialized data access component - it displays multiple records simultaneously in a table-like structure. You'll find that this component is useful for database and data-aware application testing, as you can see the results of your work or the contents of a database very easily. This type of component is even easier to set up than the Table component. Just tell the component where to find the data to display, i.e. which DataSource component to look at, and the data will magically appear on your form, even at design time.

The third and probably most confusing component that you need for a database application is a DataSource. This component handles the interface between a set of data-aware visual components and a Table component. Why do we need it? Well, suppose you have two Tables and a whole set of data access components displaying the data that they contain. Just think about all the property values you would have to change if you wanted to display the data from Table2 instead of Table1 - you would need to redirect each and every data access component towards the other table.

To simplify this task, Borland decided to make all us database application developers use a third type of component as an intermediary between these two 'extremes'. This meant that, instead of having to redirect all the data-aware components to the new table, you just changed the focus of the DataSource (i.e. you change one property value) and the new table's data simply flowed into the data access controls which display the data completely oblivious to the change.

At this point, you might be thinking "Why don't you just change the table that the **Table** component is connected to?" Well, the answer to this becomes really obvious when you know a little more about what the **Table** component actually does. As you'll see later on, the **Table** component actually keeps a marker against the current record in the database table so that the single record data access components (such as **DBEdit**) know exactly what they're supposed to be displaying. If you mess around with the connection information, de-activate the table component, or run a search using this type of component, you run the risk of losing that current record marker. This can do unspeakable things to the integrity of the displayed data and cause you untold problems when the user asks to update the 'current' record. Consequently, unless you don't care to protect your application and the data that it's accessing, try not to mess around with a **Table** component once it has been set up at design time.

Changing DBGrid's Default Display

When you fired up this application, did you notice how all the database fields were displayed? (Even the rather cryptic Contact_ID field which is used internally by the database and is therefore useless to the user.) Fortunately, Delphi makes it quite easy for you to edit which fields you want the grid to display.

Right-click on the grid and you'll see a pop-up menu appear:

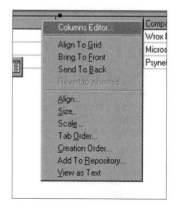

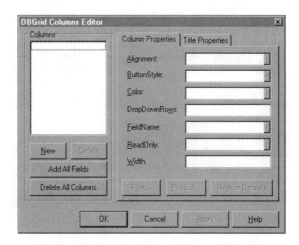

Clicking on that top item, Columns Editor, runs up a fully featured editor dialog which lets you to totally configure the grid, the data it shows, how it shows it and much more. Try it now... right-click on the grid and then select Columns Editor to run it up:

The grid component actually works in two modes: a default mode in which all the fields from the data source are displayed and a custom mode in which you specify the fields by hand.

At the moment, the grid is in default mode (it automatically shows all the fields from a data source), so when the Columns Editor comes up, no columns are shown in the list. There are two ways you can add fields (**columns** in grid-speak) into the grid. You can either click on the Add All Fields button, or you can click on the New button and edit the fields by hand.

For now, click on the New button:

On the right-hand side of the Columns Editor, all the column properties on the right should instantly light up, as you can see here. Notice that the properties area on the right of the Columns Editor has two tabs: Column properties and Title properties.

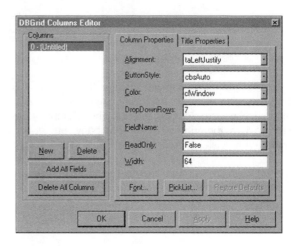

The Column properties let you change the alignment of the data in the grid (for example, numbers normally look better if they are right-aligned, text is normally centered or left-aligned), the width of the column and even allows you to set whether or not a column should be editable. Should you desire to spice up the grid a little, you can even change the color of the data in a column.

Notice the drop-down list box attached to the FieldName property. If you drop it down now, you'll see a complete list of all the fields in the selected table.

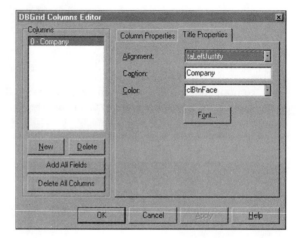

For now, select the Company field from the list and then click on the Title properties tab:

The Title properties let you change the caption of a column in the grid, as well as the color of the column title and how it's aligned. Since you've just selected the Company field, the caption is automatically set to Company, but you can change this if you wish.

Repeat this process and add in the Surname and PhoneNumber fields:

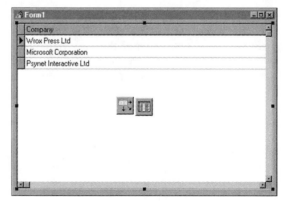

When you're done, click on the OK button on the dialog to return to the form:

The grid has now changed to only display the three columns that you included in the editor's list, something that will be reflected in the application at run time.

Note that the **Company** field soaks up a lot of screen real-estate quite unnecessarily. This is because the width of the columns is based on the maximum number of characters that the field can contain in the database - check out the **Size** column in the Database Desktop's description of the table. Delphi works out the size of the column by multiplying the number of characters the field can contain by an approximate factor of six (assuming you haven't changed the font, each letter needs about six pixels to be laid out nicely) and applies this number to the width property of the column.

You can change this value very easily by returning to the **Column Editor**, selecting the **Company** field and manually altering the content of the **Width** property.

Use One Component, Get Loads of Features Free

The grid is actually a lot more powerful than it first appears, something that will become apparent when you run the application. If you click on the small buttons to the left of each row in the grid, you'll find that you can select the entire row. Hitting the *Delete* key on your keyboard actually delete entries from the table.

You can also move down beneath the last entry in the grid to add new records. In short, the grid provides you with a single component to allow you and your users to add, edit and delete data, as well as moving around the data supplied by the data source. In fact, the only thing that it does not allow you to do is search through the data - more on this later.

Of course, not all the data controls are as powerful as the grid - the DBEdit component for example. All that allows you to do is to display and edit the data in a single field, something that you can do just by setting two properties in the Object Inspector.

Exploring the Simple Data Controls

If you intend to create data maintenance forms with little or no code, you'll need to drop a control onto the form that allows the user to navigate around your data source. You have already seen that the grid can let you do this, but, if don't want to use a grid, the only other component-based solution is to use the DBNavigator control.

If you decide to follow this option and you drop one of these components onto your form, apart from the usual setup properties (Name, Top, Left, etc.), you should take an interest in some others:

Property	Description
ConfirmDelete	When set to true, the Navigator will pop up a message box if you tell it to delete a record, just to make sure.
DataSource	Our old friend from DBGrid. Set this property to the name of the DataSource component that the navigator will work with.

Table Continued on Following Page

Property	Description
VisibleButtons	If you don't want the user to have access to all of the navigator's facilities then you can turn individual buttons on and off in the Object Inspector by double-clicking this property to display a list of possible buttons. Simply double-click the appropriate property to toggle it on or off.

Okay, so now we know how to let our users navigate round the data source and use the grid to display a selection of columns from the data source with only a single control. However, there are far more data controls to cover and judicious use of them can turn a humdrum database application into a work of art. Almost all of the remaining controls exist for one purpose: to display data from a field and allow you to change it, at the same time updating the original data in the data source.

Using the Common Data Editing Components

One of the beauties of Delphi is its consistency in terms of the way the components work, the methods they use to implement their functionality, the properties that control the component's data (remember a component is just a class with a visual front end) and generally how they look and feel.

Nowhere is this more evident than in the more common data components on the Data Controls tab of the Component Palette. By *common components* I mean:

Name	Description
DBText	Used to pull field names directly from a data source to label the components containing the actual field data.
DBEdit	Big brother to the traditional edit box, the DBEdit component is used to display alpha, numeric, or both, data from a field in a table and allow the user to modify it, just as if they were using a normal edit box.
DBMemo	Used to display data from a memo field in the data source and allow the user to make changes to it.
DBImage	Used to show graphic data held in a BLOB type field in the database.
DBCheckBox	Used to easily show yes/no, true/false values from these types of fields in the data source.

Of course, there are other data controls, but these can be a little more complex to set up, so I'll take a look at them in a short while.

If you're dealing with a lot of fields and want to use these common controls to display and deal with their data, you really will save yourself a great deal of time and effort by setting running the Database Form expert that we covered in the last chapter. Once the wizard has run, you can go through the components that it just created and move them around to your heart's content.

However, setting them up by hand is incredibly easy, since they all follow the same principles and support the same set of database properties. It's just that it can become a little tedious at times.

Looking at a Data Access Component's Basic Properties

The two important properties are our old friend the DataSource property into which you place the name of the DataSource property that you want to pull the data out of and the DataField property which you use to specify the name of the field that you intend to deal with.

> Remember that if you're using single record, single field data access components, the component looks at the **Table** component to identify which record it should look at and its own **DataField** property value to identify the appropriate field.

I won't go into a great deal of detail about the new DataField property, since you'll see a fair bit of it over the coming examples. Basically, though, as soon as you connect the DataSource property of one of these components to a data source, you'll find that the drop-down list attached to the data field property of the component instantly fills up with the names of all the fields in the data source. From there, you're just a small wave of the mouse away from selecting the field that you want to deal with.

For those instances where you want to use these components to just display information rather than allow changes to it, you'll be interested to know that all the data controls have a ReadOnly property which prevents users from updating the information in the underlying database.

By ensuring that these properties have been set, you will always be certain that your database application will come alive, even if it doesn't quite work as you originally intended! Look out for examples of how we have used these properties in the future example. The remaining data controls that I have not mentioned here deal with lists of data, either lists in terms of entire tables or queries, and can take a little more effort to set up.

Dealing with the Data List Components

By data list components I actually mean those components that belong to the same family as the grid, components which are designed to list the entire contents of a data source in one go, components such as the DBListBox, DBComboBox and so on, except that they're limited to one field. All these controls are exactly the same as their non-data-aware cousins, except that you have to set up the DataField and DataSource properties to connect components to the database.

However, there is one rather special control worth covering before we look at the others: the DBRadioGroup. Whereas the other list controls enable you to present your users with a complete list of data from within the data source, the DBRadioGroup lets you limit the data your users can enter in a field to a specific list of items.

> In this example, we're going to use the **ContactType** field attached to the Contacts table. This field has been designed to allow the user to enter a small string about the kind of contact this particular record refers to.

Using the DBRadioGroup component, you can provide a set of radio buttons on a data entry form which, when clicked, fire a preset value into the database field. This ensures that the data in that field is always consistent, which, as you will see later on, makes searching for a records a lot easier.

Let's try it out with a simple example to see exactly how to use it.

Try It Out - Using the DBRadioGroup

1 Start up a new application and drop a Table and DataSource component onto the form.

2 Point the DatabaseName property at the Contacts table, then set up the DataSet property of the DataSource component to the name of the Table component (Table1).

3 The final stage in setting up the database connection is, of course, to set the Active property of the Table component to true to enable the data flow.

4 Now drop a DBNavigator, DBEdit and DBRadioGroup component onto the form, so that your form now looks like this:

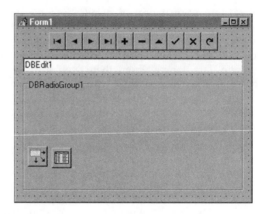

5 The next step is to set the data source of all these new components so that they all point at the data source component you dropped onto the form a little earlier. There's actually a very easy way to do this. First, click on the DBNavigator component to select it. Then, hold down the *Shift* key and click on each of the other components, with the exception of the DataSource and Table components. You should see all the components that you clicked on selected together. Now you can bring up the Object Inspector and double-click the DataSource property to select the only DataSource on the form.

FYI   If you have more than one **DataSource** on your form, simply choose the appropriate **DataSource** from the drop-down list.

6 As you should be aware by now, the next step in building the form is to set up the fields that the two data controls (the DBEdit component and the DBRadiogroup component) are going to deal with. Set the DataField property of the DBEdit component to the Company field and set the DataField property of the DBRadioGroup to the ContactType field.

Since the table should be active, you'll see the edit box change instantly to show you the Company field of the first record in the database. However, the DBRadioGroup doesn't. The reason for this is that the DBRadioGroup doesn't yet know how to interpret the values in this field and thus which radio buttons to show.

326

7 To solve this problem, double-click the Items property to start up the Items Editor and enter the following values so that it looks like this:

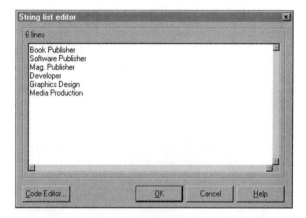

Each string represents not only a radio button and its caption, but also the values that the buttons will recognize in the field and which will be fired into the field when the user clicks on a radio button.

8 If you click OK to leave the editor, you'll see the radio group has changed on the form:

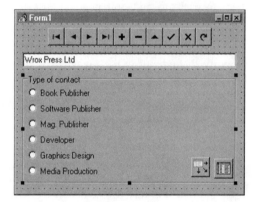

When you run the application, you'll the see the radio buttons change to reflect the values in the ContactType field in the data source. If you take a look at the table using the Database Desktop, you can see the same values that you just entered into the Items property of the component in the ContactType field:

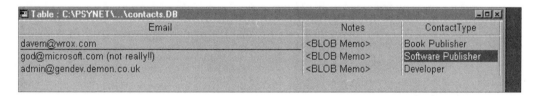

Note that, occasionally, you don't want the entry into the database table to be the same as the caption on the radio button. To get around this problem, simply add the appropriate entries to be fired into the database field into the Values property. The order in which you enter the values into this property should correspond directly to the order in which the radio buttons appear in the radio group box.

Handling the RadioGroup with Code

Since the Items and Values properties of the component are both string lists, you can also deal with them in code just as you would any other kind of string list. For example, you could set the strings up with code like this:

```
With dbRadioGroup1 do
begin
    Items.Add('Book Publisher');
  Values.Add('1');
    Items.Add('Software Publisher');
    Values.Add('2');
    Items.Add('Developer');
    Values.Add('3');
end;
```

There may also be times when you need to fire off code in response to a button being pressed. For example, setting a contact in the table as a Software Publisher may mean that you want to create a greetings record so that the rest of your system will send an automated letter telling them to pack up and quit now because they'll never be able to compete with your own technical expertise.

The OnChange event on the group can let you do this, inside which you can use the **Value** property to find out exactly what was just selected. If you added the following line of code to this event, the user would see a message box documenting exactly what had just happened:

```
ShowMessage('You just changed ' + dbRadioGroup1.DataField + ' to ' +
dbRadioGroup1.value);
```

You can try this example out by running **radiogrp.dpr**.

Be very careful with the **OnChange** event. You'll see when you run the program that the event not only fires when you click on a radio button, but also when the user navigates through the records in the data source using the **DBNavigator**.

A much better place to put this code is in the OnClick event, but that brings with it its own set of problems. Try moving the OnChange event handler code to OnClick:

```
procedure TForm1.DBRadioGroup1Click(Sender: TObject);
begin
    ShowMessage('You just changed ' + dbRadioGroup1.DataField + ' to ' +
                dbRadioGroup1.value);
end;
```

Now if you run the program, the message box pops up whenever the user clicks on an option in the group, which is exactly what we want. The problem, though, is that **Value** still holds the value of the previously selected option, not the new one.

The solution is to use the ItemIndex property in association with the **Items** string list to pull the value out by hand:

```
ShowMessage('You just changed ' + dbRadioGroup1.DataField + ' to ' +
dbRadioGroup1.items[dbRadioGroup1.ItemIndex]);
```

If you try this new solution out, the program should run correctly.

Data-aware Lists and Combo Boxes

Just to make things a little more interesting, Delphi provides two different types of list and combo boxes. Going along the Component Palette, left to right, the first two you arrive at are the standard DBListBox and DBComboBox controls. Bind these to a data source and a field in that data source and they will list all the values in that field.

The DBLookupListBox an DBLookupComboBox components on the right are a little more complex, but far more useful, effectively enabling you to list the contents of a field from one data source and feed a corresponding value into a second.

If you were to code a Contact Manager that only allowed a fixed number of contact types then you're users would pretty soon begin to feel limited by the application - it simply wouldn't be very flexible to use; it would also be awkward to maintain if every time a new contact type was found, you had to go and change the program code.

A much better solution would be to store the contact type strings in a separate table and store just a small number relating to that contact type record inside the contact record itself. This is where the lookup lists come into play. You could easily drop a DBLookupComboBox onto a form to list the contact types from the second table and fire the ContactTypeID value into the ContactType field in the first table. Confused? Let's take a look.

If you load up **dblookup.dpr**, you'll be presented with the following form design:

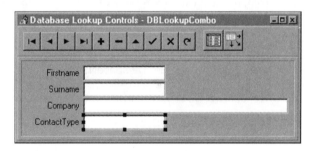

This form was obviously created with a great deal of help from the Database Form expert. Before you can run this program you'll need to point the data source at our old friend the Contacts table, supplied with the sample code for this chapter - mine probably lives in a very different location on my hard disk to yours.

However, we haven't quite finished the form yet. We can change that Contact Type edit box to a DBLookupCombo and display the strings from the Types table in the combo, while feeding the **Type ID** from that table into the Contacts table for reference.

329

Try It Out - Adding a Lookup to Your Application

1 Select the Contact Type edit box and hit *Delete* to remove it:

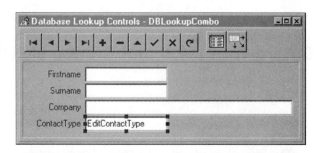

2 In its place, drop a DBLookupCombo control:

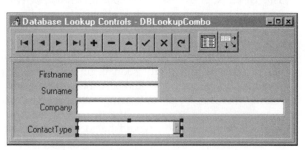

3 The first step in setting this puppy up, as with most of the other database components, is to set up the DataSource and the DataField properties. Since there's only one DataSource component on the form, you can set the DataSource just by double-clicking on that property, but you'll have to select ContactType from DataField's drop-down list.

4 Now drop a new set of Table and DataSource components onto the form. These new additions are going to supply the DBLookupCombo with the information to fire into the main table, so set the DatabaseName and TableName properties of the Table component to locate the Types table and set the DataSet property of the new DataSource to the new Table component. Don't forget to activate the table to get the information flowing!

5 Now for the new DBLookupComboBox properties - ListSource and ListField. ListSource holds the name of the data source that you want to pull data in the list from and ListField is, of course, the name of the field that you want to display in the list. Set up the ListSource property to point to the new DataSource component, then set ListField to the Type_String field.

6 The final stage is to tell Delphi how to relate the two tables. The component helps out by providing a useful property called KeyField. Use the combo on the property to select the Type_ID field from the list - this tells Delphi to feed the value of the Type_ID field in the Types table into the ContactType field of the Contacts table when a lookup is done at run time.

You can run the program now and see all this theory in action:

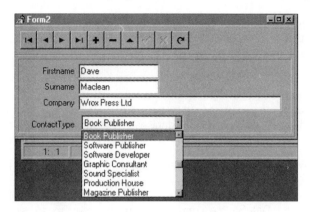

Now, instead of seeing and using contact types, we can actually see the text descriptions of each contact type while using the internal database identifiers behind the scenes. Using this technique, we can take advantage of a completely intuitive user interface while using the streamlined multitable identifiers to actually run the show!

How It Works

The most confusing part of using one of these look up components is that you're using two Tables and two DataSources. Once you've mapped out in your own mind how the tables work together and what property they should be assigned to, including their functionality into your database applications will become a snap!

The way to remember it is that a DataField maintains the connection to the field in the main table that you're interested in. That property should always point to the main table, so the component's DataSource property should also focus on this table. The other properties, ListSource and ListField, should be aimed at the other Table - the component that deals with the list or lookup table.

The DBLookupListBox works in exactly the same way as the DBLookupComboBox, the obvious difference being that the list is on permanent display with the DBLookupListBox, as opposed to being hidden until the user asks for it, like the DBLookupComboBox.

If you replace the DBLookupComboBox with a DBLookupListBox and recreate all the properties set in the previous component in the new one, you will get the same effects but with a different user interface layout:

Now as you move through the records in the table, you'll see the highlight in the list move to show you which type of contact each record is.

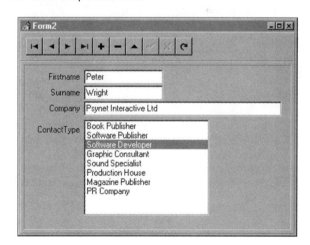

Data Modules

So far, we have actually got at the data involved in our applications by dropping Table and DataSource components onto forms and then accessing their properties and methods from code within the form. However, there are quite a few occasions where this way of working is just downright inconvenient.

For example, even the simplest contact management system would probably have more than one form that accesses the contacts table. A corporate accounts system will very frequently have an audit trail that should store a brief record of all changes to the database, no matter from which form those changes are made.

In these instances, and many others, dropping the same Table and DataSource components on lots of different forms isn't only tedious, but also a waste of time and resources. To avoid this wastage, Delphi 2.0 supports something rather special known as the **data module**. This structure allows you to store all your Table, Query and DataSource components in one, easy to access, central location within your application.

If you think back to the last chapter, you might remember that the Database Form expert offered you the option of creating a data module right at the end of its questions:

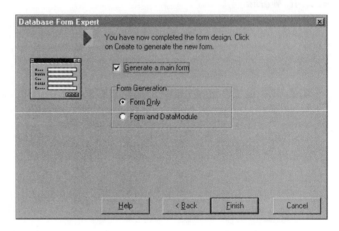

Run through the expert now and create a standard database application, but this time make sure you choose the Form and DataModule option before you hit the Finish button. This results in the creation of two new units in your application, the form itself and the new data module.

To take a look at the new data module, hit *Shift+F12* and select the form from the resulting list.

Notice how there are no data access components on the form itself - they all reside in that data module window. Click on a data-aware component and take a look at its DataSource property in the Object Inspector to see how it's set up:

As you can see, Delphi has put an explicit reference to the DataSource in this property - you'll find that this is a necessary requirement as the data module is an object and the DataSource is a member of that object's class definition. Therefore, following the rules of object-oriented programming, the full 'path' to the DataSource is required so that the other units in the application can identify where they should be looking to find the target component.

Once you've set up a data module in this way, the advantages to your application, your productivity and your users are quite dramatic. First, you no longer need to keep redrawing Table and DataSource components each time a new data maintenance form is created; you simply use the components in the data module. Second, because all the tables in your application are now being opened just once (within a single data module), the application will run a lot faster. If you have data access components on every form in your application, you will suffer from a performance hit as the overhead incurred when the connection is regularly re-established, say when the forms are created at run time is quite noticeable. This comes as a double whammy as you can avoid the hit.

Note that rather than using the Database Form expert to create your data modules, you can create them manually using the Object Repository via File | New... menu.

Using Aliases in Your Applications

Have you thought about how annoying typing in the exact path name to your database files into the DatabaseName property of a Table component really is? And have you thought that it really is more than a little annoying to have to hard code your path names into your executables (what happens if the users start renaming directories?!)? Have you thought that Borland really should have thought about this nuisance? Would you be surprised if I told you that they have?

The solution to this hard coding problem is to use a **soft coding** technique (cute name huh?). This technique is based around the idea that if you set up a temporary name that acts as a pointer to where the real name is stored and that real name is defined outside of the executable, the executable will always be robust - you only have to make sure that the external real name definition is accurate for the executable to work!

This technique is widely used and Delphi's particular incantation is called **aliasing**. You can set up an alias using the Borland Database Configuration utility which you should have on your Tools... menu by now. Just in case you haven't, you can find it under Programs/ Delphi 2.0/Borland Delphi 2.0 on the Start menu:

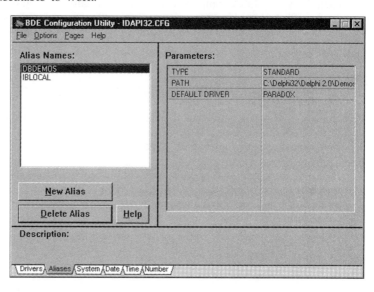

To actually set up an alias, you only need to hit the <u>N</u>ew Alias button and then choose the type of database that you want to connect to - all of the databases used in this book are based on Paradox.

When you've selected your database type, you need to tell the Borland Database Configuration utility where your alias should be pointing, i.e. the current location of your database. You can then save the changes and close down the utility.

Note that if you have Delphi running while you're adding extra aliases to your **idapi32.cfg** (the text file that holds all the important information about the aliases outside of your executable), Delphi will not be aware of any changes to the file. You must close it down and restart the application to take advantage of the new aliases.

Using Your Aliases

Once you have set up an alias, you can use it just as if it was the actual path it represents. The place where it really comes into its own is in the DatabaseName property of the Table component. By setting this value to an alias, you can compile your application and you won't have to worry about the location of the database when you distribute it to your users.

Note that when you have set up an alias, it will automatically appear in the drop-down list of options in the DatabaseName property of a Table component

Dealing with Databases through Code

Although the DBNavigator and the DBGrid allow you to edit and maintain the data in a table with little or no code, there will invariably be times when you will need to maintain a table through code, perhaps via a mass table update or perhaps to dump a whole load of test data into a database.

Thankfully, the Table component provides a wealth of methods and properties to let you easily do this. First, though, you'll want to know how to use a Table component without having to first fix its DatabaseName property at design time. Remember, it's unlikely that your users will install your application in the same directory that you develop it in, so the absolute path names that you enter at design time will cause you problems.

Just like any other property, the DatabaseName property of a table can be set up at run time simply by feeding a string into it. With that in a mind, a very common approach to solving the problem is to make sure that the database lives in the same directory on your users hard disk as the application itself. That way, all we have to do is find out where this application lives and then feed that path into the DatabaseName property.

This isn't as tough as it sounds. When your application runs, Delphi automatically creates a TApplication type object called **Application**. This object has a property, called **ExeName**, which contains the full path and filename of the current application. So, if you have a program called **test.exe** which lives in **c:\mycode**, at run time the **ExeName** property of its application object is:

```
c:\mycode\test.exe
```

All we need to do is strip the **test.exe** bit off the end of the **ExeName** property and feed the result into the **DatabaseName** property of any Table or Query component that we want to deal with to end up with a self-configuring database application.

But what if we have a data module with ten, fifty or even a hundred Table or Query components? Surely setting up the **DatabaseName** property of each at run time would be a tedious job? Well, no! Time for a slight digression I think.

Load up **showpath.dpr**, run it and click the button! When you do that, a dialog box pops up showing you the contents of the DatabaseName property of the table in the data module. Simple enough you might think. However, that's only what you see going on. When you actually click the button, the application is automatically resetting all of the Tables to point at a new database table.

Double-click inside the data module to look at the code behind its OnCreate method, code that is run as soon as the structure is created, i.e. when the application runs:

```
procedure TdmodContacts.dmodContactsCreate(Sender: TObject);
var
    sPathName : String;
    nIndex : integer;
    nComponentIndex : Integer;
begin

    sPathName := Application.ExeName;
    nIndex := Length(sPathName);
    while Copy(sPathName, nIndex, 1) <> '\' do
        nIndex := nIndex - 1;

    for nComponentIndex := 0 to ComponentCount - 1 do
        if Components[nComponentIndex] is TTable then
        begin
            tTable(Components[nComponentIndex]).DatabaseName :=
Copy(sPathName,1,nIndex - 9) + 'db\';
            tTable(Components[nComponentIndex]).Active := True;
        end
        else if Components[nComponentIndex] is tQuery then
        begin
            tQuery(Components[nComponentIndex]).DatabaseName :=
Copy(sPathName,1,nIndex - 9) + 'db\';
            tQuery(Components[nComponentIndex]).Active := True;
        end;

end;
```

The code on your screen will obviously look a lot nicer than this, with comments a plenty to help you understand what is going on. It may look nasty at first, but the ideas behind it are really simple, so let's take a closer look!

Every container object in Delphi, such as a data module, a form or a group component, has a component array attached to it. This array lets you get at every single component on a form. We can use the ComponentCount property to find out how many components are actually in this array and thus build a very nice loop to check out each component.

The first couple of lines of code figure out the path that we need to fire into the **DatabaseName** properties:

```
sPathName := Application.ExeName;
nIndex := Length(sPathName);
while Copy(sPathName, nIndex, 1) <> '\' do
       nIndex := nIndex - 1;
```

Application.ExeName is copied into the **sPathName** variable, then a loop moves through the string backwards, one character at a time, until it finds a \. Everything to the left of the \ is the path, everything to the right is the application's executable file name. I've then done a small manual fudge to remove the current directory name and replace it with the database directory.

Armed with our newly found path, the next block of code loops through all the components in the data module. When it finds a TTable or TQuery component, it fires the path into its **DatabaseName** property:

```
for nComponentIndex := 0 to ComponentCount - 1 do
    if Components[nComponentIndex] is TTable then
    begin
        tTable(Components[nComponentIndex]).DatabaseName :=
                Copy(sPathName,1,nIndex - 9) + 'db\';
        tTable(Components[nComponentIndex]).Active := True;
    end
    else if Components[nComponentIndex] is tQuery then
    begin
        tQuery(Components[nComponentIndex]).DatabaseName :=
                Copy(sPathName,1,nIndex - 9) + 'db\';
        tQuery(Components[nComponentIndex]).Active := True;
    end;
```

That's all there is to it. This actually demonstrates another important benefit to using data modules in your code. By using an OnCreate handler in the module (feel free to use this one in your own code if you like) you can easily make a location-independent application which only needs a tiny amount of code to repoint the tables and components at run time and then activate them.

Moving around the Records

Okay, so now we have our data module with a block of code to ensure the controls can always locate the database tables at run time. At this point, you are free to start creating general browsing and maintenance forms, binding data controls to the data access components in the data module. However, you are also free to start writing code to hit the tables in the database directly without having to worry about dropping controls and things.

To move around the records in a table, there are four very simple methods available to you: **First**, **Next**, **Prior** and **Last**. As their names suggest, these methods let you move to the first record, the next in the table, the previous record and to the last one in the table.

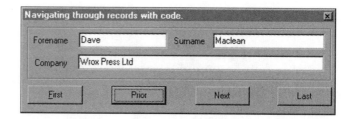

Take a look at **navigat1.dpr**:

It's a pretty simple application, but it does allow you to move around the records in the Contacts table through code, without making use of the DBNavigator at all.

When the program is running, you can click on the buttons to move through the records in the table. Reach the start of the table and the First and Prior buttons are automatically disabled. Reach the end of the table and the Next and Last buttons do the same thing.

If you stop the program running and double-click on any of the buttons, you can see the code responsible for these actions:

```
procedure TfrmNavigate.cmdFirstClick(Sender: TObject);
begin
    dmodContacts.tabContacts.First;
    Update_Buttons;
end;

procedure TfrmNavigate.cmdPriorClick(Sender: TObject);
begin
    dmodContacts.tabContacts.Prior;
    Update_Buttons;
end;

procedure TfrmNavigate.cmdNextClick(Sender: TObject);
begin
    dmodContacts.tabContacts.Next;
    Update_Buttons;
end;

procedure TfrmNavigate.cmdLastClick(Sender: TObject);
begin
    dmodContacts.tabContacts.Last;
    Update_Buttons;
end;
```

As you can see, the code is really very simple; none of the movement methods, (**First**, **Prior**, **Next** or **Last**) take any parameters - you just call them.

The code that decides whether to disable any of the buttons is held in the **Update_Buttons** routine:

```
procedure Update_Buttons;
begin
    frmNavigate.cmdFirst.Enabled := True;
    frmNavigate.cmdPrior.Enabled := True;
    frmNavigate.cmdNext.Enabled := true;
    frmNavigate.cmdLast.Enabled := true;
```

```
      with dmodContacts.tabContacts do
      begin
           if BOF then
           begin
                frmNavigate.cmdFirst.Enabled := False;
                frmNavigate.cmdPrior.Enabled := False;
           end;

           if EOF then
           begin
                frmNavigate.cmdNext.Enabled := False;
                frmNavigate.cmdLast.Enabled := False;
           end;
      end;
end;
```

The first four lines of code put the command buttons into a known state, enabling all of them before two simple **if** clauses check where we are in the table and then disable the appropriate buttons as necessary.

The Table component comes complete with two properties, **BOF** and **EOF**, which are set to true if the current record marks the beginning or end of the table, respectively. If **BOF** is true, the First and Prior buttons are disabled. Likewise, when **EOF** is set to true, the Next and Last buttons are disabled.

Don't Get Jumpy!

Sometimes, though, moving one record at a time simply isn't enough. What if you want a button that allows the user to jump say 3, 5, or 50 records at a time? You can use the **MoveBy** method. It works the same as the other methods, with the exception that it takes a number indicating the number of records to move. For example, we could change the code in the Next button's OnClick event to look like this:

```
procedure TfrmNavigate.cmdNextClick(Sender: TObject);
begin
     dmodContacts.tabContacts.MoveBy(1);
     Update_Buttons;
end;
```

In this instance, it has the same effect as the **Next** method, although that **1** could be replaced with any number to make the jumps as big or small as you like. If you want to move backwards through the records using **MoveBy**, just pass it a negative number. For example:

```
procedure TfrmNavigate.cmdPriorClick(Sender: TObject);
begin
     dmodContacts.tabContacts.MoveBy(-1);
     Update_Buttons;
end;
```

Re-ordering the Records

Remember those secondary indexes we set up in the last chapter when we created the table in the first place? Well, you can also use those to change the order in which you move through the records. By default, the Table component uses the primary key to sort the records in the table which, in our case, means we will move through the records in the same order that they were entered (since the primary key is that AutoIncrementing field that simply sets a unique number each time we create a record).

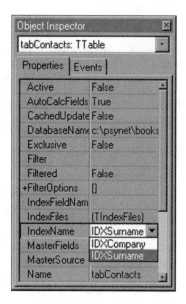

Select the table in the data module for a second and use the Object Inspector to take a look at the IndexName property:

If you select the IDXSurname index that we set up and run the program, you'll see that you can now move through the records in Surname order, rather than the previous higgledy-piggledy manner.

However, knowing how to move through records is no use at all if there are no records in the table to begin with. Let's see how to add and edit data and how to look at the fields directly through code without having to bind them to data controls.

Adding and Editing Data

There are two methods available to you for adding records to a table. Which you choose depends on whether you have components bound to the table to display data or to accept edits from the user.

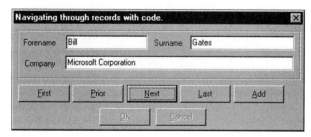

The first is the **Append** method. This tells the table to create a new record at its end and wait for data to be sent to it with the **Post** method. Take a look at **navigat2.dpr**:

This is exactly the same as the last example, except that I've added a few more buttons to cope with the addition on records to the database - an Add button to start the process and OK and Cancel buttons to allow you to save or cancel your changes.

The code behind these buttons is really simple. Take a look at the Add button code:

```
procedure TfrmNavigate.cmdAddClick(Sender: TObject);
begin
      dmodContacts.tabContacts.Append;
      Flip_Buttons;
end;
```

Flip_Buttons is just a generic bit of code that turns all the navigation buttons off and the OK and Cancel button on. The important bit of code here is the line the **Append** line. What this does is to create a new blank record which, in turn, fires blanks into any bound controls, ready for you to enter data.

Click on the OK button and this code is run:

```
procedure TfrmNavigate.cmdOKClick(Sender: TObject);
begin
    dmodContacts.tabContacts.Post;
    Flip_Buttons;
end;
```

Again, **Flip_Buttons** is called to put the buttons back to their normal state. The **Post** method posts the data from the bound controls into the new record. The alternative, of course, is to cancel the new record out:

```
procedure TfrmNavigate.cmdCancelClick(Sender: TObject);
begin
    dmodContacts.tabContacts.Cancel;
    Flip_Buttons;
end;
```

As usual, **Flip_Buttons** is used to set the buttons back to normal. The **Cancel** method cancels out any changes, restoring the data from the table back into any of the bound controls from the last record in the table. Of course, the last record does depend on which index you're using.

Using AppendRecord

An alternative way to add data to the table is to use the **AppendRecord** method. Unlike **Append**, which simply creates a blank record and waits for a **Post**, you actually hand the data that you want to feed in to the new record across to the method as parameters.

For example, you could write,

```
dmodContacts.tabContacts.AppendRecord( 'Peter', 'Wright', 'Psynet Ltd')
```

to add a new record to the table with these entries. You'll see more of this in action later in the book, in the final application chapter. It's a lot easier to explain its value and worth in the context of a full application. Basically, though, **AppendRecord** is very handy for adding records to a table and firing values into the fields, without needing bound controls to access it.

The alternative to adding new records to a table is of course to edit existing data. A change to a bound control's contents is enough to tell the table that we want to start editing some data, which you can then **Post** or Cancel in the same way you would with a new record. However, there are times when you want to edit a record through code. For example, let's imagine a scenario where we wanted to set the Country field of every contact in the database to England. This little loop would do the trick:

```
with dmodContacts do
begin
    tabContacts.First;
    while not(tabContacts.EOF) do
    begin
        tabContacts.Edit;
        tabContacts.FieldByName('Country').AsString := 'England';
        tabContacts.Post;
        tabContacts.Next;
```

```
        end;
    end;
```

This simple block of code just moves through all the records in a table, updating the country field and posting the new entry. The **Edit** method puts the current record in edit mode, ready to accept new data:

```
    tabContacts.Edit;
```

The next line then makes the alteration, changing the field with the given name. **FieldByName** simply lets you get at the data inside a field, using that field's name rather than a weird number which means nothing when you come back to read the code at a later date for maintenance purposes:

```
    tabContacts.FieldByName('Country').AsString := 'England';
```

Notice the **AsString** method. Remember, data stored in a database isn't normally handled in an identical format to the way Delphi handles data. **AsString** makes sure that the data being passed, in this case the Pascal string **'England'** is converted into the right format for the database. You could just as easily have used **AsInteger**, **AsTime**, **AsCurrency**, **AsDate**, **AsDateTime**, depending, of course, on the format of the field which you're setting. In all cases, though, you need to pass these **As** methods a string for them to be able to work with the conversion.

Once the data has been set, all that remains is, of course, to post the changes to the database, just the same as we did when we added in data earlier on:

```
    tabContacts.Post;
```

Finding Records

The next big area of functionality that all users expect to see in their database applications is, of course, the ability to rapidly search a table for a matching item of data. As always, Delphi has a whole host of searching methods which you can employ for this task:

Method	Description
Locate	Finds and selects a record based on the contents of one of more fields. You can also tell it whether or not to conduct a case-sensitive search.
Lookup	Is used to pull a field from a record in a table without selecting the record first. Useful for quick lookups of information, hence the name.
Goto	Allows you to search forwards and backwards through a table based on its indexes. A really quick way of locating records.
Find	Lets you instantly find a specific records based on index contents.

Let's look at **Locate** first. Take a look at **navigat4.dpr**. This time, we have a Locate button on the form, the code behind which uses the **Locate** method to find records based on the contact's Surname.

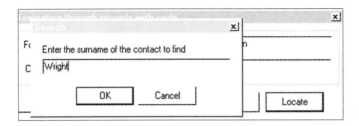

Run the program and click on the locate button and enter a surname (try Wright or Maclean) and click OK. The display will instantly change to show you the record matching your request. When you're done, stop the program running and double-click on the button to take a look at the code behind it:

```
procedure TfrmNavigate.cmdLocateClick(Sender: TObject);
var
    SearchString : String;
    Result : Boolean;
    SearchOptions : TLocateOptions;
begin
    SearchOptions := [loPartialKey];
    if InputQuery('Search', 'Enter the surname of the contact to find',
            SearchString) then
    begin
        Result := dmodContacts.TabContacts.Locate('Surname', SearchString,
                    SearchOptions);
        if not(Result) then ShowMessage('Sorry - search failed');
    end;
end;
```

The **Locate** method uses a special type, called **TLocateOptions**, to determine how it does the search. For example, it may only match the contents of entire fields or the search may be context-sensitive. The first line of code here sets up a variable, called **SearchOptions**, (which is of **TLocateOptions** type) with the set of options we require, in this case just **loPartialKey**. **LoPartialKey** means that **Locate** will treat Wright as a match for Wri.

An input query is used next to get the surname from the user that they want to search the database for. Providing they actually enter something, rather than simply clicking on OK, the code continues and the search is actually performed.

As you can see, **Locate** seems to take three parameters, the first being the field that you want to search, the second being the value that you want to search for and the third being the search options. The return value from **Locate** is true if a match is found, false if it isn't.

Cross Field Searches

However, **Locate** can do far more than that and can even be used to search for matches across a number of fields. The parameters you pass across are actually of a special data type known as **variant** (more on this in the OLE chapter) which allow you to basically pass any kind of data you want as a parameter. However, if you want to search multiple fields, you'll need to pass an array of these variants to the **Locate** method. The simplest way to do this is to use the **VarArrayOf** method. Take a look at this:

```
Locate('Surname;Company', VarArrayOf(['Wright','Surname']), loPartialKey );
```

The field names are passed to **Locate** as a single string, but with semicolons separating each entry. The field values to search for are passed as a set to the **VarArrayOf** routine which, in turn, will transform them quietly into a variant array so that the **Locate** routine can work its magic.

It's worth noting at this point that **Locate** is an extremely efficient way of locating a record. It looks at the fields on which your search is based and will try very hard to use an index if it can make a nice match between the fields you're searching on and the fields that make up the indexes in your table. If it finds that it can't use an index, it will use a slower search method.

While **Locate** is great for searching for records where you don't necessarily want to rely on an index being present, **Goto** does rely on indexes and, as such, represents a much faster method of searching your data. There are two **Goto** methods available to you from within Delphi: **GotoNearest** finds the nearest matching record to the one you require, while **GotoKey** finds an exact match and switches to that record.

Let's change the code in the previous example a little to make use of the **GotoNearest** method. Double-click on the Locate button to bring up the code window, then change the code so that it looks like this:

```
procedure TfrmNavigate.cmdLocateClick(Sender: TObject);
var
    SearchString : String;
begin
    if InputQuery('Search', 'Enter the surname of the contact to find',
            SearchString) then
    begin
        with dmodContacts do
        begin

        end;
    end;
end;
```

Specifically, the changes so far are that we have removed two of the variable declarations and the code inside the latter **begin...end**; block, to be replaced with a **with** block. The first stage in getting the **Goto** methods to work is to set up the index on the table, so add the following lines into the **with** block:

```
begin
    with dmodContacts do
    begin
        tabContacts.Close;
        tabContacts.IndexName := 'IdxSurname';
        tabContacts.Open;
    end;
```

It's very important that whenever you change or set the index on a table that the table is closed, otherwise the index change will have no effect at all. Once the index has been set, though, there's nothing stopping you from reopening the table ready for action.

The **Goto** methods themselves work in quite a strange way. Before you can use them to do a search, you need to fire the values that you want to search for actually into the fields that form the index in the table. But wait... surely that will overwrite the data in the current record? Normally, yes, but not if you use the **SetKey** method first.

SetKey

SetKey tells the table or query that we're going to fire some values into the fields of the table as a means to set up a search, nothing more. As long as you call **SetKey** first, there really is no chance of you corrupting your data:

```
begin
     With dmodContacts do
     begin
          tabContacts.Close;
          tabContacts.IndexName := 'IdxSurname';
          tabContacts.Open;
          tabContacts.SetKey;
          tabContacts.['Surname'] := SearchString;
     end;
```

Finally, all that remains is to fire off the **Goto** method to locate the record. Remember, at this point in time, you could use **GotoKey** to try to find an exact match for the data you just entered inside the index, or **GotoNearest** to find the nearest matching entry. Both return true if the record was found and false if not:

```
begin
     with dmodContacts do
     begin
          tabContacts.Close;
          tabContacts.IndexName := 'IdxSurname';
          tabContacts.Open;
          tabContacts.SetKey;
          tabContacts['Surname'] := SearchString;
          tabContacts.GotoNearest;
     end;
```

Now try running the application again and you'll find that it works just as before. Of course, this code is a little bloated just to illustrate the concepts. In a real-world application it would be unwise, for example, to keep closing and reopening the table to do index changes to search - as the amount of data in the table increases, so too does the length of time it takes to reopen the tables each time.

The **Goto** methods are also quite old and have been somewhat superseded by the much nicer **Find** methods. Take a look at this:

```
begin
     with dmodContacts do
     begin
          tabContacts.Close;
          tabContacts.IndexName := 'IdxSurname';
          tabContacts.Open;
          tabContacts.FindNearest([SearchString]);
     end;
end;
```

The **Find** methods do the same as the whole **SetKey**/**Goto** process in one neat command. Since you're using keys to search, the Table already has a pretty good idea of which fields you want to match. All you need to pass to the **Find** methods (**FindKey** and **FindNearest**) is a set holding the values that you want to match.

Deleting Data

If the mood takes you, Delphi provides a whole heap of ways for you to get violent with a table, its records and its indexes. Specifically, you have the following methods at your destructive disposal:

Method	Description
Delete	Deletes the current record from the table. The next record in sequence then becomes current.
DeleteIndex	Deletes an entire index forever.
DeleteTable	Deletes an entire table forever.
EmptyTable	Empties all the records out of a table (mass delete).

The **DeleteIndex** and **DeleteTable** methods are really meant for those of you who want to do a little database management of the sort that you would normally do in the Database Desktop, so I won't go into them in much detail here; it's far more likely that you'll want to delete records from your tables than anything else.

DeleteTable does just what its name suggests - it deletes an entire table and any indexes on that table. To use it, all you need to do is set up the Table component, deactivate the connection and then call the method:

```
Table1.Databasename := 'c:\database';
Table1.Tablename := 'MyTable';
Table1.TableType := 'Paradox';
Table1.Active := false;
Table1.DeleteTable;
```

DeleteIndex works in roughly the same way, with the exception that you need to specify the name of the secondary index as a parameter:

```
Table1.DeleteIndex := 'SurnameIndex';
```

 It's important to note that you can only delete secondary indexes.

Deleting Records

The **Delete** method allows you to delete the current record, with the table or query automatically moving onto the next available record. Take a look at **navigat3.dpr**.

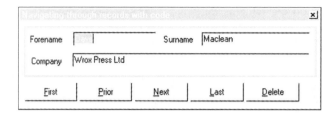

This is similar to the original n**avigat1** program that we saw earlier, but with the addition of a <u>D</u>elete button to allow you to delete the currently selected record. If you double-click that button in design mode, you can see just how simple it is:

```
procedure TfrmNavigate.cmdDeleteClick(Sender: TObject);
begin
    if MessageDlg('Are you sure you want to delete this record', mtConfirmation,
            [mbYes, mbNo],0 ) = mrYes then
        dmodContacts.tabContacts.Delete;
end;
```

As you can see, all this code does is to pop a message box up onto the screen to check that the user really does want to delete some data and then invoke the **Delete** method. The **EmptyTable** method works in exactly the same way. If you wanted to be really extreme, there's nothing stopping you from changing the last line of code to:

```
if MessageDlg('Are you sure you want to delete this record', mtConfirmation,
[mbYes, mbNo],0 )
        = mrYes then
dmodContacts.tabContacts.EmptyTable;
```

Summary

In this chapter, I've covered a lot more of the hands-on side of database application development. Throughout the chapter, I've tried to bring you to the subject based upon the knowledge you've collected from the previous chapter, focusing on the use of Tables in your database applications.

You should, however, know that you could use a Query in all the places that I have used a Table. I've not gone into any detail on those components in this chapter, as I've covered them extensively in the final application, and to be honest, once you can use a Table, you can use a Query!

Look out on the publisher's web site for more information on database application development, including some interesting ways to use a Query to achieve some quite interesting results.

In the next chapter, I'm moving on to the subject of OLE - object linking and embedding.

Object Linking and Embedding

As Windows users, you can't have failed to have noticed a lot of talk about something called **OLE 2**. In previous versions of the Windows operating system, OLE provided users with a convenient way to move data, in fact entire files (called *documents* in OLE) between totally unrelated applications.

With OLE 2, though, we have a much more powerful tool. Sure, it can still be used to move data around between applications, but OLE 2 provides developers with the tools they need to at last realize the dream of component-driven programming. Now it's possible to write applications which effectively export their functionality (using a system called **OLE Automation**) to developers and users of other applications. For example, all of the applications in the Microsoft Office suite are already OLE 2 enabled which means that, while using Excel, for example, you can call up and program Microsoft Word from within an Excel macro.

I have to admit the first time I was introduced to OLE 2, I sat back and said "Yeah... so?", but it's surface simplicity belies the incredible amount of power that it brings to developers. For example, you may need to develop an accounting package that can also print copies of an invoice. Traditionally, you would probably have to either grab the code out of another application that already prints invoices and drop it into yours, or simply write the code again from scratch. Both methods are prone to errors and can be downright inconvenient. For example, imagine trying to develop in Delphi while the other applications in the business were written in VB4!

With OLE 2, you could embed all the functionality surrounding an invoice into an OLE 2 object which can be called up and used by Delphi developers, a VB team, an Excel user, and so on.

In this chapter, we are going to look at all the issues surrounding OLE 2. You will see:

- How to make your applications OLE aware
- How to create OLE servers
- How to use OLE servers from within your code
- What all the OLE terms actually mean and how the relate to you
- What design considerations you need to make when you use OLE
- Why OLE 2 is so important to Windows, Microsoft and Windows developers

OLE - A Little Background

Originally conceived, or at least implemented, as a means for programs to swap data, regardless of the format, no-one can deny that OLE was both slow, cumbersome and really quite tedious to use. However, its heart was in the right place.

The idea behind it was pretty sound; users have long been looking for a way to pull their carefully prepared spreadsheets into their wordprocessed reports without having to resort to nasty things like exporting and reformatting. However, OLE tried to go far beyond this and allowed literally any OLE enabled application to share data with any other. If you wanted to embed a CD audio track inside a PowerPoint presentation then you could. If you wanted to whack a quick video clip inside a Word document, then hey... go ahead (I never could figure that one out!). Just select Insert | Object... from the Word menu and you're away.

However, the take-up of OLE wasn't that good. As Microsoft appeared to simply bolt OLE onto Windows, it simply made an already touchy operating system worse.

Then along came OLE 2.

OLE 2 stabilized a lot of the stuff in OLE 1 but, on the 16-bit platforms, resulted in even more performance loss as it added yet more functionality to the standard. Notice how I keep singling out the 16-bit operating systems. Windows 95 has OLE 2 built directly into the operating system and has a lot of native operating system support for it. This means that it's both more stable and a whole lot better to use.

Apart from being finally accepted into the heart of the Windows family, what's new in OLE 2? Well, quite a lot, actually!

With OLE 1, you could copy a document from one application to another, but if you then decided to update that information, you'd have to endure a nice long pause while the host application started, loaded up the document and prepared it for editing. When you were done with your editing, you invariably had to select an Update option from its File menu to make sure that the changes you just made were copied over to the application in which you had embedded the data. Okay, but a bit too much like hard work.

All this was sorted out as OLE 2 brought with it a neat little trick called **in-place activation**.

OLE 2's In-place Activation

Picture the scene. You're typing away at a report in Word and decide that you could make your point a whole lot clearer using a spreadsheet. A few mouse clicks later and you have cut and pasted the Excel spreadsheet into your Word document, just as you always could do with OLE 1. But there's a problem; you notice that some of the figures on the sheet don't quite match the work in your report, so you're going to have to make some changes to the spreadsheet. With in-place activation, you double-click the embedded object as normal, at which point the menus and toolbars on the screen change as the host application, say Excel, loads up and takes control. In our little example, you would now have full access to all of Excel's functions, menus and toolbars, but without ever leaving or losing sight of your Word report. The applications change around the document!

OLE 2 is considered by some to be the first step towards a document-centric rather than application-centric approach to working with your PC.

OLE 2's Other Toy - OLE Automation

The other main feature of OLE 2 is called **OLE Automation**. When this was first announced a few years back, the reception in the developer community as a whole was really quite lukewarm. The idea is quite simple: an application supporting OLE automation is supposed to be able to make its functionality available to other applications by basically 'exposing' the objects it contains.

 This idea builds off the concept of the client/server model, but, rather confusingly, the client, or calling program, is sometimes given the title Automation Controller, probably just to make it feel important. This controller accesses the exposed functionality of the server, rather as you can access `public` properties and methods of a Delphi object, though with no regard to the language or underlying structure of the server. This is something like the computer version of the United Nations - no matter what language a program is written in, it now has the forum in which it can sit down and work together with its fellow programs towards a common goal...

Initially, this was just taken up as a neat novelty thing. The applications in the Microsoft Office suite (such as Word and Excel) would export some of the objects that they contain (such as an Excel sheet) and allow VB developers to manipulate these objects from within their own code.

However, front-ending Microsoft Office is just a very small example of the potential of OLE automation. A much bigger benefit that it brings to the development arena is that it allows developers to wrap up core business rules and functionality in OLE 2 objects which can be reused in any application, or by any OLE automation client with very little effort.

Most commercial developers spend their time writing database applications of some kind and these invariably require some form of security system. Rather than adding the security tables to your app's database and then coding up the login form, maintenance forms, and so on, you could place all of your company's security functionality into an OLE 2 object. That way, you end up with one common compiled object used by all the applications on your PC and (by the end of this year, with the advent of Network OLE) even on your network that need these security features.

Enough of the theory. Let's take a look at OLE and OLE automation in action in Delphi.

Using the Container Control

The easiest route into the wonderful world of OLE is the Delphi TOleContainer component - check out the System page of the Component Palette.

The most basic thing you can do with OLE is simply embed or link a document from one application into another. This is what the TOleContainer component does for you.

> There are some quite important differences between a linked object and an embedded one - I'll cover them in a moment.

Dropped onto a form in design time, the container control is really nothing special:

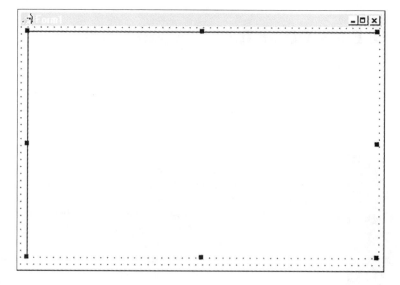

Really, it looks nothing more than a memo box or a large edit box, but its appearance when empty belies its hidden power.

This one component with little or no code attached can handle drag-and-dropped OLE objects at run time, display any OLE document format you care to name and can even activate the parent application of that document within itself, effectively giving the user complete access to a third party application from within the single form of your application - that's in-place activation for you!

For now, let's just run through a really quick example.

Try It Out - Using the Component

1 Start up a new project in Delphi and drop a TOleContainer component onto the form.

2 What we're going to do is embed a bitmap picture - you should have plenty in your Windows directory. Right-click on the new container component to bring up its pop-up menu and select Insert Object...

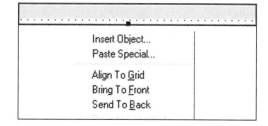

> If you have previously copied data onto the clipboard in another application, you could also select the **Paste Special** item on the menu to add this data to the **TOleContainer**.

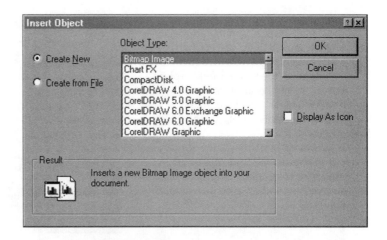

3 As soon as you select it, you should find yourself looking at the standard Windows OLE dialog:

4 From here, you can set the container up with a blank document by simply selecting a document type from the list, or you can select a file directly to load that file into the container.

Click on the **Create from File** radio button and the dialog will change:

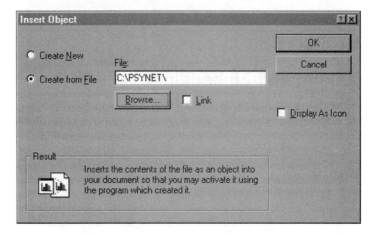

Click on the **Browse** button and select a bitmap.

5 Once you've done that, you can click on the **Link** check box to create a linked object, or leave it blank to embed the object in the container control. For now, leave it blank and click on the **OK** button.

After a short pause, your container control will come back into view, this time holding a picture of a bitmap:

If you run the program now and then try double-clicking on the container control at run time, one of two things will happen. If you embedded the new bitmap then you'll get in-place activation of the application responsible for this kind of file (MSPaint in this case), as shown here:

However, if you linked the bitmap or you try and edit it at design time then a new instance of MSPaint will be created to allow you to edit the file.

I told you that using the container control was easy enough. What you just did was create a container control, embed a document inside it and then, at run time, make use of in-place activation to edit the data-embedded file inside the container while the application was running.

Linking and Embedding

What does **object linking and embedding** mean? The object in question is normally a data file, such as the bitmap file we used in the last example, which is embedded inside a container control.

There are some important differences between linking and embedding an object inside a container component.

In the previous example, we embedded an object inside the component. If you were to take a look at the size of the compiled program, you would see that it really is quite large, since the bitmap graphic is embedded in the container and its data stored along with the application inside the .**exe** file.

The alternative to embedding an object inside the container is, surprise, surprise, to link it. This means that, rather than storing the entire graphic inside your compiled program ready for when the program runs, a small link between your container control and the file on your hard disk is created and stored inside the program instead. This means that the executable program is much smaller, at the cost of slightly slower performance.

You might be interested to know about a couple of issues related to who owns the data in linked and embedded documents and when to use which. In the case of a linked object, the data lives in its original data file on the hard disk, so it's the responsibility of the application that originally created the data file to handle any changes that are made to the graphic. When documents are linked rather than embedded, because their data is held in a central file, any changes made to them are seen by other applications that make use of the documents.

In the case of embedded documents it's your application that is responsible for loading and saving changes to the document, using the **LoadFromFile** and **SaveToFile** methods. The initial state of the file is determined inside the executable program itself, so a network of eight users of your program could have eight separate copies of your program flying around and thus eight copies of the document. Yuck! Imagine the version control on that!

At design time, choosing whether to create a linked or embedded document is easy. From the OLE dialog, creating a new, blank document creates an embedded document, albeit an empty one. When you load a document in from an existing file, as we did in the earlier example, you are by default, creating an embedded object unless you click on the Link check box on the form.

Naturally, there are also ways for you to do these things at run time. Surprisingly, these methods all revolve around the same set of Windows common OLE dialogs that you see at design time. Whether you're creating links or embedding documents, or even pasting OLE data from the clipboard, your users see the same dialogs and have access to the same powerful functionality that you do at design time.

Using the OLE Dialogs

The first and most common method is the **InsertObjectDialog** function. There are others that are as simple to invoke and allow your application users access to the dialogs so they can embed the document of their choice. We'll look at those in the next example.

Such is the power of Delphi that single commands provide all that functionality, allowing users to create new embedded documents, as well as to either link in or embed existing ones. The best way to get at all these functions is to use a menu.

Try It Out - Container Methods

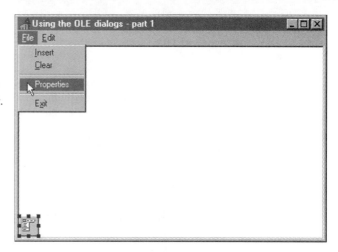

1 Load up **insert.dpr** - an application with a TOLEContainer and a MainMenu component on it. We've filled out the menu entries for you:

2 It's time to add in the code for the menu items. Starting with the File menu, add the following code to the Insert item:

```
procedure TfrmInsert.mnuFInsertClick(Sender: TObject);
begin
    if OleContainer1.InsertObjectDialog then
        mnuECopy.Enabled := True;
end;
```

3 For the Clear menu item:

```
procedure TfrmInsert.mnuFClearClick(Sender: TObject);
begin
    OleContainer1.DestroyObject;
end;
```

4 Moving to the Edit menu, we're now dealing with the clipboard. The Paste Special... item:

```
procedure TfrmInsert.mnuEPasteClick(Sender: TObject);
begin
    OleContainer1.PasteSpecialDialog;
end;
```

and the Copy menu item:

```
procedure TfrmInsert.mnuECopyClick(Sender: TObject);
begin
    OleContainer1.Copy;
    mnuEPaste.Enabled := True;
end;
```

5 And the Properties menu item:

```
procedure TfrmInsert.mnuFPropertiesClick(Sender: TObject);
begin
    OleContainer1.ObjectPropertiesDialog;
end;
```

You can now run the application and load in OLE objects from files and from the clipboard. You can copy them to the clipboard and clear them out of the container. By selecting File | Insert, you bring up the same Insert Object dialog that you saw in design mode.

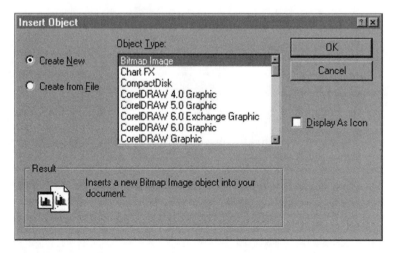

How It Works

The **InsertObjectDialog** is actually a function. It returns **True** if the user links or embeds a document and **False** if she doesn't. The method accesses the same dialog you saw at design time in the last Try It Out.

Another common dialog is the **Paste Special** dialog which allows you to paste an OLE object from the clipboard into the OLE container.

Think of this as the turbo-charged, 4x4 edition of the previous program you saw, since you can now copy objects to the clipboard, clear them and much more. We aren't going to cover all the code just yet (I'm covering the clipboard in a little while), but the Paste Special item on the file menu does show you the next powerful dialog that TOLEContainer has built in.

To bring it to life, you will, of course, need to have an object on the clipboard ready for pasting into the container. You can bring this about by inserting an object in the normal way, by selecting File | Insert and then Edit | Copy to copy it to the clipboard. At this point, you can either quit the application and come back in to do the paste, or you can select File | Clear to clear the object and then paste it in. Try it now.

As soon as you select Paste, the Paste Special dialog comes into view, a familiar sight for those of you who have spent any time playing with the Microsoft Office suite.

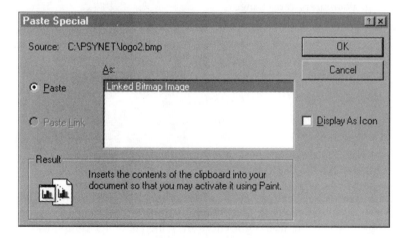

Just one more dialog remains. All OLE objects have a set of properties attached to them which you can get at run time to find out more about the object itself and to change the way it's dealt with by the container.

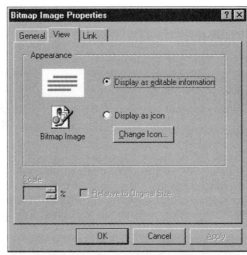

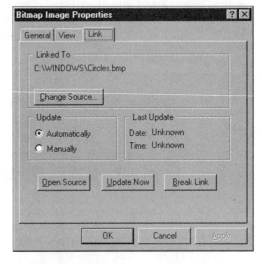

Using this dialog, your users can change almost any aspect of the linked or embedded object.

In a real-world application, in order to keep in with current Windows 95 design guidelines, you really should make the properties the very last item on a pop-up menu that appears when the user right clicks over the container component.

The OLE Container Methods

The dialogs we just saw basically provide a pretty, compact front end to a whole host of behind-the-scenes methods. For example, the Insert Object dialog provides a convenient way to get at the **CreateLinkToFile**, **CreateObject** and **CreateObjectFromFile** methods. The Paste Special dialog provides neat access to the functionality in the **DestroyObject** (which we've already met), **Paste** and **UpdateObject** methods.

358

In this section, we're going to look at all these methods and what they do individually, as well as one or two of the other less esoteric methods not front-ended by a dialog.

Linking Documents

You can link a document into the container component using the **CreateLinkToFile** method. Take a look at the **linking.dpr** project supplied with the example code:

It's a quite simple program: select File | Link and up pops a File Open dialog allowing you to select the file that you want to link into the OleContainer. However, the program does all this without once using any of its own common dialogs. It does this thanks to the **CreateLinkFromFile** method of the container control. Simply pass **CreateLinkFromFile** the name of the file that you want to link and a **True** or **False** value indicating whether or not to show the linked document as an icon.

Stop the program running and take a peek at the code behind that link item:

```
procedure TfrmLink.mnuFLinkClick(Sender: TObject);
begin
     if OpenDialog1.Execute then
         OleContainer1.CreateLinkToFile( OpenDialog1.Filename, False );
end;
```

You should be familiar with the first line - it runs up a File Open dialog and checks to see if the user actually selected a file or not. If they did, the OLE code is run - it really is as simple as that.

Handling Embedded Documents

Dealing with linked documents is a very small topic, since the only thing you can really do with these is to display them in the container - the data maintenance aspect of it all is handled by the application that created the document or file in the first place.

Embedded data is a little different, since the OLE container itself can create blank embedded documents, as well as manage changes to embedded documents pulled in from other sources.

For that reason there are a few more methods available to you to deal with embedded data. The embedded equivalent of the **CreateLinkToFile** method is the **CreateObjectFromFile** method. It takes exactly the same parameters as **CreateLinkToFile**, the result being that an embedded object is created inside the container.

You can try this out if you like, although the result looks no different to the previous example.

Try It Out - Embedding

1 Load up **linking.dpr** and save it as **ole5u.pas** and **creatobj.dpr**. Add a new menu item, **mnuFEmbed**, with the caption Embed and copy the routine we saw earlier. Change it to:

```
procedure TfrmLink.mnuFEmbedClick(Sender: TObject);
begin
    if OpenDialog1.Execute then
        OleContainer.CreateObjectFromFile( OpenDialog1.Filename, False );
end;
```

2 Add a further menu item to the File menu with caption Create and title **mnuFCreate**. Now add following code:

```
procedure TForm1.mnuFCreateClick(Sender: TObject);
begin
    OleContainer1.CreateObject('Paint.Picture', False );
end;
```

If you save and run the application and then select Embed rather than Link, the only difference you'll see is that embedding runs a fair bit slower than linking.

The second added feature is far more powerful. You can see it in action by selecting File | Create. There will be a short pause, during which the mouse pointer will turn into an hourglass to indicate the computer is busy thinking, before your application finally stops being busy and you're left looking at exactly the same form you had on screen before.

However, once you've created the new blank document, you can double-click the container control to bring the application you mentioned in the **OLEClass** parameter to life. Try it now - create the object, then double-click inside the container.

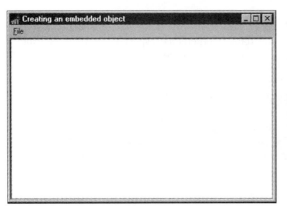 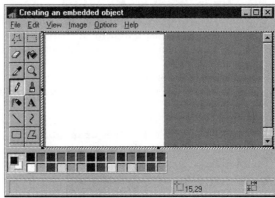

The Windows Paint program comes to life, taking over a large part of the menu bar and filling the OLEContainer with not only the document that you just created, but also with the toolbars and palettes that the user needs to maintain and edit such an object.

How It Works

This example demonstrates both loading and creating an OLE object from scratch. And it's embarrassingly easy.

The whole thing with OLE is that your application displays, and to a certain extent manages, data normally created and maintained by another application. So, in order to create a blank embedded object, we need to tell Delphi which application (Paint) and which document class within that application (Picture) we wish to create a blank of.

Embedded objects are really pretty neat. Since your application is responsible for loading and saving data held in the embedded object and basically owns the object, double-clicking an embedded object causes most host applications to take over the area occupied by your container window and run inside them just as if they were running normally. In addition, if the form with the container component has a menu attached to it, when the host application is started up, it can merge its menus with those on the form. Excellent.

CreateObject takes two parameters just like the other **Create** methods. However, this time the first parameter is definitely not a filename. Instead, what you specify is something we called an **OLEClass** above. More often than not, this is nothing more complex than the name of the OLE application that you want to deal with, in this case **Paint**, followed by a specific type of document or object that the application is able to serve, in this case **Picture**. The documentation or online help supplied with most OLE 2 enabled applications can give you a full list of the OLE class names the application supports (such as Excel's **Excel.Sheet**, etc.).

Once again, the second parameter is nothing more than a **True** or **False** value used to tell the code whether or not to display the new object in its entirety within your application, or whether to simply display an icon for it.

Dealing with the Clipboard

Something else you can do with embedded objects, but not with linked ones, is exchange them between the clipboard and your container objects. Most OLE 2 enabled applications can store information on the clipboard in object form and the Delphi OLE container component provides a couple of methods to check whether what is on the clipboard can be pasted into itself as an object and to actually carry out that operation. Of course, you can also copy embedded data from your applications onto the clipboard.

It's the Cut, Copy and Paste conundrum, and it's easy in Delphi. Show a C programmer the previous program example and then tell them that they need to modify it to support cut and paste operations and they would have a fit.

Try It Out - Editing OLE Objects

1 Load up the **creatobj.dpr** project again and double-click the menu component to start up the menu editor. Add in an edit menu and use the usual naming conventions and captions:

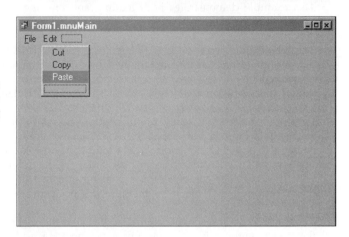

2 When you're done, close down the menu editor and select the <u>C</u>opy item in design mode to bring up the code window for its OnClick event. Change the code to:

```
procedure TForm1.mnuECopyClick(Sender: TObject);
begin
     if OleContainer1.State <> osEmpty then
        OleContainer1.Copy;
end;
```

The first line checks that there is data in the container, and if there is, runs the second line which simply copies the entire object into the Windows clipboard. Simple!

3 Bring up the code window for the <u>P</u>aste menu item and change it so that it looks like this:

```
procedure TForm1.mnuEPasteClick(Sender: TObject);
begin
     if OleContainer1.CanPaste then
        OleContainer1.Paste;
end;
```

First, we check that the data on the clipboard can be pasted and, if it can, the **Paste** method is called, which does just that. Incidentally, if the container already holds an object, when you try to paste a new one in, that old object is destroyed before the new one is pasted in.

4 All that remains is to get that **Cut** method working. The OleContainer doesn't actually contain a **Cut** method, so we need to simulate the process by first copying the document to the clipboard and then destroying the document in the container.

Change the OnClick event handler for the <u>C</u>ut menu item so that the code looks like this:

```
procedure TForm1.mnuECutClick(Sender: TObject);
begin
```

```
        if OleContainer1.State <> osEmpty then
    begin
        OleContainer1.Copy;
        OleContainer1.DestroyObject;
    end;
  end;
```

The code is now ready - try running it, creating an object, cutting it, then pasting it. You may even like to try cutting and pasting objects from one application into this one, for example cutting a media clip from the media player application and pasting it into the Delphi app.

How It Works

Cutting, copying and pasting an embedded item to the clipboard is easy - you just need to invoke the various methods of the container control. However, it's important to check that there's actually an object in the container to cut or copy, or one in the clipboard to paste into your application. Otherwise, you run the risk of hitting your users with a nasty run-time error message.

To check that we can paste data from the clipboard, we can take a peek at the container's **CanPaste** property which returns **True** if a **Paste** operation can take place.

You can check whether the container currently 'contains' an object by taking a peek at its **State** property to see if it's anything other than **osEmpty**. The **State** property is of type **TObjectState**, and can be set to either **osEmpty**, **osLoaded**, **osRunning**, **osOpen**, **osInPlaceActivate** or **osUIActive**. However, we're only interested in **osEmpty**.

Incidentally, if you didn't follow that example along, you can still take a look at the program in action and explore the code by loading up **creatob2.dpr**.

OLE Automation

The real beauty of OLE 2 is found in a feature called **OLE automation**. Using OLE automation, any application can expose its functionality to other applications through OLE objects. For example, Microsoft Word exposes all its document management facilities to other applications through an OLE object known simply as **Document**. Excel does the same, with a **Sheet** object providing programmatic access to an Excel spreadsheet.

Like much of OLE 2, it's hard to see the full potential of something like OLE automation at first glance. After all, being able to take control of an Excel spreadsheet or a Word document through code is a pretty neat thing to do the first couple of times, but then the novelty kinda wears off, right? Well it would, if all Delphi let you do was program other application's objects.

The fact of the matter is, though, that Delphi lets you create both OLE automation clients (applications that use OLE objects from other applications) and servers (applications that themselves expose their functionality through OLE objects). This is a very important Delphi feature.

Think about it. You've been used to making your Delphi code visible to other units and even other applications, but that depends on Pascal code and being able to reference other units in a **uses** clause. What about allowing any program written in any language to access your incredible Delphi database searching tool (or whatever other fruit your labors have borne). Obviously, you can't predict anything about the other program, but, by using the OLE interface, you can create an OLE object and give it methods and properties which any program using that interface can access. It's stunning in that it removes the need for you to be partisan about the software you use (though doubtless, knowing human nature, this will be as important as ever), allowing you to build on others' work.

If you could code the core rules and functionality of your business (such as invoice production, security routines, etc.) into a set of OLE automation objects then any application on the computer which supports OLE automation would be able to get at those objects and reuse them.

The key here is, of course, *reuse* and that's the main power of OLE 2. For example, by coding your database security routines into an OLE server application, you instantly make its functionality available to the Visual Basic developers, the Paradox developers, the Access developers - in fact, anyone developing in a system that supports OLE automation no longer has to worry about redeveloping your company's security routines, since they are freely available from within the OLE server application that you created.

OLE automation also lets you do one or two other sneaky things, as you'll see in a minute.

Writing a Simple OLE Client

The first and most common exposure that you will have to OLE automation will be programming an OLE client. OLE client applications are the standard applications that you and I write, but which occasionally need to make use of the functionality exposed by another application.

You'll find in most books dealing with OLE that the example that you're invited to create is a sample Excel spreadsheet; you'll fire some numbers and formula in there through code and then display the result of a calculation. Don't get me wrong, it's a great thing to do and really demonstrates the power of OLE. However, how about using Excel as a graphic filter (after all, Excel can load in most graphic file formats while Delphi can't), using Word as a spell checker, or using PowerPoint as a graphic rotation tool - all these things and more are possible using OLE automation.

Let's take a look. In the following example, I have to assume that you have an OLE automation server on your system and, to have a little fun here, I'm going to assume that the server in question is Excel. If you don't have Excel, don't fret too much; the concepts and the structure of the code are the same, no matter what OLE automation server you're dealing with - only the object and method names will change.

Try It Out - OLE Clients

1 Start a new application and save it as **convertu.pas** and **oleconv.dpr**. Drop a MainMenu component onto the form and add the following menu items - mnuFOpen and mnuFExit:

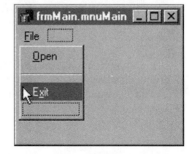

2 Add an OpenDialog and a TImage component to the form. Set the Image component's name to imgConverted, its Stretch property to True and its Align property to alClient. Bring up the OpenDialog component's Filter Editor and add the file extensions that your version of Excel supports - usually *.pcx, *.bmp, *.jpg, *.tif, *.pct, *.wpg and *.wmf. The idea here is to allow the user to see at a glance what picture formats your application can cope with.

3 On the Exit click event handler, add the following line of code:

```
Close;
```

4 For the Open menu item, add the following:

```
procedure TfrmMain.mnuFOpenClick(Sender: TObject);
begin
    if dlgOpen.Execute then
        OLEConvertImage(dlgOpen.Filename);
end;
```

5 We now need to add the procedure we've called when the Open dialog executes. First, declare it in the **interface** section:

```
procedure OLEConvertImage( sFilename : String );
```

6 Then add in the following code block, which will form the basis of our discussion in a moment:

```
procedure OLEConvertImage( sFilename : String );
var
    vOLE : Variant;
begin
    vOLE := CreateOLEObject( 'Excel.Sheet' );

    vOLE.Pictures.Insert( sFilename );
    vOLE.DrawingObjects('Picture 1').Select;
    vOLE.Application.Selection.Copy;

    frmMain.imgConverted.Picture.Assign(Clipboard);

    vOLE := UnAssigned;
end;
```

7 Lastly, we need to declare a couple of units in our program's **uses** clause:

```
uses
    Windows, Messages, SysUtils, Classes, Graphics, Controls, Forms, Dialogs,
    Menus, ExtCtrls, OleAuto, Clipbrd;
```

Now try running the program.

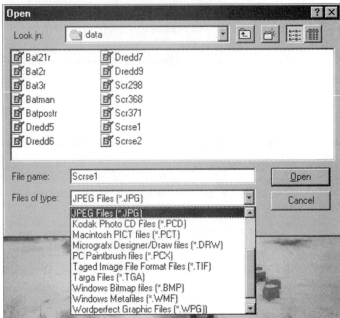

On the surface, the program is very simple; you just choose File | Open and select the graphic image that you want to see. After a pause, it comes into view. However, take a look at the File Open dialog that the program displays:

As you can see from the file extensions list, the program supports far more graphic formats than the standard **.bmp**, **.wmf** and **.ico** formats that Delphi and its components supports. The reason for this is that we're using the graphic conversion routines in Excel to load up the image, before copying it to the clipboard and dropping it into the image control in our Delphi application. This veritable plethora of formats exist as graphic filters (in the **\Windows\Msapps\Grphflt** directory), but you may have to install them if you didn't select the correct options when you installed Excel.

How It Works

As you might expect, the code calls the **Execute** method attached to the Open dialog and if it returns **True**, indicating that the user chose a filename, then the **OLEConvertImage** routine is called, with the selected filename being passed as a parameter.

This is all quite straightforward stuff - the real teeth of the program lie in that **OLEConvertImage** routine.

The first thing the routine does is to declare a variable using a new (to us) data type called the **variant**. Variants are actually data types that can hold any type of value at all, be it string, number or (as in this case) object. Flick ahead a couple of pages and you'll see that we will take a look at variants in more detail. For now, though, just take it as read that this **vOLE** variant variable is going to hold an object - an OLE object.

Although I've spoken about using objects embedded inside other applications, in actual fact, these 'objects' are really nothing more than class types. What we need to do to get at the functionality inside them is turn these embedded classes into objects at run time. That is exactly what the first real line of code in the routine does.

```
vOLE := CreateOLEObject( 'Excel.Sheet' );
```

The **CreateOLEObject** method creates an OLE Object and stores it in the variable you specify, which must be of a variant type. When you create an OLE object, you need to tell Delphi the name of the application in which the object is defined and the class that defines it. In this example, the application is simply Excel, since the example is going to use the image file converters in Excel. The class that we intend to use in Excel is the **Sheet** class, the class that contains all the functionality we need to deal with an Excel spreadsheet, including the ability to load in graphics in almost any format at run time.

What actually happens when this code is run is that Excel itself runs (although you will never see it pop into view, it just sits quietly out of sight eating up your memory) and all the functionality associated with an Excel spreadsheet, as well as the data in the sheet itself, are dumped into the **vOLE** variable.

If you skip down to the bottom of the code, you'll see that we must on no account omit to free up this object by making it **UnAssigned**. This effectively stops Excel from running and frees any memory that it was eating up.

```
vOLE := UnAssigned;
```

Remember - this is very important. You use **CreateOleObject** to create an object based on a class contained inside an OLE automation-enabled application. Then you set the object to **UnAssigned** when you're done with it, to free up any memory associated with it.

The code in between these two statements is specific to the OLE automation server that you're dealing with. In this example program, we now call methods and deal with properties and collections attached to an Excel spreadsheet. I'm not going to go into a lot of detail about this stuff, since it really is specific to Excel. You will, or at least *should*, find that any OLE automation enabled application you get hold of should also be supplied with a help file describing the classes available to you and their properties and methods that you can use through your own code.

```
vOLE.Pictures.Insert( sFilename );
vOLE.DrawingObjects('Picture 1').Select;
vOLE.Application.Selection.Copy;

frmMain.imgConverted.Picture.Assign(Clipboard);
```

In a nutshell, then, what's going on here is that we're calling the **insert** method of the **pictures** collection that all Excel **Sheet** objects have attached to them. This causes a new picture to be inserted into the collection and, in the process, goes through Excel's graphic converters - which is just the facility that we most want to make use of in this program.

Having loaded in the picture, the **Select** method of the **DrawingObjects** collection is called to select the picture we just loaded. Excel's **Copy** method is then applied to the selection to copy the picture to the clipboard. After that little lot, we can drop back into some Delphi code, calling the **Assign** method of the picture object attached to the image component to assign the contents of the clipboard to it.

Now, although this all looks a little confusing and weird, it really does illustrate how easy OLE automation is under Delphi. The code is just calling methods and properties of a second application's objects. If you're not used to dealing with Excel through OLE automation then that's why the code here may look a little weird. The concepts of what we're doing, though, is no more tricky to get the hang of than dealing with the properties and methods attached to any other component or object in Delphi.

The process of using another application then can be summarized in four simple steps:

▶ Declare a variant to hold the object at run time.

▶ Use **CreateOLEObject**, specifying the application and class you need, and store the results of the call in your new variant.

▶ Use the methods of the other application's object by calling them from the variant; i.e. **variant.Method** or **variant.Property**.

▶ Close the application down and free up the memory associated with it by setting the variant to **UnAssigned**.

Problems

If you've spent any time playing around with this sample application, you will have soon found yourself singing the age old "OLE is too slow to be useful" chant, since every time you go to load up a picture, it takes what seems like an age to actually display the picture on the screen. The truth is that, yes OLE can be slow, *very*, *very* slow, but there are steps that you can take to speed it up.

You have to bear in mind that when you're using OLE, either inside a container or by making use of OLE automation through code as here, what you're doing is loading up and using another application. If that application is a lumbering great juggernaut of an app like Microsoft Excel or Word, you are in for a fairly painful wait just to get the application to load itself.

Take a look at the example code again and you'll see that we're calling `CreateOLEObject` every time the user tries to load in a new file, the result being that same painful wait for Excel to load whenever you want to look at a picture.

The solution is simple. If you're going to be doing a lot of OLE work in your application, just as this one does, then load up the external application at the start of the program and close it down at the end.

Take a look at **fastconv.dpr** to see this in action.

This application is no different to the previous one, except that it has the benefit of being a lot faster. In this application, our variant is declared outside of any code to make it available to all the code in this unit and to any other unit you may add to the application which uses this one.

```
var
  frmMain: TfrmMain;
  vOLE : Variant;

implementation
{$R *.DFM}
```

In addition, the `CreateOLEObject` method is called when the application's form is created and it's only destroyed when the application shuts down:

```
procedure TfrmMain.FormCreate(Sender: TObject);
begin
    Screen.Cursor := crHourglass;
    vOLE           := CreateOLEObject( 'Excel.Sheet' );
    Screen.Cursor := crDefault;
end;
```

```
procedure TfrmMain.FormClose(Sender: TObject; var Action: TCloseAction);
begin
    vOLE := UnAssigned;
end;
```

Notice how I changed the mouse pointer into an hourglass before calling `CreateOLEObject` and back to normal afterwards. You would do well to do the same, or at the very least dump a status dialog of some kind on the screen, since the delay in loading up Excel can be quite significant, especially for users with slower machines.

Take a look at the File | Open code and you'll notice that it hasn't really shrunk that much and now includes calls to additional methods and properties of the Excel Sheet:

```
begin
    Screen.Cursor := crHourglass;

    vOLE.Pictures.Delete;
    vOLE.Pictures.Insert( sFilename );
    vOLE.DrawingObjects('Picture 1').Select;
    vOLE.Application.Selection.Copy;

    frmMain.imgConverted.Picture.Assign(Clipboard);

    Screen.Cursor := crDefault;
end;
```

Optimizing an OLE application nearly always results in a little more code in terms of housekeeping (here, since we're not loading and unloading Excel each time, I need to call the **Delete** method to clear any previously loaded picture inside Excel) so you really do need to figure out if speed is everything or whether you can get away with saving your fingers by doing things the slow (at run time) way.

A Little More on Variants

I have mentioned variants a fair amount in this chapter and they're not something that you have come across elsewhere in the book. So, perhaps it's time for a little digression - let's take a look at that variant type in a little more detail, before diving once more into OLE automation.

As I said, the variant type can basically hold almost any kind of data, be it numeric, string, date, OLE object, and so on. There are a number of Delphi routines that you can use to find out what kind of data is stored inside the variant and to deal with that data:

Routine	Description
VarIsArray(Variant)	Returns **True** is the given variant is an array.
VarIsEmpty(Variant)	Returns **True** if the variant is empty and contains nothing at all.
VarIsNull(Variant)	Returns **True** if the variant is **NULL**, meaning it contains an non-number - a numeric value which means nothing.
VarClear (Variant)	The same as writing **variant := Unassigned;**

Although a variant can hold any kind of value, most variants know what kind of data they hold and can tell you through the **VarType** method what kind of variant they are.

VarType returns one of the following values:

Type	Description
varEmpty	The variant contains **UnAssigned**.
varNull	The variant contains **NULL**.
varSmallInt	The value in the variant is a small integer.
varInteger	The value in the variant is an **Integer**.
varSingle	The value is a single precision floating point number (small decimal number).
varDouble	The value is a double precision floating point number (large decimal number).
varCurrency	The value is a currency value.
varDate	**DateTime** type value.
varDispatch	The variant contains an OLE object.
varBoolean	Contains a **True**/**False** value.
varString	Contains a standard **String**.

370

The interesting point about these types is, of course, the **varDispatch** type. If the **IsType** function returns **varDispatch**, you know that the variant holds an OLE object:

```
If VarType( MyObject) := varDispatch then
    ShowMessage('Yes - it holds an OLE automation object')
else
    ShowMessage('Sorry - it holds something else');
```

In all, variants provide you with a very convenient and easy way to deal with all types of data, particularly OLE objects. However, it's advisable to avoid using them on a day to day basis, unless of course, you have to (for instance to deal with OLE automation). Since they can easily deal with all types of data, they remove some of the safety nets that a strongly typed language like Pascal brings with it and they also work slower with data than the native data types such as a **String**, **Integer**, and so on.

Writing a Simple OLE Server

At its most basic level, producing an OLE automation server is really easy. Allow me to demonstrate.

Try It Out - OLE Automation Server

1 Start a new application and save it as **serveu.pas** and **oletest.dpr**. When the default form appears, select the File | New menu item. The New Items dialog will appear, asking you exactly what new item it is that you want to create.

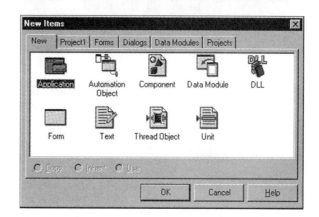

Select the Automation object and click on the OK button. A new dialog will appear - the Automation Object Expert.

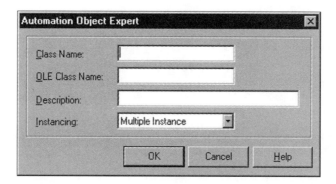

2 In this dialog, you define the name of the class that you will use at run time to call it from other applications.

The first edit box should hold the Class Name of this automation object and, like any other class you write in a Delphi application, its classiness is distinguished by the prefix T. For now fill in TTestClass as the class name.

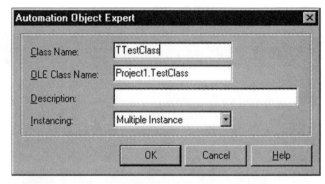

Notice that as you do this, the second edit box (OLE Class name) fills itself in. This is the name that you will use, with the **CreateOLEObject** method we met earlier, to actually bring the class to life. OLETest is our Project ID. By default, it matches the project name, but you can change it to something more memorable if you want.

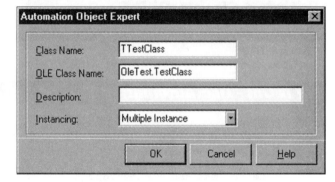

3 For now, just leave the Instancing combo set to Multiple Instance and click on the OK button. A new code window appears, containing the OLE automation object's code which looks like this:

```
unit Unit2;

interface

uses
  OleAuto;

type
  TTestClass = class(TAutoObject)
  private
    { Private declarations }
  automated
    { Automated declarations }
  end;

implementation

procedure RegisterTestClass;
const
  AutoClassInfo: TAutoClassInfo = (
```

```
    AutoClass: TTestClass;
    ProgID: 'OleTest.TestClass';
    ClassID: '{67DAD2A0-8BB1-11CF-852E-000021529426}';
    Description: '';
    Instancing: acMultiInstance);
begin
  Automation.RegisterClass(AutoClassInfo);
end;

initialization
  RegisterTestClass;
end.
```

I'll discuss what the RegisterTestClass procedure does in a little while. For now, though, all you need to know is that to bring this object to life you need to add procedure or function declarations into the automated section of the class itself, just as if you were adding event handlers to a form.

4 Let's try it. Add a procedure to the code, just above the **initialization** section (which should always be the last section of a unit).

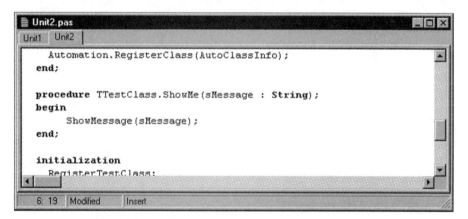

5 When you've done that, add in the procedure declaration to the **Automated** section:

```
type
  TTestClass = class(TAutoObject)
  private
    { Private declarations }
  automated
    { Automated declarations }
    procedure ShowMe ( sMessage : String );
  end;
```

6 Finally, add **Dialogs** to the **uses** clause of the **Automation** unit:

```
interface

uses
  OleAuto, Dialogs;
```

At this point, your program is almost ready to go. Save the project and then compile it with Ctrl+F9 as we don't want to run it yet - there's still one more step.

7 You need to pass the parameter **/regserver** on the command line by selecting Run | Parameters in Delphi. What you see is a combo box into which you can enter the command line parameters. So, for now type in **/regserver** and click on the OK button.

Now run the program. You should find that it will run, then immediately stop, without showing the form on the screen or doing anything.

How It Works

Doesn't seem to do much, does it? What it has done, in the background admittedly, is to register the application in the Windows Registry, run it and make our **TestClass** available to other Windows applications. If at some point you want to get rid of the application from the registry, imagine this were a commercial application and you were including an un-install program, you simply need to change the command line parameter to **/unregserver**. You can do this later when we have finished trying things out if you like, but, for now, leave things as they are, with the application registered and ready to go .

When you run **CreateOleObject**, how does Delphi, or more precisely Windows, know where the application you are after lives on the PC, and how can it check that the class you're trying to use really exists? The solution lies in the fabled Windows registry. The registry is like a central database that Windows itself uses to keep track of the hardware configuration of your PC, what software is installed and what OLE objects the various applications you have installed can serve. It makes sense, then, that you need to put information into this registry about the objects you're serving when you create an OLE automation enabled application.

The registry is normally pretty horrendous subject to deal with, but thankfully, Delphi can do all this for you and that's where the **RegisterTestClass** procedure in the application comes into play.

The first time the application is run, if you pass the **/regserver** parameter on the command line, the **RegisterTestClass** procedure runs, dumping all the information about the application and the classes that it's serving into the Windows registry. From that point on, you can take control of the automation class from another Delphi application, or indeed from any other application that supports OLE automation.

The **RegisterTestClass** procedure holds the program ID, some title that a human can easily remember, and then the **ClassID**, a unique number calculated using some strange incantation on the CPU ID number and the date. If you run the RegEdit program you'll find in Windows95, you can perform a Find to get at this registry information - just don't change anything.

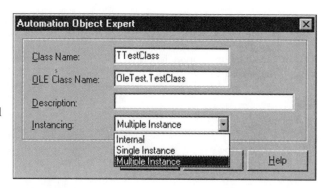

The procedure also holds the contents of the bottom two edit boxes in the expert. What do they signify? The Description edit box is just a general text entry area where you can enter a description of the class. Far more useful is the Instancing combo at the bottom of the dialog.

Instancing defines how the class can be used at run time. Set it to the default value of Multiple Instance and the class can be turned into multiple objects at run time simultaneously, by any number of applications. Set it to Single Instance and the class will only ever exist as an object at one time. For example, you couldn't run two applications that both turn the class into an object at once. The class would be used on a strictly first come, first served basis. Finally, you can set it to Internal to tell Delphi that the class can only be used internally by the application that contains it.

If you haven't followed the Try It Out so far, you can find the application with the sample code as **oletest.dpr** on the disk. Load it up and run it with that **/regserver** command line parameter as I described above, so that you can take advantage of the final example.

Try It Out - Serving the Community

1 Let's test the last application and its OLE object for real. Start up a new application in Delphi and save it as **testu.pas** and **client.dpr**. Drop a command button onto the default form that appears so that it looks like this:

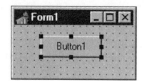

When the user clicks on that command button, we want to call up the **ShowMe** procedure in **OleTest.TestClass**, the procedure that we wrote a short while back.

2 Double-click on the button to bring up the code window and change the OnClick event handler so that it looks like this:

```
procedure TForm1.cmdShowClick(Sender: TObject);
var
   MyOleObject : Variant;
begin
     MyOleObject := CreateOleObject('OleTest.TestClass');
     MyOleObject.ShowMe('This is an OLE Test.');
     MyOleObject := Unassigned;
end;
```

3 Lastly, don't forget to add **OleAuto** to the **uses** clause of this form.

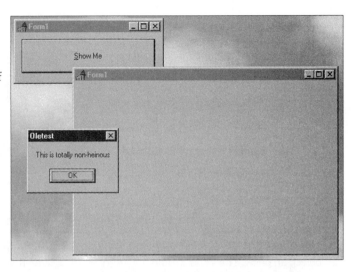

Try it now - run the program and click on the button:

A message box appears showing the string we passed to the OLE method. Notice also the how the main form in the other application appears. As we didn't change anything in the Project Options dialog, you can see when the program is running and when it's not by watching for the appearance of that form when the program starts and for its disappearance when it stops.

How It Works

Just as before, what we're doing here is first declaring a variant to hold our OLE object. Once that is done, a call is made to **CreateOleObject**, passing it the name of the project ID and class that we set up in the OLE automation object expert earlier. This allows the application to find the OLE Object's entry in the Registry.

Next, we call the **ShowMe** method of the object. Remember, **ShowMe** is the procedure that we wrote into the automation object earlier to simply take a string as a parameter and output it in a simple message box. By calling a method of an OLE automation object, we set the application containing that object's class running. So, the final step in the whole process is to set our variant to **UnAssigned**, which in turn causes the OLE application to stop running.

If you like you can prevent the automation server's form from appearing by reloading **OleServer** and using the Project Options dialog to move the main form from the AutoCreate list to the Available forms list, as I've done here:

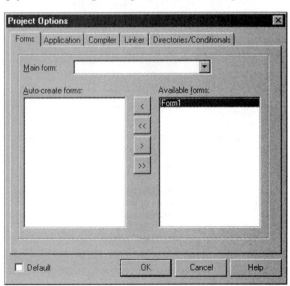

That's really all there is to it. All the tools that Delphi provides makes what could be a mind-blowingly complex application a snap. As with anything, though, the options available to you are limited only by the amount of code you want to write into the application.

Summary

In this chapter, we've met linking and embedding and OLE automation, both client and server. In all these areas, Delphi excels in making it easy for the OLE wannabee.

Linking and embedding show how we can hope and program for a document-centered future, where the tools are subservient to the information the computer user is trying to convey.

In terms of the development work you do, OLE automation objects are just the same as any other unit in your application. You add the functions, procedures and properties that bring the class to life into the **automation** section of the class and hide private, implementation code and data in the **private** section, just as if you were adding code to a form. Have a play around yourself; try changing that **ShowMe** method so that it loads up the application's form and dumps a message into label on the form. The options are limitless.

As Kraig Brockschmidt says in his book, *Inside OLE 2* (Microsoft Press, ISBN 1-55615-618-9), OLE presages the day when an object-oriented operating system (OOOS if you're excited) packages the necessary API calls in their relevant objects and previously irreconcilable applications can talk. Apart from the fact that OLE and its rival OpenDoc can't talk to each other, the picture couldn't be rosier, or more demanding of computer hardware. So you'll still have something to grumble about!

Calling the API

It's time to meet the much fabled Windows Application Programming Interface (API) which ultimately provides any Windows program with its added power and functionality. For example, the API deals with creating windows, is responsible for playing sound and video, lets you access text in a edit box, allows you to click a button and much, much more.

I'll say right at the outset that the reason why it's taken you so long to meet the API is that you've not needed it before - much of that power is gift-wrapped into Delphi's components, so insulating you from the raw API calls.

In this chapter, I'll take the ideas and code we've looked at so far and occasionally make an inconspicuous call to a procedure you've not seen before. That small call to code outside of the Delphi environment allows your application to go that extra yard, to score that vital touchdown, to soundly beat that final opponent! Once you know what facilities the API provides and how to use them, you can increase the speed of your Delphi applications, power them up with new and exciting routines and add features that Delphi can, at the moment, just dream about.

In this chapter, we're going to stroll through APIville. It's a big place, so the tour is necessarily limited, but it should give you your bearings. Hopefully, once we're done, you'll be happy with:

- The functions, procedures and messages of the API
- How to interrogate the state of Windows through the API
- How to avoid any problems resulting from an API call

You may already have strayed into the Windows API help files in your extensive help file exploration, so you might have noticed that they tend to be a little less friendly and rather terse. It often seems like you're trawling through long lists to find any sort of function that sounds as if it might do the job. It seems like it's just a question of experience... helpful I know!

Functions, Procedures and Messages

Despite the reverence with which some programmers talk about the API, it's really nothing special, nor is it hard to get to grips with. Windows was originally designed as a somewhat modular system. Rather than trying to embed all the operating system's functionality into a chip on the PC's motherboard (a ROM OS, if you will), all the functions and procedures that make up Windows are held in a collection of files on your hard disk called .**dll**s. The three core .**dll**s in Windows95 are **kernel32.dll**, **user32.dll** and **GDI32.dll**.

This module format has been a great benefit in allowing the API to be extended as new features, such as multimedia, have become standard. Additional APIs include OLE, Multimedia, Mail, Win95 Common Controls and the DirectXs. And Microsoft promise that this will continue with their latest Internet API - ISAPI...

Delphi comes bundled with several APIs of its own - for instance, there's one belonging to the BDE. Wherever the designers of a Windows system need to allow access to the nuts and bolts of the system, they use an API to provide a (hopefully comprehensive) set of access functions.

On its most basic level, dealing with the API involves nothing more than calling the functions and procedures inside these .**dll**s, just as if they were native to your Delphi application.

Delphi provides almost seamless integration with the Windows API should you choose to use it. You should think yourselves lucky - C programmers have to go through a complex process of linking numerous design-time libraries to their applications to access certain API functions. Visual Basic programmers, meanwhile, have to declare each and every API call that they intend to use. All we need to do is make a change to the **uses** clause of any unit that contains API dependent code.

Calling Windows' built-in functions and procedures is really just one side of the coin. The flip side is the Windows messaging service. Sounds like a post office, you say... but let me explain.

The events handlers that we've grown to know and love are triggered when they receive messages sent by the events. Much as I like to build up Delphi, this isn't a feature that Delphi introduced to Windows development; it is actually the way Windows works.

So, what you have in Delphi is a system that wraps up almost all the messages that Windows sends your application in nice neat events. But it's the remaining messages we're worrying about here. Read on....

Using the API

Actually using the API is really no different to using a standard Delphi method or function. All you need is to include the **Windows** unit in the **uses** clause of your unit:

```
unit Unit1;

interface

uses
    Windows, Messages, SysUtils, Classes, Graphics, Controls, Forms, Dialogs;
```

The API routines, when you use them from within Delphi look just like any normal Delphi method or function. Though they're not included in the Delphi library, Delphi's compiler aliases

Windows' API files to the **Windows** unit. As with most of the files you access through the **uses** clause, you're using precompiled code, it's just in a **.dll** rather than a **.dcu** file.

But where are the routines, what are they called, what parameters do they take and what values do they return? As far as Delphi is concerned, the answers to all these questions are held in the **Windows** unit. The code that this unit contains enables Delphi to form a link between your code and the API constants, procedures and functions that you want to use.

FYI

It's a source of never-ending surprise that once you've implemented a **uses** clause, your application can make seamless use of the API, just as if it were using a normal Delphi method.

Let's dive into a small example straight away, just to reassure you how easy it is to call an API function.

Xeyes

The **xeyes.dpr** application on the disk draws two eyes on a form which follow the mouse cursor around the screen. It's a 'port' (read as 'blatant copy') of the X windows program which I always found quite amusing:

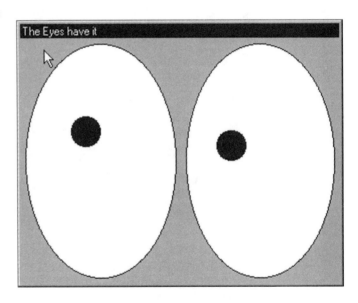

Most of the code in the two units associated with the project is concerned with calculating the position of the pupils so that they follow the cursor position, so I'll try and avoid that. Each eye is an instance of the TEye class defined in the **eyeballu.pas** unit. This class contains all the code and fields it needs to be able to draw itself when it receives the form's dimensions and the current mouse position as parameters.

Try It Out - Xeyes Pt1

1 Load up **xeyes.dpr** from the disk. It's a partially complete project which we'll add to show API calls. Firstly, because the key function of the application is, of course, to track mouse moves, it would seem sensible to see what the VCL provides to do this. If you bring up the Form's Events page in the Object Inspector, you can double-click on the OnMouseMove event to bring up the event handler:

```
procedure TForm1.FormMouseMove(Sender: TObject; Shift: TShiftState; X,
   Y: Integer);
begin

end;
```

2 **MousePosition** is a TPoint type record, declared in **eyesu.pas**, in which we're going to hold the mouse cursor's position.

So, within the event handler you've just created, add code to set up the values of the **MousePosition** record:

```
procedure TForm1.FormMouseMove(Sender: TObject; Shift: TShiftState; X,
   Y: Integer);
begin
     MousePosition.X := X;
     MousePosition.Y := Y;
end;
```

3 We now start to call TEye's procedures for each instance of our class, i.e. each eye. First, we erase the previous pupil with the following calls:

```
Eye1.ErasePupil(Form1);
Eye2.ErasePupil(Form1);
```

4 Then we pass the new value of **MousePosition** to the **TEye.MousePos** procedure. This procedure calculates the angle from the center of the eye to the mouse cursor.

```
Eye1.MousePos(Form1, MousePosition);
Eye2.MousePos(Form1, MousePosition);
```

5 Finally, we redraw the pupil in its new position:

```
Eye1.MovePupil(Form1);
Eye2.MovePupil(Form1);
```

If you now run the program, up comes the form and the eyes are drawn. If you move the cursor around on the form, the eyes will spookily follow the cursor around. Unfortunately, as soon as you move off the form, the pupils stop moving! The OnMouseMove event handler is restricted to the dealing with form events and the form only receives mouse messages from Windows when there's a mouse event over its active window.

How do we get at mouse events from the rest of the screen? The simplest way is to periodically ask Windows for the cursor's position. By going directly to Windows, I can avoid the limitations of the OnMouseMove event, instead covering the entire area in which Windows generates mouse messages, i.e. the whole screen. If I ask Windows often enough, updating the position of the eyes every time the cursor moves, I'll have some basic animation, just like we saw in Chapter 6.

FYI

There's a really snazzy, low-overhead way to 'capture' the mouse event messages from anywhere on the screen. The messages that Windows events generate pass to a message queue, where they're processed in the order that they arrived.

You have already seen this in action. Back in Chapter 4, I had to make regular calls to `Application.ProcessMessages` to 'service' any messages that were waiting around on the `Application`'s message queue.

You can think of the message queue as a stream and you can catch messages as they pass, using a Windows hook. What a picturesque name! So you can use the `SetWindowsHookEx` API call to set up a mouse-message catching hook. The only snag is that making a mistake can totally mess up Windows. One for the future, I think...

To get this information from Windows, all I need is a couple of API calls and the code to support them. Let's take a look at how it's done.

Try It Out - Xeyes Pt2

1 Load up **xeyes2.dpr** - this should be the same as the project you were left with at the end of the last Try It Out, except that the filenames are different.

2 Add a Timer component to the form and call it **timWhoMoved**. Set its Interval property to 40, representing roughly 40 milliseconds. Bring up its Events tab and double-click on the OnTimer event.

3 Now cut and paste the contents of the OnMouseMove event handler into the Timer's event handler:

```
procedure TForm1.timWhoMovedTimer(Sender: TObject);
begin
    MousePosition.X := X;
    MousePosition.Y := Y;
    {Erase old pupils, the positions of which are held in FPupilRect}
    Eye1.ErasePupil(Form1);
    Eye2.ErasePupil(Form1);
    {Process the new mouse position}
    Eye1.MousePos(Form1, MousePosition);
    Eye2.MousePos(Form1, MousePosition);
    {Draw new pupils}
    Eye1.MovePupil(Form1);
    Eye2.MovePupil(Form1);
end;
```

Then take out the two first lines which assign values to the **MousePosition** record and replace them with the following statement:

```
procedure TForm1.timWhoMovedTimer(Sender: TObject);
begin
    {API call to get mouse cursor position in screen coordinates}
    GetCursorPos(MousePosition);
    {Erase old pupils, the positions of which are held in FPupilRect}
    Eye1.ErasePupil(Form1);
```

383

4 That's it, that's the first API call. The only thing to note is that the TPoint record it returns is in screen coordinates, giving you the position of the cursor on the full screen. For the position code to work, we need to convert these to form coordinates. For this purpose, we make use of the **ScreenToClient** API function which returns the converted coordinates for the **TheForm** form to the **private** TEye field:

Call up the **eyeball2u.pas** unit

```
procedure TEye.MousePos(TheForm : TForm; const MousePoint : TPoint);
begin
    FMousePosition := MousePoint;
    {Call the protected procedure CalcAngle}
    CalcAngle(FMousePosition);
end;
```

and add the following replacement line to the **MousePos** procedure:

```
procedure TEye.MousePos(TheForm : TForm; const MousePoint : TPoint);
begin
    FMousePosition := TheForm.ScreenToClient(MousePoint);
    {Call the protected procedure CalcAngle}
    CalcAngle(FMousePosition);
end;
```

That was the second API call. Now you can run the program and the eyes will follow mouse movements around the screen. It's simple and effective and it totally transforms the application.

Getting Technical

But, and you knew this was coming, there are still a number of technical issues that you really do need to be aware of.

First of all, most of the code you will find in a **.dll** (before the advent of Delphi, at least) was written in C or C++. There are a number of reasons for this, the main one being that, for a while, the only way you could produce a **.dll** was by using a C compiler. With time, this has been adopted as something of a standard. C has some very strange ways of dealing with things, but most Windows development systems, such as Delphi and Visual Basic, now include the necessary methods to cope with these differences.

Take strings for example. In Pascal proper, a string is declared using the **string** keyword. The maximum string length is 256 bytes, with the first element (index 0) giving the actual length of the string and each byte (1 to 255) able to hold a character. So, a string is nothing more than a list, almost an array, of characters. To declare it we simply say:

```
var
    A_String : ShortString;
```

In C, strings really are arrays of characters. They're declared something like this,

```
char CString[20];
```

where the **CString** can hold up to 19 characters, the final space containing a **NULL** (\0) character to denote the end of the string. Such strings are referred to as **null-terminated strings**. When you're using an API, because they're all based around C, you must use null-terminated strings for the parameters that you pass.

Declaring a Null-terminated String

How do we declare a null-terminated string in Delphi? Quite easily; we have to do the same as the C programmers do and declare a zero-based array of characters:

```
Var
    A_Cstring : array[0..255] of Char;
```

If only things were that straight forward! Not only does C not support strings, but it also won't let you pass the whole array of characters as a parameter. Take a look at this Delphi code:

```
procedure Print_Message (sMessage : String);
begin
     ShowMessage(sMessage);
end;
```

Simple stuff in Delphi. We have a procedure that accepts an entire string as a parameter and then uses the **ShowMessage** method to put that string onto the screen. You can't do this in C, so you can't do this whenever you need to call an API function.

What you do instead is pass a pointer to the array. You what?

Pointers

Every variable you declare lives in your PC's memory somewhere. Because most PCs have quite a lot of memory, the computer uses something as an **address** to pinpoint specific things within it. Each character or byte in your computer's memory is given a unique number which, in basic terms, starts at 1 and goes up to as much memory as you have.

A **pointer** is nothing more than the memory address of something. So, when you deal with an API call that works with strings, you declare an array of characters, put your string into the array (don't panic - I'll show you how in a moment) and then pass a pointer to the array across to the API call. It's like telling people your address, instead of carrying the whole house around to show people where you live.

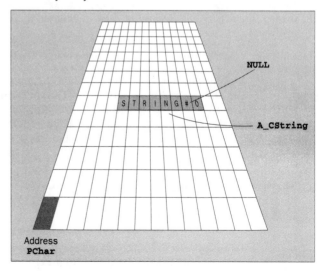

Pointers are also used in Delphi 2.0's default **string** type where the program holds the address of the string (which may be anything up to 4GB in length), rather than holding the string itself. Pointers are everywhere, but Delphi doesn't make a fuss about them - everything is handled behind the scenes for you.

When you deal with strings as arrays of characters, Delphi automatically puts a character **#0** at the end of the string so that the API code can figure out when the string has ended.

To pass a pointer, you simply pass the name of the array. In Delphi, the actual data type you are passing is called a **PChar** - a pointer to a character. Take a look at this:

```
procedure Main;
var
    A_Cstring : array[0..255] of Char;
begin
    A_Cstring := 'This is a string';
    Display_Cstring(A_Cstring);
end;

procedure Display_Cstring(A_Cstring : PChar);
begin
    ShowMessage(StrPas (A_Cstring));
end;
```

How It Works

The first routine, **Main**, declares an array of characters called **A_Cstring**. It then dumps a string of text into that array. Delphi automatically spots that we're dealing with a string literal (one enclosed in ' ') and that we want to put that string into a character array. It does the necessary conversion automatically and tacks a **NULL** character on the end of the array to mark the end of the string.

Main then calls the routine **Display_Cstring**, passing it nothing more than the name of the array. This action tells Delphi to pass a pointer to the array, a **PChar** value, rather than the array itself. **PChar**s, null-terminated strings and string literals are very closely related.

In the above code, we could declare **A_CString** as a **PChar** and the code would still work. However, this is relying on Delphi's ability to organize what's going on behind the scenes. This is something that Delphi can get it wrong, particularly when you're working with the API. However, if you stick to declaring an array of characters rather than a **PChar**, Delphi will understand and everything will be okay.

The **Display_Cstring** routine takes a **PChar** as a parameter and then uses the **StrPas** method to convert the array it has just been sent back into a normal Pascal string which can be used with the **ShowMessage** method.

Because we're now dealing with an array rather than a string literal, the code has to call a Delphi method to actually make the conversion. Delphi won't automatically convert the string in a character array to a Delphi string.

As well as including a method to convert from a null-terminated string to a normal Pascal string, Delphi also has the converse method, **StrPCopy**, which converts data in a normal Pascal string into a null-terminated string:

```
var
    A_Cstring : array[0..255] of Char;
    A_Pstring : shortstring;
begin
        A_Pstring := 'This is a string';
        StrPCopy(A_Cstring, A_Pstring);
end;
```

This code example sets up two variables, one to hold a normal Pascal string, **A_Pstring**, and the other to hold an array of characters, **A_Cstring**. The **StrPCopy** method is then used to convert from one to the other. Notice how this method takes two parameters. The first is a pointer to the destination string, our C string (or in other words, the name of the character array); the second is the Pascal string.

Variable Parameters

PChars have a very important side effect which is utilized by many of the API calls. As we saw in Chapter 3, there are three different ways of passing parameters. Passing a **variable** parameter (as opposed to a **value** or **constant** parameter) involves passing the address of the parameter's actual value, which may then be changed. You make a parameter variable by declaring it with the **var** keyword, thus:

```
procedure StringRead(var FirstString, SecondSTring);
```

When you pass a string without any prefix from one Delphi procedure to another, the second procedure sets up a temporary area of memory to hold a copy of the string. If you make changes to the string within the second procedure, these changes are only made to the copy and don't feed back to the original string. You've effectively passed the value of the string to make a **private** copy in the second procedure.

When you pass **PChar**s around, you're telling the code, "Hey, my string lives there - go get it, use it, change it, whatever - it's your responsibility". Many of the API calls you will come across utilize this feature, known as **passing by reference**. They take a **PChar** and fill it with a result. For example, in Chapter 13, I'm going to look at an API function called **mciSendString**. This returns any error code as an integer, but can also modify the strings you pass it to give you additional result information.

When you call an API routine, pay special attention to whether that routine can modify the parameters you pass it. If it can, never assume that the string at the end of the call is the same string that you passed into the call.

One final word of caution before we dive into some more examples. In Delphi, if you make a mistake in the parameters you send to a built-in method, or if the parameters you pass cause that method to fail, the chances are that Delphi's run-time library (RTL) will catch this and either display an error message or tell an exception handler in your application that there was a problem.

If you pass an illegal value to an API call, however, it can crash the machine. If you intend to use a lot of API calls in your applications, make sure that you thoroughly test your code and that you are happy with everything going in and coming out of the API before you ship the product. Also, since different versions of Windows normally include subtle changes in the API, it's a good idea to test your application on all targeted versions of Windows. Remember that Delphi 2.0 can work in both Windows 95 and Windows NT. That's why the API help has a Quick Info box so you can check whether the call is applicable to both OSes.

In the epilogue, *Where Do I Go Now?*, I mention something called the Microsoft Developer Network. If you join, Microsoft will actually supply you with any operating system patches, or, on some occasions, even the whole kit and caboodle.

My Pet API Calls

Enough theory - it's time to get down to business. Whether you want extra functionality or a leaner, meaner application (you know best), what you want are further examples of the API in action. Control, power and flexibility is the motto of this chapter.

So what can you do with the API? You can fire up other applications and watch to see when they complete. You can do simple things like flash the title bar of your window. You can do more serious things like tell Windows to shut down, or find out exactly what kind of machine your app is running on. The official Microsoft guides to the API consume six rather weighty tomes.

Those at Wrox enjoy seeing an author get personal in their books, so here are my Top Four API calls (cue chart music):

Call	Description
`GetDriveType`	Ever wanted to know if your app is running on a floppy disk, hard disk, CD-ROM, network drive or RAM disk? If so, this is the call for you.
`GetVersionEX`	Great for telling you which operating system your code is running on. You don't really want to try and fire off Explorer or run an DOS game on Windows NT do you?!
`GlobalMemoryStatus`	Just how much memory does this PC have? Will my app run? Help is one call away.
`GetSystemInfo`	Want to engage in a spot of processor recognition? For some reason, users love it when an app insults or compliments them on the power of their system. And who are we to disappoint?

Time to see what each of these calls can do.

Looking at Drives

A common question on the Internet newsgroups is, "How do I find out what kind of drive my application is running on?" The equally common response is, "Why would you want to know?"

An example of why you would want to use this call could be when you're getting into CD-ROM burning - something we need to do to as we near the release of an application to get beta copies reviewed, or when we archive source code. If the load speed of the burning process is too low, the new CD will be corrupt - and you can't patch a failed burn. This is especially likely if you're copying from CD to CD, so code which could automatically determine if this were the case and then perform some load speed check could be helpful. The **GetDriveType** call would form part of the first of these check stages.

Another example: if your app is running off a floppy disk, you could make it install itself using a setup program, but if it resides on a network drive, you can ask the user if they would prefer to store data on their local hard disk or directly on the server. Convinced?

Try It Out - Drive

1 With Delphi running, call up the online help and type in GetDriveType to see the API page. Why does it always look worse than it actually is?

From here you can deduce that the **GetDriveType** function can tell you the type of the drive associated with a letter. To do this, **GetDriveType** takes a single **PChar** parameter, a null-terminated string holding the path to the root directory of the disk you are interested in.

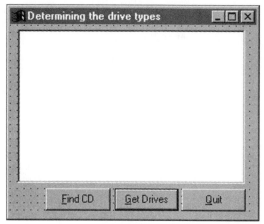

2 Load up **drives.dpr** from the disk, which should look like this:

3 The Find CD button runs a small amount of code to scan the system for a CD drive and then shows a message box telling you if it found one or not and if it did, what the drive letter is.

Bring up the **cmdFindClick** event handler and add the following code:

```
procedure TfrmDrives.cmdFindClick(Sender: TObject);
var
    bFound : bool;
    nDrive : integer;
    sCRoot : array[0..3] of char;
begin
    nDrive := 64;
    bFound := False;
    sCRoot := ' :\';
end;
```

The **bFound** variable is initially set to **False** and is only set to **True** when a CD drive is found. The **nDrive** variable is used to loop through the letters **A** to **Z**. Finally, the **sCRoot** array is set up to hold the path of the current search drive's root.

As we saw in Chapter 3, every character in the ASCII set has a unique number attached to it so that the computer can deal with it internally. It's reassuring that it's easier for your PC to think in terms of numbers than shapes - so inhuman. The letter *A* for example is equal to 65, while the letter *Z* is number 90.

4 Having initialized the variables, we need to add a **while** loop that goes through each of the letters of the alphabet and checks it against the letter stored against the CD-ROM, if you have one on your system:

```
while (nDrive < 91) and not(bFound) do
begin
    nDrive := nDrive + 1;
    sCRoot[0] := Chr(nDrive);

    if GetDriveType( sCRoot ) = DRIVE_CDROM then
        bFound := True;
end;
```

5 Finally, we report our findings, something like this:

```
if bFound then
    MessageDlg( 'CDROM found at ' + Chr(nDrive), mtInformation, [mbOK], 0)
else
    MessageDlg( 'You don''t have a CDROM - go get one', mtInformation,
                [mbOK], 0);
end;
```

How It Works

What this code does is to loop from 65 to 90 and, on each pass through the loop, send the appropriate character with ':\' tacked on the end to the **GetDriveType** routine. If at any time the call returns the code **DRIVE_CDROM,** we know that a CD-ROM drive has been found and **bFound** can be set **True**.

The **sCRoot** array only needs to be four characters long in order to hold the drive letter, followed by :\ and terminated with character **#0**. The name of the array is passed to the **GetDriveType** in the **while** loop, where it effectively gets passed as a **PChar**.

The loop ends as soon as it reaches Z, or as soon as **bFound** is set to **True**. Inside the loop, we check the return code from the **GetDriveType** API call to see whether or not we have found a CD drive.

GetDriveType always kicks out an integer which we can check against a number of Windows constants defined in the **Windows** unit. These include **DRIVE_REMOVEABLE**, **DRIVE_FIXED**, **DRIVE_REMOTE**, **DRIVE_RAMDISK**, **0** (unknown) and **1**(doesn't exist - who has a Q drive?). Let's add to our program so that it makes more use of the return integer value.

Try It Out - Making the Most of the Call

1 With your last example loaded, we'll now make use of the Get Drives button which sets code in motion to interrogate every possible drive letter in your system and output the result to the memo. It's on the disk as **drives2.dpr** if you're not fussed at typing.

Bring up the event handler and add the following variables:

```
procedure TfrmDrives.cmdGetClick(Sender: TObject);
var
    nDriveCounter : integer;
    sRootPath     : string;
    nDriveType    : integer;
    sCRoot        : array[0..255] of Char;
begin

end;
```

2 In the code block, clear the memo and set up a **for** loop to skip through the letters of the alphabet. Build the string of the root path within the loop and then, since this is a Pascal string, use the **StrPCopy** method to convert it to a null-terminated string:

```
lstDrives.Items.Clear;
for nDriveCounter := 65 to 90 do
begin
    { Now we can start to build up the root path }
    sRootPath := chr(nDriveCounter) + ':\';

    { Convert the string to a C type string }
    StrPCopy(sCRoot, sRootPath);
end;
```

3 Now add the API call to the **for** loop, passing the newly created C-string as a parameter. The return value now forms the input to an exhaustive case statement, the result of which is outputted to the memo **lstDrives**:

```
nDriveType := GetDriveType( sCRoot );

{ Now we can check the return code and update the list box }
case nDriveType of
    0             : lstDrives.Items.Add( sRootPath + ' = UNKNOWN ');
    1             : lstDrives.Items.Add( sRootPath + ' = Does not exist');
```

391

```
     DRIVE_REMOVABLE : lstDrives.Items.Add( sRootPath + ' = removeable drive');
     DRIVE_FIXED     : lstDrives.Items.Add( sRootPath + ' = fixed hard disk');
     DRIVE_REMOTE    : lstDrives.Items.Add( sRootPath + ' = Network drive' );
     DRIVE_CDROM     : lstDrives.Items.Add( sRootPath + ' = CDROM Drive');
     DRIVE_RAMDISK   : lstDrives.Items.Add( sRootPath + ' = RAM Disk (very flash)');
  end;
```

You should now be able to peruse every drive on your system.

Dealing with Version Numbers

Quite often, particularly if you're dealing with API calls, it can be handy to know on which version of Windows your program is running. This is because there are subtle differences between API calls and such things as the common dialogs in Windows 95 and Windows NT.

Normally, you would use conditional compilation to shield the user from the perils of running an application on a system it wasn't designed for by compiling a number of different versions of your project, each targeted to a single system. However, you may have a problem with 32-bit operating systems, so being able to gracefully shut your Windows 95 program down when Windows NT is detected may well be a feature you want to include in your app.

The **GetVersionEx** API call is really quite powerful. Let's show you an example of how you can use it:

Try It Out - Different Versions of the Story

1 Start a new application, saving it as **versionu.pas** and **versions.dpr**. Set it up so that it looks something like this, which you can find already on the disk if you want to:

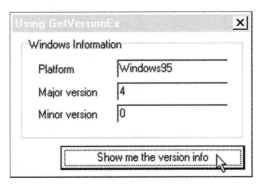

2 Bring up the **cmdGetVersionClick** event handler and add in the variable declaration and the first line that initializes the record's size:

```
procedure TfrmVersion.cmdGetVersionClick(Sender: TObject);
var
    VersionInfo : TOSVersionInfo;
begin
    VersionInfo.dwOSVersionInfoSize := SizeOf( TOSVersionInfo );
end;
```

3 Now comes the API call. The variable **VersionInfo** will receive the information returned by the API by reference:

```
GetVersionEx(VersionInfo);
```

4 The value of the **dwPlatformID** double word (one of the fields of the record) after this call determines the text that's displayed in first edit box. How do we know those obscure constant names? They're in the API's help file:

```
case VersionInfo.dwPlatformID of
     VER_PLATFORM_WIN32S:
                    txtPlatform.Text := 'Win32s on Windows 3.1';
     VER_PLATFORM_WIN32_WINDOWS:
                    txtPlatform.Text := 'Windows 95';
     VER_PLATFORM_WIN32_NT:
                    txtPlatform.Text := 'Windows NT';
end;
```

5 Lastly, the other fields of the record are displayed:

```
txtMajor.Text := IntToStr( VersionInfo.dwMajorVersion );
txtMinor.Text := IntToStr( VersionInfo.dwMinorVersion );
```

Run the program and click the Show me the version info button to see what platform you're operating under. Hopefully, there are no surprises.

The Major and Minor version numbers indicate how recent your operating system is. The major version number is obviously the true version of Windows - Windows 95 is effectively Windows 4. The minor version number indicates the release and, if you had access to the Microsoft Tech Support database, you'll be able to use it to find out which bugs have been fixed and which haven't.

How It Works

GetVersionEx takes just a single parameter of type TOSVersionInfo. This is defined in the **Windows** unit as a record. You pass it to **GetVersionEx** and it returns the record filled with various bits of information, some useful and some not. As for the **OSVersionInfo** data structure, it's listed in the online help:

```
typedef struct _OSVERSIONINFO{

    DWORD dwOSVersionInfoSize;
    DWORD dwMajorVersion;
    DWORD dwMinorVersion;
    DWORD dwBuildNumber;
    DWORD dwPlatformId;
    TCHAR szCSDVersion[ 128 ];
} OSVERSIONINFO;
```

You must be careful with many of the API calls that take a record - they normally expect you to set up a field in the record to hold the total size that the record takes up in memory. It's time to explain that first line where we set the size of the first field of the data structure to the size of the **TOSVersionInfo** record type.

If you think about this for a while, you might come to the conclusion that it's a little odd. Surely a structure knows its own size? But this initialization has another, deeper and darker purpose which I will now unfold. You see, a future API, a 64-bit, distributed-processing Windows, might need a larger **OSVersionInfo** structure to adequately categorize the OS. And this might happen with a lot of API calls - same name, but you pass different sized data. What would happen if you used a Windows 95 program in this new Windows? It would be helpful if it could still run. The way to allow this is to pass the **OSVersionInfo** size in which we're interested.

 You should always use the **SizeOf** method to set up the record's size so that future versions of Delphi, which will of course be up to date with the latest API, can recompile the code with ease.

The application just converts the major and minor versions to strings and dumps the results into the two relevant edit boxes on the form. **DwPlatformID** is just that - an ID. It's a number which we need to decode to figure out which platform the application is running on. Thankfully, there are three Windows constants that we can use to easily determine the platform from this ID:

- **VER_PLATFORM_WIN32S** for Windows 3 users running Win32s
- **VER_PLATFORM_WIN32_WINDOWS** for Windows 95
- **VER_PLATFORM_WIN32_NT** for Windows NT

There are only two other fields in the TOSVersionInfo structure that we could deal with and, really, they're not worth worrying about. **dwBuildNumber** returns a number which is nothing more than a combination of the information from **dwMajorVersion** and **dwMinorVersion**. The last field is a C-type string which returns 'arbitrary additional information about the platform', whatever that means.

Handling Memory

You have to admit that memory is a big issue in Windows applications - you never seem to have enough. Too little, and the apps may not run, or worse still, they'll run like one-legged dogs. And have you ever noticed that people get more upset at a really slow application on their system than they do at one that simply says "I can't possibly run on that pile of junk" and quits?

You can see, then, that it's pretty useful to know how to interrogate the memory in your system. At start-up, you could check it to see if the PC meets the minimum requirements of your application. During the development process, it's quite easy to write an application that watches memory while your development project runs and then returns to you average figures on memory consumption. How about something simple like a system info box? Let's try this as a quick project:

Try It Out - Memory Test

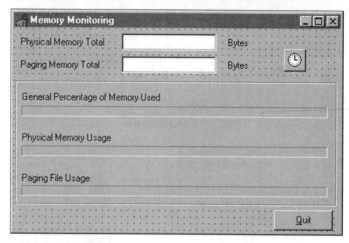

1 Load up the **memory.dpr** project from the disk. It contains the form as shown here:

Here we have quite a neat foundation for a system information box. It contains progress bars showing you the current usage of system memory in general, more specific information about the computer's physical RAM and how much of the user's memory area is currently in use (the memory area set aside to run our applications).

2 The progress bars on the form update a number of times a second, based on the code to handle the OnTimer event of the timer control. Bring up the Timer's event handler and, as before, set up the record that will get the information from the API call:

```
procedure TForm1.timUpdateTimer(Sender: TObject);
var
    MemoryStatus : TMemoryStatus;
begin
    Form1.Show;
    MemoryStatus.dwLength := SizeOf(MemoryStatus);
end;
```

3 The API, number two in our chart, is an easy call:

```
GlobalMemoryStatus( MemoryStatus );
```

4 Now we have to use the various fields of the record to set the values for the edit boxes and progress bars:

```
txtPhysMem.Text := IntToStr(MemoryStatus.dwTotalPhys);
txtVirtMem.Text := IntToStr(MemoryStatus.dwTotalPageFile);

prgTotalMem.Position := MemoryStatus.dwMemoryLoad;

prgPhysMem.Position  := 100 - trunc((MemoryStatus.dwAvailPhys /
                                MemoryStatus.dwTotalPhys) * 100);
```

```
    prgPageMem.Position  := 100 - trunc((MemoryStatus.dwAvailPageFile /
                                        MemoryStatus.dwTotalPageFile ) * 100);
  end;
```

How It Works

Like many of the information 'inquiry' API calls, **GlobalMemoryStatus** takes a record as its parameter (or more precisely a pointer to a record) and fills that record with information. In this case, the record is of type *TMemoryStatus* and includes the following fields:

```
typedef struct _MEMORYSTATUS { // mst

    DWORD dwLength;        // sizeof(MEMORYSTATUS)
    DWORD dwMemoryLoad;    // percent of memory in use
    DWORD dwTotalPhys;     // bytes of physical memory
    DWORD dwAvailPhys;     // free physical memory bytes
    DWORD dwTotalPageFile; // bytes of paging file
    DWORD dwAvailPageFile; // free bytes of paging file
    DWORD dwTotalVirtual;  // user bytes of address space
    DWORD dwAvailVirtual;  // free user bytes
} MEMORYSTATUS, *LPMEMORYSTATUS;
```

FYI   TMemoryStatus isn't documented in the help files, but it's a fair bet that it exists because there's an API data structure called MEMORYSTATUS. If you have the source code to Delphi, you can also do a search in the Windows.pas unit file (found in the \Delphi 2.0\Source\RTL\Win directory) to allay your fears.

The last two fields in the record allow you to calculate the percentage of the total address space available to the chip - which is 2GB! It's not included in the example, since it doesn't seem so useful to know what proportion of 2GB you're using if you haven't got that much memory installed in your machine.

What the code in the timer event does is to turn the available memory figures into percentages of the totals and dump the results into the **Position** property of the appropriate progress bar and the text of the edit boxes on the form. High school math. To see the demands that Delphi makes on your system, run the executable while Delphi is up and shut Delphi down - all of a sudden you have physical memory again!

Learning about the System

One of the tricks many game and multimedia developers (including Psynet, my company) have up their sleeve, is to check the processor in the system to see just how much the code is likely to be able to get away with. The **GetSystemInfo** call fills a record of type *TSystemInfo* with information about the processors in the system, who made them, and so on.

If you were working on a game, for example, you might want to fire off a neat background animation thread on a multiprocessor Pentium or lose some of the colors for a 386 machine.

FYI   What's a thread? Well, just as wonderful Windows 95 and Windows NT allow you to have several tasks (programs) running simultaneously, without chewing up the CPU, so they allow you to split your program into processes, or subtasks, which can work independently of each other and at the same time. Each thread controls one of these tasks.

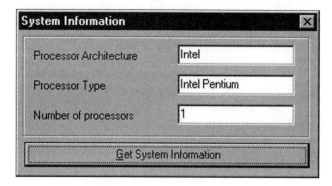

Take a look at the **sysinfo.dpr** application:

As soon as you click on the <u>G</u>et System Information button, the code behind the button goes away and calls the **GetSystemInfo** API routine. A TSystemInfo record is passed to the API routine and is returned, filled with information about the system which can then be dissected and displayed in the edit boxes on the form:

```
procedure TForm1.cmdGetClick(Sender: TObject);
var
    SysInfo : TSystemInfo;
begin
    { Grab the system details }
    GetSystemInfo (SysInfo);

    case SysInfo.wProcessorArchitecture of
        0 : txtArch.Text := 'Intel';
        1 : txtArch.Text := 'MIPS';
        2 : txtArch.Text := 'Alpha';
        3 : txtArch.Text := 'Power PC';
    end;

    case SysInfo.dwProcessorType of
        386          : txtType.Text := 'Intel 386';
        486          : txtType.Text := 'Intel 486';
        586          : txtType.Text := 'Intel Pentium';
        4000         : txtType.Text := 'MIPS R4000';
        21064        : txtType.Text := 'Alpha 21064';
    end;

    txtNum.Text := IntToStr(SysInfo.dwNumberOfProcessors);
end;
```

There are quite a lot of fields in a TSystemInfo record, but many of them cover esoteric stuff that isn't really of much use to anyone except a hardware engineer. For example, do you really care about stuff like Allocation Granularity!?

Of all the fields in the record, though, the most useful are as follows:

- **dwProcessorType** is set up with a number when the routine returns. As you can see from the code, 386 means we have a 386 in this machine, 486 and 586 mean that the processor is a 486 or Pentium. 4000 and 21064 should really only come back for machines running Windows NT, since these values tell you that you are using a MIPS R4000 or Alpha 21064 processor.

- **dwNumberOfProcessors** is simply a number telling you how many processors there are in the system. This isn't as weird as it sounds, since there are more and more PCs hitting the market these days with more than one CPU installed, the result being a phenomenal amount of available power.

- **dwProcessorArchitecture** returns a number between **0** and **3** which tells you the family of processors in your machine. **0** indicates that this is an Intel based machine, **1** means a MIPS machine, **2** for an Alpha and **3** for a PowerPC-based machine.

Summary

The point I have tried to make in this chapter is that, while using the API may scare VB and C programmers, you've got a friend in Delphi. If you want more information on just what's available inside the API then you could do a lot worse than look at *The Visual Basic Programmers Guide To The Windows API*, ISBN 1-56276-073-4 from Ziff-Davis. Although aimed at the VB developers, most of the reference material in the book is applicable to Delphi programmers.

You may also be interested to know about the *Revolutionary Guide to Delphi 2.0 and The Win32 API*, ISBN 1-86100-053-7 from Wrox Press. This book is aimed at the Delphi programmer who wants to get into the Windows API in a serious way, whether they're working on Windows 95 or Windows NT. Keep an eye on the press for details of its release date.

In the next chapter, I'm going to build upon the API knowledge that you've picked up here by taking you for a guided tour around one specific Windows API, called MCI, that allows you to control an incredible number of multimedia effects on your desktop. I'm also going to introduce you to Delphi's multimedia component, MediaPlayer, the tool that Delphi provides for you to get quick and easy access to the wonderful world of multimedia.

Multimedia

Let's face up to some facts here. Employee maintenance systems, contract administration systems, accounts systems and so on can be pretty boring in terms of both development and presentation. When was the last time a friend or spouse looked over your shoulder at the latest version of your accounts system and said "Wow - that looks really cool!"?

Adding multimedia elements to your applications can bring them to life in a way that many would never dream possible. Why throw up message boxes when your users do something wrong when you can just as easily get Windows to scream at them? Using the multimedia facilities in both the Windows API and through Delphi's multimedia component, you can add some very powerful stuff to your application. Throwing video clips around the screen really is easy and requires little or no more effort than playing a sampled sound or a music file.

In this chapter, we are going to blow open the world of multimedia. You'll learn how to:

- Play sampled sounds
- Play music files
- Play video files
- Link sound and video into your applications

You're not going to be a multimedia master by the end of the chapter (that requires a little more time and space than these few pages), but you will know everything you need to start your journey into this most fascinating area of Delphi programming. Hopefully, you should also have some fun along the way.

Using the Multimedia Component

The easiest way to build multimedia into your Delphi applications is to use the MediaPlayer component - check out the System page of the Component Palette. This one small component provides you with all the power you need to play any standard multimedia file (such as a sound sample, music file or video clip) and also record data from whatever multimedia input devices you may have.

Before we go any further, it's worth clearing up a few basic ideas that lie behind the weird multimedia files you're going to encounter in this chapter. If you read computer magazines, or spend much time on the Internet, you'll probably have come across files with a wide variety of file extensions that you don't normally see on a day to day basis. What do they mean and how do you use them?

Checking Out those File Extensions

On your normal travels through the world of multimedia, you'll find that you have to deal with a large number of files, including **beep.wav**s, **tocatta.mid**s and **movie.avi**s galore.

A **.wav** file is used as a container for a sampled sound, usually taken from a microphone or some other prerecorded format. A **.mid** file is used to contain MIDI format music tracks, generated by your sound card or an external synthesizer, while an **.avi** file is used to contain video clips taken from CD (for source images) and an animation package (for the missing scenes) or directly from a camera.

Providing you have the necessary hardware attached, the TMediaPlayer component can deal with all these types of data. You should note, however, that this component is really quite flexible. As long as Windows can identify and therefore communicate with the hardware, Delphi and the TMediaPlayer component can use it. For example, I have a video capture card in my PC which I can use to both capture and playback video using the TMediaPlayer component.

As well as being able to record and playback multimedia data from your hard disk, the TMediaPlayer component is also pretty adept at dealing with raw multimedia data taken directly from a source device. For example, you can use the TMediaPlayer to play video tracks directly off a laserdisk (providing you have a laserdisk attached, of course), or music tracks from a standard music CD.

Introducing the MediaPlayer: Dealing with CDs

One of the easiest multimedia applications to create is a CD player. It's so easy, I've already created it! Load up **cdplayer.dpr** and run it:

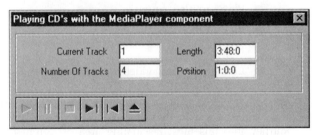

If you have a play with a CD in your CD drive, you'll find that you can do all the normal CD player type stuff: jump around the disk to the start of a given track, see the information in it, play it, jump to the start or end of the CD, eject it, and so on.

By normal standards, it's a pretty basic CD player, but when you see how easy it is to create, you'll understand that it has got quite a lot going for it. In fact, the program is based around one single component (surprise, it's a TMediaPlayer) with a supporting cast of thousands just to handle user interaction - I've always found that my applications are better received if you include this extra stuff!

Let's take a look at how easy it is to put this application together and, while we're at it, let's have a look at some of the features that make the TMediaPlayer into such a great component.

Try It Out - Building Yourself a CD Player

1 Create a new application and save it as **playu.pas** and **cdplayer.dpr**.

2 Draw up a new form and add a GroupBox containing four Labels and Edit boxes, a Timer and a MediaPlayer, aligning them to look like this:

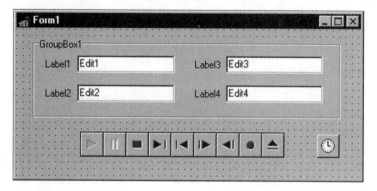

3 The next step is to rename the various elements of our application, following these changes to the letter: GroupBox1(grpDisplay), Edit1(txtCurrent), Edit2(txtNoTracks), Edit3(txtLength), Edit4(txtPosition), MediaPlayer1(mpPlayer), Timer1(timUpdate) and Form1(frmCDPlayer).

4 While you're here, let's change the captions of a few components: grpDisplay (delete it all together), Label1(Current Track), Label2(Number of Tracks), Label3(Length), Label4(Position) and frmCDPlayer(Playing CDs with the MediaPlayer Component).

After all that, you might want to re-align your components to improve the layout. You could resize the edit boxes to a width of 60 (remember that if you select all the components, then right-click and select the Size menu option, you can change the Width of all the components at the same time), so that the user interface now looks like this:

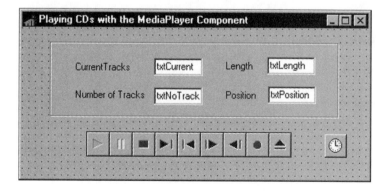

5 The interface design is almost complete, except for the issue of the MediaPlayer's buttons. We won't need all of them, so being able to hide some of them would be nice. Would you be surprised if I told you that this component has a property for this very task? Check out the Object Inspector for a property called VisibleButtons. Double-click on it to take a look at its subproperties:

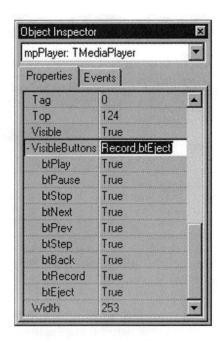

We only need the following buttons: Play, Pause, Stop, Next, Previous and Eject. Double-click on the unwanted button properties and they should disappear from the MediaPlayer on the form as the property value changes to False.

6 Code time! The first thing to consider is the display of track information in the user interface. We'll need to initialize the display as it should automatically update while the track is running. We'll also stick it to run on a timer event. We'll put this code into a support procedure, so put the following line into the form's OnCreate and the timer's OnTimer event handlers:

```
procedure TfrmCDPlayer.FormCreate(Sender: TObject);
begin
    UpdateTracks;
end;

procedure TfrmCDPlayer.FormCreate(Sender: TObject);
begin
    UpdateTracks;
end;
```

7 Now we need to set up this support procedure, so add this new procedure to your unit, just under the compiler directive in the **implementation** section:

```
implementation

{$R *.DFM}

procedure UpdateTracks;
var
```

```
        nCurrentTrack : integer;
begin
    with mpPlayer do
    begin
            TimeFormat := tfTMSF;

            nCurrentTrack := Position and 255;

            txtCurrent.text  := IntToStr(nCurrentTrack);
            txtNoTracks.text := IntToStr(Tracks);
            txtLength.text   := BreakDown(TrackLength[nCurrentTrack]);
            txtPosition.text := BreakDown( Position );

    end;
end;
```

You might notice that I've used a custom procedure call (**BreakDown**) in here. We need to break down the track information that we get back from the MediaPlayer before we can display it, so I've implemented another specialized function to deal with this. Add this function to the unit, just above the **UpdateTracks** procedure after the compiler directive:

```
implementation

{$R *.DFM}
```

```
function BreakDown( nValue : longint ) : string;
var
   nTrack            : integer;
   nMinutes          : integer;
   nSeconds          : integer;
begin
    nTrack := nValue and 255;
    nMinutes := (nValue div 256) and 255;
    nSeconds := (nvalue div 65536) and 255;

    Result := IntToStr(nTrack) + ':'
              + IntToStr(nMinutes) + ':'
              + IntToStr(nSeconds);
end;
```

```
procedure UpdateTracks;
var
```

8 As always, the final bit of code to add is just housekeeping - add this line to the form's OnClose event handler to safely handle the MediaPlayer when the form is closed down:

```
procedure TfrmCDPlayer.FormClose(Sender: TObject; var Action: TCloseAction);
begin
    mpPlayer.Stop;
end;
```

9 The last couple of things to do before you try and run the application is to further refine the workings of the MediaPlayer. Change the component's AutoOpen property to True and its DeviceType property to dtCDAudio.

10 Okay, run the application and see if it works. By the way, if you've got any other CD player running, you might get one of these really informative dialogs:

How It Works

So there you go. You've just created an application that can control the CD drive, at least to the extent of playing an audio CD through your sound card. That wasn't too difficult, was it? However, the idea wasn't to create a professional CD player application, it was to introduce you to the MediaPlayer. Let's take a closer look at this application to see how the MediaPlayer's functionality helped us out.

When the application is run, the first thing we do is set up the user's display with information taken from the CD about the tracks held on it. This information is automatically loaded into the MediaPlayer if the component's AutoOpen property is set to True.

Next comes decoding of that information. By assigning a constant to the **TimeFormat** property, you can then make you requests to the MediaPlayer for it to perform specific tasks, such as moving to the next track, or jumping to a position five minutes through track eight. In this example, we have set the property to **tfTMSF**, which, according to the appropriate help file (TMediaPlayer and then TimeFormat property), means that we'll be able to communicate with the component in terms of track number, minutes, seconds and frames (usually 24 per second) to get to any point of the CD.

From here, it's a small step to work out the value of the current track if you know that **Position** gives the current place the drive is reading from on the CD. As the information about the content of the CD is passed to us in a 4-byte variable, by performing a logical **AND** on the **Position** we can extract the current track number directly out of the **Position** property:

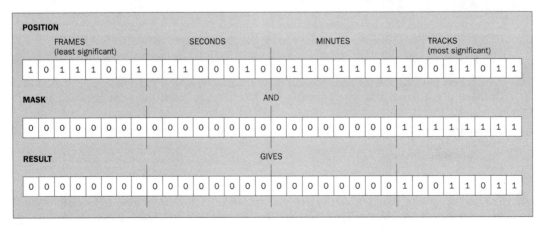

txtNoTracks is given a value by directly querying the MediaPlayer for the number of tracks held on the CD. This information is held in the **Tracks** property as an integer, so with a quick **IntToStr** conversion, the information is displayed.

Unfortunately, as I mentioned before, the other two edit boxes cause slightly more of a problem and require a further specialized function to provide them with the information we need. We can draw the current length of the track directly from another MediaPlayer property, **TrackLength**, and the current track elapsed time from **Position**, but both return a 4-byte result following the **TimeFormat** convention.

To translate both of these results, I've included a function that takes in an integer of this format and returns the appropriate results in a more understandable structure, in this case **track:minute:second**. The function achieves this conversion by simply applying a different mask to the passed parameter, before building the new format ready to be passed back to the calling procedure:

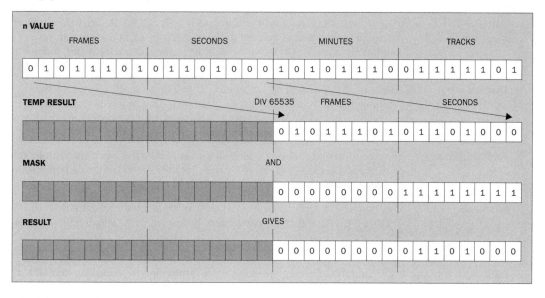

After all this reformatting, the display is complete, so we can let the user into the equation. We don't need to put any more code into the form's OnCreate event handler - the rest of the application's functionality can be safely locked away in other event handlers.

All of the work with the CD, such as which track should be playing, how far we are through the CD, what to do if the user clicks on the Play button, and so on, is all controlled by the MediaPlayer component itself. In other words, we don't have to worry about what happens once the MediaPlayer is up and running - all we need to do is to get the component to this position.

In our example, the component setup was really quite easy - just by setting a few properties using the Object Inspector, everything was ready for the code. The first property to consider is called DeviceType - it prepares the component for the type of information you want it to deal with. In our example, dtCDAudio indicates that it should be prepared to deal with an audio CD. There are a number of opinions for this property, all of which appear in the property's drop-down list. Most of the options are self-explanatory, but if you are looking for more information, check out Delphi's help files under DeviceType.

407

The only other property that we need to set is VisibleButtons. This limits the user's options by hiding some of the buttons that the MediaPlayer displays by default. Simply by double-clicking on the property you can display the entire list of buttons that the component supports, and, in turn, by double-clicking on those properties, you can remove a button from the display - nothing to it really!

Other MediaPlayer Properties

The component does have a couple of other interesting properties that we didn't need in our applications, so while I'm here...

Property	Description
AutoEnable	If set to True, the component will automatically disable or enable buttons, depending on the status of the device to which it is attached.
AutoRewind	If set to True, the device will automatically 'rewind' the device before it starts playing. For example, if you are halfway through a CD track when the component loads, it will move to the start of the CD track list and, indeed, the start of the first track, before it allows the media to run.
Display	This is used when dealing with video. If you don't set this property, the component will dynamically create a new window in which to play the video. The alternative is to specify the name of a form or panel in which you would rather have the video playing.
EnabledButtons	This is another set, but one which should only be used when the AutoEnable property is disabled. You can fire values into the set to tell it to automatically enable or disable certain buttons on the fly at run time.
Shareable	This property determines if more than one application can share the multimedia device that the component is dealing with. The default value of this property is False.

Note that if you put a CD into your drive, Windows 95 will attempt to AutoPlay the CD if your CD drive supports this feature. This may cause you problems with our example. Unfortunately, the Windows 95 CD Player isn't that friendly - it won't allow anyone else near your CD, so setting this property in your application won't help - it takes two to tango!

To see the Shareable property in action, change the property to True, recompile the project and start two instances of the application by double-clicking on the executable in Explorer. You'll see some problems with this property, but at least you can run multiple instances of the application - what you're looking at is a coding problem, so get your thinking cap on!

Dealing with Multimedia Files

Okay, you now have a pretty good idea of the sort of facilities that the **MediaPlayer** component can offer you, its run-time and design-time properties and how to use them. It's time to move on and look at some more of the methods attached to it and to find out how to use the component to deal with multimedia files.

Take a look at **fileplay.dpr**:

This project works a little differently from the CD player we saw earlier, simply because it deals with a different kind of data. The CD player dealt with **raw** multimedia data. As long as there is a music CD in the drive, the MediaPlayer component is able to get at the sound data on that CD and play it.

Fileplay, on the other hand, deals with disk files on your hard disk. Because of this, the project takes a bit more setting up, including the use of the **Filename** property and run-time methods, such as **Stop** and **Open**. Once you understand what each of these settings does, you'll find this application just as easy to put together as our CD Player.

Describing the File Player

When the program first loads, the MediaPlayer is disabled. This is because you don't really want users playing with the buttons until they have actually loaded in some data. Disabling a component provides good visual feedback to your users, indicating that they still have to do something before they can use the program properly:

In **FilePlayer**'s case, this involves clicking on the Browse button to select the multimedia file that you want to deal with:

```
procedure TfrmFilePlayer.cmdBrowseClick(Sender: TObject);
begin
    if txtFilename.text <> '' then
        mmPlayer.Stop ;
    timProgress.Enabled := false;

    if dlgOpen.Execute then
    begin
        txtFilename.text := dlgOpen.Filename;
        mmPlayer.Enabled := True;
```

First of all, we need to stop the TMediaPlayer component running and temporarily disable the application's timer. Then, as usual, I've used the OpenDialog component as the quickest way to give the user the ability to select an appropriate file.

409

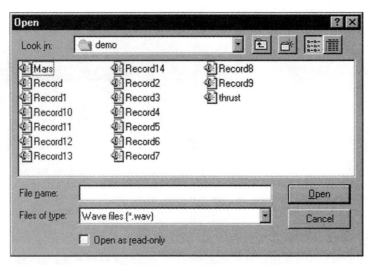

If the user successfully manages to select a file, the event handler sets up the TMediaPlayer component, loads in the appropriate file and opens it ready for execution. It then uses the information that the TMediaPlayer component has garnered from the media to update the workings of the TrackBar, before starting up the Timer that controls the movement of the TrackBar in relation to how far you are through the track:

```
procedure TfrmFilePlayer.cmdBrowseClick(Sender: TObject);
begin
      if txtFilename.text <> '' then
         mmPlayer.Stop ;
      timProgress.Enabled := false;

      if dlgOpen.Execute then
      begin
            txtFilename.text := dlgOpen.Filename;
            mmPlayer.Enabled := True;
            trkProgress.Enabled := True;

            mmPlayer.Filename := txtFilename.Text;
            mmPlayer.Open;

            mmPlayer.TimeFormat := tfMilliseconds;
            trkProgress.Min := 0;
            trkProgress.Max := mmPlayer.Length;
            trkProgress.Position := 0;
            timProgress.Enabled := true;
      end;
end;
```

As the MediaPlayer component's AutoEnabled property is set to True, the component takes care of the buttons (so we don't have to), enabling those that are appropriate to the type of file the user has just loaded and the device's capabilities. For example, a sound card can record sounds as well as play them back, so the component would enable both the Play and Record buttons.

If you play around with the program, you'll notice that you can move the track bar's slider to change where playback starts, while, during normal service, it represents the current position of the playback through the media. That's quite a combination of features in one component, but isn't it a little complicated code-wise?

Actually, to produce this effect, you need a total of two event handlers and three lines of code! The first event handler deals with the playback position of the slider and so is attached to the timer's OnTimer event handler:

```
procedure TfrmFilePlayer.timProgressTimer(Sender: TObject);
begin
    if mmPlayer.Mode = mpRecording then
        trkProgress.Max := mmPlayer.Length;
    if (mmPlayer.Mode = mpPlaying) or (mmPlayer.Mode = mpRecording) then
        trkProgress.Position := mmPlayer.Position;
end;
```

The timer control really has quite a tricky job on its hands. On the surface, it would appear that all it has to do is to move the track bar's slider as the file plays to give some graphical indication of the progress of playback. However, since the user may decide to use the MediaPlayer to record data into the current file, the timer also needs to adjust the value of the TrackBar's **Max** property accordingly.

FYI

To display the length of the recording, I'm using the track bar's tick marks rather than the slider, because while you're recording, you don't know the length of the media until you've finished - not a happy state of affairs when you want an up-to-the-millisecond display. Therefore, by changing the maximum length of the track bar while keeping the frequency of the tick marks at a constant, the track bar will automatically add more tick marks to denote the recording time.

It's quite easy to find out what the MediaPlayer is up to; simply look at the **Mode** property. This returns a number that we can check against some Delphi constants to see exactly what is happening:

Status Constant	Description
mpNotReady	The component is busy and not ready to accept any more instructions.
mpStopped	Playback or recording has stopped, either because that was ordered by the application, or because the end of the file was reached.
mpPlaying	The component is currently playing back some data.
mpRecording	The component is currently recording some data.
mpSeeking	The component is moving to a different part of the data, normally as directed by the application or the user.
mpPaused	Playback has been paused and the component is waiting to be told what to do next.
mpOpen	The component is in the process of opening a multimedia file or device ready to let the user loose.

So, in this case, the timer's OnTimer event first checks to see if the user is recording data. If she is, the TrackBar's **Max** property is reset:

```
if mmPlayer.Mode = mpRecording then
       trkProgress.Max := mmPlayer.Length
```

No matter whether the user is playing or recording data, the position of the drag handle in the TrackBar must always be updated:

```
if (mmPlayer.Mode = mpPlaying) or (mmPlayer.Mode = mpRecording) then
       trkProgress.Position := mmPlayer.Position;
```

Remember that while recording, the current position of the **MediaPlayer** is the same as the maximum length of the recording, so this code will superglue the slider to the right end of the track bar while recording is taking place.

As well as using the slider and track bar combination to display information about the media, you can also use it to dynamically move around. Fortunately, Delphi can handle this feature if you include just one line of code in the right event handler - in this case, the track bar's OnChange event handler:

```
procedure TfrmFilePlayer.trkProgressChange(Sender: TObject);
begin
     mmPlayer.Position := trkProgress.Position;
end;
```

All this code does is to move the current position of the media to reflect the current position of the slider on the track bar. Remember that these two properties are synonymous, as the length of the track bar is based upon the overall length of the media.

Using an Invisible MediaPlayer

So far, we have just looked at using the MediaPlayer as a visible component - users find it easier to cope with it in this state! However, using the component's run-time properties and methods, you can actually take complete control of the component without ever needing to bring the component's buttons into view - of course, you do still need to have the component on your form, but you can leave it invisible.

Some of the MediaPlayer's properties that make this a valid option, not including those that I've already covered, are given on the following page.

Property	Description
Capabilities	This returns a set giving the capabilities of the current device or file. You can check in the set for **mpCanEject**, **mpCanPlay**, **mpCanRecord**, **mpCanStep**, **mpUsesWindows**. Check for the value like this: **If mpCanEject in mmPlayer.Capabilities then**
Error	Returns a number representing the error or result code of an operation. If the number returned is **0** then no error occurred. You can also check the **ErrorMessage** property for a more meaningful value, or look in **Mmsystem.hlp** for full details of the error codes.
ErrorMessage	A string defining the error number, ideal for displaying in a message box if **Error** is not **0**.
Filename	Set this property at run time, before calling the **Open** method to load the file in. If you also set the **DeviceType** property to **dtAutoSelect** then the component will handle the details of deciding which multimedia device should be used to handle the file.
Start / End	**Start** and **End** can be used to set up a segment of a file or device to play back. Using **Start** and **End** you can effectively reduce the useable size of the file for as long as it remains loaded.
StartPos / EndPos	**Startpos** and **Endpos** can be used to set up a section of a file to play or record into for the next **Play** and **StartRecording** methods only. Once the methods have been run, the playable area returns to either the full file or the area specified by **StartPos** and **EndPos**.
TrackPosition	Like **TrackLength**, **TrackPosition** is another array, this time returning the position reached by the playback through the specified track.

In addition to these properties, there are, of course, a number of methods that you can use at run time to supplement and even replace the visual side of the component:

Method	Description
Close	Tells the component to release the currently selected device and any file that it may have loaded in for that device.
Eject	For devices which can eject (like a CD), this method will cause them to do just that.
Open	Opens a file or device ready to be used. If you are dealing with a device, though, such as a CD player, it's probably best to simply set AutoOpen to True to make the device available as soon as the component loads up.
Pause	Pauses playback or recording.
Play	Starts playback.

Table Continued on Following Page

Method	Description
Resume	Resumes playback or recording.
Rewind	Rewinds the current file or track to the beginning ready to start playing or record form the start again.
Save	Saves the current file to the filename specified in the **Filename** property.
StartRecording	Have a guess!
Stop	Stops playback or recording.

To see how some of these properties and methods can by used in a production-ready application, take a look at **cddb.dpr** on the Wrox Press web site. This application is effectively a multimedia front end to a database that contains information on your audio CD collection. By adding the appropriate information into the database, you can use the front-end Delphi application to definite a play list of tracks over any of the CDs in your collection.

The application should prompt you to put the next appropriate CD in your drive, check to see if it's the right CD and then auto-play the appropriate track - cool, or what?

I'm not going to describe the application in any detail here - you should be okay on the basic design and the database side of the equation should be a snip after the two earlier database chapters. To help you out, I've been a little more verbose on the comment in the code and I've added in a few interesting features to help you out - check out the Help menu for more details.

Using the API

So, if the MediaPlayer component is so powerful, why bother with the API at all? Well, whenever you deal with a component, you are effectively adding another layer of complexity between you and the lower level of Windows itself. When you send commands to a component like MediaPlayer, it has to translate what you are telling it through properties and methods into something native to the appropriate Windows API, in this case, the Multimedia Control Interface (MCI).

Since multimedia is such a speed-intensive area, why not just cut out the middle man altogether and go straight to the API? In addition, there are times where you simply don't need all the power (and resource overhead) that comes with the MediaPlayer component. You might want just to make a quick beep sound, or quickly fire off a sound bite. Since you can do these things with just one API command, there isn't really the need for the complete functionality offered by the MediaPlayer component!

The Multimedia Control Interface

The **Multimedia Control Interface** (MCI) provides you with a very low level interface to all the multimedia systems in your PC. In fact, the MCI actually gives you a complete 'programming language', specifically designed for you to gain total control over your PC's multimedia hardware.

So how does it work? You use the **mciSendString** API call to send requests to the MCI, each call telling the API exactly what you what to it do. For example, if you wanted to open a multimedia file, you simply pass the following call to the MCI:

```
mciSendString('Open myfile.wav Type WaveAudio', '', 0, 0);
```

You shouldn't have too much trouble with the parameters that need to be passed to the API call, as they closely resemble the MediaPlayer component's properties and methods, but just in case, let's take a closer look at the syntax of the **mciSendString** API call.

Using mciSendString

The format of the **mciSendString** command is really quite simple and is listed in the online Multimedia Developers Reference under mciSendString (supplied with Delphi as **mm.hlp**) as:

mciSendString(*<Command>*, *<ReturnString>*, *<Return>*, *<hwndCallback>*);

What the help file doesn't immediately make obvious is that **mciSendString** is, in fact, a function and passes out a long integer value which can be used to check whether the call was successful.

The first parameter, *<Command>*, is the command that you want to send to the MCI. You should note that the MCI expects this parameter as a string, so watch out! As I said earlier, the MCI bears a strong resemblance to a programming language in that you can issue commands to it in a similar way to those aimed at an interpreted development system, like Basic.

There are certain MCI calls which can be used to return a string packed with useful information. For example, with the MediaPlayer component you can take a look at the **Capabilities** property to see what a device can do. Working directly with the MCI, you can send a **Capabilities** request and get a string back describing the capability you were interested in.

Whatever the return string contains is returned as the contents of the fixed length string variable that you specified in the *<ReturnString>* parameter (more on this later). Because this must be a fixed length, you need to pass the length of the string to the API using the *<Return>* parameter.

Finally, *<hwndCallback>* is the address of a function that you want the MCI to call when certain events occur. It's a feature of the API that's a little beyond the scope of this discussion, so you'll probably not be surprised to see it set to 0 in all my examples. This effectively tells the API that it can forget about callback functions.

Command Parameter Options

I have already said a few times that we can send commands to the MCI using **mciSendString**, but just what are these commands? There are a lot, but the more useful ones are listed on the following page.

MCI Command	Description

`Open <filename>`
`Type <Type>`
`Alias <a name>`
	Opens the specified file. **Type** tells MCI what type of data the file contains (**WaveAudio**, **AviVideo**, or **Sequencer** by default). **Alias** allows you to assign a name to the loaded file which you can use in subsequent MCI calls.

`Play <Alias>`	Begins playback of the file.
`Stop <Alias>`	Stops playback of the file.
`Pause <Alias>`	Pauses playback so that it can be rewound, restarted, and so on.
`Seek <Alias> To <position>`	If the file is playing, this continues playback from the position you specify. You don't have to pass a numeric position to this call, you can just as easily say **Start** to move to the start of the file, or **End** to move to the end. If the file isn't playing then the next **Play** command will begin at the newly determined position.
`Status <Alias> <keyword>`	Asks the MCI to give you status information about an element of the file. For example, if you specify **Mode** as the keyword, the MCI will tell you whether the file is playing. **Position** returns the current position, **Length** the length, and so on.
`Rewind <alias>`	Rewinds a stopped file to the beginning, ready for you to start playing again.

Time to see these commands in action I reckon. Let's take a look at an application that loads and plays a **.wav** file using direct calls to the MCI.

Try It Out - Calling the MCI Directly

1 Load up **mci1.dpr**:

At present, the program does nothing - it just gives you a button to press at run time. We'll have to add some code to bring the button to life, to fireup the common dialog, to hunt out an appropriate file and play a sound.

2 Add the following local variable declaration to the button's OnClick event handler:

```
procedure TfrmMCi1.cmdPlayClick(Sender: TObject);
var
   sCommand : array[0..255] of char;
```

We're going to use this temporary variable as the transport for a null-terminated C-style string, the default format required by the MCI (and indeed by all Windows APIs).

3 Next, add the following lines of code to enable the file open dialog - this is the usual structure to check whether an OpenDialog component has been accessed by the user:

```
procedure TfrmMCi1.cmdPlayClick(Sender: TObject);
var
     sCommand : array[0..255] of char;
begin
     if dlgOpenFile.Execute then
     begin

     end;
end;
```

4 The next logical step is to add the code to deal with the MCI call. Remember the three steps to interacting with a multimedia file using the MediaPlayer component? Open it, play it and close it. Add the following lines of code to our event handler:

```
begin
     if dlgOpenFile.Execute then
     begin
          StrPCopy(sCommand, 'Open ' + dlgOpenFile.FIlename + ' Type WaveAudio
                    Alias Wave');
          mciSendString(sCommand, '', 0, 0);

          StrPCopy( sCommand, 'Play Wave Wait');
          mciSendString(sCommand, '', 0,0);

          StrPCopy( sCommand, 'Close Wave');
          mciSendString(sCommand, '', 0, 0);
     end;
end;
```

5 The application is now nearly complete. Add the following entry to your unit's **uses** clause and compile the application:

```
uses
     Windows, Messages, SysUtils, Classes, Graphics, Controls, Forms, Dialogs,
     StdCtrls,
     mmsystem;
```

On compilation, you will be presented with the original dramatic form and, when you click the unassuming button and select a **.wav** file, you'll get a sound coming from your speakers, all without the help of the MediaPlayer component.

How It Works

There are really three points to consider when you look at this code - why do we need a temporary variable, how do we make a MCI API call and how do we build the parameters to pass to the API call?

The answer to the first question is that all API calls operate with null-terminated strings, not Pascal-style strings. Therefore, in order to switch the string's style, we need a temporary storage place for the new format, at least until the call to the API has been made.

The second question has already been answered - you simply pass the API call the appropriate parameters, in this case, a variable and three constants, that define exactly what you want the API to do and wait for its reply. If you get anything wrong, one of two things will happen. If the syntax of the parameters is wrong, the compiler will complain - you know - you get those annoying Incompatible types or Missing Semicolon messages.

If it's not the syntax, but the contents of the parameters that are incorrect, you'll have to rely on the API to handle the problem. Fortunately, when you're dealing with the MCI API, you're working with a professional. If you attempt to open a file that doesn't exist (or it can't find), the API will do.... absolutely nothing! The MCI is one of the safest API interfaces that Windows provides - it's actually quite hard to crash your program by firing garbage at it - it just ignores you, kind of sulks!

The third answer is one of the most interesting things about the **mciSendString** API call. In fact, it can deal with a variety of parameters - we used three:

```
'Open ' + dlgOpenFile.Filename + ' Type WaveAudio Alias Wave'
'Play Wave Wait'
'Close Wave'
```

The first of these is a construction based upon the file that the user selects in the file open dialog that the application presents - I could have replaced this dynamic line of code with a more hard coded version, something like this:

```
Open c:\test.wav Type WaveAudio Alias Wave
```

In essence, you can read this line of code just like a paragraph from a novel:

'Please open the file called **test.wav** from the root of the **C** drive. It's an audio wave file and if anyone talks to you about a file called **Wave**, they are in fact talking about this one.'

This is what I meant by the MCI supporting its own language. Simply by talking to the API in the correct tongue, you can get it to jump through hoops for you. Take, for instance, the second and third calls that we make in our example. Simply by coding up a request to play the aliased **Wave** and then close it down, we can get MCI to generate a sound and clear the decks for the next caller.

Play's Wait Command

You should note that the **Wait** command at the end of **Play** is quite important.

As you probably know, Windows is a multitasking operating system which means that it can easily do two things at once, including dealing with multimedia. If you tell the MCI to play something, but don't pass the **Wait** command across, the MCI goes away for a very short while, starts playing the file and then returns control to your application. The file could still be playing at that point, but your code is free to continue doing whatever it needs to do.

With our application, all we're going to do is to close the file down. This means that, without the **Wait** statement on the end of the **Play** line, you will hear a very short burst of sound before it gets cut off. Putting **Wait** on the end of the **Play** line tells the MCI to stop everything until the file has finished playing, to **Wait** until the file has finished before returning from the **mciSendString** call.

The only other element of this application that might trip up the unwary is the need to manually add the multimedia unit reference to the **interface**'s **uses** clause. Normally, when you are dealing with API calls, all you have to do is to make sure that the **Windows** unit appears in the **uses** clause, but for some reason, MCI doesn't live there. This means that, before the application will compile, you've got to make an explicit reference to its resting place. If you get the following compiler error,

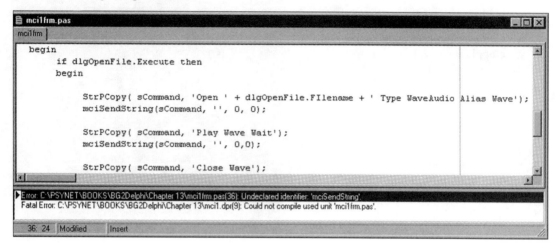

you will know that you've forgotten the **uses** clause entry.

The Flexibility of mciSendString

One of the beauties of the MCI is that it allows you to deal with different formats of multimedia data without changing the code too much. For example, if we wanted this program to deal with video clips, we would only have to make two changes.

Change the filter property of the common dialog so that it shows ***.avi** files:

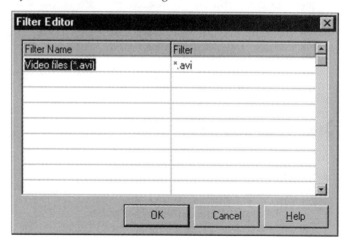

The only other change that we need to make is to the **Type** specifier on the **Open** line to reflect that the media format has changed to **AviVideo**:

```
StrPCopy( sCommand, 'Open ' + dlgOpenFile.FIlename + ' Type AviVideo Alias Wave');
mciSendString(sCommand, '', 0, 0);
```

There's no need to change the `Alias` at all, since that's a user-defined name, just like a variable name. You can assign whatever `Alias` you want to a file - neither Delphi or the MCI really care what you call it.

If you make these changes to the code, your application will be able to play video instead of just sound. If you can't be bothered then just load up `mci2.dpr`:

Another Interesting MCI (Video) Parameter

There is another interesting parameter which you can tack on the end of a **Play** command for video - **FullScreen**. If you specify this

```
StrPCopy( sCommand, 'Play Video Wait FullScreen');
```

then the video clip will be resized as much as possible to take up the whole screen. Depending on your video card, the amount of memory you have and the speed of your system, it may not always work and you may find yourself looking at a slightly larger image in the center of a black screen, but it can be quite handy sometimes.

Try it - change the play line to the one above in **mci2.dpr** and run the app - see what you think.

Querying the MCI

You may remember reading earlier that there are MCI commands that actually ask for detailed information about a file or device. The information can include a file's length, the device's capabilities, and so on. This in itself is nothing strange, but the way that it works is. The MCI returns this information in a parameter that you pass to it. Worse than that, though, the parameter is a **PChar**, a pointer to an array of characters, so getting the data out involves a little thought and effort. A valuable educational experience!

The most commonly used MCI command that returns information is **Status**. With **Status**, you need to tell the MCI which **Alias** you want status information for and exactly which kind of information you want.

With the obvious exception of items which return numeric information, such as **Position**, **Length**, and so on, this information comes back as a piece of text which doesn't look all that out of place in a message box or in a component on a form somewhere.

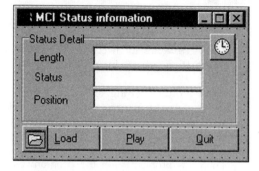

Load up **mcistat.dpr** to see what I mean:

This program builds a little on the previous two by allowing you to load up a file as normal. It then uses a **Timer** component to query the MCI at regular intervals to find out the status of the selected file and feed that information into the text boxes on the form.

The code behind the Load and Quit buttons should be quite familiar to you by now, so I won't bore you with any details. The code that handles the Timer's OnTimer event handler, though, is very interesting. Double-click on it to take a look:

```
procedure TForm1.timUpdateTimer(Sender: TObject);
var
    sReturn : array[0..255] of char;
begin
    mciSendString('Status Wave Mode', sReturn, 255, 0);
    txtStatus.text := StrPas(sReturn);

    mciSendString('Status Wave Position', sReturn, 255,0);
    txtPosition.text := StrPas(sReturn);

    mciSendString('Status Wave Length', sReturn, 255, 0);
    txtLength.text := StrPas(sReturn);

end;
```

First of all, notice how the strings being sent to **mciSendString** are not being converted into a **PChar** variable. If you're passing a constant string to an API call that expects a **PChar** variable then Delphi is intelligent enough to convert it for you. Previously, since we were joining string properties to string constants and passing that lot to a **PChar** parameter, we had to use a variable and feed the command string into it. Delphi is not intelligent enough to do that kind of conversion on its own.

Each line here looks very similar. We call **mciSendString**, passing it the command, and a **PChar** string which it uses to read in the result. The number (**255**) in each **mciSendString** tells **mciSendString** the maximum amount of data that the **PChar** can hold.

Once a value has been returned, **StrPas** is used to convert the **PChar** string to a normal Delphi string and drop the result into the text property of each text box on the form.

You should also notice that the command being sent to **mciSendString** is the same - it's always **Status** followed by the **Alias** name, then a keyword to tell the MCI which bit of information we are interested in.

Mode returns a string telling us what mode the file is in, i.e. whether it's stopped, playing, and so on. **Length** returns the length, based on the current **TimeFormat**, just like in the **MediaPlayer** component. **Position** returns the current position, again based on the current **TimeFormat**.

There's a problem with the program as it stands, though. If you load a file in and play it, when playback stops, you can't replay it. You need to 'rewind' the file before it can be played again.

Double-click the Play button to look at the code:

```
procedure TForm1.cmdPlayClick(Sender: TObject);
begin
     mciSendString('Play Wave', '', 0,0);
end;
```

To make the code replay the file from the start every time the button is pressed, we just need to add a single **mciSendString** line in above that **Play** line;

```
mciSendString('Seek Wave To Start', '', 0,0);
```

If playback has either been stopped or paused, we can use the **Rewind** command that I mentioned earlier. However, this won't work if the file is already playing. Think about a normal tape for example; you can't rewind it while it's playing.

Seek gets around this. By telling the MCI to 'seek' the file, it immediately jumps back to the start of the file and continues playing from that point - much like holding down the seek buttons on a CD player.

And Finally...

The MCI is great for having 'device-independent control' over the multimedia system, but even that is a little like overkill if you want nothing more than to fire off a quick sound sample. A much better choice would be to use **sndPlaySound**. With this one small command, you can trigger complete playback of a wave file without having to worry about first opening the file, etc.

Take a look at **plysound.dpr**:

On the surface, it looks quite similar to some of the earlier examples, but double-click the command button to expose its workings and marvel at the difference!

```
procedure TForm1.Button1Click(Sender: TObject);
var
    sFilename : array[0..255] of char;
begin
    StrPCopy(sFilename, dlgFileOpen.Filename);
    if dlgFileOpen.Execute then
        sndPlaySound(sFilename, SND_ASYNC);
end;
```

As with the MCI stuff, unless you can specify a literal filename (for example, `'c:\ding.wav'`) you need to convert the name of the file that you want to play into a **PChar** before it can be used in the **sndPlaySound** call.

SndPlaySound takes just two parameters. The first, as you can probably guess, is nothing more than the name of the file that you want to play and is, of course, a **PChar**. The second tells Windows how you want to play the file. **SND_ASYNC** is the same as telling the MCI to play without the wait clause. The alternative is to use **SND_SYNC** which locks your application up until the sound has finished playing.

Another interesting point about **sndPlaySound** is that it will always make a noise. If it can't find the file you specified, or there if is a problem with the multimedia hardware, it will make the default beep noise, either through your speakers or through the computers internal speaker. With **sndPlaySound**, you not only reduce the amount of code necessary to make a noise, but you also guarantee that a noise will occur.

Summary

This has been a whirlwind tour of multimedia in Delphi and we've certainly missed out some of the more intricate details, obscure calls, commands and functions. However, I have shown you some of the more interesting effects that you can get hold of without an awful lot of coding and, as you may agree, the results can be quite striking. You may also be interested to know that new and improved versions of the CD Player (**cddb.exe**), as well as other small applications of this type, will be made available to the general public, free of charge on my publisher's web site (**www.wrox.com**) at regular intervals - watch this space.

The Windows API is a subject that is closely related to that of multimedia, so why don't you check out Wrox Press' *The Revolutionary Guide to Delphi 2 and The Win32 API*, ISBN 1-861000-53-7. Or you might be interested in *Beginning Delphi Games*, ISBN 1-874416-88-5, also from Wrox Press.

In the next chapter, I continue to build on the use of the Windows API, although, this time, we'll focus on the Internet. By using a Delphi application as the CGI interface between your web server and your resource database, you can vastly simplify the task of setting up your own interactive web site... let's go!

Programming for the Internet

What can Delphi do for the Internet? It might not appear so at first, but Delphi is very good for writing CGI applications. What are these? Well, when a web user makes a request for some information from a server, the server in turn calls a program to produce as from a hat the requested data. The interface that all web servers use to communicate these requests to programs is the **Common Gateway Interface (CGI)**. The CGI application, which is basically any program that services a web server, then returns the information as a web page, or an e-mail, or even as a bad-tempered error message, before quitting and leaving the server to distribute the goodies.

Using Delphi applications as intermediary programs which listen patiently to web servers and then quiz databases is a wonderfully simple way of avoiding the potentially horrific problems that you're likely to have to deal with when two applications are communicating with one another.

In this chapter, you'll learn all about:

▶ The Internet and the Web

▶ HTML - What every gal should know...

▶ CGI - the signs

▶ How CGI fits into the Windows picture

▶ The part that Delphi has to play

Let's first review the background to the Internet, which will help us in our Delphi example application...

Introduction

The Internet really needs no introduction. Over the past few years, excitement over it has grown, with many people 'surfing' their way around and creating their own part of the World Wide Web. The Internet provides easy access to all kinds of information and enables people to communicate instantaneously over huge distances.

The Internet started in the 1960s as a US Defense project to link together the universities and military research establishments. About twenty years later, the Department of Defense handed the basic structure over to the US National Science Foundation, but since then it has grown so large that no one person or organization really runs the Internet as a whole.

In the last few years, the growth of the Internet has been explosive, with many new connections added to the network on a weekly basis. The majority of home pages, though, are simply linked documents providing information about the person that owns them, or about things that are of interest to that person.

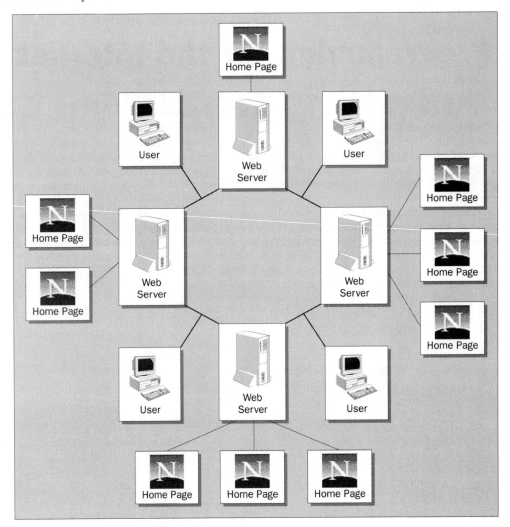

More and more sites on the Internet go beyond this simple flat-file linking and provide a certain amount of interaction to the 'surfer'. Examples of this include the multitude of search engines provided by people like Yahoo and AltaVista. Perhaps one of the most impressive sites is the one run by Federal Express which allows you to query how far your valuable parcel has got on its journey. It's this extra functionality that really brings the Internet to life and makes surfing more like using any other Windows programs, except that it operates on a global rather than an office-based scale.

This interactive ability is achieved by using applications that are run by the web server in response to a request from the user. These applications are generally called **CGI applications**, as they interact with the server by utilizing the Common Gateway Interface specification. Like most things around the Internet, this specification is subject to change, but the major areas that we shall be exploring remain fairly static. A full documentation of the original CGI specification can be found at:

```
http://hoohoo.ncsa.uiuc.edu/cgi/overview.html
```

FYI   For those of you who are completely new to the Internet, you can type this address into your URL/Location field on your browser. Note that, in most cases, the address is case-sensitive!

The original specifications for CGI were aimed at UNIX and DOS-based applications, so the workings of CGI are slightly different for Windows applications, such as those written in Delphi.

Why Use a CGI Application?

So how do we provide information on request to whoever may be looking at our pages? In the case of most companies' sites, this may be stock or ordering information, or even the ability to purchase items, information or services provided on that site. On a more individual level, a CGI application gives you the ability to create web pages that interact with the user, such as providing specific web pages based on a search criteria or a user's name. Take a look at this diagram:

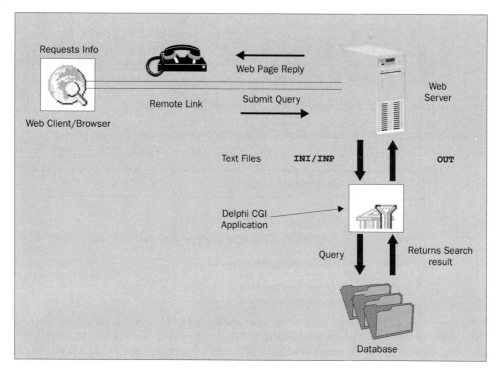

Interaction, therefore, provides a selective path through the information that you're providing. It requires the ability to create web pages ad hoc, based on information supplied by the user.

 The ability to use CGI on your own personal web pages is dictated by your friendly service-provider. You will find this information most useful if you're building information servers for your place of work, or if you're running a web server of your own.

Internet Basics

If you're an experienced surfer, I would suggest you skip through the next two sections, but if you'd like a brief explanation of the bits and pieces associated with Internet browsing, read on. I promise you it's not that complicated.

Many people regard the Internet as something a bit mysterious and complicated, but most people who use it will tell you that's not true - it's just unfamiliar territory when you set out. By far the majority of web servers that are connected to the Internet are running some form of a UNIX environment, but this is largely transparent to anyone who visits these sites utilizing any of the commercially available browsers. The only real clue you have that this is the case is generally the address of the site - you may have noticed the use of '/' instead of the more usual '\' to reference directory structures.

 By *transparent*, I mean that you can look through what the web server is doing, just to see the results.

To access any particular site or page on the Internet, you'll need to provide your browser with an address. This is generally referred to as an **URL**, or **Uniform Resource Locator** and signifies the standard laid down for addressing on the Internet, a resource being anything from a directory listing to a search engine. The URL is generally made of four main parts:

`http://super.sonic.net/ann/delphi/cgicomp/code.html`

In this address, the first reference is to the protocol you're using. This may be of a number of types:

Protocol	Description
HTTP	Hyper Text Transfer Protocol.
Ftp	File Transfer Protocol, for downloading files manually.
News	To attach to a news server.
Mailto	To send e-mail to a user across the Internet.

The second part of the above URL is **super.sonic.net**. This is the address, or name, of the actual web server that you wish to attach to. The majority of servers are addressed by name, but some still use their **IP** (**Internet Protocol**) address, such as `http://123.00.11.22/`.

FYI The IP address is a sequence of numbers allocated by a service provider to a web server, to uniquely identify that machine to the Internet. To make things easier for us mortals, most of these IP addresses are then aliased to a name.

The last part of the address, **/ann/delphi/cgicomp/code.html**, is the name, including directory path, of the file you wish to view on that server.

Given this address, a web browser can locate and query the appropriate server for the information you want - note that it's the server's job to provide that file back to the web browser. In this case, the actual file name specified above is **code.html**, so our browser will be expecting an HTML document in return - I'll be looking at those briefly in the next section.

FYI If you had simply entered the protocol and server name, such as **http://super.sonic.net/**, the server would return to you its default page, which is usually **index.html**. Note that files can have virtually any extension, although the normal ones are .html or .htm.

When you use any of the search engines that are available on the Internet, you may see a URL on your browser that looks something like this:

```
http://www.search.com/Engine?Query=Find+CGI+Documents
```

The last part of this URL, **Engine?Query=Find+CGI+Documents** is the call to the CGI application, and therefore the key to dynamic client/server communication over the Web.

The Basics of HTML

HTML stands for the **Hyper Text Markup Language** and is used to create the web pages you see as you surf your way around the Internet. The language itself is very simple and the documents can be created in virtually any editor that can output a standard text file:

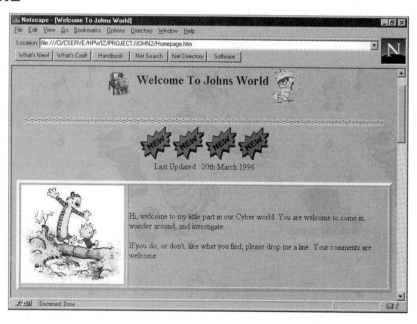

The fact that the documents are just standard text files means that creating documents ad hoc is relatively easy, and indeed, it's this that provides much of the functionality that we use in our CGI applications.

There are many and varied publications available on the HTML language and, with the advent of new and more powerful browsers, the language is being extended all the time. Consequently, I'll only provide a brief listing of the basic items required to generate a page with our CGI application.

It's easy to learn how to include the other parts of the language by finding a web page that you particularly like and viewing the source to it, via your browser.

Reviewing a HTML Document

In an HTML document, if you issue a command to turn a feature on, you must issue another to turn it off. Take a look at the following extract:

```
<HTML><HEAD>
<TITLE>Wrox Press Developers' Reference</TITLE>
</HEAD>
<BODY BACKGROUND="http://www.wrox.com/redbar2.gif" ALT=" ">
<UL><UL>
<CENTER><IMG BORDER=1 SRC="http://www.wrox.com/wrox/images/smallogo.gif" ALT="
"><P>
<B><FONT SIZE=+2>Wrox Press Developers' Reference</FONT><BR>
<I>Programming books written by programmers</I></B>
```

As you can see, this means that all commands come in pairs, like **<Head></Head>**. Any information contained between these two commands will have the appropriate formatting applied to it.

Note that each command is surrounded by <> and, to end a command, you precede it with /.

Below, I have listed some of the more useful HTML commands:

Command Pair	Description
`<A></A>`	Anchor marks around a link.
`<B></B>`	Bold.
`<BODY></BODY>`	Marks out the body of the document.
` `	Line break, used to start a new line within a paragraph.
`<FORM></FORM>`	Marks out the form part of a document, containing fields.
`<H?></H?>`	Header style, ? = 1 to 6 for size/level.

Table Continued on Following Page

Command Pair	Description
`<HEAD></HEAD>`	Defines the header information section.
`<HTML></HTML>`	Optional, but defines the document as being HTML.
`<I></I>`	Italics style.
`<IMG SRC="file">`	Defines an image, requires `SRC="file"`.
`<INPUT>`	Defines an input field, see later sections for options.
`<OPTION>`	Defines an option list.
`<P>`	Paragraph break.
`<TITLE></TITLE>`	Defines the title to display in your browser.

Some of these, like **IMG**, **INPUT** and **OPTION** warrant a little more explanation, which we will come to later in the chapter.

You can familiarize yourself with creating web documents by inserting the above commands, along with some text, into a text file and loading it into your browser using the File | Open File menu option.

Calling a CGI Application

Once you've created a standard HTML document, you can allow your users to browse through the page. If you include links, like,

you can allow the user to skip between pages. The above link would take the user to your Index page and is achieved by including the following code in your document (assuming that all your pages are in the same directory on the server):

```
Go to my <A HREF="index.html">Home</A> page
```

The anchor points around the word **Home** define it as the link item and the **HREF** statement defines the page that should be loaded when that word is selected by the user. You can include as many links as you like in your page; on the web, you could find pages that consist almost entirely of links to other pages.

What happens if we want the user to select a link that shows them an up-to-date price list and a list of up-and-coming events? The answer is to create the page dynamically, based upon the contents of a database. For this, you wouldn't use the normal form of linking, but would ask the page to submit a request for a page.

The administration of something this simple could be a nightmare if your site is receiving a large number of visits, as you must create a new page for each user. There is no easy way to tell the server to delete the page once it has been read, as the user's browser will maintain a link to the page. If they hit the 'go back' button, they may wish to reload the page. The removal of obsolete pages could be built into your application, which is something that we'll show you later, or you simply bite the bullet and do regular site spring-cleaning by hand.

To give your application the ability to respond to requests from the user, you must use the **FORM** command to create an interactive part to your document. In the case shown below, the user can hit a button to view the price list:

```
<HTML>
<FORM   ACTION="CGI/DELPHCGI.EXE" METHOD=POST>
To view our prices click this button <INPUT TYPE="submit" VALUE="Our Prices">
</FORM>
</HTML>
```

This places the text To view our prices click this button in front of a Windows-style command button control, with the text Our Prices as a caption. If the user clicks on the button, the web server will run the application **delphcgi.exe** which is located in the subdirectory **CGI/.**

It's then up to this application to create a price list and a new web page, output the file and terminate before the web server can return the file back to the user's browser. Let's take a look at how that works.

How Information is Passed Back and Forth

Now we're getting into the nitty-gritty of CGI. We know that the CGI application is spawned as a process from the server. The server passes information from the submitted form to the application, then the application passes back the information that the server needs to perform its next action, as in the figure we saw earlier. But how is this dialogue actually conducted?

Back in the days when DOS applications ruled the PC world, this information was passed via environment variables, which meant the flow of information was relatively transparent. In those heady days, setting something like **PATH=C:\DOS\ETC** in the **autoexec.bat** file, meant that **PATH**, an environment variable, could be used to simplify your DOS commands that made use of your file and directory structure. Instead of typing,

```
C:\DOS\ETC\MYGAME.EXE
```

you could type,

```
MYGAME
```

and get away with a transparent filing system.

Windows-based applications, however, found it difficult to access environment information, so a new standard was developed - the request and answer being brokered using text files.

If you were being really cunning about this forthcoming CGI program, you could make it a `Console` application and use `StdIn` and `StdOut` methods.

All the information passing to and from the server is written to text files, of which there will usually be three for any given operation:

▶ The first of these takes the form of a standard Windows **.ini** file, contains all the information the application needs to find the requested data and returns it in a suitable format.

▶ The second file, with a **.inp** extension, contains any large queries. More formally, these are the contents of any defined form fields. Although it always exists, the file doesn't have to contain any information and we won't be using it in our simple example.

▶ The third file, with the extension **.out**, is created by the application to pass information back to the server.

The **.ini** file is the most important of the three. It contains data about the type of information being requested, the server which is sending it, the document that called the application, and so on. An example of an **.ini** file sent by the server looks something like this:

```
[CGI]
Request Protocol=HTTP/1.0
Request Method=POST
Executable Path=/cgi-win/project1.exe
Server Software=WebServer Version 1.0
Server Name=john
Server Port=80
Server Admin=http-admin
CGI Version=CGI/1.1 WIN
Remote Host=pc17.123.00.11
Remote Address=195.130.16.217
Content Type=application/x-www-form-urlencoded
Content Length=0

[System]
Debug Mode=No
Output File=C:\WINDOWS\TEMP\HS2CE880.OUT
Content File=C:\WINDOWS\TEMP\HS2CE880.INP
```

The **Request Protocol** relates to the standard Hyper Text Transfer Protocol, while the **Request Method** informs your application if the call is a **POST** or a **GET**. The difference between these two is that **POST** sends information to the CGI application in support of the query, while a **GET** action just tags any query fields onto the end of the CGI call as a command line parameter. You normally see **GET** requests in action on search engines, where the request is only a couple of fields long.

There's a load more information, most of which seems spectacularly worthless. We'll discuss some of it after the excitement of our first Delphi CGI application.

The last two lines in the `.ini` file above are quite important because some servers have now stopped passing the content and output file names as command line parameters. You should, therefore, look for their names in the `.ini` file, rather than relying on them being on the command line.

It's also very important to remember that all these files must be passed with their full paths, as shown above. The application won't find them otherwise.

As a number of users could be using the CGI application at any one time, the server gives each of these sets of files a unique name. The server passes the filenames to be used in each case to your application as a command line argument. So the code,

```
<FORM ACTION="CGI/DELPHCGI.EXE" METHOD=POST>
```

would result in your application being called by the server using the following convention:

```
CGI/DELPHCGI.EXE IniFile InputFile OutputFile
```

The `Inifile`, `InputFile` and `OutputFile` all have the same name, varying only in their extensions.

A CGI Program

For starters, all that we're going to do with the `.ini` file is to read it and extract some data. The Delphi application will then create an output file, to complement the content it finds in the `.ini` file.

Having achieved this modest goal, I'll create a mock-up of a query form, which I can test by cheating and using a ready-made `.ini` file, so eliminating the need for a server which I haven't got yet. I'll then add the ability to deal with queries and dynamically create a reply web page as the output to the Delphi application.

This mock-up will always be necessary when you are developing CGI applications if you want to test the program at compile time under the Delphi IDE. The web server demands a stand-alone executable, so you have to iron out as many bugs as you can before you can link the CGI application to the server.

I'm only mentioning this because we've got used to sorting out all the bugs from within the IDE and linking to other applications (for example, a Paradox database) at design time.

While you're building the application, you can test it in the Delphi IDE, but only by calling it directly and passing it the command line parameters yourself. You can set this up, the path and file name of the `.ini` file in this case, using the **Run | Parameters...** menu item.

You must also bear in mind that different servers will react differently to any CGI application, so you must test the application thoroughly on each web server that you're using.

The last preliminary to note is that, as our application will run on a web server, we don't want it to produce any visible components on screen. One way of achieving this (although by no means the ideal way) is to perform the main actions of your application within a **Form**'s **OnCreate** and terminate the application before the form has a chance to display itself:

Try It Out - Basic Considerations - the First Steps

1 Start a new Delphi application. Save it as **cgiu.pas** and **webserv.dpr**.

2 In the **interface**'s **uses** clause add **IniFiles**, a Delphi unit that allows you to use the **TIniFile** object. Then declare a global variable, **WebIni**, of type **TIniFile**, and one called **fOutput** of type **TextFile**, whose purpose should be fairly self-explanatory. Your unit's code should now look like this:

```
unit cgiu;

interface

uses
   Windows, Messages, SysUtils, Classes,
   Graphics, Controls, Forms, Dialogs, IniFiles;

type
  TForm1 = class(TForm)
  private
    { Private declarations }
  public
    { Public declarations }
  end;

var
  Form1    : TForm1;
  WebIni   : TIniFile;
  fOutput  : TextFile;
```

3 Now double-click on the form to bring up the form's OnCreate event handler. Add the following code to open the **.ini** file:

```
procedure TForm1.FormCreate(Sender: TObject);
var
   sFileName : string;
begin
   sFilename := ParamStr(1);
   WebIni    := TIniFile.Create(sFileName);
end;
```

435

4 Now add code to set the string **sOutput** to the output file's name, from information gleaned from the **.ini** file, and then use this to open and prepare an output file:

```
procedure TForm1.FormCreate(Sender: TObject);
var
    sFileName : string;
    sOutPut   : string;
begin
    {Open the INI File}
    sFilename := ParamStr(1);
    WebIni    := TIniFile.Create(sFileName);

    {Get the Output File Name}
    sOutPut   := WebIni.ReadString('System','Output
                                    File','Error');

    {open the output file}
    AssignFile(fOutPut, sOutPut);
    ReWrite(fOutPut);
end;
```

5 For this, our first CGI-aware application, all we want to do is to tell the web server to send the next web page to the client where the query originated, much as if they had clicked on a link.

In the output file we just created, we need only insert the file name of that page. Just add the following line to what you've just typed in:

```
WriteLn(fOutPut, 'LOCATION : page2.html');
```

6 The web server responds once the application it called has terminated and it can reasonably assume that the output file is available for it to read. The normal Delphi **Close** or **Halt** methods won't work in this case. We have to use a special Windows API call to ensure the application terminates cleanly. Add the last three lines to the **FormCreate** procedure:

```
WriteLn(fOutput,'');

CloseFile(fOutput);
CloseApp(Application);
```

7 Now, in the form's **type** declaration, add the following procedure declaration:

```
type
  TForm1 = class(TForm)
    Procedure FormCreate(Sender: TObject);
    Procedure CloseApp(App : TApplication);
```

8 Then implement the following code:

```
procedure TForm1.CloseApp( App : TApplication );
begin
     PostMessage(App.Handle, WM_Close, 0, 0);
end;
```

9 Finally, in the **cgitest1.ini** file provided on the disk, change the **Output File=** entry in the **System** section to the full path of your **cgitest1.out** file. To recap on setting a parameter in Delphi's IDE, select <u>R</u>un | <u>P</u>arameters... and type in the full path of the **.ini** file. Then you can run the application.

You'll find that it creates an output file containing the line **LOCATION : Page2.html**. If you send this file back to the web server, the server will interpret it as if you had written,

http://www.[servername]/page2.html

and will load in that next page. Hey presto, your first CGI application is running!

How It Works

As with all the Try It Outs in this chapter, we're going to see a lot of string and file handling routines.

The first line of the **FormCreate** event handler uses the Pascal function **ParamStr(1)** to read in the first of the command line parameters you specified after specifying the program to run. The function is a zero-based index of each separate part of the command line - text parsing couldn't be easier! In real life, these parameters would be passed by a web server - but, for now, it's a manual thing.

The application then needs to be able to read the information supplied to it by the (hypothetical) web server. That information comes as an **.ini** file and you can deal with it with yet another convenient feature of Delphi - the **TIniFile** object. We need the **.ini** file information to be available to our entire unit, so we declare a variable of the new **TIniFile** object type to have global scope. Then we instantiate **WebIni** and pass the name of the actual **.ini** file, now **sFileName**, to the **Create** method.

Having initialized the **.ini** file object, we can read the data supplied to it by the server. For this, we utilize the methods made available through the **TIniFile** object. First of all, we want to get the output file's name, so we call the **WebIni**'s **ReadString** method. Passing it the section heading, **System** and the identifier within that section, **Output File**, the function returns the output filename to the appropriately named string. The last parameter we supply, **'Error'**, is the default string value of **sOutput**. That's the sort of no-nonsense error handling I like...

The last of the global variables is the text file variable, **fOutput**. Now we can assign our variable to the output file whose name we just extracted. The **Rewrite** method gets ready to write the file from scratch, overwriting if need be.

For this first program, the output is just one line which gives the next page's location. After this, though, we need a further blank line to inform the server that any commands have finished.

CloseFile breaks the association between the output file and the **fOutput** variable. Then the application calls the **CloseApp** procedure we added to the unit's **interface** section.

I have used the termination method suggested by Charlie Calvert and Ann Lynnworth. Visit Ann's site at HREF tools corporation on the **Super.Sonic.Net** URL I mentioned before to see her excellent Delphi CGI components.

This procedure calls the Windows API function `PostMessage()` - which pops a message in the Windows message queue, but doesn't wait for it to be processed. It passes the `Application`'s handle and the `WM_Close` message. The last two parameters, which add any message-specific data, aren't needed here. Windows then knows that the Delphi application (on which it now has a handle) is just waiting to be closed - couldn't be cleaner.

But why the special command? Well, the server is waiting for notification (via an application message) that the CGI application has finished. One problem with Delphi 2.0 is that the normal shutdown can take a prodigious amount of time, causing some servers to time out. We circumvent this with one direct call that tells Windows that it's all over.

An On The Fly Web Page

As you can see, there's a lot of information that you can extract from an `.ini` file, simply by using the `ReadString` method of the `TIniFile` object. But we've not really begun to add functionality to our program - rather than sending some predefined page, we want to create a page and send it to the user.

First, a note on how to keep the dynamically-created web page that we promised you earlier.

You can either write the output to the `.out` file or to a temporary file and then put the temporary files name in the `.out` file. The difference between the two methods is that the web server will normally delete all `.ini`, `.inp` and `.out` files automatically once it has finished with them, but, if you create temporary files, they will remain in the directory. This can be useful if you want to keep track of the way people are using your site. The information that has been requested and its requester are still present as a clutter of temporary files.

In our next example, we will create a web page on the fly and send it to the user:

Try It Out - Dynamic World Wide Web

1 Load up the project **webserv.dpr**. Save it as **cgi2u.pas** and **webserv2.dpr**. We now need to add three new procedures. Let's start by declaring them in the **public** section of the form's type:

```
procedure SendHeader;
procedure SendHTML(sString : string);
procedure CreatePage;
```

2 The first one will write out the standard header information that the web browser and the server expects to find in order for it to process the file correctly:

```
procedure TForm1.SendHeader;
begin
    SendHTML('HTTP/1.0 200 OK');
    SendHTML('SERVER:'+WebIni.ReadString('CGI','Server Software','Error'));
    SendHTML('CONTENT-TYPE: TEXT/HTML');
    SendHTML('');
end;
```

3 The code for the second procedure, **SendHTML**, is now rather urgent. It writes out the lines of HTML code that we require to build the page:

```
procedure TForm1.SendHTML(sString : String);
begin
    WriteLn(fOutPut, sString);
end;
```

It's more usual to write a separate procedure for each of the varying HTML commands and just send it the parameters it requires, but, as I don't want to send you to sleep, I'll confine the initial procedure to a simple output command.

4 The third procedure, true to its name, builds the page itself:

```
procedure TForm1.CreatePage;
begin
    {Send the Header information}
    SendHeader;

    {Put some text into the document}
    SendHTML('<HTML>');                    {Start of document}
    SendHTML('<H1>');                      {Header style 1}
    SendHTML('My Web Page');
    SendHTML('</H1>');

    {You can send multiple commands on one line!}
    SendHTML('<P><B>Hello World !</B><P>');

    SendHTML('</HTML>');                    {End of document}
    SendHTML('');                          {Terminate the document}
end;
```

5 Now replace the **WriteLn** calls in the **FormCreate** procedure with a call to the **CreatePage** procedure:

```
{open the output file}
AssignFile( fOutPut, sOutPut);
ReWrite( fOutPut );

{Create the new page}
CreatePage;
```

```
WebIni.Free;
CloseFile(fOutPut);
CloseApp(Application);
```

6 Now if you run the application as before, your output file should look like this:

```
HTTP/1.0 200 OK
SERVER:WebServer Version 1.0
CONTENT-TYPE: TEXT/HTML


<HTML>
<H1>
My Web Page
</H1>
<P><B>Hello World !</B><P>
</HTML>
```

Load the file into your web browser and you will see the result, just as if the server had 'sent' the page to you:

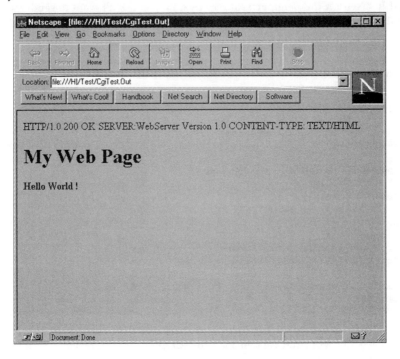

How It Works

CreatePage orchestrates the writing of the web page. It calls **SendHeader** first, which, in turn, calls the **SendHTML** procedure to insert the required header information for the new HTML document. **SendHTML** simply writes out a line of text to the output file. Then the information specific to this particular web page is added - at the moment, this is only a cheesy title, but in the none-too-distant future it will be much, much more...

It couldn't be simpler! Isn't Delphi programming difficult!

Creating Data-driven Pages

To recap, what we've achieved so far is to create and send a web page to a user, but we have yet to send the user any answer to their request, whatever that was. In this section, I'll show you how to read data from web pages and write data from a database to a page.

Web pages often contain 'fields' (edit boxes) for the user to enter information. This can obviously be useful in many ways, but, in our example, we're going to ask the user to enter a keyword to search our database. Then we'll return the search results to them in the form of a personalized web page.

To prepare for this task, I've created a web page called **search.htm**, simply by opening my favorite text editor and typing in the following HTML commands - note that you can do the same, or you can find it on the accompanying disk:

```
<HTML>
<TITLE>Delphi Search Page</TITLE>
<H1><CENTER>Welcome to our<BR>
Delphi Search Page</H1></CENTER>
<P>
<HR>
<P>
<H4>
Enter the item to search for:
<BR>
<FORM ACTION="CGI/DELPHCGI.EXE" METHOD="POST">
<INPUT TYPE="TEXT" NAME="Query" SIZE=10>
<P>
<INPUT TYPE="SUBMIT" VALUE="START SEARCH">
</FORM>
</HTML>
```

There are a couple of new HTML commands included here: the **<Center>** command centers text in the browser and the **<HR>** command provides a horizontal line across the page to separate the various sections.

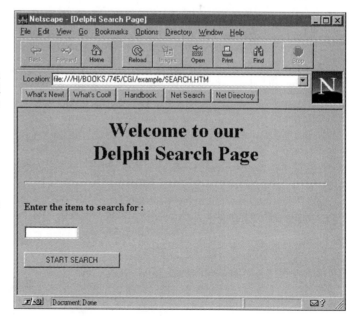

Load the file into your browser. It should look like this:

What Does it all Mean?

If this page were running on a server, when the user presses the Start Search button, the server would call your CGI application (it will eventually be called **delphcgi.exe**). It would put the entry in the query field into a section of the **.ini** file, using the format:

```
[Form Literal]
<Key>='<Value>'
```

where *<Key>* is the name you gave the field, in this case **Query**, and the *<Value>* would be the text that the user has typed into that field. The *Key/Value* pairs are stored by the server in the **[Form Literal]** section of the **.ini** file.

Other sections, such as **[Form External]**, are present when you're using large text fields, as the server will store larger data elements in external files and provide you with the file name and size in the *Key/Value* pair.

We now need to read in that data from the **.ini** file, adding a little more functionality to our project.

Try It Out - Interpreting the Request

As we would like our program to be a little bit intuitive, we're going to add a function that reads in the keys no matter how many there are, so enabling you to add and remove fields from the main form at will. For the purposes of this Try It Out, we're going to use the file provided on the disk, **cgitest.ini**, the exact same file as before, but with the following addition:

```
[Form Literal]
Query='Joe Bailey'
```

1 Load up **webserv2.dpr** and save it as **cgi3u.pas** and **delphcgi.dpr**. Add this line to the global variable declarations, to allocate a string list to hold the key names:

```
var
  Form1      : TForm1;
  WebIni     : TIniFile;
  fOutPut    : TextFile;
  KeyNames : TStringList;
```

2 Then add the following procedure to read the key names into the string list and add the procedure's heading to the form's type declaration:

```
procedure TForm1.ReadKeys;
begin
    KeyNames := TStringList.Create;
    WebIni.ReadSection('Form Literal',Keynames);
end;
```

3 What we now need to do is to activate this procedure and then read in the values associated with those keys, as and when we need them. In our example, where only one field is defined, that's the only value stored in the string list.

Modify the **TForm1.FormCreate** procedure so that it calls the **ReadKeys** procedure and then shows you the result:

```
procedure TForm1.FormCreate(Sender: TObject);
var
    sFileName : String;
    sOutPut   : String;
begin
    {Open the INI File}
    sFilename := ParamStr(1);
    WebIni    := TIniFile.Create(sFileName);

    {Get the Output File Name}
    sOutPut   := WebIni.ReadString('System','Output File','Error');

    {open the output file}
    AssignFile( fOutPut, sOutPut);
    ReWrite( fOutPut );

    {Retrieve the input value}
    ReadKeys;
    ShowMessage(KeyNames[0]);

    WebIni.Free;
    CloseFile(fOutPut);
    CloseApp(Application);
end;
```

Now when you run the program, you should get a message box showing you the value, **Query**. This is the key name of the input field from the form.

How It Works

The additions to our application simulate the user entering the name Joe Bailey into the text field on the page and then hitting the Start Search command button.

The new procedure will read in the names of the fields that are defined on the form. We can, therefore, use it for any forms we may want to create.

Connecting to the Data

Our example so far has been limited to searching one field of a database, but this need not necessarily be the case. You can have multiple input and output fields on any form.

What we now want to achieve is a simulation of the user typing in their name, the CGI application searching the **Customers** database for their details and then displaying these to the user as a web page.

Try It Out - Queries

1 With the last example loaded, add a TQuery component to the form. Set its Database property to point to the DBDemos database alias.

2 Now we'll set up a query that reads in a parameterized value, this being the value of the **Key** field **Query** from the **.ini** file, and then returns the customer's details.

In the **FormCreate** procedure, add a new string variable:

```
procedure TForm1.FormCreate(Sender: TObject);
var
    sFileName     : String;
    sOutPut       : String;
    SQueryString  : String;
begin
```

3 Where we showed the **Key**'s value in the last example, we will now insert the value of the web page's input field into this newly declared variable. Replace the **ShowMessage** command with the following line:

```
sQueryString := WebIni.ReadString('Form Literal', KeyNames[0], 'Error');
```

 FYI You can see from the code how you can then use the string list to access any number of key values simply by incrementing the index of **KeyNames** to **KeyNames[1]**, **KeyNames[2]**, and so on.

4 Now that we have the query's value stored in **sQueryString**, we need to pass this to the **TQuery** component. Now for a parameterized query:

```
Query1.Close;
Query1.SQL.Clear;
Query1.SQL.Add('Select * from Customer where contact= :NameStr');
```

5 We then pass it the value for that variable:

```
Query1.Prepare;
Query1.Params[0].AsString := sQueryString;
Query1.Open;
```

This will return to us a cursor containing the record details of Joe Bailey.

6 Now we want to return these details to the browser. In your **FormCreate** procedure, insert the call to **CreatePage** after the SQL statements.

7 Alter the **CreatePage** procedure so that it looks like this:

```
procedure TForm1.CreatePage;
var
   iCounter : Integer;
begin
     {Send the Header information}
     SendHeader;

     {Put some text into the document}
     SendHTML('<HTML>');                 {Start of document}
     SendHTML('<H1>');                   {Header style 1}
     SendHTML('Search Result');
     SendHTML('</H1>');

     SendHTML('<P>');
     SendHTML('<Center>');

     For iCounter := 1 to Query1.fieldCount -1 do
         SendHTML(Query1.Fields[iCounter].AsString+'<BR>');

     SendHTML('</HTML>');                {End of document}
     SendHTML('');                       {Terminate the document}
end;
```

Once you've done this, run the CGI program and open the output file in your browser. Your output file should have created a web page like this:

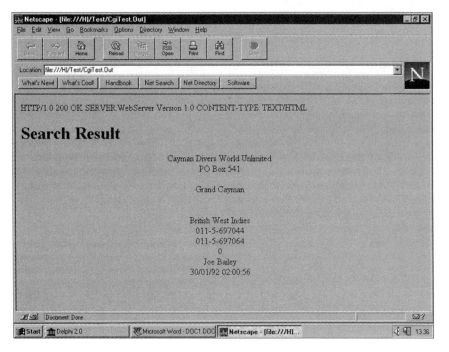

How It Works

To recap the **TQuery** statements:

▶ You must ensure that the component is inactive, so we call **Query1.Close**.

▶ Then clear out any old SQL queries, **Query1.SQL.Clear**.

▶ Add in the new SQL statement, which in this case means 'Get all the records in the customer table where the field **contact** is equal to a variable, **:NameStr**, the details of which I shall give you as a parameter in a moment.'

▶ Prepare the query to receive the variable.

▶ Insert the contents of **sQueryString** into the variable. Note the use of **AsString** to convert all values to text values.

▶ Execute the query, **Query1.Open**.

These few lines return the subset of the database, if any, that matches the search criterion.

All the modified **CreatePage** procedure does is to traverse the fields return by the TQuery component and output them to file.

Extending Interaction

We now have a very simple input/output program to interact with a web server. As you can see from the code, the CGI program is just like any other Delphi program, with the exception that it doesn't have a visual interface. Instead, it communicates with the outside world via a text file.

The most flexible and interactive pages, though, will allow you to perform multiple operations. Furthermore, an entire site may be build around CGI interaction, so your application may have to perform many different types of operations, providing personal pages, log-on screens, stock lists, inquiry screens, and so on.

It's reminiscent of the story of the computer science department where you can check how full the staff coffee machine is across the network, before making that 200 yard trek in search of restorative. But, in order to work such technological feats, you may need to use some more features of CGI. This will be the substance of the rest of this chapter.

The Web Page

With what you've already learned, you can soon build up some very effective and useful search engines and other types of interactive pages. For example, the page below is used to generate customer requests for information and stores the request in a database. Once the customer has sent the form, the CGI program stores the data and then returns a page to the user containing a customer order number.

As we know from our previous examples, the code required to create this page is very simple:

```
<HTML><BODY BACKGROUND="MARBLEBG.GIF">
<TITLE>
Customer Service Request
</TITLE>

<HEAD><CENTER><H1>
Welcome to our Customer Services Page
</H1></HEAD></CENTER>

<P><CENTER><IMG SRC="BLUELINE.GIF"></CENTER>

<H4>Enter the details set out below, and our customer services representative
will be in contact with you as soon as possible.</H4>
<P><B>
<FORM ACTION="DELPHCGI.EXE" METHOD="POST">
<TABLE>
<TD>Customer Name<TD><INPUT TYPE="TEXT" NAME="Name" SIZE=30><TR>
<TD>Account Number<TD><INPUT TYPE="TEXT" NAME="Account" SIZE=30><TR>
<TD>Telephone<TD><INPUT TYPE="TEXT" NAME="Tel" SIZE=30><TR>
<TD>Product Name<TD><INPUT TYPE="TEXT" NAME= "Product" SIZE=30><TR>
<TD>Nature of Enquiry<TD><INPUT TYPE="TEXT" NAME="ENQ" SIZE=60><TR>
</TABLE><P>
<INPUT TYPE="SUBMIT" VALUE="SEND">
</FORM></HTML>
```

The new commands you see above are **BODY BACKGROUND**, which tells the browser what image to use as a background for the document, and **TABLE**, which is used to place text and images or fields on the same line. The **TD** stands for table data and shows what is placed in each column; **TR** is used to end a row.

Once the customer has filled in the relevant fields and sent the form, the CGI application can read the entries to the **Form Literal** section of the **.ini** file and extract the customer's name and their product order. Almost as a receipt, your application then creates a personalized web page:

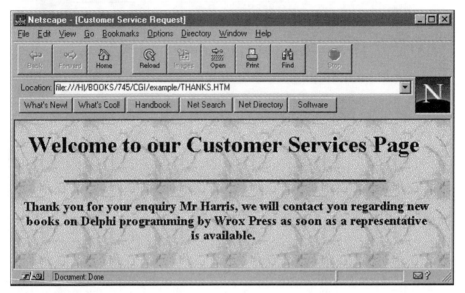

What Else Can CGI Do?

You can control multiple services by making use of the extra path information that the server can provide to your application. You can set the various command buttons that you place on your web pages to call your application and pass a specific parameter simultaneously. This is achieved by adding a 'path' variable to the end of your CGI call:

```
<FORM ACTION="DelphCgi.Exe/DoSomething" METHOD="POST">
```

The **/DoSomething** part of the command line gives the extra path information which will be passed to your application as the **Path Info** variable in the CGI section of the **.ini** file.

If we used such variables, we could process them with a **case** statement in our **FormCreate** procedure, so all the possible events that can be called by the page are handled.

There are two types of path, physical and logical, which the CGI script can specify. They depend on the web server's aliases. For example:

```
c:\windows\programs\mywebserver\cgi\data  =  cgi\data
```

Another method of passing data to the application is by using the '**?**' character:

```
<FORM ACTION="DelphCgi.Exe?DoSomething" METHOD="POST">
```

In this case, the item **DoSomething** will be stored in the **CGI** section of the `.ini` file under the **Query String** item. We would simply read this value to find out what the user wanted to do next. This method is the one most commonly used by the big search engines and though, at first, it might appear that the engine is being unduly skeptical about your request, you now know it's doing exactly what you want.

Where Requests Live

Depending on whether you make a **GET** or a **POST** request, you'll have to look in a different part of your `.ini` file to find out the nature of the request. A **GET** request is stored as,

```
Extra Path=<Field>=Key&<Field2>=Key2&<Field3>=Key3...
```

which contrasts with the **POST** method, which would place the query in the **Form Literal** section:

```
[Form Literal]
<Field>=<Key>
<Field2>=<Key2>
```

Other Input Types

Standard web page forms allow you to enter three different types of text fields: **Form Literal**, **Form External** and **Form Huge**.

The Form Literal field is the basic field type and may be up to 255 characters long. If you have a field on the form that is larger than this, the data to that field will be stored in the Form External section of the `.ini` file. In this case, the values will be stored as:

```
[Form External]
<Key>=<Path> <Size>
```

The *<Path>* variable contains the name of an external, input file and the *<Size>* variable contains the size of the data stored in that file. To find out the values stored in that field, you must first read in the file name and then open the file to examine its contents.

Lastly, there are Huge fields, fields that are commonly over 64KB in size. If you feel the need to use a field of this size, the server will pass information regarding this field to you in the `.ini` file, thus:

```
[Form Huge]
<Key>=<Offset> <Length>
```

Here *<Offset>* is the offset from the beginning of the content file (the one with the `.inp` extension), at which the raw value string for this key is located, and *<Length>* is the length in bytes of the raw value string.

 You can use the *<Offset>* to perform a 'seek' to the start of the raw value string and use the *<Length>* to know when you've read the entire raw string into your variable.

As for different types of input fields on forms, it almost puts Delphi to shame - you can have selection boxes, radio buttons, check boxes or simple text fields. It's worth noting that a check box will only be listed in the `.ini` file's **Form Literal** section if it has been checked. So, in your code, you must first check to see if a key exists to the variable before trying to read in its value.

Errors

This last warning, trying to access a field value that doesn't exist, is one of the major stumbling blocks you may encounter. Another peach is dealing with the user inputting incorrect values into a field (integers in a text field, etc.). Errors will be returned to the application in the normal way and should be handled as such - use a **try/except** block.

You need to be able to handle errors that can occur in your database operations and in the general file input/output routines. In general, your error routine should at least create an output file telling the user that an error occurred and terminate appropriately.

Error handling leads naturally enough to debugging - a major issue with CGI applications, as the web server will only respond to executable files, so there's no way to easily see what's happening whilst your application is running. It's for this reason that we have been building our example application using the command line Parameters option and adding items to the `.ini` files ourselves.

If you can get your application to work correctly via the IDE and have checked all its responses thoroughly, you should have reached the situation where the application will work correctly once it's attached to the web server. If your application isn't responding correctly to web server requests, the only real option is to include debugging information into your executable.

Many programmers have different methods of achieving this. One can be writing all information to an output file, or, my preferred method, is to encase the offending area of code with **ShowMessage()** calls so that you can see easily the internal state of the variables you're interested in.

 Check out the chapter on debugging for some more interesting techniques.

You must remember that the web server will wait for your application to terminate before proceeding, so if you include these calls, remember to keep hitting the OK button!

Grown-up Applications - Considerations

When you're building a large CGI application, you must remember that the application may be called a number of times by the same user. To keep track of what's going on and to ensure that you are offering the correct information, you need to identify each user.

The **CGI** section of the `.ini` file contains a reference to the remote user address. As this is normally unique, you can use it as a key to your users, or you could assign a value yourself. This value can then be 'built' in to your web page so that you can keep track of who's doing what to whom.

You must bear in mind that if you have multiple pages that call the CGI application, it will be loading and terminating many times. If your application needs to perform complicated lookups, or is extremely large to load, this delay can be quite considerable. You should also remember that you may have multiple instances of your application running at the same time. It's important to manage any database activity so that conflicts don't arise between the various instances of your application.

FYI

One other optimization we can make is to try and remove some of the memory overhead from all those units listed in the **uses** clauses. We don't need a form as such, just a CGI object, and we can set the whole thing running using the **initialization** section of the unit's **implementation**.

It's a bit like the old Pascal programs, where the main code from which all those subprocedures were called was placed at the bottom of the code and just delimited by **begin** and **end;**, with no header. Then you can wow your boss with some terms like 'non-form parameterised executable'!

An Explanation of the CGI Data Type

The CGI data type is defined in the **.ini** file created by the server. The main sections included in the **.ini** file are:

Section Heading	Description
CGI	Standard CGI variables.
Accept	What the client browser can read.
System	Windows interface specifications.
Extra Headers	Any extra information provided by the browser.
Form Literal	The main input values on the form.
Form External	The file names of the Large fields.
Form Huge	The offsets to the Huge fields.

The CGI standard variables will normally be set as follows:

Identifier	Description
CGI Version	The version of CGI spoken by the server.
Request Protocol	The server's information protocol (e.g. **HTTP/1.0**).
Request Method	The method specified in the request (e.g. "**GET**").

Table Continued on Following Page

451

Identifier	Description
Executable Path	The physical path name of the back-end (this program).
Logical Path	The extra path information in logical space.
Physical Path	The extra path information in local physical space.
Query String	The string following the "**?**" in the request URL.
Content Type	The MIME content type of information supplied with request.
Content Length	The length, bytes, of information supplied with request.
Server Software	The version/revision of the information (HTTP) server.
Server Name	The server's network hostname (or alias from **config**).
Server Port	The server's network port number.
Server Admin	The e-mail address of server's admin. (**config**).
Remote Host	The remote client's network hostname.
Remote Address	The remote client's network address.
Authenticated Username	The username used for restricted access.
Authentication Method	The method used for authentication (e.g. "**Basic**").
RFC-931 Identity	The TAP identity of client user.

As you can see, about 80% of the above information is of no real use to you in your application. The fields you will be interested in are:

▶ The **Logical Path** or **Query String**, which will hold the parameters that you have supplied via the extra path information.

▶ The **Remote Address**, so that you can identify which machine is asking for information necessary on a secure system.

The **System** section may contain the following information:

Information	Description
Debug Mode	If the server is running in debug mode.
Output File	The name of the output file you must create.
Content File	The name of the content file, for holding Huge data.

The **Accept** section heading lists the types of file that the client browser can handle and are listed as **xxx/yyy=Yes**. In our example **.ini** file, the lines in this section state all the image types the browser will accept:

```
image/x-xbitmap=Yes
image/jpeg=Yes
image/pjpeg=Yes
*/*=Yes
```

The **Extra Headers** section will inform you of any extra information that is available from the browser or server. For our example, the following information was supplied:

Information	Description
Referer	The web page that called the application.
Connection	To maintain or destroy the client's connection.
User-Agent	The type of operating system running, Windows 95, etc.
Host	The name of the host web server.

Obviously, the data and variables held in the **Form** section will depend on the fields you have included on your web page.

Summary

I must mention Bob Denny and Ann Lynnworth here, as the two people who have been at the forefront of integrating Delphi into the world of the Web. You can gain a good insight into CGI programming from Ann's Delphi Component site (**http://href.com**) at HREF Tools corporation.

There are several useful components there, available as shareware and freeware, as well as demonstration systems built around them. There's even a free trial download of their web server. These and the documentation that comes with them provide an excellent introduction to the world of CGI over and above what you've learned here.

In this chapter, we've been to the web frontier... I hope you're enthused enough to return as a pioneer and that you consider Delphi an essential tool in this enterprise. In the next chapter, I finally get round to putting all this information together into one big application and, hopefully, show you some of the pitfalls to beware of as you design your own applications.

One Final Application

Within this book, we've explored most of the significant features of Delphi 2.0 and, along the way, learned how to build small applications, using components and Object Pascal to determine the look and add functionality.

This approach is very common in tutorial books and can often leave you feeling "OK - so now what?" Well, the next logical step for anyone has got to be starting to build complete, useable applications that either service a need in your business or satisfy you as a hobbyist. The problem, then, is how to bring all the disjointed topics that we've covered in the book together into one application.

That's exactly what we're going to take a look at in this chapter. Included on the disk is an application called **conman.exe**, a simple contact manager. It's an MDI application with child windows that handle browsing data in the database, as well as searching, printing, and so forth. In short, it's a simple, but complete, application.

Throughout this chapter, we're going to pull it apart, see exactly how it does what it does and how Delphi made writing this application so easy. Along the way, we'll also answer some of those inevitable questions you still have, such as:

 How do we create cool toolbars?

 How do you add simple reporting to an application?

By the end of the chapter, you should have a pretty good idea of everything that goes into writing a complete program. Although ConMan is quite small and very simple, it really does include everything you might expect to find in a much larger, much more sophisticated database application - so it's great teething ground for us.

Read on...

A First Glimpse of the Application

You'll find **conman.dpr** on the disk. Load it into the Delphi IDE, but before you can compile it, you'll need to set up a database alias, company. This alias refers to the location of the three databases used in the application. The easiest way to do this is to add the Borland Database Engine Configuration utility to your menu bar and then run it from there.

To add this utility to your menu bar, simply select Tools | Tools... and then the Add button. Delphi will then let you browse for the file that you want to add to the menu bar (you're looking for the **\Common Files\BDE** directory and a file called **bdecfg32.exe**) and a suitable name for the application on your menu (I suggest BDE Config!!).

When you've got this set up, if you haven't already, run the app by choosing it from the menu. Add the alias to your database configuration file (**idapi32.cfg**) by selecting the Alias tab, clicking the New Alias button, selecting the standard Paradox 7 database format and giving the resulting dialog the full path to the databases, such as **C:\BegDel\DB**.

Before we dive into how ConMan does what it does, it's probably a good idea to take a look at it from a user's point of view. By exploring its features, you're bound to come up with some questions about how it works which the rest of this chapter will (hopefully) answer:

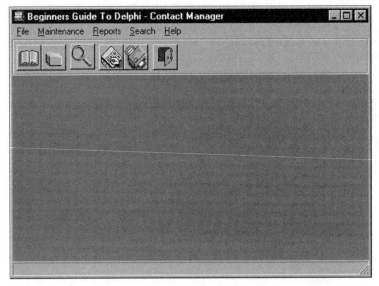

When you first start up the application, you should find yourself looking at a screen much like this, an MDI form with a menu bar across the top and a rather neat toolbar underneath. You can use the menu items to access any part of the application. The toolbar, as in any Windows application, just gives you quick and easy access to the most commonly used menu items.

The Forms

ConMan, like any self-respecting contact manager, helps users to keep track of contacts they might come across in business, allowing them to store details of the contacts themselves, the companies they work for and any work they do with them.

For that reason, the bulk of the application revolves around three forms:

- The Company Maintenance form, where you can enter details of the companies that you comes across
- The Contact Maintenance screen, where the people get dumped
- The Action List, where you can record any dealing you have with them

Click on the far left icon on the main toolbar and you'll see the Company Maintenance form:

The Company Maintenance Form

One of the most important things you can do in developing an application like this, particularly if the people who are going to use it are not really all that computer literate, is to keep a fairly standard look and feel, not only from application to application, but also from form to form. That was Chapter 2's lesson - hope you learned it well!

 Doesn't this stunt creativity? Well, making your users' lives as easy as possible with a well thought-out application that actually enhances their work should keep you on your toes - that's where the real creativity of computer programming lies.

For just that reason, notice how the Company Maintenance form looks quite similar to the MDI parent. We have a very similar looking toolbar and, once again, if you slowly wave the mouse over the buttons on the new toolbar, you'll see hints popping up just as they do on the MDI form. You'll also see in a little while that the Contact Maintenance form also bears a remarkable resemblance to this form.

The toolbar on the Company Maintenance form is basically my own version of the DBNavigator component, with improved icons and the addition of pop-up hints:

The four icons on the left of the toolbar should be pretty easy to understand - they allow you to move to the first, previous, next and last companies respectively. The next two let you create a new company record and delete the one currently on display. Clicking on the Add button simply causes all the data entry areas on the form to blank out, ready for you to enter new company information. When you're done, you can either click on the check mark button on the toolbar to accept (post) the new data, or the cross button to cancel it.

Clicking on Delete simply pops up an obligatory message box asking if you're extra-specially sure you really want to go ahead and delete the record:

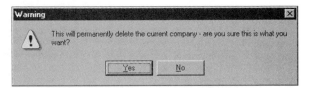

The two right-hand buttons (Accept and Cancel) are also used for simple editing. When a record is on display, there's nothing stopping you changing the data shown. Closing the form down or moving to a new record in the database causes the changes to get posted to the table, as does clicking on the Accept button on the toolbar. However, clicking the Cancel button forfeits any changes you made and restores the previous record to all its glory.

The Contact Maintenance Form

As I mentioned previously, in terms of how it looks and what it does, the Contact Maintenance form is almost identical to this. Select Contact Maintenance from the Maintenance menu to bring it into view and see what I mean:

Same toolbar, same options, just different data.

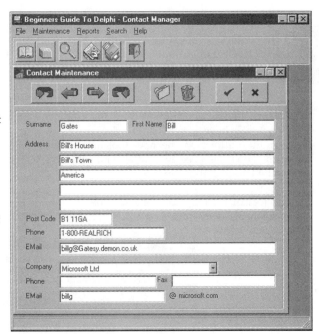

The Action Lists Form

In fact, the only thing that does work differently is the Action List window. In ConMan, the Action List window lets you record details of any action that you've taken with a contact in your database, or any dealings you've had with them. As you move through the contacts in the Contact Maintenance window, the Action List changes to reflect those records that are in the actions table for this contact:

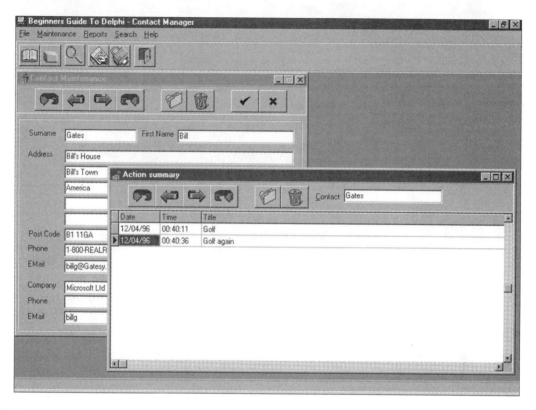

Notice our old friend, the toolbar, at the top. Again, the functionality is exactly the same as it is on the other maintenance forms, the only difference being that, this time, when you click on the Add button, a separate form is loaded up to allow you to enter far more information than can be displayed in the grid:

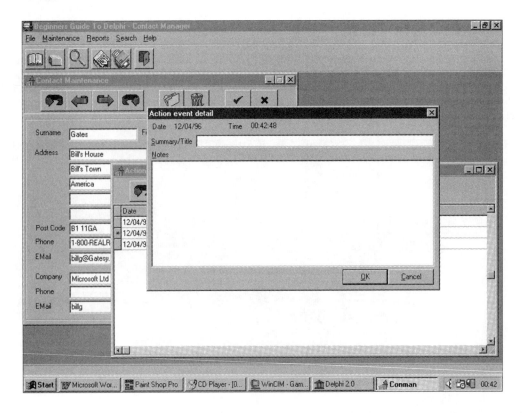

There's also a little more code to this, as the date and time that the action record was created are automatically fired into the database for you. I'll discuss those few lines of code in a moment.

Of course, no database application would be really complete without facilities which make it easy for users to locate data from what could grow to be an immense pool of information. In ConMan, we use a single search form to allow the user to quickly locate either a contact or a company by entering either the whole name (or even part of the name) of that contact.

You can get to the search form simply by selecting Find from the Search menu:

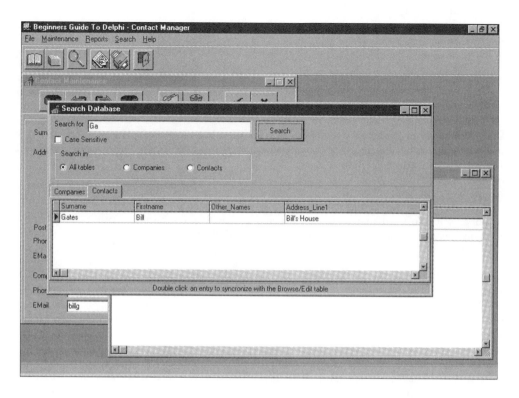

Here, you just enter the information you want to search for in the edit box at the top of the form and then click on the **Search** button. The radio buttons beneath the edit box tell ConMan exactly what you want to search for and allow you to tell the application to look for both matching companies and contacts, or one or the other.

The final real feature of the application is its reports. All the reports work in the same way, just select the type of report that you want from the **Reports** menu and a **Report Preview** window appears allowing you to see what the report is going to look like before you consign a rainforest to its production.

The reports in ConMan are intentionally simplistic and don't allow you to limit the amount of data that is printed each time. However, as you'll see, Delphi's QuickReport controls give you an incredible amount of control over exactly what information is included in the report, as well as the how the report looks and much more besides.

That's basically all there is to it.

If you keep the user interface consistent for all the forms in the application, you can see that you soon end up with an application which, despite the amount of functionality it contains, is very easy for a user to get to grips with. More than this, the sheer power of Delphi and its vast array of prebuilt components makes actually writing such an application a relatively painless and quick affair. Let's continue our tour with an in-depth look at exactly what's going on behind the scenes.

Toolbars

When Visual Basic first hit the shops, it created an enormous spin-off market of suppliers of VBX (and later OCX) controls. One of the most common controls from third-party developers was the ubiquitous toolbar control not included in VB - a control that could easily dump an attractive graphical toolbar on a form, complete with pop-up hints on the buttons and such like.

Delphi doesn't have a standard toolbar control either, but, since it's light years ahead of Visual Basic in terms of flexibility and power, it should come as no surprise that Delphi makes it easy to create one, exactly as I've done here.

The toolbars that you see on the forms actually consist of two types of components. The first is a Panel which, like the GroupBox we saw earlier in the book, is a container component. Drop components inside the panel while it's selected and wherever the panel moves to on the form, the components it contains will follow. Notice the sunken border on the toolbars in the application.

We created this border by playing with the BevelInner and BevelOuter properties of the panel. There are two very thin lines around the outside of the panel, called **bevels**, each of which you can either leave invisible, raise to cast a shadow, or sink down into the panel. By raising the inner bevel and sinking the outer one, we soon end up with that attractive sunken border around the toolbar. Without these, the toolbar stands a good chance of just merging in with the rest of the controls on the form, which rather misses the design point.

The panel also has a Caption property, since by default it can display a small text message in its center. In all the toolbars used in this application that simply isn't very useful, so I emptied it, leaving just a nice plain empty panel. I've also set the Align property to alTop so that the toolbar is glued to the top of the child form and resizes with it.

The toolbar buttons themselves are quite unique, though I do say so myself! The component I used is the SpeedButton (since it's normally used to provide speedy access to an area of functionality in the application) and can be found on the Additional tab of the Component Palette.

Basically, these are very similar to the bitmap components we've be using, except that they can form part of a group. Just by specifying that each speed button in a set should have the same **GroupIndex**, you can ensure that only one can be selected at any one time. This is one of the speed button's coolest features, hardly relevant here, but I thought you might like to know.

If you click on one of the SpeedButtons on the toolbar and then double-click the Glyph property, you'll see the following editor. The bitmaps I've used are included on the disk:

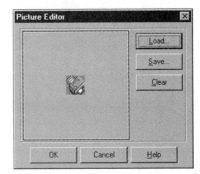

FYI

Delphi also does some interesting stuff in the background here which many people don't even notice, although I'm certain that some poor Borland programmer probably spent hours implementing it.

When you load in a picture, the **Picture Editor** takes a look at the border of the picture and treats the color it finds as changeable. So, if you load in a picture of a printer on a red background, for example, Delphi will figure that red is a color that you really aren't interested in. Then, when the picture is actually dropped onto the speed button, Delphi will change that red (or whatever other color it finds) to the same color as the face of the button.

The result, of course, is that you don't have to spend hours mucking about with graphics editors changing the colors to match the buttons. More than this, though, your application will automatically respond to any color preference changes that the user makes in Windows without the images on your speed buttons looking completely naff as a result. So your applications will always be in vogue.

The fun doesn't stop at simply loading in the graphic, though. Scroll down through the properties attached to a SpeedButton and you should come across a rather neat property called NumGlyphs.

The bitmap images you load in can actually contain more than one picture. For example if you had loaded in a bitmap containing an image to display when the button isn't pressed and another right beside it to display when it is, you would set the NumGlyphs property to 2. Delphi will split the graphic you just loaded in half and display the left-hand image when the button isn't pressed and the right-hand image when it is - neat, huh?!

Now what about those pop-up hints that appear at run time - how do we add them?

Pop-up Hints

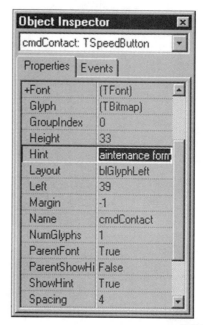

It's very easy to get Delphi to display pop-up hints over most of its visual components; all you have to do is play with the two Hint properties. Try selecting a button on the toolbar, then take a look at its properties in the Object Inspector:

The two properties in question are Hint (simple enough) and ShowHint. You need to do nothing more than type the Hint string into the Hint property and then double-click on the ShowHint property to enable the hints to pop up at run time.

I actually lied a little there (what a fibber); there is a third hint property which can come in handy sometimes. What if you want all the components on a form or inside a container to show the same hint? You can do this by setting up the Hint properties on the form or container and then setting the ShowParentHint property to True for each relevant component. At run time, Delphi will display the hint that is set for the parent or container object, rather than looking at the Hint property of each child component.

Accessing the Data

If you have spent any time wandering around the application's forms at design time, you'll have noticed a complete lack of Data Access controls on most of the forms. Where are the Table and DataSource components?

Rather than duplicating Table components and the code necessary to set them up to point at the right alias or directory for each form, almost all the Data Access components in this application are held in a single data module:

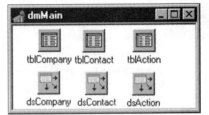

In ConMan, this brings with it a number of benefits, some obvious and some not so obvious. Firstly, all the forms in the application, as well as any code that may be flying around in a unit not attached to a form, can easily access the data that the application is designed to maintain. Secondly, as I already mentioned, there's no need to duplicate Data Access controls on the forms at run time.

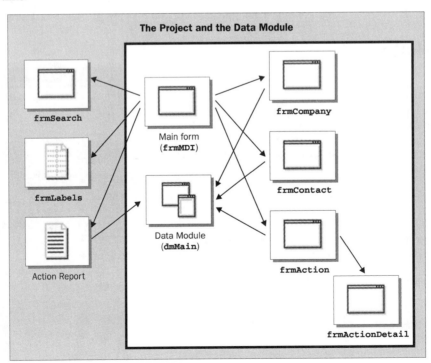

The Project and the Data Module

A not-so obvious benefit of this approach is speed. Each time a Table component is enabled (such as when a form containing it is created) there's a small amount of work going on in the background to check that the DatabaseName and the TableName are valid. This is all handled for you by Delphi and, on a fast machine, (basically, any machine with a lot of memory, or any decent Pentium) this delay goes unnoticed. On slower or less capable machines, though, the delay each time a data enabled form is loaded can soon become very tedious.

In Delphi 1.0 there was no way around this problem other than to have a single form containing all the data access controls and then write a lot of code to provide front-end access to them, or simply access the controls on the form directly by making all the units in the application reference that form in their **uses** clause. These are valid things alternatives, but not really all that apt in an object-oriented world. Delphi 2.0's new data module component is a far more elegant approach.

Another less obvious benefit is one that you can see at run time. Remember the Action List? As you move through the contacts on the Contact Maintenance form, so the Action List (which is on a separate form, remember?) changes too, to reflect the action records related to the new contact. This is because both forms reference the same data controls. In other visual development systems, this little touch can be a real pain in the butt. As for synchronizing updates from one form to another… well, go make some coffee and settle in for the night.

In Delphi 2.0, we need do nothing more than point the components on these separate forms at a central data module.

Breakdown the Forms

Time to look at some of these forms in a little more detail.

The Company Maintenance Form

The first of the actual data maintenance forms is for company maintenance:

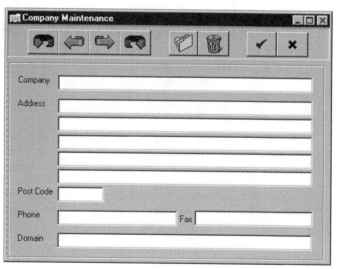

If you haven't already read the database development chapters then you'll probably look at a form like this and panic; all those controls to display and edit data, all bound together by that toolbar. What a tough job! If you have, though, it should come as no surprise to learn that the amount of actual code in this unit is really tiny.

As you might expect, all the controls on the form are bound to the dsCompany DataSource in the data module that we saw just a short while ago. Take a look at the Object Inspector if you need a little more convincing:

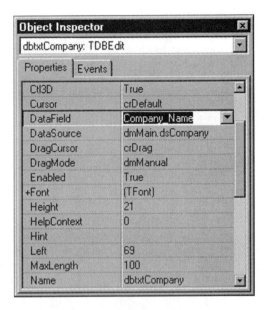

The DataSource property is set to dmMain.dsCompany, meaning the DataSource component called dsCompany, which is contained in the unit called dmMain (which, as you may have guessed, is the name of our data module).

Just as if you were to reference the components in that unit through code, the forms need to add the data module unit to their **uses** clause in order to work. Setting up properties to reference other units is as good as writing code to do the same. The good news here, though, is that, more often than not, Delphi will remind you of this and add the appropriate statement to your **uses** clause itself. It will only do this when you set up properties such as DataSource, though, not when you write code:

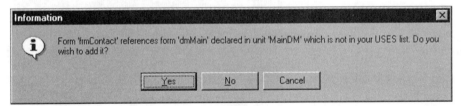

Since all the edit boxes on the form are bound to a data source, there's no need for you to add any code to them to manage the updates the user makes at run time, nor to pull the data from the database and display it. The only code in the form is attached to the buttons on the toolbar.

The first four buttons on the toolbar, the navigation buttons, do nothing more than call the **First**, **Prior**, **Next** and **Last** methods of the Company table in order to move from record to record.

This statement does contain a very important, but subtle, point. Even though the components on the form are bound to a DataSource control, the methods you call to move around the table, add and delete records, and so on, still need to be applied to the original Table component, tblCompany. The DataSource component just provides a means for those bound components to do their thing (displaying data, dealing with the updates, and so on). The code you write must deal with the underlying Table component directly.

The next button, the Add button, is just as simple. When the user clicks on it, all that happens is that the **Insert** method of the Company table is called:

```
procedure TfrmCompany.cmdAddClick(Sender: TObject);
begin
    dmMain.tblCompany.Insert;
end;
```

This single statement has quite a profound effect at run time. Starting an **Insert** like this tells the table to create a blank record and move to it. In response, the DataSource that's linked to it tells all the edit boxes on the form to clear themselves, instantly causing a form devoid of data to be displayed to the user ready for them to enter new record information.

The next button, Delete, is only slightly more complex. After the check that the user really is awake, a **MessageDlg** box asks the user if they are really sure that they want to delete the company record currently selected and the code checks that the user hit the Yes button before it calls the table's **Delete** method to permanently remove the record:

```
procedure TfrmCompany.cmdDeleteClick(Sender: TObject);
begin
    if MessageDlg('This will permanently delete the current company -
                  are you sure this is what you want?',
                  mtWarning, [mbYes,mbNo], 0) = mrYes then
    dmMain.tblCompany.Delete;
end;
```

If the user edits the data on display, or chooses to add a new record, they will probably want some clear way to save that data to the table or back out of the changes they just made. Think about that for a second...

The user decides that they're going to edit the data in the current company record, so they quite happily trot through all the edit boxes on the form, changing data as they go. Then, someone comes into their office and says "Hey, you don't need to make those changes after all", so the user starts hunting around for a Cancel button.

From a programmer's point of view, this could be a real nightmare. We need to spot when the user starts to change information and if they hit an OK button to fire the changes into the database. If they decide to cancel, though, we need to pull all that original data back and pretend nothing happened.

In Delphi, as usual, it's easy. As changes are made to the data on display, the DataSource component automatically dumps the information into a temporary storage area attached to the table. From there, the **Post** method can be called on the Table to copy the contents of this storage area into the Table proper. Alternatively, the **Cancel** method can be called. **Cancel** does just what we want it to do in that nightmare scenario. It copies the unchanged record information back into the temporary area. The DataSource spots this and automatically updates all the components on the form to restore the data that was there before the user started messing.

467

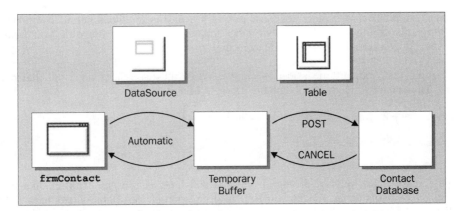

It's important to note something here; if you try to post unchanged data to a table, or cancel changes that haven't actually taken place, you'll get a run-time exception. For example, if you simply move to a new company record, then fire off a call to the **Post** method, the application will crash unless you have code in there to stop it.

```
procedure TfrmCompany.cmdPostClick(Sender: TObject);
begin
    if dmMain.tblCompany.State in [dsEdit, dsInsert] then
        dmMain.tblCompany.Post;
end;

procedure TfrmCompany.cmdUndoClick(Sender: TObject);
begin
    if dmMain.tblCompany.State in [dsEdit, dsInsert] then
        dmMain.tblCompany.Cancel;
end;
```

That's what we have here. You can check the **State** property of a table to see what state the table is in; for example, you can find out whether the user is inserting or editing data. In this example, all that is happening is that we're checking the value in the **State** property against a set of values using the Delphi **in** keyword. If Delphi finds the **State** is either **dsEdit** (meaning the user has edited some data) or **dsInsert** (meaning the **Insert** method was called a while back) then either **Post** or **Cancel** can be called without any problems.

The Contact Maintenance Form

The Contact Maintenance form is very similar to the Company Maintenance form:

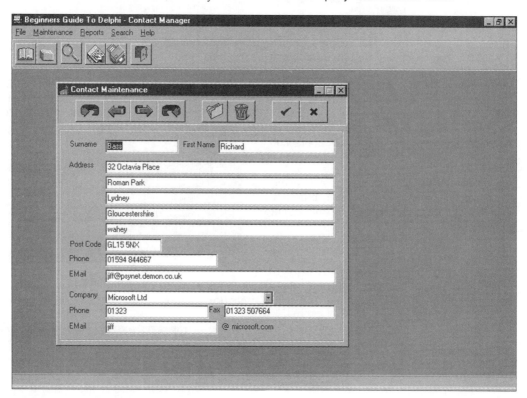

All the buttons on the toolbar perform exactly the same functions that they did back on the Company Maintenance form, the obvious difference being that this time they deal with the Contacts table in the data module. For example:

```
procedure TfrmContact.cmdAddClick(Sender: TObject);
begin
  dmMain.tblContact.Insert;
end;

procedure TfrmContact.cmdDeleteClick(Sender: TObject);
begin
  if MessageDlg('This will permanently delete the current contact - are you sure
this is what you want?'
    , mtWarning, [mbYes,mbNo], 0) = mrYes then
    dmMain.tblContact.Delete;
end;
```

The only other difference between this and the previous form is that this one actually pulls in data from more than one data source; notice next to the bottom e-mail name, the system automatically displays the e-mail domain name of the company that this person works for. The DBText component there points to dsCompany rather than to dsContact:

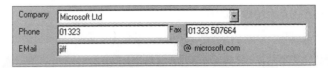

This is really easy to do and requires nothing more than pointing the DataSource of the appropriate control at a different DataSource in the data module - no problems there!

That bottom part of the form also lets you choose the company that the contact works for from the complete list of companies. Take a look at the actual definition of the Contacts table in the Delphi Database Desktop by selecting Tools | Database Desktop. Within the Database Desktop window, select File | Open | Table... and set the Alias combo box to Company to quickly get to the right directory, and then select contact.db.

You'll then see that the company field in the contact record is actually a number, but we've seen that the form displays the textual name of the company:

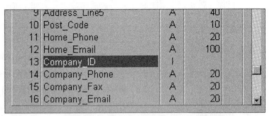

The form is able to link the number to the actual company name from the Company table simply by using our old friend the DBLookupComboBox component that we saw in Chapter 10.

In design mode, click on that component, then bring up the Object Inspector to see what has been set:

Remember that with the lookup controls we need to specify two data sources and a field from each. One is the data source and field that we want the control to actually update, the other is the data source and field from which we want to display data in the combo box at run time.

In this case, we want to update the Company_ID field in the dsContact DataSource, the field that holds the company ID that this contact actually works for. To do this, the DataField is set to Company_ID and the DataSource property itself is set to dmMain.dsContact.

The field that we want to display in the combo box that relates to this is the Company_Name field from the dsCompany DataSource. To set that up, we just fire Company_Name into the ListField property and dmMain.dsCompany into the ListSource property.

The only remaining field that needs to be set up is the Link field, the field in the second data source (dsCompany) that corresponds to the field we're actually updating in the first data source (dsContact). The field that links the contact records and the company records is the Company_ID field. We already set the DataField to Company_ID so that is taken care of. To form the link in the company DataSource Company_ID is fed into the KeyField property.

So, by using this arrangement, the user sees data that makes sense (in this case, a company name), instead of some cryptic number.

Searching for Data

Aside from the ability to actually enter and edit data in a database, most users will expect your database application to provide them with some way to easily locate information in the database - a search facility of some kind. Here's a form:

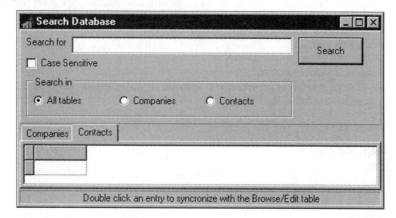

The radio buttons on the form let the user choose whether to search for just a contact or a company or both. The edit box at the top of the form provides an area for the user to enter the string that they want to search for and the Search button kicks off the search. It's set to be the default button, so pressing *Enter* after the search term will start the request.

The bottom of the form holds a PageControl, as we saw in Chapter 4. In our search form, each page of the control contains a grid. The company page holds a grid bound to the Company table that you can also see on the form, while the contact page holds a grid bound to the Contact table that you can see.

 Hang on a second! If we're using a data module to centralize all the tables and stuff that the application deals with, why do we need to have two more table controls on this form? Read on - all will be revealed.

What we want to do in the search is look at each field in every record of the Company and Contact tables and display the records with one or more matching fields in the relevant grid. If we were to do this and consequently limit the records actually available from the tables in the data module, we would run the risk of losing our hard won position in both tables. Therefore, it's a lot safer to create new tables for the search.

So, how exactly can we reduce the records that are actually made available from a table? A little coding is necessary.

If you set the Filtered property of a Table to True, each time the table is refreshed, the OnFilterRecord event fires for each record in the table, allowing you to check out the contents of each record using an event handler something like this:

```
procedure TfrmSearch.tblContactFilterRecord(Dataset : TDataSet; var Accept :
Boolean);
begin

end;
```

As you can see, one of the parameters that your code gets if you write an OnFilterRecord event handler is **Accept**. Set this to **True** and the record is available, set it to **False** and the record is hidden from view.

If you take a look at these actual event handlers in the code, you'll see the whole thing in action:

```
procedure TfrmSearch.tblContactFilterRecord(DataSet: TDataSet;
  var Accept: Boolean);
var
  I: Integer;
begin
  Accept := False;
  I := 0;
  while (not Accept) and (I < tblContact.FieldCount) do
  begin
    if not (tblContact.Fields[I] is TMemoField) then
    begin
      if CaseSensitive then
        Accept := (Pos(Searchfor, tblContact.Fields[I].AsString) > 0)
      else
        Accept := (Pos(Searchfor,
                       UpperCase(tblContact.Fields[I].AsString)) > 0);
    end;
    Inc(I);
  end;
end;
```

This code loops through all the fields in the table (except the memo fields which are far too complex to deal with here) and checks to see if anything in them, in the current record, matches the data that the user asked to search for.

The **FieldCount** property of the table helps here - it tells us how many fields there are in a record. All we then need to do is to loop through these fields and increment the loop counter, **I**, until we hit this value. When we do, we know that there are no more fields to search:

```
while (not Accept) and (I < tblContact.FieldCount) do
  begin
    if not (tblContact.Fields[I] is TMemoField) then
    begin
```

472

The **(not Accept)** part of the **While** condition makes sure that we only bother to check a field as long as one of the others hasn't already matched. If it has, the record will be included in the table, **Accept** will be set to **True** and the loop will terminate.

The actual searching is done using the Delphi **Pos** method:

```
if CaseSensitive then
        Accept := (Pos(Searchfor, tblContact.Fields[I].AsString) > 0)
     else
        Accept := (Pos(Searchfor,
                        UpperCase(tblContact.Fields[I].AsString)) > 0);
```

Now when the user hits the Search button, the event handler code (which we see in just a minute) checks to see if they want a case-sensitive search or not, i.e. whether or not the letters 'W' and 'w' should be treated differently. If it's a **CaseSensitive** search, the search term is copied into a variable called **SearchFor** as is. Otherwise, the text is first converted to uppercase letters before being copied into the same variable.

 A similar thing happens in the **OnFilterRecord** event handler code above, but here it's the current field we convert to uppercase if the search is case-sensitive.

Pos takes two parameters, both of which need to be strings, and then searches for an occurrence of the first string in the second.

If a match is found, **Pos** will return the number of characters from the left of the string that the match was made. If not, it will return **0**. Armed with this, you should be able to see what the code is doing here:

```
Accept := (Pos(Searchfor, tblContact.Fields[I].AsString) > 0)
```

What is actually happening is that the result of the **Pos** call is being checked to see if it's greater than **0**, meaning that we have at last found a field in a record that matches what the user is searching for.

If it's greater than zero, **Accept** is set to **True**, meaning that this record will make it into our grid. If the result isn't greater than zero (meaning the search failed, no match was found) then **Accept** remains **False** and the loop keeps on looking, at least until it runs out of fields.

So there you have it - a search routine that searches every field in every record and displays matching records in a grid.

And There's More

There's a little more functionality to this form that you might find useful to explore. Take a look at the code behind the search button, the code that actually starts off the filtering process:

```
procedure TfrmSearch.cmdSearchClick(Sender: TObject);
begin
  CaseSensitive := Checkbox1.Checked;
  if CaseSensitive then
    SearchFor := Edit1.Text
```

```
    else
      Searchfor := UpperCase(Edit1.Text);
    case rgSearchIn.ItemIndex of
      0: begin
           tblCompany.Active := True;
           tblCompany.Refresh;
           tblContact.Active := True;
           tblContact.Refresh;
         end;
      1: begin
           tblCompany.Active := True;
           tblCompany.Refresh;
           tblContact.Active := False;
         end;
      2: begin
           tblCompany.Active := False;
           tblContact.Active := True;
           tblContact.Refresh;
         end;
    end;
  end;
```

The first few lines you know about already. First, we look at the check box on the form to see whether the user requested a case-sensitive search. If they did, the **CaseSensitive** variable is set to **True**, otherwise it's set to **False**. **SearchFor** is then set up accordingly.

Now the seemingly tricky part. The radio buttons on the form are actually a radio group. If you click on this component and take a look at properties, you'll see that its **Column** property is set to **3**, so you get three columns of radio buttons on the screen.

When you double-click the **Items** property, it lets you edit the caption of each of the radio buttons:

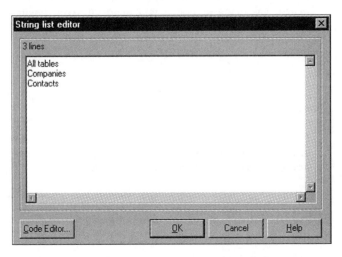

At run time, all we have to do to see which button was pressed is take a peek at the RadioGroup's **ItemIndex** property. It will be set to **0** for the first button, **1** for the second, and so on. And we make use of a **case** statement to code for each value **ItemIndex** can take.

What we need to do is to refresh the tables, depending on which button was pressed. Refreshing tells Delphi to go away and make sure that all the records that are in the actual table on the disk are available through the Table component. This, in turn, fires off our OnFilterRecord event handlers which perform the actual searching for us.

The final piece of functionality in the puzzle is the grids themselves; when you double-click an item in the grid, the record you double-click is made the current record in the data module, which in turn affects any currently loaded data maintenance forms loaded at the time.

This is actually very easy to do - take a look at the code yourself to see:

```
procedure TfrmSearch.DBGrid2DblClick(Sender: TObject);
begin
   dmMain.tblContact.GotoCurrent(tblContact);
end;
```

All that happens here is that the **GotoCurrent** method of the **tblContact** table is called. **GotoCurrent** is designed to synchronize two Table components so that they point to the same record. By passing the Table component that is on the search form (**tblContact**) as the parameter to **GotoCurrent**, we're telling the relevant Table component in the data module to display exactly the same record as is currently selected in our local Table component. We, therefore, ensure that the current record is available in full from the data module.

The Action Lists

The Action List form provides you with a means to not only to see all the dealings that you have had with a contact, but also to enter and edit existing records using Delphi's DBGrid.

The Action List form actually represents a more realistic view of the way you would structure information in a fully fledged business application and so contains some useful points. For example, if you were developing some kind of financial accounting system, it would be unlikely that the user would really want to scroll through the detail of every invoice in the system. Instead, many would prefer to see a summary list of all the invoices in the system, using the addition detail screen to view the ones they were interested in.

This is exactly how the Action List form works. The grid displays a summary of all the action that has taken place with a contact. Double-clicking an entry, perhaps to edit it, takes you to a separate form where the actual detail information is stored. Since we have all the data that's on display in the grid stored centrally in the data module, this is quite easy to do. We just need to pop up a detail form with controls bound to fields in the data module table to display more information than is currently on display in the grid.

However, there's another important consideration. Like the DBNavigator component, the grid allows the user to move around the records in a table without you having to write code for them to do so. If they pop up an edit form or a detail form for a record in the grid, there's a chance that they could still be able to use the grid and change the data on display in the detail form.

There are two solutions to this. The first is to drop a new Table component on the detail form and synchronize it to the one in the data module, using our old friend the **GotoCurrent** method. This means, though, that we start along a path of decentralizing the data. A better option is to use a modal form.

Modal Forms

A **modal form** is one which is not an MDI child and which is displayed on the screen floating above any other forms on display. The user must respond to the modal form before they're allowed to continue to use the forms in the background.

You can do this quite easily by playing with the **FormStyle** property that you would normally use to turn a form into an MDI child. By setting the value of **FormStyle** to **StayOnTop**, the form in question instantly becomes modal. Whenever this form comes into view, the user will be unable to use any other form in the application until they close this one down.

Actually displaying the form at run time is simple enough - take a look at the code attached to the Insert button on the Action List form:

```
procedure TfrmActions.cmdAddClick(Sender: TObject);
var
    Detail_Form : TfrmActionDetail;
begin
    dmMain.tblAction.Insert;
    dmMain.tblAction.FieldByName('Contact_ID').AsString :=
            dmMain.tblContact.FieldByName('Contact_ID').AsString;
    dmMain.tblAction.FieldByName('Date').AsDateTime := now;
    dmMain.tblAction.FieldByName('Time').AsDateTime := Now;

    // Load up the action detail form as modal
    Detail_Form := TfrmActionDetail.Create(Application);
    Detail_Form.Show;
end;
```

The Action table actually has a few fields which aren't normally set up by the user, specifically the **Contact_ID** field and the **Date** and **Time** fields which tell the user when the record was created.

Whenever a new action record is created, it needs to be automatically linked to the current contact, so after triggering the **Insert** method, the first thing you need to do is to copy the Contact_ID field from the Contact table into the Contact_ID field of the Action table.

The **AsString** methods are used to ensure that the data types of the Contact_ID field in the Contact table are properly converted to the data type of the Contact_ID field in the Action table. Remember, the Contact_ID field in the Contact table is an auto-incrementing field, whereas the one in the Action table is a number. So, when they're copied, the actual Contact_ID is first converted to a string and then the Contact_ID field in the Action table is fed the value.

The next step is to set up the **Date** and **Time** that the record was actually created. This is quite easy - we just copy the value of the Delphi **Now** operator (which contains the current date and time) into the relevant fields, using the **AsDateTime** operator to ensure that it's converted to a value with which the database can cope.

Finally, the Detail form is loaded up in exactly the same way that you might load any other. Since the **FormStyle** property has been set to **StayOnTop**, there's nothing special that you need to do to it to get it to show up as a modal form.

If the user had double-clicked in the grid to bring up the edit form, the code is even simpler:

```
procedure TfrmActions.grdActionsDblClick(Sender: TObject);
var
    Detail_Form : TfrmActionDetail;
begin
    Detail_Form := TfrmActionDetail.Create(Application);
    Detail_Form.Show;
end;
```

Here, the Detail form is created and displayed on screen. Remember, the user is double-clicking a record in the grid, which means that the record already exists. Since we're using bound controls on the detail form, we don't need to do anything else to get the form populated with the appropriate data.

Take a look at the detail form for a second:

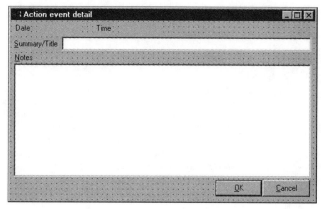

The next obvious step from our point of view is to ensure that the user does, in fact, have some way of saving their changes to the database and closing the form down. These functions are, logically enough, provided by the OK and Cancel buttons on the form (did you notice that there are no Post and Cancel buttons on the main Action List form - we don't need them since the user will be editing the data on the detail form, not on there). Here's the code behind both buttons:

```
procedure TfrmActionDetail.cmdCancelClick(Sender: TObject);
begin
  if dmMain.tblAction.State in [dsEdit, dsInsert] then
    dmMain.tblACtion.Cancel;
  Close;
end;


procedure TfrmActionDetail.cmdOKClick(Sender: TObject);
begin
  if dmMain.tblAction.State in [dsEdit, dsInsert] then
    dmMain.tblAction.Post;
  Close;
end;
```

Just as on the other maintenance form toolbars, we first check that the table is in edit or insert mode before issuing either the Post or Cancel method to save the changes or cancel them. In both cases, though, the form is closed down and the user returns to the main Action List.

Back to the Action List form. One very interesting feature of the form is that, as the user scrolls through the contacts in the Contact Maintenance form, the Action List also changes to reflect the actions attached to the newly selected contact. How is this done?

In the description of the search form, you saw how setting the **Filtered** property of a table to True caused an event to fire for each record in the table, thus allowing you to determine whether to allow that record to be visible.

You can do the same thing for simple filters using the **Filter** property. In the filter property of a table, you can place a clause which will be checked at run time for each record to see if that record should be visible.

At run time, as the user pages through the contacts in the table, the contact edit box at the top of the Action List form changes, causing a OnChange event to fire. In there, we simply change the filter to match the newly selected contact and then **Refresh** the data set. Take a look:

```
procedure TfrmActions.dbtxtContactChange(Sender: TObject);
begin
     // The user has clicked in the combo and selected a new contact.
     // We need to rebuild the query at this point to reflect actions
     // that have taken place with this new contact only.
     dmMain.tblAction.Filtered := false;
     dmMain.tblAction.Filter := 'CONTACT_ID = ' +
             dmMain.tblContact.FieldByName('Contact_Id').AsString;
     dmMain.tblAction.Filtered := true;
     dmMain.tblAction.Refresh;
end;
```

The first thing that happens when a new contact is selected is that the table filter is turned off. This lets us safely go ahead and change the filter in the next line, telling the table to only allow records through where their Contact_ID field matches a certain value. In this case, it's the value copied across from the same field in the Contact table.

Finally, the filter is turned back on and the table refreshed, which, of course, means that the grid gets refreshed at run time with only the action records for this contact.

Simple Reporting with QuickReports

The final most important area of an application like ConMan has to be the reporting side of things. Most users expect their database applications to perform some kind of printing. Thankfully, Delphi comes with two very powerful ways to create your reports; the QuickReports components and an application called ReportSmith.

ReportSmith is a fully fledged stand-alone report generator that Borland also sell as a separate product. It really is immense - far too big, in fact, to cover in a humble guide such as this. However, if you're going to create powerful client server applications or really big database applications then you could do worse than take a run through the tutorial ReportSmith exercises in the ReportSmith manual.

The QuickReports components, on the other hand, are designed to be quick and simple to use and are ideal for creating simple, yet effective reports in all but the largest database applications. Indeed, we're going to explore these here, since they are used in ConMan for its reporting.

ConMan provides its users with two reports: a contact label printer designed to print contact names and addresses on labels:

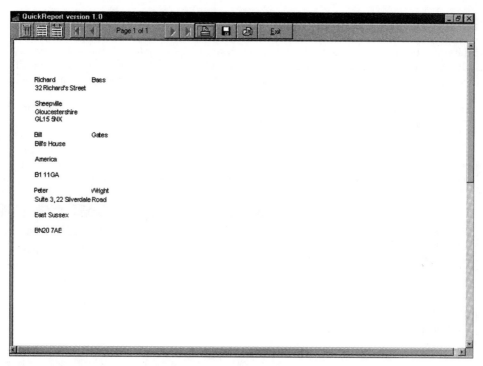

and an action summary report which lists all the actions attached to each contact in the database.

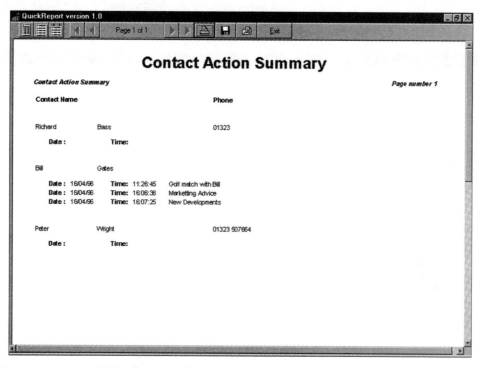

Both reports are available from the Reports menu on the MDI form.

Simple Reports

QuickReport components basically allow you to draw a report onto a form, and then, by calling either the **Print** or **Preview** methods of the main QuickReport component, you can either print the report out, or produce an on-screen preview of the report. The latter (creating a preview on screen, as opposed to just printing it) is preferable, since from there the user can very easily click on the Print button to go ahead and dump the report to the printer, or simply hit the Exit button to cancel the operation before any paper gets wasted.

Since producing the report consists of nothing more than calling the **Print** or **Preview** method of the QuickReport component, the trickiest part of the code is actually producing the report itself. Thankfully, Delphi's Object Repository can do a lot of the work for you.

By selecting File | New... from the Delphi menu and choosing the Forms tab of the New Items window, you can access a range of preset QuickReport forms to drop onto your application. It's these forms that are a good starting point for your own reports:

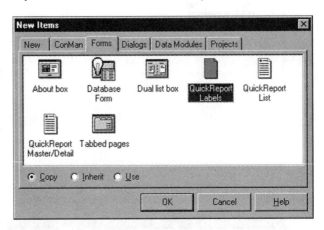

Take a look at the contact labels report (**frmLabels**) to see what a QuickReport looks like:

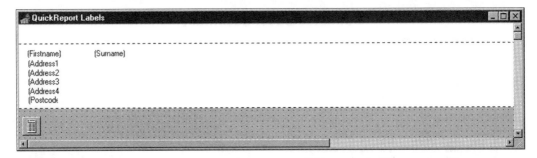

Notice that the form is split into two large white areas known as **bands** which are used to split the pages of your reports up into easily identifiable segments. You can get at the QRBand component yourself and drop new bands onto a form by simply selecting it from the QReport tab of the Component Palette.

Although there's only one band component (QRBand) in Delphi, you can set up the BandType property in the Object Inspector to tell it what kind of band it is and how it should work at run time.

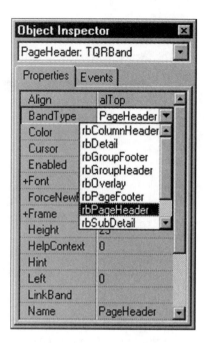

For example, setting a band to be a rbPageFooter or rbPageHeader type band means that it will print just once per page, either at the top or the bottom depending on your choice. The top band in the contact label report form, for example, is as a PageHeader band. The actual content of your report (the most important part), is usually set up to be of type rbDetail, since it contains the detail of the report. I've used this setting for the second band in our report.

Actually, defining the report itself is really quite easy once you have the bands on the form. Simply drop a QuickReport component onto the form and set its DataSource property to the DataSource component that will be supplying the bulk of the information for the report. At run time, the QuickReport component is responsible for getting at each record through the DataSource and firing the values of the fields in the records to the controls in your report.

Inside each of the bands, you can then drop QuickReport detail components, such as the QRLabel to set up a label on the page, or the QRDBText component to actually display a value from within a field. Just as if you were using standard data-aware components (which, incidentally, you can't do on a QuickReport form), you then set up the DataSource and DataField properties to tell the components where to get the data that they will print out. To see all this in action, take a look at some of the controls on the Contact Label report and their properties.

The Contact Label report is actually a very simple report if the truth be told, since it only has a header and detail band and it simply drags information out of a single table. When the user wants to see or print the report, they just choose it from the Reports menu and the following code kicks into action:

```
procedure TfrmMDI.mnuRContactsClick(Sender: TObject);
var
   CReport : tfrmLabels;
begin
    CReport := tfrmLabels.Create(Self);
    CReport.QuickReport.Preview;
end;
```

Master/Detail Reports

The Action Summary report, though, is quite a bit more complex:

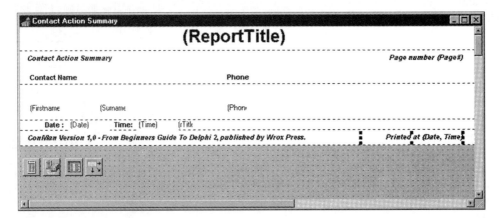

This time, the report consists of five bands. The first is known as a **title band** - it prints just once at the start of the report. The second band is the header band we saw previously that prints at the top of each and every page. Header bands, as you can see here, are ideal for putting QuickReport labels in to tell your users what each column of data in your printed report actually means. The final band on the page is nothing more than a footer band, very handy indeed for printing out a copyright message or some other information which must sit at the bottom of every page.

However, it's the third and fourth bands on the page which are the most interesting. This kind of report is actually known as a **Master/Detail** report, since it usually displays information from a master file, in this case contact names and phone numbers, and then lists for each master record (again, each contact record in this report) detail information from a separate data source. In this report, that detail information is the action records attached to each contact.

When we looked at the Action List form, we saw how to pull action records for a contact by hand, by changing the **Filter** property of the Action table each time a new contact is pulled up. However, you can get Delphi to do this for you automatically - it just involves a little thought and leg-work, as we shall see in a moment. For now though, let's get back to those bands.

The third band, then, is the master band and contains nothing more than a couple of QuickReport labels and some QuickReport text components to pull information from the dsContact data source in the data module. No great problems there.

The fourth band is the detail band and contains QuickReport components that pull information from the Action table via new DataSource and Table components on this form. Rather than write code to change the filter property on the main Action table in the data module, this form actually has a new Action Table component and DataSource. The Action table that you see on this form knows how to select records matching the current contact automatically, without any help from you other than setting up a few properties at design time.

The way that we do this sounds terribly complex, but is actually very easy get used to. I already had a tblContact table component in the data module, so all that was necessary to implement the detail side of the Master/Detail report was to drop a new table on this form to look at the Action table. The **DatabaseName** properties and **TableName** properties are both set up as normal to look for the Action table.

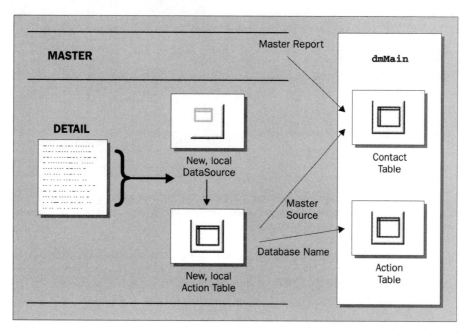

Now, in addition, at run time, this table needs to know about the Contact table. You do that using the new table component's **MasterSource** property:

As you can see from the screenshot, the name of the data module and Contact table's data source are dumped into the **MasterSource** property which instantly tells the new Action **Table** component that it's linked to the Contacts table in the data module elsewhere in the application.

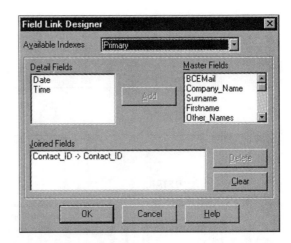

All that remains is to tell the Action table how it's linked. This is done using the MasterField property. Double-click that property and you'll get a list of fields in both the Action and Contact tables:

To form the link, you just select the field or fields in the Action table on the left and then select the fields they are related to in the Contact table on the right, clicking the Add button to drop the links into the box at the bottom of the dialog.

And that's all there is to it. Once those things have been done you end up with a new Action Table component on the form which knows that it's linked to the Contact table, and knows how. At run time, you will only ever be able to access the action records that are related to the current contact. We could have used this same approach on the Action List form that we looked at earlier, but then you wouldn't have seen both sides of the coin?

There's still one more tiny step to make. While the new Action table provides access to the related action records at run time, it won't automatically trot through them and update the detail band in our report. To get that working you just have to drop a QRDetailLink component onto the form.

Once you have done that, you can tell the DetailLink which band to affect and which data source to use by filling in the DataSource and DetailBand properties. Don't forget that the data source needs to be the new data source that is on this form, not one of the data sources from the data module.

Finally, set the Master property of the DetailLink component to the main QuickReport component on the field, and voila, everything is linked up and you're ready to rumble. At run time, the detail link will use the new Action table and data source to move through all the related records in that table and dump the results into the controls you have in the detail band.

More QuickReport Components

Take another look at that report - there are still a couple of components that we haven't covered. For example, the ones that print the page number, the current time and date and the report title.

QRSysdata components are designed to display a piece of text, specified in the QRText component, and an item of system information. You can choose exactly which piece of system information to display using the drop-down combo attached to the Data property in the Object Inspector:

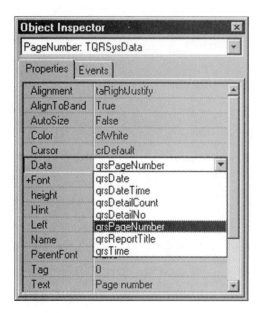

On the whole, these should all be quite self explanatory. The only one that takes a tiny bit of explaining is the qrsReportTitle value which is what that large report title heading at the top of the report is supposed to display. This isn't really that complex, though: it just pulls the report title from the main QuickReport component's ReportTitle property.

And that's all for QuickReports. As with all the topics in the book, it's impossible to cover absolutely every eventuality, property or method; there are tons and the combinations you can set to achieve different results and effects are almost limitless. Normally, this wouldn't be a problem, since as you gain experience, you will probably start to resort to the reference manuals that come with Delphi to augment your expertise. However, in the case of QuickReports there is no supplied manual.

Why? Because for some unknown reason Borland decided to include the manual in electronic form. You can find it in the **Delphi 2.0\QuickRpt** directory.

Summary

And there you have it - a basic, but totally functional program. As well as reviewing what we've learned in the rest of the book, we've even sneaked a few new tricks into the program. This learning thing just never stops.

In this chapter, you've seen how to:

▶ Create an overall look for your application

▶ Maintain your contacts

▶ Search for data

▶ Report the data to paper

And with that final application, you've completed the book - congratulations to all those who made it, commiserations to those that didn't. Before I leave, I would recommend that you take a look at the next section, it's just a small something you may be interested in covering - you can go from here. And on that note, goodbye...

Where Do I Go Now?

By now, you have a pretty good grounding in Delphi basics. You should have a reasonable grasp of how to write stable Delphi code, use the VCL components, dive into databases, interface with other applications and so on...

But, your journey on the road to becoming a Delphi expert is really only just beginning. This book is a beginner's guide - it was designed to take novice developers to a stage where they could start to stand on their own feet and begin developing applications for their paymasters, or even just for fun. However, in order to keep the book focused on key issues, there are a number of peripheral issues that have been avoided.

In this epilogue I'm going to give you a roadmap to the world of Delphi. I want to point you in the right direction for additional reading, technical support, additional software purchases and much, much more. You should be able to start developing Delphi applications now, but should you come up against a wall, an impasse which your knowledge and this book can't help you through, this chapter will at least be able to point you in the right direction when it comes to finding a solution.

In this chapter, we'll look at:

▶ Additional reading for Delphi and development theory

▶ Which online resources are available to you and which are the best

Have fun.

Quality Control

Whether you're writing a public domain utility or a full blown commercial application, the quality of your application is paramount. It's vital that as many bugs as possible are out of the system, that you have decent error handlers in place to capture the unexpected, and, on a higher plane, that the application is both easy to use and maintain.

The last point is important - more important than many people realize. Windows users have come to expect certain things of programs which claim to be Windows applications. They expect certain form layouts, certain actions take place when an OK or Cancel button is clicked or that the *Enter* and *Esc* buttons work as per usual.

Although you can't buy tools to instill these standards into your applications, there's one book that will be a great help. *The Windows Interface Guidelines To Software Design*, published by Microsoft Press (ISBN 1-55615-679-0), is the ideal companion for developers of Windows applications, no matter which development tool they use.

Written by various development teams within Microsoft, the book walks you through the standards that Microsoft themselves use when they design a user interface for one of their applications. Issues such as the spacing between buttons, standard menu and toolbar layouts, default actions and behavior of components, windows and dialogs are also covered in quite some detail. Whether you love or loathe Microsoft, you have to admit that, as far as Windows applications go, this is the team that set the standards and the trends, especially in terms of usability. This book can help you aspire to their heady heights.

Testing

Okay, assuming you have your user interface done now, and the application looks really sweet, how can you be sure of its reliability in the field? Well, we covered a number of steps back in Chapter 7, such as field tests, code reviews, and so on, all of which you can use to ensure the stability of your code and that it matches the application's specification. However, there are a number of tools available that you can use to help you, including MS Test and Nu'Mega's Bounds Checker.

Both are fully automated and programmable testing applications that will put any Windows application through its paces, entering data, simulating key presses, hitting buttons, and so on. Every test they do can be programmed, and the results recorded. MS Test in particular is quite a veteran in the field and even incorporates a subset of Microsoft's Basic programming language to let you really take control of the whole testing process.

However, automated testing tools and design standards still don't represent the whole story when it comes to ensuring the quality of your application. There are three more books, again from Microsoft (sorry, but they are the best) that go a long way towards imparting years of knowledge in testing, debugging and coding to ensure that you get in just the right mindset.

Code Complete, by Steve McConnell (ISBN 1-55615-484-4), is rapidly becoming the software developers bible, with one of the most readable texts available today on how to improve the coding, testing and debugging phases of any development. The book covers everything from coding standards, to debugging strategies, to the various testing methods and is backed up by literally hundreds of horrifying facts, figures and statistics, as well as some valuable case studies.

Writing Solid Code (ISBN 1-55615-551-4) and *Debugging The Development Process* (ISBN 1-55615-650-2), both by Steve Maguire, combine to form an excellent roadmap to common development pitfalls, both while sitting in front of the computer and while wearing the managerial hat. *Writing Solid Code* focuses squarely on writing C code, although the techniques and theories Maguire imparts in the book are valuable no matter what development system you use. *Debugging The Development Process* on the other hand is a sweeping study of some of the problems Microsoft encountered in the development of a number of leading commercial packages, the lessons they learnt and useful advice and anecdotes that we can all learn from. Ignore these three books at your peril.

As for problems with Windows development, we promised you the address of the Microsoft Developer Network. Call 1-800-662-9065 or use the URL **http://www.microsoft.com/msdn**. They promise to keep you up to date, for a fee, and, like any good game, there are a number of levels of membership.

Further Reading

The Delphi book market is growing at a phenomenal rate, due in part, some would say, to the poor documentation that is actually supplied with Delphi. However, separating the wheat from the chaff can be a mammoth task.

In a blatant advert for Wrox Press which, as you already know, produce excellent books, I recommend their *Revolutionary Guide to Delphi 2* (ISBN 1-874416-67-2), and their best selling *Instant Delphi Programming* (ISBN 1-874416-57-5). Written by masters of the art, in a clear concise, easy to follow style, they form part of a growing series of books devoted to Delphi programming.

The Revolutionary Guide is high-powered, and aimed at the Delphi programmer who knows the basics and wants more detail. Written by a nine-man author team whose expertise is drawn from real-world programming, technical support, international speaking and teaching, it covers the creation of components (data-aware, and non-data-aware), using the Open Tools API to create your own editors and experts, detailed databases, debugging, application interfacing, application design, optimization - basically, everything, in detail. All the source code, a complete electronic version of the book (as a 32-bit help file), and a broad selection of tools, information and demos make the CD as useful as the book.

Instant Delphi Programming, though written for Delphi 1, still has a lot of mileage in it. It's a speed-learning guide, full of tips and tricks, and will give you a different angle on Delphi. Dave Jewell, the author, is an avid exponent of Delphi and regularly appears in a whole spectrum of magazines.

Going Online

It really doesn't matter how good a developer you think you are, there will always be a technique that you haven't come across, as well as the inevitable problems and walls that we all have a problem solving on our own.

Online services, in particular the various Internet newsgroups, can go a long way to helping you dig yourself out of a rut in a very short space of time. Using an online service you get the opportunity to pick the brains of literally thousands of developers, many of whom have probably crossed the same Delphi terrain as you may be struggling with. There really is no better, quicker way to get support with Delphi these days, as well as sample code, new components and much more besides, than by hooking up a modem to your computer and getting at least one online account. But which service do you choose, and where, once you're connected, should you go to look for help?

Although most online service providers have areas on them for Delphi users (such as America Online, MSN and so on) the two most popular are CompuServe and, of course, the Internet.

On Compuserve, the DELPHI sections (GO DELPHI and the new Delphi 2 forum, GO BDELPHI32) are very active and are regularly frequented by some of the industries most revered Delphi experts. It also has a vast and growing software library attached to it from where you can download sample code, new components and much, much more.

On the Internet, while there are hundreds of Delphi web sites providing you with tricks and tips, as well as vast FTP libraries from where you can download even more sample code and such like, the best places to go are the Internet newsgroups, in particular:

> `alt.comp.lang.borland-delphi`
>
> `comp.lang.pascal.delphi.components`
>
> `comp.lang.pascal.delphi.misc`
>
> `comp.lang.pascal.delphi.databases`

Your local Internet access provider can help you get connected and provide you with the necessary software to get at these gems, as can Compuserve.

As a point of interest, though, most online service providers also now allow their users access to these Internet newsgroups, only Compuserve can provide you with access both to the Internet newsgroups and its own vast Delphi resources.

For UK readers (though it's spreading), there's a lively forum on CIX. The best method of access is to get one of the many off-line readers, such as Ameol, which are available from a variety of sources including the cover disks of a number of computer magazines.

A selection of favorite web sites can be found at the Wrox website:

> `http://www.wrox.com`

and I've included my bookmark sites on the disk as an HTML file. For goodness' sake, check out these and other links before you commit yourself to reinventing the wheel. It's components galore out there...

Summary

You're not alone, you're never alone, and everything that yet remains to be learned (or even written) about Delphi is out there waiting to be laid bare by the patient questioner, or even by the arrogant flame.

Dig around, don't be afraid to ask questions and above all, have fun!

Naming Conventions

Long awaited, it's now time to summarize the naming conventions we meant to adhere to in the book. These are based partly on common sense, partly on the deliberations of British-based Delphi Developers Group and partly on my opinion.

Basically, there are two types of prefix: those for components and those for data types. They help you and others (assuming someone wants to read your code) to follow the sudden appearance of an essential word in code and follow it back to its source.

But they don't replace the need for a good initial name to describe a component or data type's function - which almost always seems to demand as much creativity as the actual programming! This may have something to do with clearing your head sufficiently to identify precisely what variables are needed to do what - but it's all a bit of a haze. I think they call it development.

Component Prefixes

Prefix	Applies to...
bar	TProgressBar, TStatusBar, TrackBar
bat	TBatchMove
bev	TBevel
bn/btn/cmd	Button, BitBtn, SpeedButton, SpinButton
cal	Calendar
cb	ComboBox, DBComboBox, DriveComboBox, FilterComboBox
ck	CheckBox, DBCheckBox
db	DataBase
dde	DDEClientConv, DDEClientItem, DDEServerConv, DDEServerItem

Table Continued on Following Page

Prefix	Applies to...
dg/dlg	All dialogs
ds/dsc	DataSource
ed/txt	Edit, DBEdit, SpinEdit
fm/frm	Form
gg	Gauge
gd/grd	StringGrid, DBGrid, DrawGrid, ColorGrid, DBCtrlGrid
grp	Group
hdr	Header, HeaderControl
hot	HotKey
img	Image, DBImage, ImageList
lbl	Label, DBText
lst	ListBox, DBListBox, StringList, FileList, DirectoryList
lk	DBLookUpList, DBLookUpCombo
mu/mnu	Menu, PopupMenu
msk	MaskEdit
mem	Memo, DBMemo
mp	MediaPlayer
nav	Navigator
nb	Notebook, TabbedNoteBook
ocx	All OLE controls
ole	OLEContainer
out	OutLine, DirectoryOutline
pnt	PaintBox
pn/pnl	Panel
pc	PageControl
qu/qry	Query
qr	All QuickReport components
rdo/opt	RadioButton, RadioGroup, DBRadioGroup
re	RichEdit
scr	ScrollBar, ScrollBox

Table Continued on Following Page

Prefix	Applies to...
shp	Shape
sp	StoredProc
tb/tbl	Table
tim	Timer
vw	TreeView, ListView
ts	TabSet, TabSheet, TabControl

Variables, Objects, Types

In order to keep track of the data types you've got floating about in your code, these prefixes may help:

Prefix	Applies to...
ar#/a#	Arrays, with **#** indicating the variable type
b	Boolean
h	Handle
e	Enumerated variable
f	Floats
i	Integers
p	Pointer
s	String
r	Record
T	Type declarations (Class, Record, other user-defined types)
v	Variant

I hope you find these naming conventions of some help. If you have any comments to make, please forward them to my publisher by e-mail on **feedback@wrox.com**.

Beginning
Delphi
2.0

Database Desktop

files

G

H

I

ShortString

Revolutionary Guide to Delphi 32

This book deals with Win95 and Delphi 32 straight out of the gate. Written by a plethora of experts and tested by a world-wide web of Delphi developers to ensure accuracy and completeness, the book provides you with megabytes of coding examples, source materials and demo applications for this new programming environment.

By providing you with in-depth background information on such subjects as the Win95 API, inline assembly language and multithreading, this book explores the problems you might face when recompiling your 16-bit apps. On the environment side of the equation, check the chapters on the Delphi Tools API that allow you to customize the workings of the user interface by adding extra experts and editors to your arsenal, while the Object Pascal tutorial will allow you to brush up your rusty code.

Author: Various   ISBN: 1874416672

Price: $44.95 C$62.95 £41.99

The Beginner's Guide to Visual Basic 4.0

The sequel to the best selling 'Beginner's Guide to Visual Basic 3.0' this is a practical guide to 32-bit programming with Visual Basic 4.0 Standard Edition. After a walk through the VB4.0 environment, it will take you straight into the Common Controls and writing real code for Win95. The book contains practical lessons in object-oriented programming, utilizing graphics and interacting with the Win95 API. You will also learn how to write powerful database applications with the Jet database engine. By the end of this book you will understand dialogs, handling data and list controls, OLE and DLLs and how to manipulate them in useful Windows applications.

Every topic is illustrated with 'Try It Outs' - real code examples that augment each concept as you progress.

Comes with a disk containing all the source code from the text.

Author: Peter Wright   ISBN: 1874416559

Price: $34.95 C$48.95 £32.99

Instant SQL Programming

This is the fastest guide for developers to the most common database management language. If you want to get the most out of your database design, you will need to master Structured Query Language. SQL is the standard database language supported by almost every database management system on the market. This book takes you into the concepts and implementation of this key language quickly and painlessly, covering the complete ANSI standard SQL '92 from basic database design through to some of the more complex topics such as NULLS and 3-valued logic. We take you through the theory step-by-step, as you put into practice what you learn at each stage, gradually building up an example database while mastering essential techniques.

Author: Joe Celko   ISBN: 1874416508

Price: $29.95 C$41.95 £27.99

Revolutionary Guide to Office 95 Development

The book initially has primers for WordBasic and Visual Basic for Applications (VBA), and gives details of DDE and OLE technology which is the 'glue' which holds the Office 95 applications together. Stand-alone applications in Word, Excel and Access are developed to complete the readers understanding of these applications. The book then goes into detail of client/server design, before developing applications hosted in, again, Word, Excel and Access, that show how it is possible to combine functionality of the host application with the other applications in Office 95. Information on mail-enabling applications is also provided, using Exchange as well as the built-in mail capabilities. A detailed explanation of the workflow paradigm is given, before showing a complete office system built from the components so far discussed. The book finishes off with how to extend Word's capabilities by writing a WLL (using C), and finally considers what is required to make an application ready for distribution.

Author: Steve Wynkoop   ISBN: 1874416699

Price: $49.95 C$69.95 £46.99

WIN FREE BOOKS

TELL US WHAT YOU THINK!

Complete and return the bounce back card and you will:

- Help us create the books you want.
- Receive an update on all Wrox titles.
- Enter the draw for 5 Wrox titles of your choice.

FILL THIS OUT to enter the draw for free Wrox titles

Name _____

Address _____

_____

_____

_____ Postcode/Zip _____

Occupation _____

How did you hear about this book?

- ☐ Book review (name) _____
- ☐ Advertisement (name) _____
- ☐ Recommendation
- ☐ Catalogue
- ☐ Other _____

Where did you buy this book?

- ☐ Bookstore (name) _____
- ☐ Computer Store (name) _____
- ☐ Mail Order
- ☐ Other _____

I would be interested in receiving information about Wrox Press titles by email in future. My email/Internet address is:

_____

What influenced you in the purchase of this book?

- ☐ Cover Design
- ☐ Contents
- ☐ Other (please specify) _____

How did you rate the overall contents of this book?

- ☐ Excellent
- ☐ Average
- ☐ Good
- ☐ Poor

What did you find most useful about this book? _____

What did you find least useful about this book? _____

Please add any additional comments. _____

What other subjects will you buy a computer book on soon? _____

What is the best computer book you have used this year? _____

Note: This information will only be used to keep you updated about new Wrox Press titles and will not be used for any other purpose or passed to any other third party.

Please do not put me on your mailing list ☐

WROX

WROX PRESS INC.

Wrox writes books for you. Any suggestions, or
ideas about how you want information given in
your ideal book will be studied by our team.
Your comments are always valued at WROX.

Free phone in USA 800-USE-WROX
Fax (312) 465 4063

Compuserve 100063,2152.
UK Tel. (44121) 706 6826   Fax   (44121) 706 2967

——————— *Computer Book Publishers* ———————

NB. If you post the bounce back card below in the UK, please send it to:
Wrox Press Ltd. Unit 16, 20 James Road, Birmingham, B11 2BA

NO POSTAGE
NECESSARY
IF MAILED
IN THE
UNITED STATES

BUSINESS REPLY MAIL
FIRST CLASS MAIL   PERMIT#64   LA VERGNE, TN

POSTAGE WILL BE PAID BY ADDRESSEE

WROX PRESS
2710 WEST TOUHY AVE
CHICAGO IL 60645-9911